Return to Babylon

From Adam to Antichrist

David Patrick Harry

Logos Academic Press

Return to Babylon: From Adam to Antichrist
David Patrick Harry, PhD

Copyright © 2025 by David Patrick Harry, PhD

All rights reserved. No part of this publication may be reproduced, stored in a retrieval system, or transmitted in any form or by any means—electronic, mechanical, photocopying, recording, or otherwise—without the prior written permission of the publisher, except for brief quotations used in scholarly or critical works.

Publisher: Logos Academic Press
ISBN: 979-8-9999249-0-2

First Edition: Paperback

Printed in the United States of America

Logos Academic Press
Indianapolis, Indiana

Electric information environments, being utterly ethereal, foster the illusion of the world as spiritual substance. It is now a reasonable facsimile of the mystical body, a blatant manifestation of the Antichrist. After all, the Prince of this World is a very great electric engineer.

— **Marshall McLuhan**, *Letter to Jacques Maritain*, May 6, 1969

Preface

Western civilization stands at a crossroads: to code divinity into machines, or to walk into God's grace. *Return to Babylon: From Adam to Antichrist* emerged from my doctoral dissertation in Religious Studies and reflects years of investigation at the intersection of intellectual history, theology, and the philosophical foundations of modernity. It is a study of the ideas that shape our understanding of humanity, destiny, and the divine, and of the profound tensions arising when technology claims the role once reserved for God.

At its core, this work traces the historical and metaphysical currents that give rise to contemporary transhumanism. Paradoxically rooted in the intellectual and spiritual soil of Christian history, transhumanism envisions technological apotheosis, offering the Singularity as a new utopia. In contrast, the premodern doctrine of *theosis*, preserved in Eastern Orthodox theology, presents a radically different vision: human participation in divine life through grace, mystery, and communion with the Logos, Jesus Christ. These trajectories are not merely different – they are inversions. Whereas God became flesh to redeem humanity, transhumanism seeks to revert the flesh into digital code, attempting human transformation through rational, utilitarian, and technological means. *Theosis*, by contrast, is a mystical anthropology that preserves personhood, freedom, and participation in the uncreated energies of God.

This book presents a premodern Orthodox critique of transhumanism. Its eschatological imagination, the AI god, the Singularity, and the pursuit of posthuman immortality, all of which resonates with the ancient warning of Babylon and prefigures the stage-set for the Antichrist. *Theosis* offers a counter-narrative, safeguarding human dignity, moral order, and spiritual communion. By juxtaposing these visions, the work illuminates the choices that define our age: the pursuit of human ingenuity severed from grace, or human flourishing fulfilled in divine participation.

My aim is twofold. First, to map the intellectual and historical genealogy of transhumanist thought, tracing how it emerges from centuries of Christian intellectual and metaphysical frameworks. Second, to illuminate the enduring wisdom of *theosis* as a transformative anthropology, capable of guiding humanity through the moral, spiritual, and existential challenges of our time. This is not merely a critique of a contemporary movement, it is a meditation on civilization's ultimate trajectory.

I offer this work to scholars, theologians, and reflective readers in the hope that it provokes thought, fosters discernment, and clarifies the stakes of our era. May it illuminate the tensions, challenges, and possibilities that lie before humanity as we navigate the precarious intersection of technology, theology, and the enduring mystery of divine life.

—David Patrick Harry, PhD

Table of Contents

INTRODUCTION 1

    A.   METHODOLOGY AND SCOPE 7
    B.   CULTURAL RELEVANCY 9

1. TECHNO-MILLENARIANISM: THE RETURN TO EDEN 15

    A.   THE MECHANICAL IMAGO DEI 19
    B.   MEDIEVAL ESCHATOLOGICAL INNOVATION 32
    C.   WESTERN ESOTERICISM AND TECHNOLOGY 43
    D.   THE ROYAL SOCIETY AND MODERN SCIENCE 61
    E.   FREEMASONRY AND THE PRIEST ENGINEER 85
    F.   AMERICA AND THE SECOND EDEN 95
    G.   CONCLUSION 107

2. TRANSHUMANISM: RELIGION WITHOUT REVELATION 111

    A.   ORIGINS OF TRANSHUMANISM 115
    B.   EXTROPIANISM: IN PRAISE OF THE DEVIL 133
    C.   EPISTEMOLOGY, METAPHYSICS, AND ETHICS 138
    D.   RELIGION IN OUR POSTSECULAR MOMENT 149
    E.   VISONS OF A POSTHUMAN FUTURE 157
    F.   IS TRANSHUMANISM RELIGION? 165
    G.   EMERGENCE OF THE AI GOD 174
    H.   IMMACULATE CONCEPTION: BORN OF TECHNOLOGY 196
    I.   NATURAL MAGIC AND GNOSTIC ILLUMINATION 200
    J.   TECHNO-APOCALYPSE: THE EXISTENTIAL RISKS 213
    K.   CONCLUSION 216

3. THEOSIS: THE LADDER OF DIVINE ASCENT 219

    A.   ESSENCE-ENERGY DISTINCTION: PERSONHOOD & PARTICIPATION .225
    B.   LOGOS THEOLOGY 248
    C.   EPISTEMOLOGY, METAPHYSICS, AND ETHICS 263
    D.   CONCLUSION 287

4. TRANSFIGURATION: GODMANHOOD VS MANGODHOOD 289

    A.   PATHS TO DIVINITY: GODMANHOOD VS MANGODHOOD 293
    B.   IMMORTAL EXISTENCE: MIND VS SOUL 309
    C.   METAPHYSICS: THEOSIS VS HENOSIS 327
    D.   POSTSECULAR MOMENT: THE SEARCH FOR MEANING 338
    E.   RETURN TO BABYLON: FROM ADAM TO ANTICHRIST 359
    F.   CONCLUSION 379

CONCLUSION: THE BATTLE ENSUES 383

INDEX 391

BIBLIOGRAPHY 400

Introduction

As Orthodox Christian philosopher Brandon Gallaher states "Transhumanism is Satanic."[1] Transhumanism tempts humanity with a pathway to self-deification that recapitulates Lucifer's false promise that by transgression "you will be like God" (Gen. 3:5). Today, transhumanism promises human transcendence and deification not by way of moral discipline, sacraments, and ascetic practice but by augmenting the human body with technology. This work utilizes the premodern worldview of Eastern Orthodox Christianity, specifically its doctrine of *theosis*, as a critical lens to examine contemporary transhumanism and its opposing methodology for human deification.

Transhumanism is the offspring of Enlightenment humanism and incorporates a religious faith in the evolution of technology as a salvific means of human transcendence. In the pursuit of such goals, transhumanism diminishes personhood to functionalist definitions of cognition, drawing equivalence between the computational methods of computers and the subjective experience of human embodiment. In contrast, the Eastern Orthodox doctrine of *theosis* rejects any notion of deification being related to technical prowess. Instead, Orthodoxy understands deification as a gift of uncreated grace, in which people are able to directly participate in divinity by way of God's uncreated energies

---

[1] Brandon Gallaher, "Technological Theosis? An Eastern Orthodox Critique of Religious Transhumanism," in *Religious Transhumanism and Its Critics*, eds. Arvin Gouw, Brian Patrick Green, and Ted Peters (Maryland: Lexington Books, 2022) 161.

(love, truth, order, logic, longsuffering, mercy, and so on) and, in so doing, become ontologically transformed.

The Orthodox Christian worldview is an important and interesting critique of transhumanism as it did not experience the same intellectual history that characterizes Western traditions. Not being influenced by Scholasticism, the Renaissance, or the Enlightenment, Orthodox Christianity preserves the Patristic onto-relational framework that prioritizes experiential knowledge of God as opposed to rational apprehension. While transhumanism desires to be remade in the image of superintelligent machines, Orthodoxy aims to become like Christ, the Godman, who has already sanctified human nature with the divine. This theanthropic paradigm emphasizes that Christ is the bridge to eternity, and entrance is gained by acquiring the image and likeness of the transcendent Creator.

The juxtaposition of these frameworks sets the stage for a deep philosophical and theological inquiry into how each understands the transformation of the human condition, and under what metaphysical assumptions and eschatological hopes each project operates. Central to the transhumanist vision is a monistic materialist metaphysics, in which the end goal of humanity is to be augmented and plugged into a centralized digital network. Transhumanist religions, such as Yuval Noah Harari's Dataism, posit that reality is fundamentally composed of bits of information, and all life, biological or synthetic, are essentially algorithms that process information at various speeds based on their position on the evolutionary spectrum. Whereas Christianity believes the Word was made flesh, Dataism attempts to reverse the Incarnation by seeking to turn flesh back into data. The Singularity functions as a secularized Christian eschatology. Instead of anticipating the return of Christ, they eagerly await the emergence of God from machines.

This work adopts "Rebuilding the Tower of Babel" as a guiding metaphor to explore two starkly different approaches to human deification. Babel's biblical story addresses how the pursuit of a god-like status through human ingenuity ultimately leads to catastrophe and destruction. While on the one hand transhumanism is an avowedly secular techno-scientific movement for improved augmentation of humanity, on the other hand it employs unambiguous religious rhetoric concerning *apotheosis* through technology. Despite their superficial similarities, eschatologically these two paradigms are mutually exclusive. Transhumanism aligns with modernity's optimism for unlimited linear progress, culminating in a technological transition into utopian existence. This belief is reinforced by a combination of Darwinian evolutionary theory and Pierre Teilhard de Chardin's Omega Point theory. From this perspective, material evolution is a cosmological process of information complexity that is teleologically pulled forward until the arrival of ultimate intelligence.

Orthodox Christian eschatology is amillenial, believing that the kingdom can already be glimpsed in the Church, and understands the historical movement toward the eschaton as defined by the moral lives of individuals and societies. As people abide by the moral commands of God and seek repentance, so too is the arrival of Antichrist and his New Babylonian empire pushed back by the mercy of God. Any effort to dehumanize individuals or violate their God-given free will is seen as part of a larger spirit of Antichrist. While transhumanism pursues its goals for a total centralization of power, knowledge, and authority, as well as dehumanizing people to simple inputs and outputs, Orthodoxy understands these aims as luciferian and contributes to a one-world order in which personal privacy, autonomy, and true divine union are abolished.

  The presuppositions that undergird transhumanism originated from a Western Christian thread of theological developments from the Middle Ages, which viewed technology as a means to restore the lost perfection of Adam and Eve. Techno-millenarian beliefs are traced throughout Chapter One from late antiquity through the Middle Ages, the Renaissance, Enlightenment, and modernity. It argues that a unique strand of Western Christian thought progressively sacralized technological advancement as a means of restoring humanity's lost Edenic perfection. What humanity lost in the Fall, technology was believed to restore. This salvific hope in technology begins with John Scotus Eriugena's ninth-century theological elevation of mechanical arts as a redemptive means to human perfection. This vision was later fused with Joachim of Fiore's millenarian eschatology, culminating in a techno-religious impulse that saw scientific and mechanical progress as preparatory for the Kingdom of God. Figures such as Roger Bacon, Francis Bacon, and Robert Boyle are shown to have advanced this synthesis, promoting empirical science as a spiritual enterprise aimed at recovering Adamic knowledge and dominion. Chapter one further explores how this techno-millenarian trajectory was institutionalized through the Royal Society, Freemasonry, and engineering academies, positioning the engineer as a priest-like figure of societal transformation. In the American context, this vision was secularized and nationalized, casting the United States as a Second Eden destined to fulfill humanity's redemptive telos through technological innovation. The narrative culminates in the emergence of transhumanism as a postsecular heir to this tradition, wherein scientific aspirations for immortality, omniscience, and bodily perfection echo the theological promises of Christian eschatology, now reframed in secular, technoscientific terms.

Chapter two presents a comprehensive analysis of transhumanism as a postsecular faith, exploring its historical roots, philosophical underpinnings, and cultural impacts. It elucidates how transhumanism, while often perceived as secular, exhibits explicit religious dimensions in its eschatological narrative and salvific promises. This chapter traces the movement's origins from Julian Huxley to the thoughts and aspirations of contemporary transhumanists. It examines transhumanism's incorporation of elements from older spiritual traditions, its explicit framing as a new religion by certain groups, and the continuity of its religious faith with techno-millenarianism. The analysis also addresses critiques and potential risks associated with transhumanist aspirations, ultimately positioning transhumanism as a postsecular faith offering meaning and transcendence through technological rather than traditional religious frameworks.

Chapter three elucidates the intricate theological framework of Eastern Orthodox Christianity, centering on the concept of *theosis* (deification) and its multifaceted implications. It explores the essence-energy distinction in Orthodox theology, emphasizing the unknowability of God's essence, while affirming the accessibility of divine energies for human participation. It delineates *theosis* as an ontological transformation, encompassing the entirety of human existence in union with the Divine. The chapter further delves into *Logos* theology, noetic epistemology, and therapeutic ethics, presenting a holistic worldview that integrates metaphysics, epistemology, and moral philosophy. The Orthodox understanding of sin as ontological privation and salvation as synergistic cooperation with divine grace is juxtaposed against Western theological models, highlighting the distinctive features of Eastern Christian thought. This analysis not only elucidates the foundational principles of Orthodox theology, but also demonstrates its capacity to harmonize philosophical tensions and offers a coherent framework for understanding the relationship between God, humanity, and creation.

Chapter four provides a comprehensive analysis of the divergent approaches to human transcendence and deification between Eastern Orthodox Christianity and transhumanism. It examines their contrasting metaphysical frameworks, anthropological assumptions, and eschatological visions within the context of the postsecular moment and modern crisis of meaning. The Orthodox concept of *theosis*, centered on synergistic communion with God, is juxtaposed with the transhumanist pursuit of technological *apotheosis* and posthuman transformation. Whereas the techno-millenarians of old aimed to restore the prelapsarian perfection of Adam, transhumanists pursue the same project, but with the Posthuman being the new Adam. Orthodox critiques frame transhumanism as a misguided attempt to recreate Edenic perfection and build a New Babylon, warning of its potential to facilitate an antichrist figure. In this sense, Orthodoxy understands transhumanism as a parody of *theosis*, placing their hope in uniting with a pseudo-messiah. Ultimately, the analysis reveals profound philosophical and theological differences between these two paradigms of human transcendence, with significant implications for understanding personhood, ethics, and the ultimate destiny of humanity in a technological age.

A. Methodology and Scope

This work employs an intellectual historical approach and explores the body of Western thought concerning technology as having a deifying and salvific purpose. Intellectual history attempts to identify unit ideas and trace their permutations and persistence through different eras. In this sense, the current work adopts a perennialist approach akin to Arthur Lovejoy, who believed that ideas are enduring entities that can be traced across long time spans among different centuries and cultural settings.[2] This approach highlights how later thinkers inherit and recombine elements of earlier thought, revealing a long-term genealogy of concepts.

Concerning intellectual history, this study incorporates an internalist method by focusing on the internal logic that drives the development of ideas. An internalist approach explains intellectual change principally in terms of the ideas themselves: new theories arise in response to previous theories, and arguments evolve through an inherent dialectic or logical progression. In contrast, the externalist approach situates ideas with their broader social, cultural, and material contexts and places an emphasis on the external factors that shape ideas. While cultural contexts are not entirely discarded, this work attempts to find a balance by prioritizing continuity and internal logic while also recognizing how ideas evolve based on social circumstances.

---

[2] The perennialist approach is opposed to the contexualist approach, most identifiable with Quentin Skinner, who rejected the existence of timeless ideas or questions and believed ideas could only be studied by the embedded context of their language and societal circumstance. Thus, while perennialists focus on the continuity of ideas, contexualists emphasize discontinuities and specific usages.

The scope of this work is concentrated on how Christian concepts concerning technology were seen in theological terms and how these ideas still inform the current project of transhumanism as a postsecular religious narrative. By incorporating what Jürgen Habermas and Charles Taylor have deemed the postsecular moment – a time when the distinctions between the secular and the religious are blurred, allowing secular ideologies to function as totalizing worldviews of ultimate meaning – this work labels transhumanism as a postsecular re-enchantment narrative regarding human transcendence, techno-divinity, and planetary utopia. In this light, although transhumanism is typically described as a secular movement, it can be analyzed as a theological construction and contrasted with the theological paradigm of Eastern Orthodoxy.

Therefore, the scope of this work is not focused on detailing the current state of various technologies, how they function, or their incorporation into biomedical applications. Neither is this work concerned with documenting the extent to which transhumanist ideas have saturated pop culture by way of Hollywood films, science fiction novels, or video game culture. Much scholarship has already been conducted to address these developments and their impacts.

Of the various strands of Christian thought, Orthodox Christianity is most notably labeled a "mystical theology" due to its unique emphasis on direct participation in God and the deifying process of *theosis*. Many attempts to place transhumanism and Orthodoxy into conversation have failed to recognize the significant differences between these paradigms, and have overemphasized the shared pursuit of transcendence as being one and the same thing. Part of this confusion is due to the mutual origins of techno-millenarianism and *theosis* in

Christian thought. However, due to the Great Schism of 1054 and the relative isolation of Orthodoxy from Western scholasticism, the Renaissance, and Enlightenment, the intellectual trajectories of these two paradigms significantly diverge. Orthodoxy is not characterized by the same rationalism that has shaped Western thought and thereby offers a unique perspective through its premodern disposition. Orthodoxy shares the postmodern critique of the modernist project, but instead of relativizing truth, Orthodoxy sees the postmodern turn as an opportunity to return to a premodern outlook that both values subjective experiences and provides a metaphysical basis for objective truth, empiricism, and logical foundations. This work prioritizes the discontinuities and mutual opposition between Orthodoxy and transhumanism and outlines why the first millennium Christian faith sees techno-salvation as a rebuilding of the Tower of Babel.

B. Cultural Relevancy

In recent years, both transhumanism and Eastern Orthodox Christianity have received significant public attention. This convergence is not coincidental; it reflects a cultural moment in which secular visions of human "upgrade" and religious visions of human glorification openly compete and converge.

Despite being a small minority in the United States, Eastern Orthodox Christianity has seen a recent surge in interest and conversions, especially among young adults. According to one report a "78 percent increase in converts to Orthodoxy in 2022 compared with prepandemic levels," marks a striking increase.³ This trend, highlighted in a viral New York Post article about young men "converting in droves," suggests that Orthodoxy's traditional spirituality and mystical orientation resonates in modern culture.⁴ Cultural visibility and curiosity in Orthodoxy have risen since the COVID-19 pandemic and gained members at higher rates than other Christian churches in America.⁵ All of which has marked Orthodox Christianity as a notable player in the American religious landscape after 2020.

The 2020s saw rapid advances in AI, biotech, and space technology that fuel the public's imagination about posthuman futures. Silicon Valley oligarchs and industry leaders openly discuss the goals of life extension, human enhancement, and even immortality in ways that would have seemed far-fetched a decade ago. Investment into anti-aging science, for example, hit record levels in 2012-2022 with over $7 billion each year in private funding, and companies devoted to longevity (Altos Labs, Calico, etc.) have received billion-dollar backing.⁶ Brain computer

---

³ Trevin Wax, "Is Eastern Orthooxy the New Thing for Young Men," *The Gospel Coalition* (January 7, 2025) accessed March 30, 2025, https://www.thegospelcoalition.org/blogs/trevin-wax/eastern-orthodoxy-young-men/#:~:text=picture,7%20percent%20of%20the%20population.

⁴ Rikki Schlott, "Young Men Leaving Traditioanl Churches for 'Masculine' Orthodox Christianity in Droves," *New York Post* (December 3, 2024) accessed March 30, 2025, https://nypost.com/2024/12/03/us-news/young-men-are-converting-to-orthodox-christianity-in-droves/.

⁵ Meagan Saliashvili, "Orthodox Church Boomed During Pandemic, Study Finds, but Calls Growth 'Mixed Bag,'" *National Catholic Reporter* (August 26, 2024) accessed March 30, 2025, https://www.ncronline.org/news/orthodox-churches-boomed-during-pandemic-study-finds-calls-growth-mixed-bag#:~:text=The%20Orthodox%20tendency%20to%20,declines%20in%20participation%20and%20volunteering.

⁶ Kate Goodwin, "Investors Fuel Fountain of Youth Research with Longevity Company Funding," *Biospace* (October 3, 2023) accessed March 30, 2025, https://www.biospace.com/investors-fuel-fountain-of-youth-research-with-longevity-company-

interface research likewise leapt forward, and in 2023, Elon Musk's Neuralink received FDA approval for human trials of its brain implants.[7]

At the same time, transhumanist ideas have been moving from niche futurist circles into mainstream discourse. If Elon Musk exemplifies applied transhumanism through his corporate endeavors, Bryan Johnson is a case of personal transhumanism, and treats his own body as a project of enhancement and life-extension. Johnson, a tech entrepreneur and founder of Braintree/Venmo, is a self-proclaimed professional rejuvenation athlete and has gained fame for his extreme anti-aging regimen known as Project Blueprint. He has amassed millions of followers on YouTube and across his social medias, with a devoted community following his example in pursuit of technological immortality. This goes to show how influential and popular transhumanist ideas have become, and that the ancient quest for immortality is very much alive in the secular sphere.

In the 2024 presidential election, famous tech billionaires such Elon Musk, Peter Thiel, Marc Andreeson, Ben Horowitz, David Sacks, and the Winklevoss brothers voiced public support for Donald J. Trump, and backed his run with significant political donations. Vice President J. D. Vance was mentored under Peter Thiel and worked at Mithril Capital. Demonstrating an interesting realignment among Silicon Valley moguls and the Republican party in recent years. All of which has been noted by political theorists and cultural commentators, with one article stating

---

investments#:~:text=Over%20the%20past%20five%20years%2C,to%20be%20by%20Jeff%20Bezos.

[7] Sissi Cao, "Six Companies Owned by Elon Musk: How the Tech Mogul Manages Them All," *Observer* (October 23, 2023) accessed March 30, 2025, https://observer.com/2023/10/elon-musk-companies-key-people/#:~:text=match%20at%20L213%20Musk%20has,its%20brain%20chips%20in%20humans.

"Trust in artificial intelligence makes Trump/Vance a transhumanist ticket."[8] Within the first month in office, President Trump signed the Stargate Project, a $500 billion investment for AI dominance with Sam Altman, CEO of OpenAI, Larry Ellison, Chairman of Oracle, and Massayoshi Son, CEO of SoftBank. This project aims to win the global AI race and promises to provide Americans with personalized vaccines and cancer treatments tailored to their DNA.

Despite championing transhumanist projects that traditionally religious conservatives find blasphemous, Elon Musk has become a darling among many political conservatives and MAGA supporters. This paradox highlights a broader cultural tension. On the one hand, Musk's critique of "woke" culture and his stance on free speech has endeared him to many on the political right. He is celebrated in MAGA circles as a tech tycoon who stands up to liberal elites, promotes American innovation, and fights for the traditional values of having children and domestic prosperity. Yet on the other hand, Musk is precisely the kind of Silicon Valley transhumanist Christian thinkers have warned about – someone who pushes for the merger of humankind with the machine and pursuing projects such as brain chips, human genetic experimentation, space travel, and sentient AI.

However, not everyone on the right has been swept up in Musk-mania. Influential voices like Steve Bannon and Joe Allen have issued stark warnings about Musk's transhumanists endeavors. Bannon, a populist Catholic and political ideologist, has derided Musk as a hardcore

---

[8] Filip Bialy, "Trust in artificial intelligence makes Trump/Vance a transhumanist ticket," *The Loop* (October 2024) https://theloop.ecpr.eu/trust-in-artificial-intelligence-makes-trump-vance-a-transhumanist-ticket/#:~:text=ideological,Rationalism%2C%20Effective%20Altruism%2C%20and%20Longtermism.

technofeudalist who does not value humans for being humans, but treats people as raw material for a digital utopia. In Joe Allen's book, *Dark Aeon: Transhumanism and the War Against Humanity*, he describes Musk as a cyborg billionaire whose techno-religious vision threatens to undermine human dignity. He describes how currently we are merging with our machines through billions of people using smartphones; however, in the future, this merger will entail a full rewiring of human brains to artificial intelligence systems.[9]

This odd confluence – a billionaire transhumanist icon embraced by segments of the Christian right – is emblematic of a postsecular entanglement in our culture. Because he is seen as an opponent of the globalist left, some religious conservatives overlook their profound worldview differences and reflect a certain techno-utopianism creeping into conservative Christianity, where being pro-Western Civilization and pro-technology can override theological caution. It also sows the seeds for future conflict, forcing conservative Christians to face a reckoning between following the world's richest man and political champion into a transhumanist future, or heed the warnings of people like Bannon and Christian theologians and draw a line. This tension is of great interest to scholars of religion and society, as it reveals how postecular society scrambles usual alignments, forcing ancient faiths to grapple with futuristic aspirations. It also suggests a latent instability between one movement aiming to serve God and another serving a Techno-Mammon entity, so to speak. Eventually, this fundamental incompatibility between Christian *theosis* and technological self-deification will demand a clearer resolution. For now, Elon Musk sits as the fulcrum of the debate, making

---

[9] Joe Allen, *Dark Aeon: Transhumanism and the War Against Humanity* (New York: Skyhorse Publishing, 2023).

the cultural conversation around transhumanism and Christian faith not abstract but concrete and urgent.

1. Techno-Millenarianism: The Return to Eden

During the Carolingian era, John Scotus Eriugena coined technology as the *"artes mechanicae,"* and imbued them with salvific connotations as redeeming the divine attributes Adam lost after the Fall. Combine these developments with the millenarian prophecies of Joachim of Fiore in the twelfth century, and a novel techno-religious perspective emerges. This impulse envisions technology as a means of regaining lost Edenic perfection and achieving transcendence, effectively blending Christian eschatological expectations with the pursuit of technical mastery.

Within the Christian context, millenarianism is the belief that Christ's second coming will inaugurate a thousand-year utopia of human flourishing, supernatural peace, and abundance.[10] What is meant by the term "techno-millenarianism," is the distinct trajectory in Western Christianity that weds technological progress with millennial hopes of salvation. The following analysis examines how this techno-millenarian strand developed within Western Christian thought, how it shaped ideas of redemption through knowledge and dominance over nature, and how it laid the groundwork for contemporary transhumanism as a secularized form of salvation.

---

[10] Millenarianism is distinguished between "pre-millennial" – meaning Christ comes before the arrival of the millennial kingdom – and "post-millennial" – meaning Christ comes after the millennial kingdom. Both strands are incorporated within the history of "techno-millenarianism;" as the central focus in not when Christ will come, but that notion technology is the catalyst for human advancement toward the kingdom to come.

Historian David Noble famously termed this phenomenon "the religion of technology," arguing that modern technoscience carries an unconscious religious impulse. Beginning in the Middle Ages, theologians believed that Adam's fall deprived humanity of both spiritual and material perfection, but through human ingenuity, we could recover our original prelapsarian state. Thereby, what Adam lost, technology would redeem. In the Benedictine monastic tradition, work and its technological tools came to be seen as a means of grace to assist in restoring fallen creation. By the twelfth and thirteenth centuries, this redemptive view of technology fused with Joachim's apocalyptic expectations. Franciscan Friar Roger Bacon exemplifies this fusion: he inherited the idea that advancing the arts and sciences could restore humanity's lost divinity and placed it within a millenarian framework, viewing technological progress as a means of preparing for the kingdom to come. Bacon's vision was influenced by theologians John Scotus Eriugena and Hugh of St. Victor.

Late-medieval and early modern thinkers increasingly saw the scientific-technical enterprise as part of God's providential plan to redeem creation. This inspiration fueled the Age of Discovery with a religious impetus to improve the world and fulfill mankind's destiny. Sir Francis Bacon, the prophet of modern science, explicitly cast the pursuit of scientific knowledge in theological terms. As Lewis Mumford notes, Francis Bacon preached "science as technology" and insisted that knowledge must have practical, world-improving applications.[11] The Baconian reforms brought with it a new science with the aim of alleviating the material miseries of the human condition. In Bacon's

---

[11] Lewis Mumford, *The Myth of the Machine: Pentagon of Power* (New York: Harcourt Brace Jovanovich, 1964) 106.

formulation, scientific progress would reverse the consequences of the Fall, so that spiritual and material restoration would establish a new divinely created order.

Redemption through knowledge is a central characteristic of Western thought. By the Enlightenment and Victorian eras, this outlook was secularized while retaining millenarian optimism. Even within its post-Christian context, utopian hopes for perfection of the individual and society through technology have endured, albeit in a secularized idiom. In late nineteenth-century America, Edward Bellamy's techno-utopian novel *Looking Backward* symbolizes how deeply the Western imagination had come to link technological progress with eschatological fulfillment. Bellamy's vision of the year 2000 depicted a veritable heaven on earth achieved by industrial efficiency and scientific organization, representing a society modeled after machines, where technology transforms a living hell into a Garden of Eden.

By the twentieth century, techno-millenarianism had fully emerged as a guiding ideology in the West if often unconscious. Its spirit can be felt in the development of atomic bombs, space travel, artificial intelligence, and genetic engineering, all propelled by utopian promises of transcendence. This religious faith in technology has been held tenaciously for over a thousand years and seeks salvation within history through human hands. The legacy of this Western Christian trajectory is profound: it sacralizes technological progress as central to human destiny, paving the way for modern secular ideologies that preach human perfectionism through *techne*.

Contemporary transhumanism can be viewed as a direct heir of the techno-millenarian drive, and is a secular outgrowth of Christian eschatology. Concepts of radical life extension, bodily immortality, and even resurrection of the dead abound in transhumanist literature; however, they are now framed in scientific terms rather than divine ones. The search for the Elixir of Life and perfect knowledge from the Philosopher's Stone are now promises of a religious faith that aims to transform humanity in the impending evolutionary eschaton.

This chapter begins by describing the ways in which scientific and mechanical knowledge was categorized in the ancient period. Historically, for the Greeks, philosophical knowledge (*episteme*) was deemed higher than practical science (*techne*). The intellectual thread of techno-millenarianism is then traced from the Middle Ages through Renaissance magicians, esotericists, alchemists, and fraternities, such as the Rosicrucians and Freemasonry, who also saw mechanical arts as contributing to God's kingdom. By the time of Sir Francis Bacon, the empirical foundations of science had become more fully established and unified with the Christian impetus to perfect humanity and society through scientific improvement. Bacon's methodological reforms undermined the Aristotelean tradition of the medieval period and moved in favor of a utilitarian approach concerned with practical application. Knowledge became associated with doing and making, rather than the contemplation of Aristotelean metaphysics and syllogistic logic.

Utopian visions of a scientifically advanced society spread throughout the sixteenth and seventeenth century in works such as Francis Bacon's *New Atlantis*, Thomas More's *Utopia*, Tommaso Campanella's *City of the Sun*, and Johann Andreae's *Christianopolis*. Wanting to strip away some of the magical baggage science had been associated with in previous centuries, the founding of institutions such as the Royal Society and the Ecole Polytechnique placed science in a context divorced from the taint of superstition. What eventually emerges from Masonic lodges and scientific societies is the new profession of the engineer. The engineers, with their technological and scientific know-how, became the avant-garde and priest-like figures who were anticipated to bring about the total transformation of society. These were the expectations of thinkers such as Henri de Saint-Simon and Augustus Comte's positivist philosophy, which influenced both European and American thinkers.

The chapter ends by presenting how techno-millenarian beliefs played a significant role in the formation of the American mythos of progress and technological advancement. Many influential figures have viewed America as the endpoint of the techno-millenarian journey throughout history. America was seen as the divinely inspired "City on a Hill," the fulfillment of the second Eden to come. The American ethos of technological progress and scientific betterment still holds a significant sway in American culture. Silicon Valley plays an important role in the development of transhumanist ideals and technological innovation, which color their eschatological hopes regarding human perfection. What follows are the historical foundations of many presuppositions that shape transhumanism as a postsecular faith that fulfills the promises of human transcendence and deification.

A. The Mechanical Imago Dei

Before tracing the old idea of techno-millenarianism, it is important to understand how scientific knowledge was first classified in antiquity. What will eventually be known as the "mechanical arts" by the ninth century was deemed inferior to the pursuit of philosophical knowledge in the ancient period. Philosophical knowledge was perceived to be universal, abstract, and thereby more encompassing than any particular skill or technique. The reclassification of knowledge that occurred during the Middle Ages and Enlightenment elevated useful arts to a novel place of primary importance. Addressing these intellectual shifts is important for analyzing how and why technical knowledge took on religious significance for the recovery of humanity's lost divinity after the Fall.

Beginning with the Greeks, philosophical (*episteme*) and scientific (*techne*) knowledge were relegated to two separate domains. Philosophical knowledge was understood as speculative or theoretical and viewed higher and more revered than that of practical or technical arts. The natural course of an individual's education was thought to carry them from the lesser arts to greater wisdom, and from techniques to philosophical understanding.

Plato (428-348 BC) is a prominent example of this epistemological hierarchy. He believed that branches of knowledge were not solely determined by their content, but by their relationship between the subject and Being. Plato believed that physics and knowledge of the relationships between objects in the physical world were among the lower tiers of intellectual insight. In contrast, mathematics applies hypotheses with the aid of physical models to better understand mental objects. This progression was seen as a step away from the mere opinion (*doxa*) of the physical world towards true universal knowledge. As Aristotle (384-322 BC) states in *Metaphysics*, Plato perceives mathematics as an intermediary between ideal forms and physical things.[12] Plato's highest form of knowledge is metaphysical and can be apprehended directly

---

[12] Aristotle, *The Basic Works of Aristotle*, ed. Richard McKeon (New York: The Modern Library, 2001) "Metaphysics," *Met.* 987b14, 701.

without the mediation of material forms. Because ideal forms are apprehended through metaphysics, they obtain both ontological and epistemological states, meaning that they are not only objects of knowledge but also the sources of knowledge itself.

The Platonic distinction between philosophical and scientific knowledge was challenged by his student Aristotle. Aristotle's division of knowledge is more complex than that of Plato. Aristotle directed his focus on the content and methods of the different branches of learning, as opposed to their relationship with ultimate Being. Essentially undercutting the Platonic hierarchy and classification of learning. Aristotle's division of sciences is a distinction between speculative and practical. His classification of learning provided students with practical self-edification during their lifelong process of mastering discrete disciplines. The fruits that Aristotle believed aided the students of science in obtaining moral and practical wisdom for everyday life. As seen in his *Metaphysics* and *Nicomachean Ethics*, Aristotle provided a tripartite distinction to the sciences in the productive arts (medicine, gymnastics, music, logic, grammar, statuary, rhetoric, and poetics), practical sciences (politics, economics, and ethics), and speculative sciences (metaphysics, theology, mathematics, arithmetic, geometry, astronomy, harmonics, mechanics, and physics or natural science).

Despite these differences, like Plato, Aristotle believed that "the highest science must deal with the highest genus, so that the theoretical sciences are superior to the other sciences."[13] However, unlike Plato, he more fully explicated the methods and proof whereby knowledge can be obtained, stating "Knowledge, then, is a state of capacity to

---

[13] Aristotle, "Metaphysics," 1026a 21.

demonstrate."[14] He maintains a strict distinction between what can and cannot be objects of knowledge. In his *Posterior Analytics*, Aristotle described a universal methodology whereby certain knowledge may be attained in any science, so that the various divisions of learning are not a model obtained from a lower form of knowledge, but a method applicable to all sciences.

Neither Plato nor Aristotle developed a sufficient place for the mechanical arts in their division of knowledge. Plato makes it clear in *Sophist* 266a-d, that human craftsmanship is, in fact, the lowest kind of knowledge. Aristotle's discussion of *techne* in *Ethics* (114oa) highlights the fact that craftsmanship is intended to be productive, and while they can be taught, they must be distinguished from the higher forms of theoretical knowledge because their object is experience rather than causation. Knowing how to create a writing utensil is very different from philosophical understanding of the nature of writing and language. A fully developed classification and analysis of mechanical arts did not develop until the twelfth century with Hugh of St. Victor.

Although the focus of this work is not the classification of knowledge per se, it is the distinctions between the sciences and approaches to knowledge laid by Plato and Aristotle, which had a reverberating impact on Western Civilization and its relationship to technology. By the fifth century, an important allegorical work titled *De nuptiis Phiologiae et Mercurii* (On the Marriage of Philology and Mercury) by Martianus Capella (430-500) laid a new basis for the seven most important disciplines of learning. Cappela describes the courtship and wedding of Mercury and his bride Philology. Among the wedding

---

[14] Aristotle, "Ethics," 1140b31ff.

gifts, seven maids were gifted as servants to the new bride Philology, including grammar, dialectic, rhetoric, arithmetic, astronomy, and harmony. The two arts present at the wedding feast, but not elevated as gifts to Philology were architecture and medicine. As Capella clarifies, these two arts were deemed to care more about earthly things than about the celestial realm of Mercury. Architecture and Medicine were considered lower arts and did not serve transcendent purposes for knowledge acquisition. This indicates that the Greek division of knowledge was still present during the early Middle Ages in the Latin West. The useful arts, architecture, and medicine were often deemed to be the priority of clever slaves rather than that of the learned echelon of Roman society.

Capella's work belongs to a Latin tradition, going back to Marcus Terentius Varro's (116-27 BC) *Disciplinae*, in providing a comprehensive survey on the liberal arts that humanity should wield and command. The negative disposition towards manual labor in regard to the arts of architecture and medicine was an echo back to the foundations laid by Greek philosophers. As Aristotle states, "We think that the manual workers are like certain lifeless things, which act, indeed, but act without knowing what they do, as fire burns."[15] However, Benedict of Nursia (480-547) soon reenvisioned this attitude in the West. It is his monastic order, the Benedictines viewed manual labor not as a practice of slaves, but an activity that spiritually uplifted and combined with prayer became essential to their daily devotion. Benedict's new monastic rule, *ora et labora* (prayer and labor), established a new precedent and spiritual reframing around labor and craftsmanship. For the life of a Benedictine

---

[15] Aristotle, "Metaphysics," 981b1ff.

monk, daily practices were balanced by both religious prayers and manual labor. By the Carolingian era (800-887), Benedictines were the hegemonic standard among monastics in Western Europe. Recognizing the influence this had in reshaping perspectives on the arts and crafts, David Nobel writes,

> "the Benedictines eventually turned their religious devotion to the useful arts into a medieval industrial revolution, pioneering in the avid use of windmills, watermills, and new agricultural methods. In the process, the monastic elevation of technology as a means towards transcendent ends gained wider currency. By investing them with spiritual significance, the Benedictines lent a new dignity to the useful arts, which was reflected in the Carolingian calendar illustrations and scriptural illumination."[16]

One of the earliest examples of changing medieval attitudes towards the useful arts is the illuminated Utrecht Psalter, composed near Rheims around 830. In it, is seen an illustration of Psalm 63, which symbolizes that those in God's favor are graced by technological advancement. Historian Lynn White describes the illumination as "In each camp a sword is being sharpened conspicuously. The Evildoers are content to use an old-fashioned wetstone. The Godly, however, are employing the first crank recorded outside China to rotate the first grindstone known anywhere. Obviously the artist is telling us that

---

[16] David Noble, *The Religion of Technology: The Divinity of Man and the Spirit of Invention* (New York: Penguin Books, 1997) 14.

technological advance is God's will."[17] The Utrecht Psalter signifies a significant change in Christian theological dispositions towards technology. If technological advancement can aid the faithful in defeating God's enemies, technology must be a divine gift granted to do so.

To this point in Christian history, both in the Greek East and Latin West, the *imago Dei*, the image of God within humanity as described in Genesis 1:26-27, was understood to reside in the soul and humanity's noetic capabilities. In the Greek East and Latin West, the recovery of humanity's lost divinity after the Fall of Adam and Eve was understood as a purely spiritual phenomenon. "In the Augustinian view, therefore, technology had nothing whatsoever to do with transcendence; indeed it signified the denial of transcendence. Transcendence, the recovery of lost perfection, could be gained only by the grace of God."[18] During the Patristic period, Eastern and Western church fathers would never have recognized material technological advances as having redeeming qualities for humanity's salvation. As Jacques Ellul, theologian, and philosopher of technology argued, technology existed only for mankind in its fallen state; it had no significance beyond it, nor would it have for the renewal of that perfect prelapsarian state.[19]

The first person to fully advance the notion the mechanical arts are in fact essential to the soteriological destiny of humanity was John Scotus Eriugena (815-877), the Irish Neoplatonist and Christian theologian of the ninth century. Under the invitation of King Charles the

---

[17] Lynn White, "Cultural Climates and Technological Advance in the Middle Ages," in *Viator*, vol 2 (1971) 198.
[18] Nobel, *Religion of Technology*, 12.
[19] Jacques Ellul, "Technique and the Opening Chapters of Genesis," in *Theology and Technology*, eds. Carl Mitchum and Jim Grote (Lanham: University Press of America, 1984), 135.

Bald, Eriugena succeeded Alcuin of York as head of the Place School, becoming the leading philosopher of the Carolingian Renaissance. He was one of the few scholars in the Carolingian Empire who knew both Greek and Latin and translated many works. He was greatly influenced by Eastern theologians such as Maximus the Confessor, the Cappadocian Fathers, Pseudo-Dionysius the Areopagite, and Augustine of Hippo. Eriugena's most important work is *Periphyseon* (866-67), in which he uses a neoplatonic approach to discuss the hierarchical divisions of nature and classifications of knowledge. Incredibly influential, this work has been considered by some scholars the final achievement of ancient philosophy. In book three, Eriugena divides wisdom into four main distinctions:[20] practical wisdom is concerned with ethical behavior; natural wisdom is concerned with the causes and effects of nature; theology is concerned with the causes of all things; and rational wisdom is concerned with the methodology through which such investigations should be pursued.[21]

With Eriugena, we see the notion of obtaining the image and likeness of God to begin taking on corporeal meaning. Historically, the Christian pursuit of spiritual perfection involved cleansing the rational soul through moral and ascetic practices. However, for Eriugena, humanity's restoration of Edenic perfection incorporates the expansion and perfection of the useful arts. Departing from Augustine's view, Eriugena argued that the useful arts were indeed part of mankind's original endowment, his God-like image, rather than merely a necessary

---

[20] John Scotus Eriugena, *Periphyseon: On the Division of Nature*, Translated by Myra L. Uhlfelder (Eugene: WIPF & Stock, 1976) 123-206.

[21] George Ovitt, *The Restoration of Perfection* (New Brunswick: Rutgers University Press, 1986) p.116.

byproduct of his fallen state. Thereby, he honors the mechanical arts as a redemptive method to restore the lost attributes of prelapsarian perfection. As Eriugena states, he viewed technology as "man's link with the Divine, their cultivation a means to salvation."[22] The novelty of Eriugena's theology signifies an important turning point in the ideological history and classification of technology. Regarding the significance of this shift, historian Elspeth Whitney writes, "It would be difficult to over-estimate the significance of this development. The new emphasis on the place of the arts in Christian education must be seen as one of the chief factors animating the ninth century's intense interest in the arts."[23]

Another significant work by Eriugena was the rewriting of Capella's fifth century, *The Marriage of Philology and Mercury*. However, instead of the mechanical arts being deemed too mundane to be of celestial significance, Eriugena describes medicine, architecture, and five other mechanical arts as gifted back to Mercury from his new bride Philology. Eriugena coined the generic term "mechanical arts" to denote all technological arts as a distinct human activity. By contrast, Augustine had no vocabulary at his disposal. The earliest known use of "*artes mechanicae*," to define the arts collectively appears in Eriugena's work. Departing from the Patristic view, Eriugena argues that mechanical arts are part of mankind's original endowment, the *imgo dei*. Therefore, knowledge of the technical arts was regarded as divine *gnosis*, allowing a return to that already known by Adam. As one scholar wrote about

---

[22] Elspeth Whitney, *Paradise Restored: The Mechanical Arts From Antiquity Through the Thirteenth Century* (Philadelphia: American Philosophical Society, 1990) 70-72.
[23] Whitney, *Paradise Restored*, 70-72.

Eriugena's theology, "In pursuing the study of the arts ... one progresses in perfection since the arts are innate in man. Knowledge of them has been clouded by the Fall. Their recovery by study helps to restore man to his pristine state."[24]

Eriugena provided a new view of the useful arts as distinct, dignified, divinely inspired, and central to God's salvific plan. Mechanical arts had a rightfully honored place in the divine creation of God. Eriugena invested technology with spiritual significance and identified it as the vehicle for collective redemption. The arts were "man's link with the Divine, their cultivation a means to salvation." Knowledge of the mechanical arts was primordially imprinted upon the human soul and had been clouded by the corruption of sin. Eriugena writes,

> ... it follows that all men by nature possess natural arts, but, because, on account of the punishment for the sin of the first man, they are obscured in the souls of men and are sunk in a profound ignorance, in teaching we do nothing but recall to our present understanding the same arts which are stored deep in our memory.[25]

The new Christianization of mechanical arts provided, for the first time, a framing that technology was not only a means crucial for mortal survival, but essential to the realization of immortal salvation.

---

[24] John J. Contreni, "John Scotus, Martin Hiberniensis: The Liberal Arts and Teaching," in *Insular Latin Studies*, ed. Michael W. Herren (Toronto: Pontifical Institute of Medieval Studies, 1981), vol. 1, 25.
[25] As quoted in Contreni, "John Scotus," 26.

Although scholars are not certain of the later life and death of Eriugena, the legend is that he eventually became a Benedictine abbot at a monastery in England. Whatever may be the case, his influence remained, and Eriugena's theological elevation of the mechanical arts was reiterated by Remigius of Auxerre (841-908) in his own commentary on Capella's *The Marriage of Philology and Mercury*. Remigius's notion that mechanical arts were divinely inspired was illustrated in a new iconography of the creator God as a master craftsman, which first appeared in the tenth century in Winchester. This portrayal was the first time God's hand was seen holding scales, a carpenter's square, and a pair of compasses, which later became the Renaissance masonic symbol of the Great Architect. Winchester was an important site for Carolingian-inspired monastic reform. It housed the first giant organ built by Benedictine monastics, which was the most complex machine known at the time and was only surpassed by the invention of mechanical clocks.

By the twelfth century, the spiritualization and exaltation of the mechanical was reinforced by the extremely influential work of the Augustinian canon, Hugh of St. Victor (1096-1141). His innovative and incredibly important work, the *Didascalicon,* is a medieval encyclopedia for the classification of sciences. Written in Paris in the late 1120s, his work builds upon the fourfold Aristotelian division of the sciences. However, unlike Aristotle, this work provides a further elevation of the mechanical sciences as an important domain of knowledge. His four branches include theoretical science, which focuses on the contemplation of truth; practical science, which considers the cultivation of morals; mechanical science, which orders the actions of this life; and logical science, which provides knowledge for correct thinking and effective argumentation. Hugh further divides mechanical arts into seven subordinate arts: fabric making, armament, commerce, agriculture, hunting, medicine, and theatrics. He even asserts that these mechanical arts are on par with the trivium and quadrivium to further legitimate "the inclusion of the mechanical arts in the classification of learning."[26]

Hugh identified technology exclusively with a fallen world, with the first act of technological craftsmanship by Adam and Eve being the making of clothes. Departing from Patristic and Augustinian teachings, he established the useful arts as a means for the recovery of mankind's perfection and his original divine image. Following Eriugena, Hugh viewed prelapsarian perfection as not just spiritual, but also physical. As medievalist Elspeth Whitney states, "the mechanical arts supply all the remedies for our physical weakness, a result of the Fall, and like the other branches of knowledge, are ultimately subsumed under the religious task of restoring our true prelapsarian nature."[27] Addressing the ultimate telos of technology, Hugh of St. Victor writes, "This, then, is what they intend, namely, to restore within us the divine likeness."[28]

It is difficult to quantify the impact of Eriugena's shift in the theological importance of the mechanical arts in the Middle Ages. With Hugh of St. Victor, the monastic reception of useful arts as a means for a divine union with God, became fully articulated. Describing the impact Eriugena's reclassification of the arts had, David Noble writes,

> According to recent studies, the earliest known use of the term *artes mechanicae* to describe the arts collectively appears in Eriugena's work, and thereafter, as interest in

---

[26] Ovitt, *Restoration of Perfection*, 117-118.
[27] Whitney, *Paradise Restored*, 81.
[28] Ovitt, *Restoration of Perfection*, 120.

craftsmanship grew, the term came into common usage. Borrowed from Eriugena, it was later used by Hugh of St. Victor in his enormously influential classification of knowledge. By the end of the twelfth century, the rubric had been fully absorbed into the mainstream of medieval thought and become the normal term for technological arts, used by such philosophers as Abelard, Duns Scotus, Bonaventure, Albertus Magus, and Raymond Lully.[29]

In the thirteenth century Michael the Scot held that "the primary purpose of the human sciences is to restore fallen man to his prelapsarian position."[30] According to historian George Ovitt, Bonaventure, like Hugh of St. Victor, "sanctified the mechanical arts and placed them within the context of knowledge whose source goal is the light of God."[31]

To reiterate the main point, from the Greeks to the rise of the Carolingian Empire, mechanical arts were not deemed to be of spiritual importance regarding the actualization of humanity's divinity. Manual labor was often associated with the activities of salves and lower-class people. Patristic theology had no place for the technological arts to be redemptive in any way. With the rise of the Benedictine monastic community and the rule of *ora et labora* (prayer and labor), a new association between spiritual enrichment and manual labor began to take root. Like the Benedictines, monastic labor and ascetic practice are also part of the Eastern Christian tradition, but divorced from any

---

[29] Nobel, *Religion of Technology*, 15.
[30] Whitney, *Paradise Restored*, 76.
[31] Ovitt, *Restoration of Perfection*, 121.

understanding of technological salvation. Rather, manual labor was understood as an ascetic practice that disciplined the body and mind.

With the emergence of new technologies such as heavy plows, windmills, watermills, and new agricultural methods during the Carolingian Renaissance, manual labor became easier and more productive. Water-powered machinery for milling, fulling, tanning, and blacksmithing constituted what has been described as the medieval industrial revolution. Combining these industrial innovations with a change in theological attitudes towards the mechanical arts – from Eriugena forward – many thinkers saw technology as constituting a recovery of prelapsarian human perfection. The soteriology of the mechanical arts went further than the spiritual benefits of manual labor and asceticism; they became the vehicle for humanity's full restoration.

B. Medieval Eschatological Innovation

Millenarianism is the expectation that the end of the world is soon at hand and that a new earthly paradise is about to commence. For millenarian Christians, theologically, this meant a thousand-year reign of Jesus Christ on Earth. Christian believers of millenarian eschatology taught that Christ would descend from Heaven, return to Earth, defeat evil, and resurrect the righteous to enjoy temporal life within a thousand-year utopian reign. A second resurrection would take place after this millennial period, and the rest of humanity would be resurrected before the Universal Judgement, where the righteous would be rewarded and unrepentant sinners would be punished. Various interpretations of the twentieth chapter of the Book of Revelation form the basis of this ideology.

Also known as chiliasm, coming from the Greek chiliasmos (χίλιασμος) meaning a thousand years, this belief was deemed heretical by the Second Ecumenical Council of Constantinople in 381 as well as the Third Ecumenical Council of Ephesus in 431. During the second council, the church fathers inserted into the creed that "His kingdom shall have no end," in an attempt to dispel the notion that Christ's kingdom would be interrupted in anyway once it began with His church. In contrast to pre- and postmillennial eschatology, both the Greek East and Latin West taught an amillennial eschatology.[32] The church wanted to dismiss notions of two separate resurrections: one for the righteous and the other for sinners. The Patristic teaching of the first resurrection referred to the baptism of believers in the body of Christ, the Church. They pointed to the epistles of St. Paul for further reference "Awake, you who sleep, arise from the dead, and Christ will give you light ... You are risen with Christ."[33] The allusion to a thousand years was understood as symbolic of a long period of time and not a literal thousand years, as millenarians have often taught. The "righteous," who are said to be reigning with Christ in Revelation before the Universal Judgement, according to Patristic teaching, are the saints who have died for their faith (martyrs).[34]

---

[32] Amillennial eschatology teaches that the "thousand years" mentioned in *Revelation* 20 is to be understood symbolically rather than literally. The "thousand years" refers to the current age of the New Testament church during which Jesus Christ reigns as the eternal King from Heaven. Amillennialists see the binding of Satan as a reference to the victory of Christ over Satan during his earthly ministry, which is continued as the Gospel is preached throughout the world. They emphasize the "already/not yet" tension of the Kingdom of God, which had been inaugurated with Christ's incarnation and ascension but has not yet been fully realized. Amillennialism avoided the extremes of over optimistic or pessimistic interpretations of the future.

[33] Eph 5:14; Col. 3:1 and 2:12; Eph. 2:5-6.

[34] Ernst Benz, *Evolution of Christian Hope: Man's Concept of the Future from the Early Fathers to Teilhard de Chardin* (New York: Doubleday & Company Inc., 1966) 22-30.

Church fathers did not teach an elect group of righteous people who would enjoy a utopian existence to bring about God's millennial kingdom.

Many heretical groups and various gnostic sects taught chiliasm based on the expectations of a literal utopian kingdom. However, none was as influential within the history of Christian thought as the teachings of the Cistercian abbot from Calabria, Joachim of Fiore (1135-1202). Historian Ernst Benz described Joachim's prophecy concerning God's kingdom as the most influential prophetic system known to Europe until Marxism. Describing Joachim's importance Benz writes,

> Joachim's doctrine of the Spirit became the basis for one of the greatest spiritual revolutions of the Middle Ages. Those circles of reformers who, in the thirteenth and fourteenth centuries, adopted his teachings of the coming status of the Holy Spirit became the protagonists of the revolution through which ecclesiastical feudalism in the Middle Ages was overcome. This doctrine also was the starting point for many social and political ideas of modern times. There is a direct connection between Joachimite Spiritualism and the criticism which radical Franciscans directed against the ideological basis of the medieval Papacy. Up to the sixteenth century it also influenced the beginnings of most of the reforming and revolutionary movements.[35]

---

[35] Benz, *Evolution of Christian Hope*, 36.

On the morning of Pentecost in 1190, while meditating upon the *Book of Revelation*, Joachim was struck by what he believed to be an inspired illumination to "understand the complete cause of the history of salvation."[36] His basic insight was that history itself was abiding by the progressive development of successive periods corresponding to the three persons of the Holy Trinity. The first period was that of the Father, the *ordo conjugatorum*, initiated by Adam and symbolized by marriage and the family; the second was that of the Son, the *ordo clericum*, initiated by Christ and embodied in the priesthood of the Church; the third and final stage was that of the Holy Spirit, the *ordo monachorum*, initiated by Benedict and is represented by the monk. This final stage of millennial preparation inaugurated the appearance of *viri spirituales*, spiritually advanced men who were at the forefront of humanity's redemptive arch. Joachim believed that these men would aid in the liberation of humanity from misery and suffering through spiritual contemplation and inspired preaching.[37]

Joachim became a spiritual consultant for three popes and preached that the millennium was to arrive in 1260. His prophecies ignited a spiritual fever among monastics, most specifically the more radical Franciscans, followers of Francis of Assisi (1181-1226), who saw their job as preachers to the world rather than cloistered away in contemplative prayers. Joachim's message asserted that the Holy Spirit was fully present to illuminate the faithful and worked within "the pure principle of inwardness."[38] This was in contrast to the official teaching of

---

[36] Benz, *Evolution of Christian Hope*, 36.
[37] Frank E. Manuel, *Freedom from History* (New York: New York University Press, 1971) 127; also see Richard K. Emerson and Bernard McGinn, eds., *The Apocalypse in the Middle Ages* (New York: Cornell University Press, 1992).
[38] Benz, *Evolution of Christian Hope*, 41.

the Roman Catholic Church, which taught that the Holy Spirit works through the church and is personally met in the holy sacraments. Due to his belief in the interiority of God's presence in the third age, he called into question the validity of holy scripture and sacraments, arguing that they were historically restricted to the second age of the Son. The age of the Spirit was an age of freedom, personal communion with God, and the beginning of a social utopia. Joachimite prophecies not only influenced Catholic thinkers for centuries, but also had a significant impact on the Protestant Reformation.[39]

In addition to elevating evangelism over contemplation, Franciscans acknowledged another means of anticipating the millennium: advancement of the arts. By the thirteenth century, the millenarian inspiration behind technological development had been fully expressed by many cathedral builders. Their stone images were to bring acknowledgment of divine judgement and acted as a millennial symbol for the world to come. Their focus on the technical arts was an effort to create works that symbolized the restoration of humanity. As Arnold Pacey wrote, "Rather, they were reaching forward to meet an eternal order, a New Jerusalem, which the cathedral itself symbolized."[40]

No one in the thirteenth century more fully synthesized the mechanical arts and Joachimite prophecy than the Franciscan friar Roger

---

[39] Ernst Benz, *Evolution of Christian Hope*, "But when he describes the community organization of the third age, he outlines certain social-utopian ideas. These emerge most clearly among the radical Spiritual Franciscans in their fight for an uncompromising realization of the Franciscan ideal of poverty. Significantly enough, the social-utopian elements of Joachimitism are particularly noticeable among the Hussites of Bohemia and among those in Germany who were influenced by them as well as in the Joachimitism of the time of the Reformation." 48.

[40] Arnold Pacey, *The Maze of Ingenuity: Ideas and Idealism in the Development of Technology* (Cambridge: The MIT Press, 1992) 30.

Bacon (1219-1292). Following the path laid by Eriugena and Hugh of St. Victor, Bacon inherited the medieval view of technology and placed it in the context of Joachimite prophecy. Bacon not only understood the technical arts as restoring humanity's lost divinity, but in light of Joachimite millenarianism, Bacon also envisioned them as a means to anticipate and prepare for the millennial New Jerusalem. According to Bacon "All wise men believe that we are not far removed from the times of the Antichrist."[41] Sensing the eschaton's approach, Bacon urged his fellow monastics to study the works of Joachim of Fiore to understand the final events of history.

Roger Bacon was a monastic scholar who taught at Oxford and Paris. He was an ascetic reformer who spoke out against the corruption of the Roman Catholic Church and the decadence of his contemporary world. Being a Joachimite, Bacon saw the religious infighting of his day as a sure sign of the impending Antichrist. Bacon held a privileged position with Pope Clement IV, who not only commissioned but approved of Bacon's *Opus Majus*; an attempt to incorporate Aristotelian logic and science into a new Christian theology. He is often accredited as the first advocate of empirical investigations into nature, the first European to describe the prerequisite mixture for gunpowder, and expanded knowledge concerning calendrical reform, optics, and linguistics.

Bacon believed technology was essential for the Christian defeat of the enemies of God and the kingdom of Antichrist. When counseling the Pope, Bacon warned, "Antichrist will use these means freely and effectively, in order that he may crush and confound the powers of this

---

[41] Roger Bacon, *The Opus Majus of Roger Bacon,* trans. Robert Belle Burke (New York: Russel and Russel, 1962) 417.

world," and thereby advised that "the Church should consider the employment of these inventions ... because of future perils in the times of the Antichrist which with the grace of God it would be easy to meet, if prelates and princes promoted study and investigated the secrets of nature and art."[42] Bacon believed, like Eriugena and Hugh of St. Victor, the scientific and mechanical arts, were the birth rights of the sons of Adam. These arts were being remembered through scientific *gnosis*, as they were fully known and understood by prelapsarian man. The steady advancement of technological knowledge has redeemed what was lost in the Fall.

    The advancement of technology served two primary initiatives for Bacon: on the one hand, it was a means for the recovery of knowledge that had been the birthright of humanity, and on the other hand, it was a means to triumph over the machinations of Antichrist and fully establish God's millenarian kingdom. If monastics elevated the mechanical arts as a means of restoring the divine image and likeness to its original perfection, mendicants like Bacon dignified them further for their providential purpose of defeating evil and preparing for the millennial redemption of mankind. What made Bacon even more interesting was the fact that he was an alchemist, astrologer, mystic, and, according to the legends, attempted to create a mechanical brazen head who could answer all questions with yes or no answers. The medieval mechanical oracle is reminiscent of twenty-first-century expectations regarding the capabilities of advanced artificial intelligence, an anticipation that the machine will provide answers to all human questions and problems.[43] The

---

[42] Roger Bacon, *Opus Majus*, 633-34.
[43] Stuart Armstrong, Anders Sandberg, and Nick Bostrom have an article on the expectation, potentialities, and dangers of an Oracle AI whose sole purpose is to

symbol of a mechanical oracle was not unique to the legends about Roger Bacon but was in fact a common motif in medieval romance.

The first appearance of such a pursuit can be found in the *Chronicles* of William of Malmesbury around 1125.[44] Although scholars have questioned the validity of Bacon's mechanical oracle, the lore of Bacon as an erudite wizard was cemented in the English zeitgeist. This was due primarily to the anonymous sixteenth century work *The Famous Historie of Fryer Bacon*, and further by Robert Greene's 1590 pre-Shakespearean comedy *Friar Bacon and Friar Bungay*. Robert Greene's play is often cited as the central source for the myths concerning Roger Bacon's attempt to animate an all-knowing mechanical oracle. The play explains that after seven years of perfecting his invention, Bacon falls asleep at the decisive moment the Oracle awakes and utters three short cryptic phrases, "Time is, Time was, Time is past." Then, a hand appears on stage that smashes the mechanical head with a hammer in one of the more spectacular scenes in Elizabethan drama. The mechanical oracle represents a visual symbol of the intellectual and technological aspirations of the early modern era. As Todd Borlik states, "the play delivers a stern judgement not only on contemporary fantasies of technological dominion, but also a drama itself as an aesthetically and morally dubious form of animation."[45]

Following Bacon, Joachimite Franciscans continued the millenarian message further through men such as the triumvirate of

---

answer humanity's questions titled "Thinking Inside the Box: Using and Controlling an Oracle AI."
[44] Todd Andrew Borlik, "More than Art: Clockwork Automata, the Extemporizing Actor, and the Brazen Head in Friar Bacon and Frian Bungay," in *The Automaton In English Renaissance Literature*, ed. Wendy Beth Hayman (Routledge, 2011), 130.
[45] Borlik, "More than Art," 130.

Catalan science, Raymond Lully (1232-1316), Arnau de Villanova (1240-1311), and John of Ruspescissa (1310-1370). One of the preconditions for the New Jerusalem was a worldwide conversion to the Christian faith. To bring about the millenarian kingdom, Joachimites were convicted to spread the gospel as far and as wide as possible in order to convert nonbelievers. As Franciscan missionary efforts spread to the New World, Geronimo de Mendieta (1525-1604) stated, "Tis vocation of God shall not cease until the number of the predestined is reached, which according to the vision of Saint John must include all nations, all languages, and all peoples."[46] The evangelical effort to extend the Christian faith with the eschatological expectations of the Kingdom to come was a major catalyst for European exploration efforts in the fourteenth, fifteenth, and sixteenth centuries. As historian Pauline Moffit Watts has noted, the apocalypticism of explorers, particularly that of Christopher Columbus, must be recognized as inseparable from their geography and cosmology because it not only inspired their technological innovation, but also shaped their scientific understanding.[47]

Most notably, during the oceanic phase of the age of discovery, is the Italian messianic mariner Christopher Columbus (1451-1506). Columbus believed "himself divinely sent to open up a new way for the friars to fulfill the prophecies of the apocalypse, to convert the heathen, and to hasten the arrival of the millennium."[48] Columbus dedicated his life to his evangelical undertaking, which can be seen in his *Book of*

---

[46] John Leddy Phelan, *The Millennial Kingdom of the Franciscans in the New World* (Berkeley: University of California Press, 1970) 1.
[47] Pauline Moffitt Watts, "Prophecy and Discovery: On the Spiritual Origins of Christopher Columbus' Enterprise of the Indies," *American Historical Review* 90 (1985), 73-102.
[48] Noble, *Religion of Technology*, 30.

Prophecies. Columbus believed himself to be uniquely chosen by God for this particular mission. According to his son Ferdinand, Columbus lived such a pious and ascetic life that he could be mistaken as being a "member of a religious order."[49] His closest companions were friars and monks, especially Franciscans, and Columbus spent a considerable amount of time preparing for his missionary efforts at monasteries.

Intellectually, Columbus was greatly influenced by the works of Cardinal Pierre d'Ailly (1351-1420). Cardinal Pierre was not a Franciscan nor a monastic, but his 1410 work *Imago Mundi*, echoed the same sentiments of Roger Bacon's technologically infused millenarianism. In it, d'Ailly supported his earnest advocacy of the natural sciences by discussing topics such as cosmology, geography, astronomy, meteorology, and calendar reform. Like Bacon, d'Ailly defended the use of astrology as a guide for interpreting prophecy – much like that advocated by Bacon to Pope Clement IV – and was highly invested in the anticipation of the Antichrist. D'Ailly was both the chief source of Columbus's scientific geography and apocalyptic outlook.

> Columbus carefully read and annotated the *Imago Mundi*, and used the knowledge it provided both to guide him on his voyages and to situate them in the divine millennial scheme. Through d'Ailly, Columbus became aquatinted with the writing of Roger Bacon and the prophecies of Joachim of Fiore, which shaped his own reading of events.[50]

---

[49] Watts, "Prophecy and Discovery," 73-102.
[50] Noble, *Religion of Technology*, 32.

Columbus was fully convinced that the world would end in approximately a century and a half. Therefore, believing that all prophecies must be fulfilled, he was adamant that his explorations should end with the conversion of Muslims and the recovery of Mount Zion. He proclaimed himself the Joachimite messiah commissioned by God to prepare the world for its divine renewal. According to his son, Columbus's given name, Christoferens (Christ-bearer) – which was symbolized by the dove of the Holy Spirit – provided further providential connection in Columbus's mind to himself being the fulfillment of Joachim's third age. Like his patron St. Christopher, Columbus too would carry the message of Christ across distant waters to be evangelized to the world.[51]

Fifteenth-century Spain understood itself in the light of Joachimite millenarian eschatology. The Spanish monarchs "assumed the mantle of Joachimite messiah-emperors of the third age, leading the righteous into the millennium."[52] Franciscan Friar Geronimo de Mendieta believed that God specifically chose the Spanish race to undertake the final conversion of Jews, Muslims, and Gentiles before the end of the world. Viewing himself guided by divine prophecy, Columbus dubbed his voyages the "enterprise of Jerusalem" and insisted that his explorations be capped by a religious crusade to conquer the Holy Land and rebuild the Temple. "God made me the messenger of the new heaven

---

[51] After converting to Christianity, St. Christopher is believed to have devoted his life to carrying travelers across a river. One of which was an unknown boy who upon crossing revealed himself to be Christ. Due to his efforts, St. Christopher is considered the patron saint of travelers. Within Western iconography, St. Christopher is depicted with a staff carrying the infant Jesus across a rover on his shoulder.
[52] Noble, *Religion of Technology*, 31.

and the new earth" wrote Columbus in his *Book of Prophecy*.[53] Columbus was a virtuoso of marine arts, furthering the connection between his technical achievements and the millenarian destiny of humanity. The discovery of the New World signaled the promised recovery of adamic perfection. His voyages to the New World inspired Renaissance humanists and magi, who saw these events as sparking a religious revival and further advancement of science and the useful arts.

C. Western Esotericism and Technology

Humanist scholars Marsilio Ficino (1433-1499) and Giovani Pico della Mirandola (1463-1494) are two key figures who attempted to acquire the lost secrets of hermetic natural philosophy and the occult arts in light of Joachimite prophecy. Florence Italy was the site of the failed ecumenical council in 1449; an attempt to repair the schism between Eastern and Western Christendom. As Constantinople was bombarded by Ottoman Turks and full defeat came in 1453, manuscripts preserved only in the Greek East were brought to the Latin West for the first time. The translations of various works were commissioned by Cosimo de Medici (1389-1464) and led primarily by Marsilio Ficino. By 1463, Cosimo requested that Ficino immediately stop his translations of Plato – yet fully translated into Latin – and begin at once on the newly received *Corpus Hermeticum*. Hermes Trismegistus, the purported author of the *Corpus Hermeticum* was believed to date before the time of Moses, and ignited intense effort among Renaissance humanists to unpack the ancient wisdom as a new source of divine inspiration. Despite being redated to

---

[53] Kirkpatrick Sale, *The Conquest of Paradise* (New York: Alfred A. Knopf, 1992), 188-190.

the fourth century by Isaac Casaubon (1559-1614) in 1613, Hermeticism sparked a sixteenth-century fascination with esoteric and occult knowledge that further catalyzed intense interest in the advancement of scientific arts. The alchemical pursuits for the elixir of immortality and deciphering the secrets of nature were understood as spiritual scientific investigations and gave rise to the archetype of the Renaissance magus.

Technological advancement and the useful arts were core features of this new hermetic science. According to Todd Borlik, "the *Corpus Hermeticum* provided a decisive stimulus to the Renaissance fascination with automata."[54] Renaissance humanists read the Hermetic Treatise *Asclepius* and saw ancient theurgic rituals involving statues ensouled with consciousness that could foretell of future events. Reminiscent of similar legends for Roger Bacon's mechanical brazen head. Occult theories have spurred technological innovations. Scholars such as Cesare Vasoli, Pamela Long, Anne Blair, and Anthony Grafton have attempted to demonstrate how humanism, once considered irrelevant to scientific advance, actually was a catalyst that abetted its development.[55]

Heinrich Cornelius Agrippa (1486-1535), a German Renaissance polymath and occult writer, drew inspiration from Joachimite commentary, and saw Joachim as one who gained prophetic knowledge from the occult meaning of numbers. Agrippa believed that because of the Fall and sin of Adam, mankind cannot truly know God without esoteric revelation. That which was lost by Adam, the illuminated soul of the magus could recollect. When the soul was illuminated through esoteric knowledge and practice, Agrippa argued "it returns to something

---

[54] Borlik, *"More than Art,"* 130.
[55] Borlik, *"More than Art"* 131.

like the condition before the Fall of Adam, when the seal of God was upon it and all creatures feared and revered man."[56]

The medieval millenarian legacy and spiritualization of technology also greatly influenced Swiss alchemist and theologian Phillip von Hohenheim, more commonly known as Paracelsus (1493-1541). Often credited as the founder of modern pharmacology, Paracelsus foresaw "the dawning of the Joachimite age of the Holy Spirit in which nothing would remain hidden and the arts and sciences would attain their greatest perfection."[57] The alchemist, for Paracelsus, belonged to the spiritual and scientific vanguard of humanity. Many saw Paracelsus as a prophet, not just as a student of Joachim. Acquiring the attributes of the Creator was a central element of Paracelcian alchemy. In addition to the pursuit of the Elixir of Life and the transmutation of lead into gold, Paracelsus elevated the creation of homunculi as the ultimate prerogative of the alchemist. According to William Newman, Paracelsus saw the creation of the homunculus to likening "the alchemist to a demiurge or lesser god."[58] Through alchemical investigations into nature, man could create and fashion life just as God created humanity. This attribute is still the primary focus of contemporary transhumanism, although packaged in the secular rhetoric of genetic engineering and advanced artificial intelligence. In his own book of prophecy, the *Prognosticato*, Paracelsus closes with an Edenic scene, depicting a man reclining under the tree of knowledge, where the sun of divinity shines forth, illuminating the restored perfection of God's creation. "All things will be revealed. From

---

[56] Marjorie Reeves, *The Influence of Prophecy in the Latter Middle Ages: A Study in Joachimism* (Oxford: Oxford University Press, 1969), 102.
[57] Reeves, *Prophecy in the Latter Middle Age*, 454.
[58] William Newman, *Promethean Ambitions: Alchemy and the Quest to Perfect Nature* (Chicago: University of Chicago Press, 2004) 199.

the lowest to the highest, from the first to the last ... and everything that is in the world will be disclosed and come to light."[59]

The fifteenth century saw the invention of the printing press and ushered in an innovative era of mass communication and increased literacy. The ability to mass-produce written works catalyzed European hopes in technology and its inventive spirit. "What happened during the Renaissance was that this inventive spirit achieved self-consciousness. The pursuit of novelty and technical improvement became a goal and indeed, an established ideal."[60] The history of invention in Europe can be seen as a succession of movements, each characterized by its cluster of ideas and techniques. The invention of printing by moveable type expanded rapidly in Europe. Beginning with only a few pioneer presses in 1450, 1500 saw thousands of presses, demonstrating how a series of inventions could grow rapidly, furthering both technological development and commercial exploitation.

Historians of technology have noted that these technological shifts during the Renaissance was the first emergence of the "technical inventiveness that so strongly characterizes Western culture."[61] The multitude of technical advancements that occurred during and after the Renaissance left an enduring impact on Western civilization's presuppositions on the relationship between technology and human progress. The shift in societal attitudes towards technological innovation also provided a new understanding of humanity's creative relationship

---

[59] Jolande Jacobi ed., *Paracelsus Selected Writings*, trans. Norbert Guterman (Princeton: Princeton University Press, 1979) 296.
[60] Pacey, *The Maze of Ingenuity*, 59.
[61] Pacey, *The Maze of Ingenuity*, 58.

with God and His creation. Humanity was no longer a passive player in history, but a coworker with God to fulfill its telos.

> The idea that men could truly be creative was a new and exciting idea at this time. Creation had previously been thought of as the prerogative of God; now it was seen to be an activity in which mankind could share...Stress on the individual as creator was very characteristic of Renaissance art, and it affected technology also, because at this time, artist, architect, and engineer were often one and the same...The idea of invention soon came into such prominence that it was taken to represent the essence of technical progress.[62]

With the spread of printing technology, Bibles, prophetic books, and apocalyptic speculations became more accessible than ever before. The first printing of Joachim of Fiore's millenarian prophecies was in Venice in the early sixteenth century, coinciding with Martin Luther's break from the Roman Catholic Church. As the Protestant North began to secede from the Catholic Church, millenarian eschatology fueled the reformation project. They were not just critical of papal corruption, but viewed themselves as fighting against Antichrist.[63] From the Protestant

---

[62] Pacey, *The Maze of Ingenuity*, 56-7.
[63] Nobel, *Religion of Technology*, "Martin Luther, who studied Joachimite Franciscan prophecy, "revived the apocalypse as a pattern of history, an illumination of events past and ... prophecy of things to come," while identifying reformers as the chosen people confronting persecution but destined to triumph in the end; in the fourteenth century John Wycliffe identified the papacy as Antichrist; and in the fifteenth, the Cambridge friar John Bale "placed Antichrist's identification with the papacy in a historical scheme influenced by Joachim and based on the book of Revelation." For many in the sixteenth and

perspective, reformers were the millenarian frontline breaking free from the Antichrist Papacy, which held back the fulfillment of Christ's kingdom to come. "The utopian yearning to bring heaven down to earth" greatly stimulated the Protestant Reformation as noted by historian John Phelan.[64]

Not only were the aspirations for an earthly utopia fervent among Protestant reformers, but it also ignited a utopian literary genre throughout the sixteenth and seventeenth centuries. Utopian novels reenforced Eriugena and Roger Bacon's beliefs in the transcendent and salvific abilities of technology. Notable examples of such novels include Thomas More's *Utopia*, Tommaso Campanella's *The City of the Sun*, Francis Bacon's *New Atlantis*, and Johann Andreae's *Christianopolis*. These works describe a future point in which the advancement of scientific discovery would ease, if not eliminate, human suffering. This effort was pioneered by the scientific priest class, who held the divine gnosis of the natural world and the material workings of God.

Thomas More (1478-1535) was an English lawyer, author, social philosopher, and Renaissance humanist. Unlike others in this utopian literary genre, he was a staunch defender of the Catholic Church. More opposed the Protestant Reformation, along with King Henry VIII's separation from Roman Catholicism; a stance that would eventually lead to his execution and veneration as a Catholic saint. Nevertheless, his work *Utopia* (1516) emphasizes many of the themes addressed in this chapter. More's vision of earthly paradise included a monastic vision of austerity, a disciplined egalitarian community, and an elevated belief in

---

seventeenth centuries, the rupture in the Church signaled the coming apocalypse, the prophesized end of the world and recovery of paradise." 38-9.

[64] Phelan, *The Millennial* Kingdom, 70-2.

the salvific power of the useful arts. Every man in More's utopia had to practice a craft for the advancement of knowledge and betterment of society. Technology was clearly seen by More as a means of personal and collective salvation. Technology not only elevated living conditions and capital but was also believed to prolong human life and bring about prosperity and happiness to the whole of humanity. This notion became central to all utopian writings in the sixteenth and seventeenth centuries.

The sixteenth century cemented the idea that technology and mechanical arts were privileges granted to Adam's decedents for the restoration of their *imago Dei*. Spiritual emphasis on technology and technical advancement became a central theme within art, philosophy, esoteric spirituality, and theology. God endowed humanity with superior intelligence and the capacity to refashion the world with his hands, distinctive features that separate mankind from the animal kingdom. Emphasis placed on scientific and technological achievements became a preeminent factor, in which humanity transcended his animal nature and enabled deification. Addressing this sentiment in the sixteenth century Giordano Bruno (1548-1600) wrote,

> This capacity consists not only in the power to work in accordance with nature and the usual course of things, but beyond that and outside her laws, to the end that by fashioning, or having the power to fashion, other natures, other courses, other orders by means of his intelligence, with that freedom without which his resemblance to the deity would not exist, he might in the end make himself god of the earth… And always, from day to day, by force of necessity, from the depth of the human mind arose new

and wonderful inventions. By this means, separating themselves more and more from their animal natures by their busy and zealous employment, they climbed nearer the divine being.[65]

Like Joachim of Fiore, Dominican friar Tommaso Campanella (1568-1639) was also a native of Calabria, and ardent preacher of the approaching millennium. During the seventeenth century, in an attempt to accelerate the apotheosis of history, Campanella led a rebellion to establish an ideal heavenly city. Upon facing his inquisitors for his belief, Campanella "identified himself as the embodiment of Joachim's third age" of the Holy Spirit.[66] His utopian work *City of the Sun* (1602) enshrined the worship of science and technological arts as core principles for social and moral perfection. Science and technology possessed the power to recover the knowledge of creatures and creation once enjoyed only by Adam. Thereby, once humanity could reacquire this perfect knowledge of creation, the second Eden would soon commence.

In Johann Andreae's (1586-1654) utopian work *Christianopolis* (1619), all 400 inhabitants assiduously studied and practiced technological arts. Andreae was a student of Joachim's prophecies, as well as those attributed to Paracelsus and other esotericists. He was a fervent believer in the approaching millennium along with the total restoration of human perfection through scientific advancement. Resonating with the corporal deification first postulated by Eriugena,

---

[65] Gordano Bruno, "The Expulsion of the Triumphant Beast," as quoted in *The Philosophy of Francis Bacon*, Benjamin Farrington (Chicago: University of Chicago Press, 1964), 27.
[66] Nobel, *Religion of Technology*, 40.

Andreae believed that humanity's mind and soul may unfold itself through "different sorts of machinery, or by which, rather, the little spark of divinity remaining in us may shine brightly in any material offered."[67] Technology is not only a means of redemption but also the unfolding of the human soul itself. Andreae argued that practice of the useful arts of science and technology allowed for men to "return to themselves." The divine image and likeness of a redeemed Adam.

One of the most influential expressions of millenarian yearnings present in the sixteenth and seventeenth centuries was the Rosicrucian Brotherhood. Esoteric manifestos began to circulate around Europe in the early seventeenth century, announcing a new spiritual order dedicated to science and art. Their stated goals were nothing less than the reform of mankind and reunification of Christianity through the advancement of scientific and technical knowledge. They understood themselves as the latest incarnation of the Joachimite prophecy and the final reformation. According to the Rosicrucians, the new learning acquired during the Renaissance signaled a new era of spiritual enlightenment and perfection. They encouraged the learned of Europe to join their providential mission and embark on a grand enterprise to fulfill human destiny. The third reformation proclaimed by the Rosicrucian brotherhood was one they believed would sweep over the entire world. In their three founding manifestos, which are often believed to have been written by Johann Andreae, they asserted clear opposition to the Jesuit order and referred to the Pope of Rome as the Antichrist. Their explicit aim was to establish a new era of advanced spiritual and scientific learning. If the great men of Europe were to unite under their banner, they would "collect out of the

---

[67] Francis Yates, *The Rosicrucian Enlightenment* (New York: Routledge Classics, 2002) 119.

Book of Nature a perfect method of all arts."[68] Science, as was common for the period, were thought of in Renaissance Hermetic-Cabalistic terms, relating to the work of "magia" and "Cabala."[69] The brotherhood was built upon the fictional legend of Christian Rosenkreutz and his miraculous travels to distant places, such as the Far East, to discover the wisdom of ancient esoteric truths. Like many of the individuals mentioned previously, this total restoration brought humanity back to the Edenic, prelapsarian perfected state of Adam and Eve. As historian Francis Yates writes,

> …this general reformation has millenarian overtones; it will bring the world back to the state in which Adam found it, which was also Saturn's golden age. So, in the *Confessio*, the second Rosicrucian manifesto, the general reformation is said to presage "a great influx of truth and light" such as surrounded Adam in Paradise, and which God will allow before the end of the world. And, in the verses of the print, this millennium, this return to the golden age of Adam and Saturn, is said to be assisted by "the high society of the Rosicrucians who wish to turn all the mountains into gold." The satire here associates the whole movement with a "Rosicrucian" type of alchemy, for the gold referred to is not the material gold of alchemical transmutation but the spiritual gold of a golden age and a return to Adamic innocence.[70]

---

[68] Yates, *The Rosicrucian Enlightenment*, 60.
[69] Yates, *The Rosicrucian Enlightenment*, 67.
[70] Yates, *The Rosicrucian Enlightenment*, 79.

According to Rosicrucians, Renaissance learning became a new era of enlightenment, an anticipation for the millenarian kingdom to come, and a true recovery of Adam's divine powers. These divine powers are attained not only through the ancient wisdom of magic but also through the advancement of science and technology. Rosicrucians of the European continent, Protestant reformers, and Catholic monastics, all drew inspiration on the millennial advancement of learning from the biblical prophecy of Daniel 12:4, that "many shall run to and for, and knowledge shall be increased."[71] Therefore, they read the *Book of Revelation* as a historical script depicting contemporary events of the sixteenth and seventeenth centuries. The end of history was already at hand. The Reformation was not a problem to be resolved, but a project awaiting millennial fulfillment. Highlighting apocalyptic fervor among Protestants, historian Charles Whitney writes,

> the British Reformation spawned a great revival of historical interpretation of the Book of Revelation … Protestants as a group believed that they were living near the end of the world, during the time prophesized in Daniel and Revelation, and made their fight against the Pope that of a righteous remnant against the Antichrist.[72]

In England, only the most erudite minds were tasked with interpreting the books of Daniel and Revelation. King James I of England

---

[71] Daniel 12:4 King James Version.
[72] Charles Whitney, *Francis Bacon and Modernity* (New Haven: Yale University Press, 1986) 44-45.

(1566-1625) was infatuated with writing extensive commentary on Revelation and Biblical prophecy. British attempts to encourage scientific knowledge and build new educational systems were colored by their millenarian anticipation. Science and education are the means to a perfect society. As scholar Richard Popkin has noted, "it is striking how all pervasive the theme was, and how influential it was ... Efforts to accomplish this great end are part of the making of the modern world and of the making of the modern mind."[73]

Perhaps no one better signifies the bridge into modernity from the Renaissance, along with defining modern science, than King James's Lord Chancellor, Sir Francis Bacon (1561-1626). Often referred to as the father of empiricism, Francis Bacon was an English philosopher and statesman who professed his faith in the millenarian spiritualization of technology. Bacon wrote extensively about the place and importance of science and laid the foundation for scientific methods. Science was a means to understand the Creator, and through the use of scientific inquiry, humanity could now come to perfect knowledge of God through His creation. What Bacon meant by "science" was always "science as technology."[74] Bacon wrote *The Advancement of Learning* in 1605 to further change attitudes towards the utility of science and technology. He stressed the social ideal of technological knowledge as a historical force of progress for the development and blessing of mankind. In *The Great Instauration*, published in 1620, Bacon viewed the great renewal of knowledge and creation as an imitation of the divine work of God's creation. The work is divided into six parts, symbolizing the six days of

---

[73] Richard Popkin, *Millenarianism and Messianism In English Literature and Thought* (Leiden: E. J. Brill, 1988) 6-7.
[74] Lewis Mumford, *The Myth of the Machine*, 106.

creation, with the seventh day of rest emblematic of Adam's divine dominion over creation.

For Bacon, the kingdom of man should be founded on the sciences, being itself the entrance into the kingdom of Heaven. In the same vein as his progenitors, he wanted to elevate the useful arts of technology to the prestigious position of other liberal arts, and explicitly associate them with the means to human deification. This entailed the recovery of mankind's original image and likeness of God; and addresses what he fully intended by "the great instauration." As biographer Paolo Rossi states, Bacon's overarching aim "was to redeem man from original sin and reinstate him in his prelapsarian power over all created things."[75] Reiterating this point Frances Yates writes, "His 'great instauration' of science was directed towards a return to the state of Adam before the Fall, a state of pure and sinless contact with nature and knowledge of her powers. This was the view of scientific progress, a progress back towards Adam."[76]

Baconian science was not just a speculative enterprise but was grounded in a utilitarian focus on practical applications. Bacon desired to reform natural philosophy. In *Novum Organum*, he further explicates this relationship between the useful arts and natural philosophy, as two separate enterprises that should provide feedback and nourish each other. Still tainted by previous classifications of knowledge, some philosophers of his day had a contemptuous attitude towards the mechanical arts, deeming them unworthy of being the sole focus of philosophical inquiry.

---

[75] Paulo Rossi, *Francis Bacon: From Magic to Science* (Chicago: University of Chicago Press, 1968) p.127-29.
[76] Yates, *The Rosicrucian Enlightenment*, 158.

The ultimate goal of Bacon's scientific reforms was to close the gap between technological enterprise and elite disdain held by philosophers.

Bacon's biblically inspired vision reflected the anthropocentric assumptions of his seventeenth-century Protestant faith, as well as that of Renaissance humanism. Human ascendency was central to the divine plan, and knowledge of creation was a rich storehouse for the glory of God and the relief of man's estate. Bacon wrote "Man, if we look to final causes, may be regarded as the center of the world insomuch that if man were taken away from the world, the rest would seem to be all astray, without any aim or purpose."[77] Like Roger Bacon, Francis Bacon referenced the biblical narratives of Noah, Moses, and Solomon, as well as the progressive development of technology, as providing "sufficient evidence for the belief that the restoration of mankind's original powers was part of the divine plan."[78]

Towards the end of his life, Bacon articulated his ideals between technological utopia and Christian eschatology in the posthumously published work, *The New Atlantis* (1626). In it, he presents a utopian society regulated and led by a scientific priesthood located at his ideal college, Solomon's House. The story takes the form of an allegory concerning the discovery of a new land and society by storm-tossed mariners. What they discover is a perfect society built on the principles of brotherly Christian love and investigations into scientific knowledge. This advancement in knowledge occurred at their great college called Solomon's House. Here, the order of priest-scientists pursued research in all domains that would benefit the whole of humanity. This work

---

[77] Charles Webster, *The Great Instauration: Science, Medicine, and Reform 1626-1660* (London: Gerald Duckworth, 1975) 329.
[78] Nobel, *Religion of Technology*, 51.

indicates to which subjects research should be devoted. Such topics include but not limited to gardening, agriculture, baking, botany, astronomy, alchemy, psychology, and economics; but specifically concerning the mechanical arts, "research on flying machines, submarines, and methods of refrigeration, subjects related to 'natural magic' on which several of Bacon's contemporaries speculated."[79]

    Bacon's utopia is an egalitarian society in which generosity, enlightenment, dignity, and piety prosper among inhabitants. To create such a society, Bacon clarifies that spiritual knowledge is the highest degree of scientific knowledge. Science, for Bacon, not only aids our empirical understanding of nature, but also brings with it the spiritual gnosis of God's creation. Therefore, not only does the mechanical arts perfect society, but they also perfect humanity and move them towards union with God. Technical domination over nature actualizes and realizes Christian virtues, which foreshadow modern technological innovation and its utopian aims. *The New Atlantis* gave readers a vision of what life would be like once the "Great Instauration" was completed. Like the Rosicrucians, Bacon believed that the advancement of science and technology was intrinsically related to the redemption of humanity's fallen state.

    The relationship between Francis Bacon and the Hermetic magical milieu of his day has been a topic of great speculation by scholars. The monumental impact of Hermeticism in Renaissance Europe catalyzed newfound interest in magical forms of spirituality. However, as mentioned previously, the delineation between what we know today as "science" compared to that of magic was blurred. Was it science or magic

---

[79] Pacey, *The Maze of Ingenuity*, 125.

when practitioners pursued the alchemical transmutation of gold, the quest for the elixir of immortality, or the creation of homunculi? In "A History of Transhumanist Thought," transhumanist philosopher Nick Bostrom concludes that these activities were in fact early iterations of the transhumanist project. Alchemy is often credited as a precursor in modern chemistry. As Nick Bostrom highlights, Renaissance humanism offered a new depiction of man, one that was impowered by natural investigation, was highly developed scientifically, and concluded man was "responsible for shaping himself."[80] Technology remains a mechanism through which humanity redefines in light of their own scientific knowledge.

During Queen Elizabeth's reign, considerable interest was garnered in the study of alchemy, divination, and hermetic philosophy. The most emblematic of her support was the backing of the works and expeditions of her court astrologer, John Dee (1527-1609). John Dee was an English mathematician, cosmographer, alchemist, and occultist. He was an incredibly learned man with an enormous library, which scholars have described as the greatest personal library in England at the time. He traveled to various European courts casting horoscopes and shared his knowledge of hermetic sciences, leading to accusations that he was an Elizabethan spy. Utilizing his "shew stone" –a black obsidian stone Dee claimed was gifted to him from heaven and fell from the sky in his backyard – he, with the help of his associate Edward Kelley, claimed to use this stone to contact what they believed were angels. This led to the construction of an entire magical practice and language known as Enochian. Believing that they were contacting divine angels that

---

[80] Nick Bostrom, "A History of Transhumanist Thought," in *Journal of Evolution and Technology* 14 (April 2005) 2.

provided spiritual gnosis, they dubbed Enochian the language of the angels.

For Dee, magic and science were intimately linked, and with the elevation of King James VI of Scotland to King James I of England, imperial dispositions towards magic and the occult shifted. King James I, did not have the same support for John Dee's magical endeavors as did Queen Elizabeth. King James had a deep "interest in, and dread of, magic and witchcraft," and in his work *Demonology* in 1597, advocated for the death penalty for sorcerers and witches.[81] It's not surprising then, that when Dee appealed to James to help clear his tarnished reputation from accusations of conjuring demons, James had nothing to do with him. The old man, who once held a prestigious position in the Elizabethan Court and garnered respect across Europe, died in shame and poverty. Francis Bacon surely took note of his King's disdain for all things magical, and likely avoided anything that would invoke the King's suspicion.

The old Elizabethan scientific tradition was no longer in favor; therefore, Bacon needed to steer a cautious course around any magical association with his advancement of scientific learning. Bacon never directly implemented himself in any esoteric brotherhood, although speculative theories have attempted to tie him with the order of the Rosy Cross. Given his historical context, Bacon must have been aware of such fraternal organizations, whether he was ever initiated or not. Nevertheless, when one reads his utopian work *The New Atlantis*, it is difficult not to conclude that Bacon was consciously aware of the Rosicrucians and their manifestations. Themes emerge eerily reminiscent

---

[81] Yates, *The Rosicrucian Enlightenment*, 162.

of the Rosicrucian manifestos. Describing many of the motifs present in *The New Atlantis*, Francis Yates writes,

> The religion of *The New Atlantis* has much in common with that of the Rosicrucian manifestos. It is intensely Christian in spirit, though not doctrinal, interpreting the Christian in terms of practical benevolence, like the R.C. Brothers. It is profoundly influenced by Hebraic-Christian mysticism, as in Christian Cabala. The inhabitants of *New Atlantis* respect the Jews; they call their college after Solomon and seek for God in nature. The Hermetic-Cabalist tradition has borne fruit in their great college devoted to scientific enquiry. There is an unearthly quality in the world of New Atlantis. Though it may be prophetic of the advent of the scientific revolution, this prophecy is made, not in a modern spirit, but within other terms of reference. The inhabitants of *New Atlantis* would appear to have achieved the great instauration of learning and have therefore returned to the state of Adam in Paradise before the Fall – the objective of advancement both for Bacon and for the authors of the Rosicrucian manifestos.[82]

Whether Francis Bacon was directly involved with the Rosicrucians or other esoteric groups is up for speculation. Given the animosity King James I had towards the magical arts, it is plausible that

---

[82] Yates, *The Rosicrucian Enlightenment*, 168-69.

Bacon would hide such evidence if there were any. Still, what is important is Francis Bacon as an essential bridge, uniting the techno-millenarian expectations of the Middle Ages with those of modern science. Bacon sanitized the magical and alchemical legacy associated with the techno-millenarian project for Edenic restoration after the Renaissance. Bacon adopted a utilitarian approach to scientific knowledge, emphasizing the role of science in practical applications and methods for uncovering truths about God's creation. "'Truth and utility here are the very same thing,' wrote Bacon, meaning the perfect knowledge acquired through science was best measured by its usefulness."[83] Science was not purely a speculative enterprise but was rooted in the utility and invention of practical arts. Science and technology were seen as essential for attaining perfection and uplifting humanity, both spiritually and physically. Having witnessed the mechanical achievements of shipbuilding, navigation, ballistics, printing, and water engineering, Bacon took these as signs that the millennial Kingdom of God was surely at hand. If Bacon's effort was utilitarian in emphasis, it was still transcendent in essence. Utilizing this practical knowledge would restore humanity's divine image and erect the New Jerusalem.

D. The Royal Society and Modern Science

Francis Bacon's enduring influence on the medieval identification of technology with transcendence now informed the nascent mentality of modernity. Baconian reforms emphasized the

---

[83] Nobel, *Religion of Technology*, 49.

importance of observation, experimentation, and induction in the scientific process. Bacon challenged the prevailing authority of Aristotelian philosophy, which dominated scholasticism and medieval Europe, using a more empirical and inductive methodology. This reform not only influenced many great scientists of the seventeenth century but also laid the foundation for the scientific method used today. Bacon's reforms were a revolution and powerfully catalyzed by the efforts of English puritans who wanted to rid England of its Catholic legacy. As capitalistic and industrial enthusiasm spread across England and parts of Protestant Europe, Puritans held tight to the millenarian promise of science as a sign of their providential favor with the All Mighty.

At the center of the Baconian reforms was the German educational reformer Samuel Hartlib (1600-1662). Hartlib was greatly indebted to Francis Bacon's contribution to the new theory of education and knowledge. Building a network of correspondence around Western and Central Europe, known as the Hartlib Circle, Hartlib aimed to bring Protestants together to further stimulate scientific, technological, and educational reforms. Like Bacon, Hartlib's advocacy for science and the arts was marked by a decidedly utilitarian spirit. Hartlib attempted to bring to life Bacon's fictional Solomon's House, a centralized institute dedicated to the study and investigation of nature described in *The New Atlantis*. Hartlib coined this the "Office of Address;" with aims of ingenuity, scientific progression, and profitable inventions. The Office of Address was a college of "Nobel Mechanisms and Ingenious Artificers" with the "express purpose of making Bacon's Solomon's House a reality through the establishment of scientific schools."[84]

---

[84] Nobel, *Religion of Technology*, 54.

Hartlib believed that the earnest development of scientific arts would prepare humanity to return to prelapsarian grace. Because of the fall, men were required to learn the arts anew. Believing that the millenarian kingdom approached, Hartlib was convinced that medical improvement would eventually restore humanity to its original Edenic immortality. He saw the development of modern science as regathering forbidden fruits from the original Tree of Knowledge. These scientific fruits constituted the coming of the new Garden of Eden. In his 1655 *Chymical Address*, Hartlib emphasizes this point writing,

> ...by which all men and all flesh shall be delivered from death, and that as truly, solidly, and surely, as at the time of the Fall, by gathering the fruit of the forbidden tree, we together with all flesh fell into sin, death, and ill. And this glory and great joy hath God reserved for us, that live in these latter days, and hath kept his good Wine until now ... I do foretell all physicians, that then their Physic shall be worth nothing, for another Garden will be found. Whence shall be had herbs, that shall preserve man not only from sickness, but from death itself.[85]

Like other Baconians, Hartlib was a promoter of practical arts and wanted to direct the advancement of knowledge and learning towards those practical ends. Therefore, great effort was placed on educational reforms, emphasizing the practical application of scientific knowledge and focusing on training in mechanics and other useful arts. John Milton

---

[85] As quoted in Webster, *The Great Instauration*, 246.

(1608-1674), one of Hartlib's closest associates in educational reform, shared these sentiments. Milton argued in his treatise "On Education," that education was above all else a means towards divine redemption. "The end of learning," wrote Milton, "is to repair the ruins of our first parents by regaining to know God aright, and out of that knowledge to love him, to imitate him, to be like him."[86] Milton, who himself had gnostic leanings, promoted a message of scientific knowledge that united humanity with God.

The Puritan initiative for practical universal education was inspired by the Moravian Protestant and educational philosopher John Amos Comenius (1592-1670). Comenius was a friend of Hartlib and part of his inner circle within the Office of Address. Comenius was a Czech theologian, philosopher, last bishop of Moravian Unity of the Brethren church, and often considered the founder of modern education. His magnus opus for education was *Didactica Magna* (The Great Didactic) published in 1657. His aim was nothing less than to teach everything to all men. Comenius was one of the earliest champions of universal education, advocating textbooks be written in native languages, the educational use of pictures in textbooks, and equal opportunity for poor children and women. Comenius saw education as central to the recovery of humanity's divinity and what it meant to be fully made in the image and likeness of God, placing rational apprehension as the meeting point between the Creator and man. Comenius placed great emphasis on applying Baconian reform principles to the education of children and the general population. His book *Orbis Pictus* (Visible World in Pictures)

---

[86] As quoted in Webster, *The Great Instauration*, 100.

was one of the first children's textbooks to utilize pictures, and was one of the most widely circulated textbooks for children for the next century.

Comenius's Baconian reform efforts emphasized the practical application of knowledge to everyday life, and focused upon training in animal husbandry, mechanics, minerology, navigation, surveying, architecture, and metalworking. Upon the invitation by Hartlib, Comenius visited England briefly before the outbreak of the English Civil War, with a goal to implement and incorporate his educational principles within Hartlib's "Office of Address." An effort shared by fellow Protestant educational reformers and members of the Hartlib circle, John Dury (1596-1680). By 1641, Comenius, Hartlib, and Dury had all found themselves in England with the hope of finally actualizing a Baconian universal school for the advancement of all humanity. Despite renewed excitement in England, 1641 was a false light. With building tensions within England, it became apparent that this new vision would not be peaceful. By 1642, Comenius had left England for Sweden and Dury for the Hague. Only Hartlib continued writing, planning, and organizing societies that would be models for the future. Dury attempted unsuccessfully to unite various Protestant churches in 1661 in anticipation of the Christian millennium.

Protestantism was filled with millenarian fervors at the time, and with notable advances in scientific and technological development, they felt the Kingdom was soon approaching. Protestants placed great hope in Frederick the Elector Palatine (1592-1632) to be that king to rule over the millenarian promise. However, by the end of the Thirty Years War, sentiment had begun to shift. With the defeat of the "Winter King" Frederick the Elector Palatine, King of Bohemia, at the Battle of White Mountain on November 8, 1620, Protestant hope for a spiritually illuminated kingdom felt lost. Frederick was an intellectual, hermetic mystic, and a Calvinist who married Elizabeth Stuart, the daughter of King James I of England. Protestants viewed Frederick's wedding to Elizabeth as more than just a union of European nobility; it was the dawn of a new beginning for humanity. Unlike his father-in-law, Frederick was greatly influenced by Hermetic philosophy and the esoteric spiritual milieu of the early seventeenth century. He was a strong patron of the sciences, and the Rosicrucian movement was fully behind Frederick, as the idealized king prophesized in their manifestos.

    The most notable among those who propagated this faith was the secret author of the Rosicrucian manifestos Johann Andreae (1586-1654). Shortly before his marriage in 1613, King James I inducted Frederick into the Order of the Garter, the most prestigious knighthood in England. An honor of significant recognition for his support of the Protestant cause and close ties to the English monarchy. When Andreae rewrote his youthful version of the *Chemical Wedding of Christian Rosenkreutz*, "he would bring it up to date by allusions to the present notable German representative of the Order of the Garter, the prince whom we have already found implied in the Rosicrucian movement, Frederick of the Palatinate."[87] The Rosicrucian hope for a new universal reform movement to advance spiritual and scientific knowledge felt lost with the disaster of war and the collapse of Frederick, King of Bohemia. Andreae and Comenius' intellectual and religious attitudes reflect each other. They and their followers began to move away from the discredited name of "Rosicrucian" during wartime. Nonetheless, Andreae's Christian vision of utopia, *Christianopolis*, still colored the hearts and minds of many

---

[87] Yates, *The Rosicrucian Enlightenment*, 94.

influential reformers. Utopianism "was one of the great subterranean forces of the wartime years, propagated by men like Comenius, Samuel Hartlib, John Dury, all influenced by Andreae, and inheritors of the reforming movement which had met with such catastrophe in its Rosicrucian disguise."[88]

Where Andreae describes the Ministry of Angels and their insistence on science, technology, and philanthropy in *Christianopolis*, Comenius makes explicit the teaching aspect of the Ministry of Angels in his work, *Labyrinth of the World and Paradise of the Heart* (1623). Inspired by the millenarian vision of Campanella's *City of the Sun* but horrified by the Thirty Years War, Comenius reverses the optimistic hope of the preceding years. *Labyrinth of the World* describes a city divided into many quarters and streets, in which all the sciences, learning, and occupations of men are represented. However, all the sciences of man lead to nothing and are futile because of the unsound foundation of knowledge. The streets are filled with quarrelsome men from different religions and sects. We read about vast armies rolling along inflicting inhumane punishments on rebels, contempt for human life, and vast swaths of death and destruction. Science, in the wrong hands of the spiritually unsound, ultimately leads to demise. The work is an insightful snapshot into Protestant attitudes during the Thirty Years War, and highlights the "failure and petering out of the Rosicrucian furor and the hopes it raised."[89]

The institutional and cultural divide between science and technology that occurred in the nineteenth century had not yet developed by the time the first permeant institutions of science were established.

---

[88] Yates, *The Rosicrucian Enlightenment*, 218-19.
[89] Yates, *The Rosicrucian Enlightenment*, 215.

The utilitarian spirit underlying Baconian reform efforts was still central to early scientific academies. The first academy, the Italian Academia dei Lincei, was formed in 1603, closed in 1630, and reopened in 1660. Coinciding with the year the Royal Society was first founded in England in 1660. According to the Italian Academia dei Lincei, and later the Royal Society, their expressed empirical aim was "to improve the knowledge of natural things and all Useful Arts, Manufactures, and Mechanical practices, Engines, and Inventions by experiment."[90]

The Royal Society desired that this new era of science be divorced from its previous relationship with magical and hermetic philosophies. However, in the years preceding the founding of the Royal Society, some important members of the Oxford Group still supported the tarnished John Dee and Paracelsian science. One such member was John Wilkins (1614-1672), an Anglican clergyman, a natural philosopher, and author. Wilkins was an important founding member of the Royal Society and author of the 1648 book *Mathematical Magick*. His work was highly supportive of the mechanical theories of esotericist Robert Fludd (1574-1637), and the mathematical work of John Dee. The book outlines Wilkins's great interest in automata and speaking statues by way of "mechanical magic"[91] Wilkins frequently mentions Lord Verulam (Francis Bacon) in this work, showing that at this point in time, he had not disconnected Baconian science from the hermetic tradition of John Dee and Robert Fludd. Wilkins claimed he titled the book *Mathematical Magic* "because the kind of mechanical inventions treated in it have been so styled by occultist Henry Cornelius Agrippa."[92] Despite these clear

---

[90] Mumford, *Pentagon of Power*, 111.
[91] Yates, *The Rosicrucian Enlightenment*, 236.
[92] Yates, *The Rosicrucian Enlightenment*, 237.

proclivities towards esoteric spirituality, by the 1660s, with the founding of the Royal Society, Wilkins later disavowed the hermetic arts.

Wilkins's book is important because it highlights his outlook on science in 1648, the same year meetings began in Oxford to form what would become the Royal Society. According to Thomas Sprat's *The History of the Royal Society*, these meetings in Oxford were held in Wilkins's room at Wadham College and ran from 1648 to 1659. Among some of the notables present, were Robert Boyle, William Petty, and Christopher Wren. Wilkins was a polymath, a serious natural philosopher, and one of the few people to head both the University of Oxford as well as the University of Cambridge. His fascination with magic and automata is understood in light of his scientific interest and research. According to John Evelyn (1620-1706), fellow founder of the Royal Society, Wilkins's office had a hollow statue which could utter "words by a long, concealed pipe, and that he possessed many other artificial, mathematical, and magical curiosities."[93]

Despite some efforts, hermetic lore had not yet fully dissipated in 1640s England. During this same period, Thomas Vaughn translated the *Fama* and *Confessio* into English, making Rosicrucian manifestos better known to the general public. Thomas was the twin brother to the influential Welsh poet Henry Vaughn. Thomas's patron is said to have been Sir Robert Moray, a founding member of the Royal Society and Freemasonry in Great Britain, demonstrating the esoteric curiosities many learned men still held.

During this early period, before the advent of the Royal Society, John Webster (1578-1632) wrote a work advocating the philosophy of

---

[93] Yates, *The Rosicrucian Enlightenment*, 237.

Hermes to be revived by the Paracelsian school and made part of the official curriculum of universities. Webster was a Jacobean dramatist, best known for his tragedies *The White Devil* and *The Duchess of Malfi*. Webster believed that the recovery of the Adamic language (language of nature) before the Fall has been made available by men such as Jakob Böhme (1575-1624), Robert Fludd, John Dee, Paracelsus, and the Fraternity of the Rosy Cross.[94] Webster argued that works of these men may be brought to perfection by the empirical methods of Francis Bacon. He advocated that educational reforms in England replace Aristotelian scholasticism with a Hermetic-Paracelsian-type natural philosophy, if the Adamic language was to be recovered. This provoked a stern rebuke by the Royal Society's founding members, Seth Ward (1617-1689) and John Wilkins. Ward was quite angry with Webster for equating Bacon to Fludd and was disgusted with his magical discourse on the language of nature and illuminated fraternity of the Rosicrucians. What is so striking, is only six years earlier, Wilkins made the same connection with Bacon and the Dee-Fludd tradition in *Mathematical Magick*.

    The shifting opinions of English intelligentsia are indicative of the public disavowal of magic and witchcraft by the time the Royal Society was founded. By 1659, Meric Casubon (1599-1671) had published John Dee's Spiritual Diary and publicly accused him of diabolical magic and demonic witchcraft. The Parliamentarians tried to suppress the work unsuccessfully, as it was thought that the publication was an attempt to discredit the sectarian Protestants in their fight against the Royalists. The result was as intended: religious passions remained high after the English Civil War, and many feared accusations of a

---

[94] Yates, *The Rosicrucian Enlightenment*, 238-39.

dreaded witch-scare that could stifle their newly found scientific enterprise. As natural philosophers moved towards the establishment of the Royal Society, efforts were made not to let the superstitions of the past discredit their Baconian reforms. Therefore, public support for John Dee waned, and a sanitized depiction of Baconianism was made as innocuous as possible. Describing the result of Meric's publication and denouncement of Dee, Frances Yates writes,

> The publication of Dee's diary was certainly part of a general campaign against enthusiasts and illuminati being worked up at the time. In his preface, Casaubon states that Dee, like Trithemius and Paracelsus, was inspired by the Devil. The mention of Paracelsus gets rid of the whole Rosicrucian movement. This campaign ruined Dee's reputation and deprived him for centuries of the credit for his important scientific work. Robert Hooke, who, as one of the best mathematicians in the Royal Society, would have known Dee's work, later tried to rescue his reputation by arguing that the Spiritual Diaries were a "concealed history of art and nature" relating to contemporary events.[95]

With the restoration of Charles II to the English throne in 1660, parliamentary armies disbanded and men were eager for peace. At this moment of reconciliation, the Royal Society was founded and Charles II was its patron. The Royal Society was composed of men on both sides of

---

[95] Yates, *The Rosicrucian Enlightenment*, 241.

the civil war, and the advancement of scientific learning brought about unity. However, certain subjects needed to be avoided, and religious matters were not discussed, only scientific problems. The Baconian insistence on experiments, with the collection and testing of scientific data, guided the society forward. The delicate existence of this enterprise required great caution.

The Invisible College, promised by the Rosicrucians, was now made visible, but with restricted aims compared to earlier movements. In his book, *The Way of Light*, published in Amsterdam in 1668 and dedicated to the Royal Society, Comenius argued that the Royal Society was the inheritor of previous labors of the Rosicrucians. He writes of sounding trumpets heralding their labors "to secure that human knowledge and the empire of the human mind over matter shall not for ever continue to be a feeble and uncertain thing."[96] Comenius feared that the restricted aims of the Royal Society may lead not to the transcendent kingdom of God, but one shackled to the earthly desires of fallen man. Echoing his cautious message in *the Labyrinth of the World and Paradise of the Heart*. He warned that the new foundations they were building for the investigation into nature be not a "Babylon turned upside down, building not towards heaven, but towards Earth."[97]

Scholars Lauren Kassell and Charles Webster have also argued the Invisible College of Rosicrucianism is the intellectual precursor to the formation of the Royal Society. The earliest direct references found regarding this matter come from three sperate correspondences Robert Boyle (1627-1691) had with his tutor Isaac Macombes, Francis Tallents,

---

[96] As quoted in Francis Yates, *The Rosicrucian Enlightenment*, 244.
[97] Yates, *The Rosicrucian Enlightenment*, 244.

and Samuel Hartlib.⁹⁸ Boyle described the aims of the Invisible College with the same utilitarian and utopian rhetoric presented by Andreae, Hartlib and Comenius. Emphasizing this point, historian Charles Webster writes "Boyle's references to the Invisible College relate to the schemes of Hartlib, Dury, and Comenius for a pansophic college and an Office of Address in which their endeavors for the reformation of education, learning, and religion were comprehended."⁹⁹ The letters from Boyle express sympathy for the ideals of the Hartlib circle. This further connects the techno-scientific millenarian aims of the previous century to the influential period of establishing modern science. The Invisible College played an important role in the development of Baconianism and "generated a whole spectrum of informal scientific groups and culminated with the formation of the Royal Society in 1660."¹⁰⁰

Robert Boyle was not just any man, but the father of modern experimental chemistry, cofounder of the Royal Society, and arguably the most influential figure in pre-Newtonian science. His scientific pursuit as a religious devotion came to him early in his life. When a young boy in Geneva, Boyle experienced a great storm that he associated with the end of the world from his reading of the Book of Revelation. Pleading with God to spare him from a certain death, he avowed to dedicate his life and work to God, and live a pious and chaste existence. A pledge that he lived up to throughout the rest of his life. For Boyle, empirical investigation into the natural world was a "form of spiritual experience, and knowing was at once a form of worship and an anticipation of millenarian

---

⁹⁸ Charles Webster, "New Light on the Invisible College the Social Relations of English Science in the Mid-Seventeenth Century," *Transactions of the Royal Historical Society* 24 (1974): 19–42. https://doi.org/10.2307/3678930.
⁹⁹ Webster, "New Light," 19–42.
¹⁰⁰ Webster, "New Light," 19–42.

resurrection."[101] In his work "Usefulness of Natural Philosophy," Boyle unequivocally called for the renewal of Adamic knowledge as a means for the anticipated recovery of prelapsarian perfection. Given his faith in scientific knowledge as spiritual gnosis, Boyle believed that his investigations could provide rational explanations for various mysteries in scripture. Later in his life, he wrote a treatise explaining the Resurrection as a natural process of chemical transmutation entitled *Some Physico-Theological Considerations About the Possibility of the Resurrection.*[102]

Fellow founders of the Royal Society reiterated similar sentiments regarding how they envisioned scientific knowledge related to the approaching millennium. John Wilkins in his book *The Beauty of Providence*, expressed a millenarian theme in which history resolves itself into a "great serenity."[103] Likewise, Robert Hooke (1635-1703), fellow polymath of the Royal Society, wrote his own continuation to Bacon's *New Atlantis*, in which he describes "a future consolidation of religious, scientific, and political leadership in the hands of a Solomonic oligarchy 'whose rule on earth corresponded to God's governance of the universe.'"[104]

Perhaps the fullest expression of the millenarian mentality of modern science comes from Joseph Glanvill (1636-1680), another founder and leader of the Royal Society. In his defense of the new science, *The Vanity of Dogmatizing*, he begins with the chapter "What Man Was," in which he depicts humanity's adamic powers lost due to the

---

[101] Nobel, *Religion of Technology*, 60.
[102] Eugene M. Klaaren, *The Religious Origins of Modern Science* (Grand Rapids: William B. Eerdman, 1977) 129.
[103] Klaaren, *The Religious Origins of Modern* Science, 129.
[104] Nobel, *Religion of Technology*, 60.

Fall. Glanvill states "We are not now like the creature we were made ... and have not only lost our Maker's image, but our own."[105] As many of the predecessors mentioned in previous centuries, Glanvill believed that technology would redeem lost endowments originally bestowed on mankind in the garden.

> The senses, the Soul's windows, were without any sport or opacity ...Adam needed no spectacles. The acuteness of his natural optics showed him most of the celestial magnificence and bravery without Galileo's tube ... His naked eyes could reach near as much as the upper world, as we with all the advantages of the arts ... His knowledge was completely built, upon the certain, extemporary notice of his comprehensive, unerring faculties...Causes are hid in night and obscurity from us, which were all Sun to him. While man knew no sin, he was ignorant of nothing else.[106]

The founders of modern science proclaim the same millenarian theme of recovering prelapsarian perfection through the advancement of the scientific and technological arts. Scientific *gnosis* was understood to elevate man to the shared perspective of God. Like the spiritual men of the Third Age in Joachimite prophecy, Glanvill even went so far as to claim that the learned men of science were already taking steps beyond mere mortals, writing, "Upon the review of these great Sages, methinks,

---

[105] Joseph Glanvill, *The Vanity of Dogmatizing* (New York: Columbia University Press, 1931) 3-5.
[106] Glanvill, *The Vanity of Dogmatizing*, 6-11.

I could easily opinion, that men may differ from men, as much as Angels from unbodied souls."[107]

As part of the Baconian tradition, seventeenth-century scientists stressed the utility of useful arts in their pursuit of empirical and experimental knowledge. Technological arts were not just the practical end of scientific knowledge, but were the concrete means of gaining an understanding of nature and how it functions. The artisan gained not only an understanding of how his various mechanisms worked, but also, in a deeper sense, why they worked. This meant that knowledge of the mechanical arts brought with it a more complete knowledge of nature. Historian Amos Funkenstein has described this subtle shift as a "constructive theory of knowledge," a novel development unique to the seventeenth century.[108] From Bacon onward, knowing became associated with the constructive process of making and doing. This is in contrast to previous theories in which knowledge is understood as a revelatory, receptive, and passive result of sensory impression. True knowledge is now akin to that of artisan makers.

It was Bacon's critique of Scholasticism and emphasis on the weakness of the deductive method, which had a profound influence on seventeenth-century views. Bacon's call was nothing less than a revolutionary restructuring of the sciences. He believed that the mechanical arts would continue to progress as long as the devices were capable of extending human control over nature. Bacon was not so focused on the contemplation of the world, but on its practical improvement.

---

[107] Glanvill, *The Vanity of Dogmatizing*, 238.
[108] Amos Funkenstein, *Theology and the Scientific Imagination* (Princeton: Princeton University Press, 1986) 298.

In Joseph Glanvill's 1668 work, *The Progress and Advancement of Knowledge Since the Days of Aristotle*, he defends the newly found institution of the Royal Society, as well as these new methods of the modern empirical school against the old Aristotelian "school of talking." Glanvill argued that Aristotle was the champion of syllogistic reasoning, and therefore, was a clear opponent to the experimental sciences. Baconian reform unified the pursuit of knowledge with an undergirding common methodology. This sentiment can also be found in Thomas Sprat, Robert Boyle, and the charter of the Royal Society. One year previous, Thomas Sprat (1635-1713) wrote *History of the Royal Society* in 1667, and defined some of the methodological changes that made the experiments performed by the society possible. His purpose was to describe the scientific progress already made by members of the Royal Society. Sprat's emphasis was rigorously utilitarian, and he believed that Scholasticism, with its focus on Aristotle, only provided useful argumentative tools against heretics, but eventually divided religion into a thousand intricate questions. Addressing this shift from scholastic understanding to that of modern science George Ovitt writes,

> Thus the history of medieval thought from the rediscovery of Aristotle onward was one of misconception: its axiomatic method could not lead to truth in the physical world but only to disputations in theology; medieval men did not observe nature, and as a consequence, they created no useful knowledge. Aside from their admirable defense of religion, the Scholastics were worthless as guides to thought; though vestiges of

their dogmatic philosophy survive, the modern critical philosophy has largely superseded them.[109]

For other seventeenth-century writers, the accumulation of scientific and technical knowledge made humanity's general progress towards a better society more apparent. In 1694, William Wotton (1666-1727) argued that it was self-evident that modern men of the late seventeenth century had outstripped the ancients in all fields of learning; "it cannot be a matter of controversy, who have been the greatest geometers, arithmeticians, astronomers, musicians, chemists, botanists, or the like."[110] He viewed the previous fifteen hundred years of European learning as stagnant in all fields except ethics. Wotton understood the competition between men and nations as a great catalyst awakening Europe from its unproductive moral slumber. The "New Philosophy" of modern science was the promise to reactive the human will towards higher endeavors. As Paolo Rossi has notes, it wasn't just defenders of the Royal Society like Glanvill, or of the "New Philosophy" of Wotton who affirmed the progressive perfection of the arts and sciences, but also Protestant theologians. Seventeenth-century theologians saw great technical accomplishments, praised mechanical inventions, and saw progress as part of a general advance and increase in knowledge of God's creation.

Knowing the mind of God by scientifically deciphering the divine blueprints behind nature, which was understood as a god-crafted

---

[109] Ovitt, *The Restoration of Perfection*, 25.
[110] William Wotton, *Reflections Upon Ancient and Modern Learning* (London, 1694) xiv-xvii,
https://archive.org/details/reflectionsupon00wottgoog/page/n40/mode/2up.

mechanism, provided further identification with God and the restoration of Adam. As scientists increasingly distanced themselves from Hermetic lore and alchemy, which posited a divinity within nature, mechanistic scientists divorced nature from any mystical presence. Deism became vogue; they preferred a transcendent rather than an immanent deity, one who was filled with divine knowledge of His mechanistic creation. Knowing came to be understood as impersonal, detached, and abstract, epitomized in the advancement of mathematics.

Deification by rational knowledge can be seen most clearly in figures such as Robert Boyle and Isaac Newton (1642-1727). Although both still held private alchemical and hermetic beliefs, they embody the scientific quest towards God as the transcendent knower. Boyle believed this was the prerogative of the scientist, a priest of nature, and a mediator between God and creation. This meant surpassing Adam's knowledge in the garden. Boyle believed in the millennium, the scientist would "have a far greater knowledge of God's wonderful universe than Adam himself could have had."[111]

Isaac newton, like Boyle, was an unmarried, ascetic, and austere man who devoted his life to the discovery of God's intricate design within nature. Like Boyle, Newton devoted himself to the study of ancient languages in order to better understand scripture. He was a fervent millenarian who spent a considerable amount of time deciphering prophecy and providing commentary on the books of *Daniel* and *Revelation*. He believed that everything foretold in *Revelation* had already perfectly come true in history. As Margaret Jacob observes, the "millenarian impulse must be reckoned as one of the main motivations

---

[111] Klaaren, *Religious Origins of Modern* Science, 105.

for the cultivation of scientific inquiry in seventeenth century England ...Almost every important seventeenth century English scientist or promoter of science from Boyle to Newton believed in the approaching millennium."[112]

For seventeenth-century millenarians, scientific knowledge and technological improvements contributed to the completion of the first creation and progress towards a new creation. Novel inventions were perceived as extensions of and improvements to God's original construction. Building a new creation meant that humanity too would ascend into a totally new creature. Scientists slowly but steadily assumed the mantle to be a divine creator in their own right. The Fall came to be viewed as a blessing in disguise. Through scientific and technical knowledge, humanity did more than just recover prelapsarian divinity, it allowed for the attainment of God's privileged perspective. Francis Bacon had predicted in *New Atlantis*, that men would in fact create a new species, one that superseded their current state and become as gods; the central impulse present in the contemporary aims of transhumanism and their pursuit for God-like power through technology. As Lewis Mumford put it, this was "the undeclared ultimate goal" of modern science.[113]

The same millenarian spirit can be found to inspire the scientific minds in the age of Enlightenment. James Burnett (1714-1799), also known as Lord Monboddo, was a Scottish philosopher, deist, and pioneer in the historical study of languages. A century before Darwin wrote *On the Origin of Species* in 1859, Burnett first posited the principal notion of

---

[112] Margaret Jacob, *The Cultural Meaning of the Scientific Revolution* (Philadelphia: Temple University Press, 1988) 34, 75.
[113] Mumford, *Pentagon of Power*, 117, 125.

natural selection and biological evolution. Decades before the French Revolution Burnett wrote,

> ... the species is to end in not so many generations. There will be a convulsion of Nature, which is to produce a new Heaven and another Earth, to be inhabited by a new race of men, more righteous and pious than the former, and who are therefore called saints ... a man must be prepared for it in this life. And it is not sufficient that he is not vicious or wicked, but he must have cultivated his understanding by arts and sciences, and so have prepared his mind for the most perfect knowledge which he will have in a future state.[114]

The great eighteenth-century scientist, theologian, and liberal political theorist Joseph Priestly (1733-1804) viewed the turmoil in Europe during the rise of the French Revolution as the inauguration of the new millennium. In a private letter written to American John Adams, Priestly stated that his view of the political upheaval was "founded altogether upon revelation and prophecies." He was an enthusiastic supporter of both the American and French Revolutions, believing the ten horns of the Beast in *Revelation* were the "ten crowned heads of Europe, and that the execution of the king of France is the falling off of the first

---

[114] As quoted in Ernest Lee Tuveson, *Millennium and Utopia* (New York: Harper and Row, 1964) 122, 128.

of these horns; and the nine monarchies of Europe will fall one after another in the same way."[115]

Priestly was best known for his independent discovery of oxygen, his studies on electricity, invention of carbonated water, contributing founder of Unitarianism, and a fellow member of the 1766 Royal Society. His investigations into electricity were closely followed by the American Benjamin Franklin (1706-1790), who was later inducted as a member of the French Academy of Sciences. Like Newton and Boyle, Priestly was a lifelong millenarian who studied the ancient languages of scripture to better understand their meaning and wrote commentaries on the books of *Daniel* and *Revelation*. He argued that the second coming of Christ would be preceded by the return of Jews to their homeland, the collapse of the Turkish Empire, and the fall of Antichrist.[116] Throughout his life, Priestly insisted on the complementarity between his religious beliefs and scientific work. Resembling his predecessors, Priestly was true to the Baconian heritage, emphasizing the practical application of science for both immediate utility and millennial preparation. He was a multi-subject educator and often taught and associated himself with people destined for work in industry and commerce, as opposed to those granted entry into universities for more learned professions. He married the daughter of an ironmaster, and together with industrial pioneers James Watt, Mathew Boulton, and Josiah Wedgewood, established the Birmingham Lunar Society to promote the application of science to industry and crafts.

Technological salvation was carried further in the age of enlightenment by Michael Faraday (1791-1867), the father of our modern

---

[115] Clark Genett, "Joseph Priestly, the Millennium, and the French Revolution," *Journal of the History of Ideas*, vol. 34 (1973), 51.
[116] Nobel, *Religion of Technology*, 70.

understanding of electricity. He was a member of the fundamentalist Sandemanian sect of Christianity, and believed science "entailed both pious service to, and a devout effort at identification with divinity."[117] James Clerk Maxwell (1831-1879), who gave mathematical expression to Faraday's theories, was a devout Christian who earnestly studied the Bible and end time prophecies. In 1865 Maxwell writes,

> Almighty God, who hast created man in thine own image, and made him a living soul that he might seek after Thee and have dominion over Thy creatures, teach us to study the works of Thy hands that we may subdue the earth to our use, and strengthen our reason for Thy service, and so to receive the blessed Word, that we may believe on Him whom Thou has sent to give us knowledge of salvation.[118]

Charles Babbage (1791-1871), mathematician, inventor, and pioneer of industrial automation, believed that advancement of the mechanical arts was one of the "strongest arguments in favor of religion."[119] Babbage was inspired by the future vision of immortality. Applying his scientific knowledge to religious beliefs, he attempted to use the Calculating Engine to demonstrate the possibility of biblical miracles and the Resurrection of Christ. Technological advances have led

---

[117] Nobel, *Religion of Technology*, 71.
[118] Lewis Campbell and William Garnett, *The Life of James Clerk Maxwell* (New York: Johnson Reprint Corporation, 1969) 323.
[119] Charles Babbage, *The Ninth Bridgewater Treatise* (London: Frank Cass, 1967) (Original 1837), 82.

to a transcendence from post-lapsarian constraints. Babbaage believed the current stage of humanity's existence was soon to end, which he "founded on an instinctive belief that we are destined to be immortal by the Creator." "In a future state ... with increased powers," Babbage writes, we could

> apply our minds to the discovery of nature's laws, and to the invention of new methods by which our faculties might be aided in the research, pleasure the unalloyed would await us at every stage of our progress ... Unclogged by the dull corporeal load of matter which tyrannizes even our most intellectual moments, and claims the ardent spirit of its unkindred clay, we should advance in the pursuit ... [with] irresistible energy resulting from the confidence of ultimate success.[120]

A great pioneer of automation, Jacques Vaucanson (1709-1782), devised some of the most ingenious automata in Europe at the time. Vaucanson invented a prototype of the automatic loom, served as the French inspector of manufacturers, and started his career as a Minim Monk. Vaucanson had a preoccupation with regeneration, and began work on "'a completely artificial man,' destined for both perfection and immortality."[121] The transhumanist desire for immortality through technological liberation can be observed in both Babbage and Vaucanson. The mechanical man, often referred to now as a cyborg, is not a twentieth-

---

[120] Babbage, *The Ninth Bridgewater Treatise*, 139-40.
[121] Nobel, *Religion of Technology*, 73.

century novelty, but can be found in the early centuries of modern science.

E. Freemasonry and the Priest Engineer

As science began to fully emerge in the seventeenth century, another fraternity grew in prominence to carry the perfectionist project of Adam and technology into a more secular age, the Freemasons. Freemasons were renowned defenders of the dignity of mechanical arts and ardent promoters of useful knowledge, and they embedded these core beliefs within esoteric rituals. Freemasonic institutions were dedicated to the advancement of the useful arts of technology known as the "craft." While modern science publicly shed much of its alchemical and magical past, Freemasonry privately inherited the same symbolic rituals, oaths, hermetic language, and lore. They viewed themselves as vanguards in the recovery of ancient wisdom and restoration of Adam. In line with the tradition of Andreae, Comenius, Hartlib, and Boyle, Freemasons actualized the Baconian vision of Solomon's House; a temple of divine knowledge dedicated to the recovery of humanity's lost divinity.

Freemasonry grew out of medieval stonemason guilds on the one hand, and their occult association with the Rosicrucians on the other. Their early history is clouded with obscurity and replete with faulty legends and mythology. Lodges during the medieval period were established as resting places for the social gatherings of itinerant stonemasons. These early beginnings were known as "operative masonry because they were comprised of practicing masons with concerns for wages and working conditions. By the seventeenth century in England, a new form of "speculative masonry" arose, mostly comprised of aristocrats with much loftier aims than labor conditions. The evolution from operative to speculative masonry shifted its focus from laborious craftwork to a moral and mystical interpretation grounded in the worship of the Great Architect.

The exact date on which speculative freemasonry arose is uncertain. As Frances Yates argues, Freemasonry certainly had Rosicrucian connections, and many of its members were instrumental in founding the Royal Society.[122] Like the brotherhood of the Rosy Cross, Masons used secretive passwords and handshakes to help identify the initiated members. By the 1720s, according to historian Margret Jacob, one in every four English Freemasons was a fellow of the Royal Society.[123]

During this time, John Theophilus Desaguliers (1683-1744) was generally recognized as the leader of speculative Freemasonry. He was himself a fellow of the Royal Society and an experimental assistant to Isaac Newton, as well as an Anglican clergyman. As an exiled Huguenot from France, Desaguliers studied at Oxford and became a prominent scientist, inventor, and engineer. He gave some of the first public lectures on natural philosophy, invented a planetarium, studied the early applications of steam engines, experimented with electricity, and translated Vaucanson's work on mechanical automata. For his industrial application of science, he was awarded the Royal Society's Copley Medal and became society's official experimenter and curator. Desaguliers was also a member of the learned Spalding Gentlemen's Society, founded in Lincolnshire, England, to promote industrial science. The Spalding Gentlemen's Society was founded in 1710 by Royal Society fellow

---

[122] Yates, *The Rosicrucian Enlightenment*, 267-77.
[123] Jacob, *The Cultural Meaning of the Scientific Revolution*, 36-7.

Maurice Johnson and physician William Stukeley, who wrote millenarian tracts on "The Creation" and "Solomon's Temple." By 1719, Desaguliers was elevated to the third grand master of the English Grand Lodge, initiated a project to collect the historic lore of Freemasonry, and commissioned the writing of the Freemason *Constitutions*.

Present in the opening sentences of the *Constitutions* is the redemptive message of technology and science restoring humanity back to prelapsarian Adam. "Adam, our first parent, created after the Image of God, the Great Architect of the Universe, must have had the Liberal Sciences, particularly Geometry, written on his Heart; for ever since the Fall we find the principles of it in the Hearts of his offspring …"[124] Freemasonry viewed itself as the modern agent of renewed Adamic perfection. "No doubt Adam taught his sons Geometry, and the use of it … for Cain, we find built a City, which he called Consecrated or Dedicated."[125] Through perfect knowledge of the laws of mechanical proportions, all scientific arts could be discovered. "So that as the Mechanical Arts gave occasion to the Learned to reduce the Elements of Geometry into Method, this noble Science, thus reduced, is the Foundation of all the Arts, and the Rule by which they are conducted and performed."[126]

Freemasons tried to avoid any religious sectarianism by tending towards anticlericalism, and required all masons to pledge a monotheistic devotion to the Great Architect of the Universe. Men were not born masons but made masons through rituals of initiation and acquiring the

---

[124] *The Constitutions of the Freemasons* (New York: J. W. Leonard, 1855) 1. https://archive.org/details/constitutionsoff00andeuoft/page/2/mode/2up?q=Babel.
[125] *The Constitutions of the Freemasons*, 2.
[126] *The Constitutions of the Freemasons*, 2.

gnosis of secret teachings. Initiates undergo symbolic death and resurrection by laying in a coffin and passing through a labyrinth of rites before their illumination of masonic membership. Most notably, this ritual was illustrated in Mozart's *The Magic Flute*, which he knew as an enthusiastic mason.

Freemasonry's privileged knowledge was believed to be heaven-sent, and they had a unique spiritual duty to disseminate such knowledge, most specifically through the advancement and development of useful arts and sciences. Belief in the redemptive power of technology places masonry in the long-established millenarian tradition outlined in this chapter. Through practical virtue, reflecting the utilitarian Baconian spirit, masons elevated to higher and more mystical positions within the lodge. Improvements in scientific, practical, and ethical knowledge are the key features of masonic salvation. This progressive ethos and gnostic advancement towards higher knowledge was the cornerstone of eighteenth-century masonry. The promotion of science and its utilitarian application have had a significant impact on all scientific education in Europe. As Margaret Jacob has noted

> In the eighteenth century, European Freemasonry played a role in relation to scientific education analogous to that of progressive Calvinists in the seventeenth. In disproportionately large numbers, Freemasons promoted the new science by organizing lectures and philosophical societies for scientific devotees like themselves. In so

doing, they exercised a role as progressive improvers, as the concrete of the highest of Enlightenment ideals.[127]

Compared to their continental counterparts, the English were ahead in the mechanical application of scientific knowledge. In 1775, William Shipley founded the Society for the Promotion of the Arts, later renamed the Royal Society of Arts and Crafts, and it became the model for other institutes in Europe. Most famous of which is the French Société d' Encouragement pour l'Industrie Nationale. Freemasonry was first introduced in France in the 1730s by Scotsman Chevalier Ramsay (1686-1743), who was also a member of the Spalding Gentlemen's Society in Lincolnshire with Desaguiliers. Ramsay clarified that the purpose and mission of French masonry was the advancement of useful arts and centered their mission on the Masonic La Loge des Neuf Soers. As Nicholas Hans has suggested, due to its renown reputation for scientific learning and education at the time, this lodge has been referred to as the "UNESCO of the eighteenth century."[128]

However, one of the most lasting and important aspects of masonry is its facilitation in the birthing of the new spiritual men of technology in the modern era, the engineer. Engineering "emerged as much out of Masonry as it did out of the military (indeed, the military itself was rife with Masonry)."[129] Similar to Freemasonry, the engineer first appeared in England a generation before its counterpart in France,

---

[127] Jacob, *The Cultural Meaning of the Scientific Revolution*, 186.
[128] Nicholas Hans, "UNESCO of the Eighteenth Century: La Loge des Neuf Soers and Its Venerable Master Benjamin Franklin," in *Proceedings of the American Philosophic Society*, vol. 9, no. 5 (Oct. 1953) 513.
[129] Nobel, *Religion of Technology*, 79.

despite France going on to exert a far greater impact on the development of engineering as a profession. The French were pioneers in professional engineering education and had set standards for the world. The first professional engineering school was the Ecole des Ponts et Chaussées and was established by the leading pioneer in engineering education Jean-Rodolphe Perronet (1708-1794). Perronet was one of the leading civil engineers of his time and was a member of the Uranie Lodge of Freemasons. Succeeding Perronet as the leader of the Ecole des Ponts et Chaussées, was Gaspard Richie de Prony (1755-1839), "the personification of the art of engineering" and was a Freemason of the L'Heuresse Réunion lodge of the Grand Chapter. Prony believed that the engineer was a "new breed of man," the full realization of the vision of the previous two centuries. In those previous centuries Prony saw "the science of the engineer began to experience the great development that prepared its current state of transcendence."[130]

During the French Revolution, Freemasons founded what would be deemed the world's premiere engineering school, the Ecole Polytechnique. All four men who formulated the plans for its establishment, Antoine Fourcroy, Jean Hassenfratz, Claude Berthollet, and Gaspard Monge, were all masons. Monge was the first officer of the military lodge at Mézières, the inventor of descriptive geometry, and a professor at the famous military school, Ecole du Corps Ryal du Génie at Mézières. Founded in 1749, this institute was state of the art, fully equipped with laboratories for physics and chemistry, and offered the most advanced education, not only in France but also in Europe. During this same period, in 1780, the Ecole des Arts et Métiers was established

---

[130] Antoine Picon, *French Architects and Engineers in the Age of Enlightenment* (Cambridge: Cambridge University Press, 1992) 346-53.

by Francois Alexandre Frédéric de la Rochefoucauld. The curriculum was formulated by a committee that included both Monge and Berthollet. The same men, with the help of Jacques-Etienne Montgolfier (1745-1799) founded the Société d'Encourgement pour l'Industrie Nationale, which was modeled after the mason-inspired English Society for the Promotion of Arts.

The French vision of engineers set the gold standard for both Prussian and American engineering education. As Freemasonry codified the Baconian millenarian vision for the utilitarian advancement of technology, it was the engineer who embodied and realized this vision. One of the first people to herald the millenarian significance of the engineer was Henri de Saint-Simon (1760-1825). Saint-Simon was a social reformer, and he and his followers became "evangelists for the engineer" and "apostles of the religion of industry," constructing a new religion, a new Christianity, envisioning humanity's redemption through the labor of science and technology.[131]

However, it was Saint-Simon's disciple Auguste Comte (1798-1857) who would carry the torch of millenarian science further to illuminate a new social order. Like Simon, Comte studied mathematics under Monge and served as a tutor and admissions examiner at Ecole Polytechnique. Amid social disorder following the French Revolution, Comte believed that chaos signified a transition to a new form of society. One that would be enlightened by the new positivist social order built on science. Discussing the importance of the engineer in constructing his utopian vision of a scientific society, Comte writes,

---

[131] John Hubbel Weiss, *The Making of Technological Man: The Social Origins of French Engineering Education*, (Cambridge, Mass.: MIT Press, 1982) 157, 182.

> ...the establishment of the class of engineers in its proper characteristics is the more important, because this class will, without doubt, constitute the direct and necessary instrument of coalition between men of science and industrialists by which alone the new social order can commence.[132]

Comte was the Bacon of the nineteenth century, a man who admired the scientific investigations of Benjamin Franklin and Marquis de Condorcet. Comte recognized that his positivist project was the continuation of Bacon's reforms, but fully actualized in himself as a scientific prophet. It is a remarkable testimony to the millenarian influence of men from the Middle Ages that the core of their ideas was reproduced in the work of Comte. "We (positivists) are the true successors of the great men of the Middle Ages," wrote Comte.[133] Like Joachim of Fiore, Comte believed that the movement of history had three deterministic stages: theological, metaphysical, and positivist. A notion that came to him through personal revelation. The advent of positivism led to the inauguration of Comte's third stage of history. Whereas, for Joachim, this third age entailed humanity's illumination by way of the Holy Spirit, Comte understood it as the restoration of the true religion, the "Religion of Humanity," the "final religion." Positivism, Comte

---

[132] As quoted in Lewis Mumford, *The Myth of the Machine: Technics and Civilization* (New York: Harcourt Brace Jovanovich, 1966) 219-20.
[133] Gertrude Lenzer ed., *Auguste Comte and Positivism: The Essential Writings* (New York: Harper and Row, 1975) 81.

declared, "will afford the only possible, and the utmost possible, satisfaction to our natural aspiration after eternity."[134]

Comte's positivist system repeats the aspirations of the old goal of techno-millenarian Christianity, pursuing a gnostic recovery of mankind's image and likeness of God. He argued that science restores man to his rightful place as "chief of the economy of nature ... at the head of the living hierarchy," with "pride of preeminence stirring with us, and above us the type of perfection below which we must remain but which will ever be inviting us upwards." Positivism's aim was the "awakening in all the noble desire of honorable incorporation with the supreme existence," attaining "perfect unity" with the Great Architect, and would usher in man's "ultimate regeneration" – the "reconstruction" of "our whole nature," "the ultimate condition" the "definitive form of his existence."[135]

According to Comte, all of history when seen from the millenarian positivist perspective reveals a "tendency towards regeneration," unescapable movement towards the "kingdom of the Great Being," and "the normal state, the advent of which is shown by the whole past to be at hand." The time had come for "the regeneration of the world by positivism," a transformation "as indispensable as it is inevitable ...No moral revolution ever existed at once more inevitable, more ripe, more urgent..."[136] Like the previous prophets of techno-millenarianism, Comte believed that the "Great Being" is "deeply stamped on all its creations, in morals, in the art and sciences, in industry," and insisted that

---

[134] Auguste Comte, "Cours de Philosophie Postive," in *Auguste Comte and Positivism*, 302.

[135] Auguste Comte, "Système de Politique Postive," in *Auguste Comte and Positivism*, 466, 457, 44, 453, 447, 457, 458.

[136] Auguste Comte, "Third Essay," in Lenzer, *Comte and Positivism*, 32.

the redeeming of these divine attributes was essential to the restoration of mankind.[137] The engineer officially became the new priest for scientific regeneration. As expressed by Bacon and reminiscent of contemporary transhumanist ideals, Comte saw a future in which mankind would ultimately become a master over both biology and cosmology.

Without religious excess, Comte's technologically inspired millenarianism was shared by nineteenth-century socialists who founded philosophical projects on the rejection of religion and the advancement of scientific rationalism. Humanism began to replace religious devotion and piety. Similar to the role Freemasonry played during the Enlightenment, it was the socialists who took techno-millenarianism further into a more secular age. Robert Owen (1771-1858), the nineteenth century Welsh reformer and founder of utopian socialism, believed that a more human use of machinery accompanied by social and cultural reform was salvific and "offered a millennial vision of the transformation of the machine."[138] As historian Maxine Berg has noted, the liberatory power of technology was something worthy or worship, machinery was viewed as "a god of the state of bliss."[139]

Of course, the most prominent nineteenth-century socialist was Karl Marx (1818-1883), who believed that technical development signaled a social revolution that would end class conflict and lead to the material transcendence of history. Despite viewing religion as an opiate

---

[137] Auguste Comte, "Système de Politique Postive," in Lenzer, *Comte and Positivism*, 458, 449.
[138] Robert Owen, *Debate on the Evidences of Christianity* (London: R. Groombridge, 1839) 28.
[139] Maxine Berg, *The Machinery Question* (Cambridge: Cambridge University Press, 1980) 271.

of the masses, Marx was still filled with the millenarian spirit outlined in this chapter. Incorporating a materialistic Hegelian dialectic, Marx believed that history would resolve itself through the destruction of class warfare and economic subjugation by capitalism. For Marx, as was the case for Owen, machines did not change society, only people did, but technological advances provided the utopian promise of deliverance. Be it Marx's socialist utopia, Christian techno-millenarianism, or contemporary transhumanism, the same utopian theme of science and technological salvation can be found.

F. America and the Second Eden

The defining American myth is rooted in the providential promise of a new start, R. W. B. Lewis (1917-2002) wrote, "The American myth saw life and history as just beginning." "It described the world as starting up again under fresh initiative, in a divinely granted second chance for the human race."[140] The American was seen as an individual emancipated from history, indicative of the typology of the new Adam and Eve. Just as Bacon expressed in *the New Atlantis*, the new utopian garden of Eden was found in Westward expansion, not continental Europe. "I, chanter of Adamic song, through the new garden of the West," wrote Walt Whitman (1819-1892), "Divine am I, inside and out, and I make holy whatever I touch."[141]

Beginning with Edward Johnson's (1598-1672) 1628 solicitation of volunteers to colonize New England, America was already viewed as

---

[140] R. W. B. Lewis, *The American Adam* (Chicago: University of Chicago Press, 1955) 4, 5.
[141] As quoted in Lewis, *American Adam*, 5.

the place of a new Heaven and a new Earth. Describing the American future, Johnson wrote it would be "the amalgamation of the City of the World into the City of God." "For all of your satisfaction, know this is the place where the Lord will create a new Heaven, and new Earth in new churches, and a new Commonwealth together." The same sentiment was shared by John White (1539-1593), the English colonial governor of Roanoke (the "Lost Colony"), who viewed the American project as blessed by God and stood as "a bulwark … against the kingdom of the Antichrist."[142]

A century later, the American myth was reaffirmed by the religious revival of the First Great Awakening; "the Millennium is begun…" exclaimed Boston minister John Moorhead (1703-1773). Johnathan Edwards (1703-1758), likewise, believed that the millennium was at hand and America was uniquely destined by God to usher in the universal restoration of mankind. The First Great Awakening signaled for Edwards "the dawning, or at least prelude, of that glorious work of God, so often foretold in scripture, which in the progress and issue of it, shall renew the world and Mankind." "Many things … make it probable this work will begin in America," wrote Edwards[143]

A century later, the even more intense Second Great Awakening swept across the United States, stimulating millenarian theology through religious revival. The premillennialist eagerly awaited and spiritually prepared for the arrival of Christ's immanent return to reign for a thousand years. The postmillennialists, believing that Christ's return was after the utopian millennium, began eagerly constructing His earthly

---

[142] Paul Boyer, *When Time Shall Be No More: Prophecy Belief in Modern American Culture* (Cambridge: Harvard University Press, 1992) 68.
[143] Boyer, *Prophecy Belief in Modern American Culture*, 71.

kingdom. Both pre- and post-millennials viewed arts and sciences as a means to their millenarian end. The second creation was accomplished through the divinely inspired work of mortal hands, an artifice built on top of and in tune with God's assembly. Thereby, it was seen as an extension of the first creation, reflecting the elevated and restored capacity of mankind, as well as signaling the new beginning of divine perfection. Man's second creation signified advances in the restoration of Adam and the completion of God's telos for humanity. The advancement of the arts and sciences was a cooperative work between man and God, and America represented the progressive fulfillment of this historical journey back to divinity.

For American millenarians, the future kingdom would be a period in which the laborious curse of Adam would be lifted and humanity would enjoy a life no longer plagued by suffering and physical labor. Deeply rooted in the millenarian mind was the belief that, by way of machines and technology, humanity would transcend the restraints of labor. As Perry Miller notes in *The Life of the Mind in America*, "it was not only in the Revival that a doctrine of perfectionism emerged; the revivalistic mentality was sibling to the technological."[144] These sentiments can be found in important American theological thinkers such as Johnathan Edwards, Joseph Bellamy (1719-1790), and Samuel Hopkins (1721-1803). Addressing this faith in the emergence of a utopian ease due to mechanical inventions, Johnathan Edwards wrote,

> Tis probable that the world shall be more like Heaven in the millennium in this respect: that contemplation and

---

[144] Perry Miller, *The Life of the Mind in America* (New York: Harcourt, Brace and World, 1960) 274.

> spiritual enjoyments, and those things that more directly concern the mind and religion, will be more the saint's ordinary business than now …because there will be so many contrivances and inventions to facilitate their secular business … including contrivances or assisting one another through the whole earth by more expedite, easy, and safe communication between distant regions.[145]

The same utopian theme was repeated by American abolitionist and Congregationalist theologian Samuel Hopkins, who understood the millennium as a relative time of ease and temporal pleasure, a time full of "outward conveniences and temporal enjoyment." In 1793, in his treatise on the millennium, Hopkins wrote,

> There will also be doubtless great improvements and advances made in all those mechanic arts, by which the earth will be subdued and cultivated, and all the necessary and convenient article of life, such as all utensils, clothing, buildings, etc., will be formed and made in a better manner, and much less labor, than they are now.[146]

While many Protestant believers were inspired by the future vision of a mechanized return to the garden of Eden, no one was more motivated than the German emigrant inventor and civil engineer John

---

[145] Joel Nydahl, "Introduction" in John Adolphus Etzler, in *The Collected Works of John Adolphus Etzler* (Delmar, N.Y.: Scholar's Facsimiles and Reprints, 1977) xi.
[146] Nydahl, "Introduction," xii.

Adolphus Etzler (1791-1846). Etzler was greatly influenced by Hegelian philosophy, Owenite socialism, and American evangelism. At the height of the Second Great Awakening in 1833, Etzler wrote what was probably the first American technological utopia, titled *The Paradise Within Reach of All Men, Without Labor, by Powers of Nature and Machinery.*

For Etzler, rationality was the signifying mark of God's stamp on the human race. "If man ever forfeited the paradise by his sin, as we are told," wrote Etzler, "it must have been the sin of neglecting the most precious gift of his maker, that reasoning faculty, that only gives him the dominion over the brutes, and may give him also the dominion over the inanimate creation, and make thereby of the earth a paradise. Man needs not to eat his bread in the sweat of his brow…"[147] Etzler described in detail how paradise would be accomplished by the rational harnessing of the powers of nature; the wind, water, ocean waves, and the sun, would be sustainable natural energy sources for America's destiny. Man's God-like powers in the paradise to come are not identical to that of the Creator but a tapping into that which exists divinely. "Powers must pre-exist, they cannot be invented," insisted Etzler. By deciphering the divine patterns of nature and mechanically utilizing these forces, he believed that the engineer could "cause a regeneration of mankind and bring humanity into an Edenic paradise of peace and abundance." It would be "a general state of sincerity, innocence and true intelligence. Mankind may thus live in and enjoy a new world, far superior to the present, and raise themselves far higher in the scheme of being."[148] Etzler's project was no other than the end of history and the fulfillment of paradise on Earth. His paradise,

---

[147] Etzler, *Collected Works*, 56.
[148] Etzler, *Collected Works*, 117-18.

like those previously mentioned in our tracing of the old idea of techno-utopia, was the divine restoration of prelapsarian Adam.

Another American enthusiast of millennial dreams was the botanist, geologist, and technological educator Amos Eaton (1776-1842). A disciple of the Baconian tradition, Eaton preached the usefulness of technology and "wandered through the New England states and New York like a religious evangelist."[149] Under his Masonic patron Stephen Van Rensselaer (1764-1839), Eaton put his preaching into practice, and together they founded the first American civilian engineering school, the Rensselaer Polytechnic Institute.

During this same period in the early nineteenth century, Harvard professor Jacob Bigelow (1787-1879), whom historian Perry Miller referred to as the "true prophet" of utilitarian science in America, coined the new word "technology," in his *Elements of Technology*.[150] Roughly a thousand years after Eriugena devised the term "mechanical arts" to signify technical crafts, Bigelow provided the generic term we use today to describe the arts of science. Bigelow, like Eriugena, saw the engineer of the mechanical arts as men who wore God's image, reconciling faith and truth in the restoration of the arts and extending man's dominion over nature. Bigelow saw technology as salvific to the human enterprise, stating to an audience at the opening of the Massachusetts Institute of Technology – which adopted the new term "technology" at the suggestion

---

[149] Ethel M. McAllister, *Amos Eaton: Scientist and Educator* (Philadelphia: University of Pennsylvania Press, 1941), 368.
[150] Miller, *Life of the Mind*, 289.

of Bigelow – that "technology has had a leading sway in promoting the progress and happiness of our race."[151]

Many American Protestants believed that the millennium was at hand, and this notion was further catalyzed by Samuel F. B. Morse's invention of the telegraph. Samuel Morse (1791-1872) was a faithful Calvinist who graduated from Yale in 1810. Morse viewed communication technology as a method by which the Gospel could spread faster and further than ever before. As Carlton Mabee highlights, the telegraph was not simply perceived as a mundane invention, "but as divinely inspired for the purposes of spreading the Christian message farther and faster, eclipsing time and transcending space, saving the heathen, bringing closer and making more probable the day of salvation."[152] The first message transmitted across the new invention was a Biblical message stating "What hath God wrought!" Witnessing the advances in steam and electrical technology, Morse was filled with hope that God's technological remedy for fallen man was about to commence. This exuberant hope is expressed in a poem addressed to "Professor Morse":

> A Good a generous spirit ruled the hour;
> Old jealousies were drowned in brotherhood;
> Philanthropy rejoiced that Skill and Power,
> Servants to Science, compass all men's good;

---

[151] Jacob Bigelow, address at MIT, 1865, quoted in Howard P. Segal, *Technological Utopianism in American Culture* (Berkeley: University of California Press, 1985) 81.

[152] Carelton Mabee, *The American Leonardo: A Life of Samuel F. B. Morse*, (New York: Alfred A. Knopf, 1944) 260.

And over all Religion's banner stood.[153]

American engineer George S. Morison (1842-1903) declared, "The civil engineer is the priest of material development ... He is the priest of the new epoch."[154] Morison was the leading bridge builder and president of the American Society of Civil Engineers. "No changes have ever equaled those through which the world is passing now," wrote Morison, "the new epoch differs from all the preceding epochs" due to it creating an entirely "new civilization." This epoch will witness the final and "inevitable" destruction of "savagery" and "barbarism," "ignorance," and "superstition." "Mankind must settle down to a long period of rest," marked by "contentment," "comfort," and "happiness." Furthermore, "it will not be the condition of a town nor of a nation but of the whole earth, with nothing to change it unless communication should be opened with another planet."[155]

Robert Thurston Kent (1880-1947), who was an expert on steam power and the leader of the new American mechanical engineering profession shared these same American senitments. He was the first president of the American Society of Mechanical Engineers, the president of the Stevens Institute of Technology, and the founder and first head of the Mechanical Engineering School at Cornell University. Thurston argued that science and engineering offered "an increase appreciation of, and familiarity with God's ways." Thurston equated science and

---

[153] James W. Carey, *Communication as Culture* (Boston: Unwin Hyman, 1989) 206-7.
[154] Segal, *Technological Utopianism*, 94.
[155] George S. Morison, *The New Epoch: As Developed by the Manufacture of Power* (Boston Houghton Mifflin, 1903) 5, 6, 11, 68, 75, 128, 130, 132-33, https://archive.org/details/newepochasdevelo00mori.

engineering to "revelation and prophecy," which he believed were now "the fruits of science."

> The astronomer watching the developments in Perseus now sees and describes to us the destruction of the world (of which heavens are seen to melt with ferment and heat) and the simultaneous beginning of the new heaven and the new world, the process of the sequence prophesied alike by Laplace and the new inspired seer, thereby confirming an old, and giving a new and more exact revelation.[156]

Thurston understood the utopian future of perfection as being fulfilled materially, spiritually, and intellectually. Human perfection is intricately related to advancements in technology and material applications. If man should bend "every law to his aid in the building of a world, he may profit in maximum degree by every force, energy and substance, by all material and spiritual laws and phenomena." Thurston wrote that mankind can advance "himself to loftier and loftier planes, perfecting himself..."[157] For Thurston, like many others, America was the place for the historic return to Eden and inhabited by the new Adam and Eve.

Perhaps the best expression of America's religious spirit of technology can be found in the utopian writings of American socialist

---

[156] Robert Thurston Kent, "Scientific Research: The Art of Revelation and Prophecy," *Science*, vol. 16 (Sept. 12-19, 1902) 402, 404, 407, 422, 423, https://www.jstor.org/stable/1628776.

[157] Kent, "Scientific Research," 457.

Edward Bellamy (1850-1898). In his enormously popular 1888 utopian novel, *Looking Backward*, Bellamy portrayed the year 2000 as a futuristic socialist utopia. Bellamy describes a future nation filled with warehouse clubs, such as COSTCO or Sam's Club, payment is made through credit cards, home entertainment through cable technology, and endorsed a universal basic income for all citizens. The work has been described as the quintessential "product of America's peak faith in technology," by historian Howard P. Segal. Only *Uncle Tom's Cabin* sold more copies than *Looking Backward*, making it one of the most important and influential works in nineteenth-century America. The popularity of *Looking Backward* highlights the intense fervor and hopes Americans place in the promise of technology. It was incredibly persuasive to many intellectuals and socialists and was one of the few books that sparked political movements immediately upon its publication. Describing the importance and vision of Bellamy's America, Segal writes,

> The United States of the year 2000 is very much a technological utopia; an allegedly ideal society not simply dependent upon tools and machines, or even worship of them, but outright modeled after them... The purposeful, positive use of technology – from improved factories and offices to new highways and electric lighting systems to innovative pneumatic tubes, electronic broadcasts, and credit card – is in fact, critical

to predicted transformation of the United States, from a living hell into a heaven on earth.[158]

A decade after the publication of *Looking Backward*, Bellamy tempered his excitement for technological advancement in his book *Equality* with a more sober and critical observation. He felt that technology was failing to fulfill its promise to alleviate human misery. Bellamy saw a paradox in which technological advancement directly contributed to human suffering. Witnessing the deficiencies of technology to improve people's lives, Bellamy lamented the serious lack of concern by the general populace as a sort of insanity. He was astonished that the lack of any apparent benefit did not diminish the American public's excitement and enchantment with new inventions and viewed this irrational behavior as a deep-seated cultural compulsion.

> This craze for more and more and ever greater and wider inventions for economic purposes, coupled with apparent complete indifference as to whether mankind derived any ultimate benefit from them or not, can only be understood by regarding it as one of those strange epidemics of insane excitement which have been known to effect whole populations at certain periods, especially of the Middle Ages. Rational explanation it has none.[159]

---

[158] Howard P. Segal, "Bellamy and Technology," in Daphne Patai, ed., *Looking Backward 1988-1888: Essays on Edward Bellamy* (Amherst: University of Massachusetts Press, 1988), 91, 104.

[159] Edward Bellamy, *Equality* (New York: D. Appleton and Co., 1897) 235-36.

Bellamy's warning still rings true today, as many scholars and technologists have warned of the doubled-edged sword technology has played in our contemporary world. Although technology has furthered the expansion of knowledge, it has also hampered it. Many studies have demonstrated that social media has had a negative effect on people's ability to concentrate for extended periods. Instead, social media is designed to condition the brain to constantly desire more dopamine, causing addictive and obsessive behaviors. In the twenty-first century, America witnessed its first decline in average IQ.[160] As more people have access to the Internet and smartphones in their pockets, shockingly, math and literacy skills are experiencing significant declines, not increased intelligence, as promised.[161] As during Bellamy's time, American fascination with the latest and greatest technological innovation is still part of American culture, where people camp outside stores to be first in line for Apple's release of the latest iPhone. Reading Bellamy's rebuke of his own techno-socialist vision is insightful concerning the engrained relationship that American culture has with technological innovation.

The twentieth century witnessed advances in chemical warfare, nuclear weapons, gene editing, nanotechnology, neuroimplants, and artificial intelligent systems. These technologies are still a central topic of contentious debate concerning their ethical use in the twenty-first century. From its foundation, America has been intricately tied to techno-

---

[160] Michael T. Nietzel, "American IQ Scores Show Recent Decline, According to New Study," *Forbes* (March 23, 2023) accessed March 26, 2025, https://www.forbes.com/sites/michaeltnietzel/2023/03/23/american-iq-test-scores-show-recent-declines-according-to-new-study/.

[161] Debbie Elliott, "U.S. Reading and Math Scores Drop to Their Lowest In Decades" *NPR* (June 22, 2023) accessed on March 26, 2025, https://www.npr.org/2023/06/22/1183653578/u-s-reading-and-math-scores-drop-to-their-lowest-levels-in-decades.

utopian hope for centuries. A foundational myth that still colors the contemporary American experience of technological innovation, especially in places such as Silicon Valley. As will be further addressed in the next chapter, it is the progressive development of such mechanical arts, along with a historic presupposition of the Christian return to prelapsarian perfection, which has paved the way for transhumanist optimism concerning the use of technology as a means of human transcendence.

G. Conclusion

This chapter has argued that the historical journey of techno-millenarianism and its theological presuppositions, founded within Christian eschatology, have shaped current expectations related to technological innovation. From the ninth century onward, technological advancement and the belief in historical progress towards perfection shaped Western civilization's relationship to the technical and scientific arts. Chilastic/millenarian assumptions about the eschaton fueled a religious devotion to the development of mechanical arts as an essential means by which humanity was believed to redeem the fallen state of human nature. Knowledge of creation and the construction of machines was understood as a gnostic restoration of God's image in man, leading back to Edenic perfection.

Some of the prophets of this religion of technology include John Scotus Eriugena, Roger Bacon, Joachim of Fiore, Hugh of St. Victor, Christopher Columbus, Francis Bacon, Robert Boyle, and Auguste Comte. In addition, societies such as the Rosicrucian brotherhood, Freemasonry, the Royal Society, and many other organizations were fueled by the hope of scientific advancement, leading towards a perfected and knowable creation. Initially, the techno-millenarian vision began within a European Christian context; after the Renaissance, it began to incorporate more esoteric and occult sentiments. The Rosicrucian goals of an Invisible College that would liberate humanity through divine *gnosis* began to fall out of favor by the end of the Thirty Years War. Science underwent a transformation from being infused with a hermetic philosophy to a sober and rationalized practice divorced from occult superstition. Baconian reforms were essential to this transformation, and education moved away from the Aristotelean tradition towards utilitarian applications. It is in this light that modern science came into recognizable forms in institutions such as the Royal Society and Ecole Polytechnique. Scientists and engineers were viewed as new priests, leading humanity to the promise land of New Jerusalem. The sacred veneer of science still colors contemporary attitudes towards the progressive march of technology today. Without this, contemporary movements, such as transhumanism and their deifying pursuit of biological liberation, omniscient AI, and genetic engineering, would not be possible.

As technology evolved, utopian and socialist thinkers anticipated that it would alleviate the laborious curse God placed on Adam after the Fall. The mechanical arts were foreseen to allow men and women to live in a millennial paradise, pursuing their own interests and pleasure. However, by the end of the nineteenth century, men such as Edward Bellamy became skeptical of technology delivering utopian assurance. He bemoaned that the American populace was so infatuated with the latest technological invention that people scarcely considered whether it actually improved human conditions.

Once the wilderness frontier in America was subdued, digital technology became a new frontier for progressive exploration. America was believed by many to be the Second Eden, with a divine destiny to bring humanity into the millennial Kingdom of God through scientific and technological progress. The First and Second Great Awakenings amplified this millenarian ethos in America and provided the foundation for the country's fascination with technological innovation. Regarding contemporary transhumanism, America has played a leading role in the research and development of these technologies and ideals. Although transhumanism is a secular movement, and thus far, our historical overview has been shaped by Christian beliefs, many of the historical qualities mentioned, such as a millenarian expectation (technological singularity), the progressive pursuit of perfection, the transcending of our biological condition, lessening human suffering, and the salvific belief in technology are still present.

2. Transhumanism: Religion Without Revelation

Medieval techno-millenarian movements have set a historical precedent for anticipating a transformative age of worldly perfection. These beliefs established a template of linear progress towards an ultimate redemption within history, rather than beyond it, and is a pattern reverberated in modern transhumanist visions. Modern secular ideologies have inherited this prototype and betray the influence of Joachimism whenever they treat humanity as moving along a linear teleology through distinct epochs, arriving at an immanent climax that transforms humanity. Transhumanism fits squarely in this lineage of techno-millenarianism, projecting an epochal transformation of humanity driven by technological advances rather than divine intervention.

The utopian sentiments of transhumanism derive much of their power from the traditional Christian eschatological hope for a transfigured future. Thus, transhumanism functions as a religious narrative in the postsecular age, preserving the structure and psychological comfort of religion even as it rejects traditional theology. Jürgen Habermas and Charles Taylor describe today's era as "postsecular," meaning in technologically advanced secular societies, the typical distinctions between the secular and religious have blurred providing secular ideologies the ability to function as religious narratives.[162] Transhumanism exemplifies this by providing meaning, faith, and eschatology for individuals who have largely abandoned

---

[162] Jurgen Habermas, "Notes on a Post-Secular Society," *New Perspectives Quarterly* 25 (2008): 17-29, https://doi.org/10.1111/j.1540-5842.2008.01017.x

organized religions. Rather than religious creeds, these secularist faiths provide narratives of salvation and transcendence in a disenchanted world. Their proclamation of an enhanced and augmented future re-enchants believers with the promise technology can deliver what religion once did.

In this sense, the transhumanist worldview strongly exemplifies what Martin Heidegger called "enframing" (*Gestell*). Enframing is a mode of understanding in which the world and everything in it are revealed primarily as a resource – a "standing-reserve" of usable raw materials to be ordered and manipulated. In such a mode, a river is no longer a majestic creation or sacred symbol, but simply water on call for hydroelectric plants; forests are enframed as merely timber available for industrial use. Critically, humanity is not exempt, "he comes to the point where he himself will have been taken as a standing-reserve. Meanwhile, man, precisely as the one so threatened, exalts himself and postures as lord of the earth."[163]

Under the transhumanist ethos, the human body and mind are treated as modifiable artifacts and objects to be optimized, upgraded, or discarded in favor of better substrates. Transhumanism enframes the human body as a technologically manipulatable product. Likewise, our consciousness and personal identity are seen as software, a configuration of data that can be enhanced by artificial intelligence while the hardware of the body is reengineered. Such an enframing exalts humanity as "lord of the earth," creating the illusion we can become masters of our own evolution and thereby seize control of our own destiny.

---

[163] Martin Heidegger, "The Question Concerning Technology," in *Basic Writings: Martin Heidegger*, ed. David Farrell Krell (Routledge, 1993) 322.

Far from being a purely rational endeavor, transhumanism is suffused with mythic and religious undertones that mark it as a form of re-enchantment in the modern world. It represents a zeitgeist of postsecular re-enchantment by constructing its own techno-theology, or what Erik Davis calls *Techgnosis*. Transhumanist works often read like modern scripture, complete with prophecies of a transformed Earth into a new Eden inhabited by cyborgs with supernatural capabilities. This resonates with what Abou Farman calls "re-enchantment cosmologies," in that transhumanism uses scientific concepts (information, intelligence, evolution) in quasi-mystical ways to restore a sense of intentional order to the universe.[164] Thus, their ideology resembles the myth of technological apotheosis, a sentiment deeply rooted in Western religious and philosophical categories. It echoes the age-old idea of a New Jerusalem, an earthly paradise, or, for Christians, the new Tower of Babel.

This chapter addresses both the secular philosophical side of transhumanism and the more religiously motivated strand. The work outlines the philosophical and theological paradigms of transhumanism concerning their metaphysics, epistemology, normative ethics, concepts of deification, and eschatology (Singularity). Those who view transhumanism as a religion of the future have acknowledged that their enterprise is religious in nature, with the aim of competing with traditional religious practices by concretizing goals that are often theologized about in older myths. Such groups include the Order of Cosmic Engineers, the Society for Universal Immortalism, and Terasem Transreligion, all driven to utilize the transhuman vision for a new religion suitable for the twenty-first century.

---

[164] Abou Farman, "Re-Enchantment Cosmologies: Mastery and Obsolescence in an Intelligent Universe," in *Anthropological Quarterly* 85 (2012) 1069-1088.

This chapter demonstrates the continuity of techno-millenarianism with contemporary aims, and the eschatological paradigm of religious transhumanism. Though typically understood as a novel secular philosophy of human enhancement, transhumanism is, in actuality, part of a long historical thread, unique to Western civilization, and infused with religious sentiments repackaged in a postsecular guise. The posthuman, emancipated from the confines of history and enhanced with potential, acts in similar ways to techno-millenarian beliefs concerning a return to prelapsarian Adam.

Many transhumanists refer directly to the future construction of advanced artificial intelligence as the emergence of God in history. They argue that all entities exist on an evolutionary spectrum of becoming, ultimately fulfilling their historical journey as superintelligent machines. Divinity is conceptualized as attaining immortality, omniscience, and omnipotence, and is couched in rebellious mythic terms, drawing on the symbolism of Lucifer and Prometheus. By Embedding age-old eschatological motifs into a materialistic narrative, transhumanism reenchants the world with its own technological myth.

The scientific details of various technologies that transhumanists envision, such as the current state of genetic engineering, nanotechnology, and advanced artificial intelligence (AI), are outside the scope of this work. Rather, the goal is to connect the historical trajectory and aspirations of techno-millenarianism with the contemporary movement of transhumanism, so that it can be seen more clearly as a competing narrative for human deification. This chapter focuses specifically on the twentieth-century origins of transhumanist thought, its philosophical paradigm, how it functions as a religious narrative in our postsecular moment, and its vision of a posthuman future.

A. Origins of Transhumanism

The term "transhumanism," as contemporarily understood, first appeared in Julian Huxley's 1957 book *New Bottles for New Wine*.[165] Beginning with his publication *Religion Without Revelation* (1927), Julian Huxley (1887-1975) wrote about the scientific rationalism he believed would replace the shortcomings of all traditional religions. Huxley argued that God, as a transcendent divine creator, was nothing more than a "stop-gap" to the full advancement of scientific progress. Throughout the book, Huxley presents the case for a new religion of rationality, scientific understanding, and human liberation. He laments that the greatest "defects of our modern world is its lack of a religion of its own, and the accompanying disruption of its thought and aims."[166] Huxley's new rational religion was believed to displace the superstitions and failed traditions of the previous generations. He argues that the process of evolution has brought humanity to a point where it can transcend its historical context and biological limitations. In opposition to traditional religion, which Huxley saw as antiquated and stagnant, he describes his rational religion of the future as truly "promethean" as it alone will bring "the fire of absolute truth" into the phenomenal world. A feat, he claimed, the religions of old only theologized about but never

---

[165] Early uses include Dante Alighieri's (1265-1321) *Divine Comedy*, which utilizes the word "transumanare" in a religious context to refer to a spiritual passing beyond the human, T.S. Elliot's (1888-1965) *The Cocktail Party*, which employed "transhumanized" to refer to personal spiritual illumination. In neither case did the word connote technological transcendence of human augmentation.

[166] Julian Huxley, *Religion Without Revelation* (New York: Harper Collins, 1929) 376.

achieved. Humanity may attain the tactile promise of eternal life through instrumental use of science and technology. Huxley writes,

> I believe that man, though not without perplexity, effort, and pain, can fulfill this duty and gradually achieve his destiny. A religion which takes this as its core and interprets it with a wide vision, both of the possibilities open to man and of the limitations in which he is confined, will be a true religion, because it is coterminous with life; it will encourage the growth of life, and will itself grow with that growth. I believe in the religion of life.[167]

Religion Without Revelation never utilizes the term "transhumanism" to describe the vehicle for Huxley's true "religion of life." However, by 1957, Huxley makes clear in *New Bottles for New Skin* that transhumanism is the promethean fire promised to humanity. In the opening chapter titled "Transhumanism," he lays out why the pursuit of technological transcendence is part and parcel of humankind's evolutionary destiny. This destiny ends with the man-made technology breathing life into the universe itself. This requires humanity to determine the "future direction of evolution on this earth" to actualize these latent potentials within human rationalism and ingenuity. Huxley calls on believers of his new faith to step into their "cosmic office" to accomplish the task at hand. Huxley writes,

---

[167] Huxley, *Religion Without Revelation*, 380-81.

The human species can, if it wishes, transcend itself – not just sporadically, an individual here in one way, an individual there in another way, but in its entirety, like humanity. We need a name for this new belief. Perhaps, *transhumanism* will serve: man remaining man, but transcending himself, by realizing new possibilities of and for human nature. "I believe in transhumanism": once there are enough people who can truly say that, the human species will be on the threshold of a new kind of existence, as different from ours as ours is from that of Pekin man. It will at last be consciously fulfilling its real destiny.[168]

Transhumanist philosophers Max More (Max O'Connor) and Nick Bostrom have both written on the history of transhumanist thought and highlighted historical figures they believe to be "proto-transhumanists." They both begin their histories by addressing the aims of Medieval and Renaissance alchemy as precursors to their posthuman goals. The transmutation of substances, creation of homunculi, search of the Philosopher's Stone, and the Elixir of Immortality are deemed a "magical form of technology capable of transmutating elements, curing diseases, and granting immortality."[169] Both men make mention of the importance of Giovani Pico della Mirandola's (1463-1494) *Oration on the Dignity of Man* (1486), due to Pico's insistence that "man does not

---

[168] Julian Huxley, *New Bottles for New Wine* (London: Chatto and Windus LTD., 1957) 17.

[169] Max More, "The Philosophy of Transhumanism," in *The Transhumanist Reader*, ed. Max More and Natasha Vita-More, (West Sussex, UK: John Wiley and Sons Inc., 2013) 9.

have a readymade form and is responsible for shaping himself."[170] Renaissance thought inspired the existential pursuit of reforming humanity into a new image.

Major consideration is also given to Francis Bacon (1561-1626) and his advocacy for inductive reason, empirical investigations, and utilization of the scientific method. As Max More notes, without the work of Bacon, the full articulation of transhumanist philosophy would not be possible. Bacon helped inaugurate a turn in Western thought from scholastic and platonic approaches towards empirical science and utilitarian application. His Baconian reforms emphasized the utility of scientific and technical knowledge in the pursuit of perfected humans and society. As science flowered during the Enlightenment, many others trumpeted proto-transhumanist lines, proclaiming a future age in which technology and science would lead to unlimited lifespans, easing of suffering, and an increase in pleasure and knowledge. Bostrom also mentions Benjamin Franklin (1706-1790) as a proto-transhumanist because he longed for a future time in which people could be recalled back to life from the grip of death. According to Bostrom this is perceived as "foreshadowing the cryonics movement."[171]

---

[170] Nick Bostrom, "A History of Transhumanist Thought," in *Journal of Evolution and Technology*, vol. 14, April 2005, 2.

[171] Bostrom, "Transhumanist Thought" full quote of Benjamin Franklin, "I wish it were possible…to invent a method of embalming drowned persons, in such a manner that they might be recalled to life at any period, however distant; for having a very ardent desire to see and observe the state of America a hundred years hence, I should prefer to an ordinary death, being immersed with a few friends in a cask of Maderia, until that time, then to be recalled to life by the solar warmth of my dear country! But … in all probability, we live in a century too little advanced, and too near the infancy of science, to see such an art brought in our time to its perfection." 3.

Transhumanism is the philosophical child of rational humanism. Figures such as Isaac Newton, Robert Boyle, Thomas Hobbes, John Locke, Immanuel Kant, and Marquis de Condorcet are all credited as scientific progenitors of the transhumanist project. Both Bostrom and More hold Condorcet (1743-1794) in a very high regard due to him echoing a salvific disposition towards the unlimited progress of science and technology. Reiterating this point, Condorcet writes,

> Would it even be absurd to suppose this quality of melioration in the human species as susceptible of an indefinite advancement; to suppose that a period must one day arrive when death will be nothing more than the effect of either extraordinary accidents, or of the flow and gradual decay of the vital powers, and that the duration of the middle space, of the interval between the birth of man and this decay, will itself have no assignable limit?[172]

More and Bostrom describe their movement as a blossoming of Enlightenment ideals and values. Unlike postmodernists and poststructuralists, who sneer at outdated human-centric ideals, transhumanism sees itself as an expressly humanist enterprise. This places transhumanism at odds with other posthumanist philosophies that want to decenter the anthropocentric subject as the primary focus of

---

[172] Jean Antoine Nicolas de Caritat Condorcet, *Outlines of a Historical View of the Progress of the Human Mind* (London: 1795) 368, https://archive.org/details/outlinesofhistor00cond/page/n15/mode/2up.

philosophical and critical inquiry. Transhumanism wants to enhance the intellectual, physical, and psychological capabilities of humans and, therefore, retain the human subject as the primary center of their movement. The humanism of transhumanist philosophy is filtered through the evolutionary perspective presented in Charles Darwin's (1809-1882) *Origin of Species* (1859). According to Max More, the theory of Darwinian evolution gave scientific credence to the concept that human beings do not have a static nature. Homo sapiens and nature exist on an evolutionary spectrum of change and mutation, without any fixed metaphysical essence. Bostrom articulates transhumanist anthropology as a combination of Darwinian theory with the work of French physician and materialist philosopher Julien Offray de La Mettrie (1709-1751). In La Mettrie's 1750 work *L'Homme Machine* (Man a Machine), he argues that "man is but an animal, or a collection of springs which wind each other up."[173] The belief that human beings are constituted solely of matter and forcibly obey physical laws provides a logical basis for viewing human composition as analogous to the parts of a machine. As science and technology provide further capabilities to manipulate nature, Bostrom concludes, "then it should in principle be possible to learn to manipulate human nature in the same way that we manipulate external objects."[174]

Another pre-twentieth-century figure credited by both Bostrom and More is Friedrich Nietzsche (1844-1900). Despite Nietzsche not being a major advocate of techno-millenarianism, his concept of the Übermensch had an enduring impact. According to Nietzsche, humans were something to be overcome, and "the Overman," by liberating

---

[173] As quoted in Bostrom, "Transhumanist Thought," 3.
[174] Bostrom, "Transhumanist Thought," 3.

himself from the slave morality of Christianity, would allow exceptional individuals to soar to the novel heights of personal growth and cultural refinement.[175] Nietzsche did not envision technology as playing a role in this transformation of humanity; however, the idea that Homo sapiens must overcome what they have historically been has remained a great impetus for transhumanist goals. Owing to the major differences between the two philosophical systems, debate ensued within transhumanist circles on how much credit should be attributed to Nietzsche. Given transhumanism's Enlightenment roots, its focus on individual liberties, anthropocentric concern, and utilitarian emphasis, it is fair to say that transhumanism may actually have more in common with Nietzsche's contemporary John Stuart Mill (1806-1873).

Nikolai Fyodorov (1829-1903) – often labeled as a proto-transhumanist – was a Russian philosopher, futurist, and founder of the Russian Cosmism movement. Fyodorov was an important nineteenth-century inspiration concerning his beliefs in the perfected future of humanity, techno-utopian society, scientific-based resurrection, immortality, space colonization, and ancestor worship. Fyodorov believed that the evolutionary process was driven by culmination in increased intelligence, resulting in the eventual scientific defeat of death, and the ability of people to be restored in an immortal form. Although Fyodorov was a Russian Orthodox Christian and attempted to reconcile his religion with science and evolution, his work blurred the lines of Orthodox teachings and ventured into the territory of heresy. Orthodox

---

[175] Bostrom, "Transhumanist Thought," "I teach you the overman. Man is something that shall be overcome. What have you done to overcome him? All beings so far have created something beyond themselves; and do you want to be the ebb of this great flood and even go back to the beasts rather than overcome man?" 4.

theologians have been critical of his work and have demonstrated how it is inconsistent with the Church's historical teachings.

A lesser-known thinker who took up the transhumanist cause was the Frenchman Jean Finot (1858-1922). Finot's *The Philosophy of Long Life* (1909) is of considerable importance because he was one of the first advocates of the technological engineering of life and living matter. He explores topics such as life extension, regeneration, the immortal body, and how living organisms can be reduced to artificial creations. Interest in longevity was prevalent in France at the turn of the twentieth century, and Finot's work exemplifies this interest by addressing the problem of death through logical and rational means.

Despite the origins of some of the proto-transhumanists mentioned above, transhumanism has emerged from an Anglo-American cultural and linguistic context. Some contributing factors to this may be the achievements of Victorian science, the English origins of the Industrial Revolution, the techno-Edenic promise of America, the legacy of Anglo-American analytic philosophy, or the fact that science fiction saw its greatest developments in the United States. Whatever the case, one cannot address the origins of contemporary transhumanism without recognizing the unique Anglo-American context from which it emerges. Three of the most important progenitors of the transhumanist movement within the twentieth century were Englishmen Julian Huxley, B.S. Haldane, and John D. Bernal.

J.B.S. Haldane (1892-1964) was a British geneticist and evolutionary biologist, one of the founders of neo-Darwinism, and taught biology at the University of Cambridge. In Haldane's 1924 book *Daedalus* (or *Science and the Future*), he argued for the immense benefits that would come from the manipulation of human genetics and foresaw a future in which humans would direct their own evolution. Haldane uses the Greek myth of Daedalus as a promethean symbol that represents the revolutionary capabilities of science. He believed that genetic manipulation of Homo sapiens would allow science to make people taller, healthier, and smarter. He was also one of the first to promote "ectogenesis" (in vitro fertilization). Haldane was a self-described Marxist atheist and secular humanist. In *Daedalus*, Haldane clarifies his awareness of the religious criticisms that would come from the future capacities of science and the transformation of mankind. Describing how the promethean potentials of genetic engineering will be viewed as religious blasphemy, Haldane writes,

> The chemical or physical inventor is always a Prometheus. There is no great invention, from fire to flying, which has not been hailed as an insult to some god. But if every physical and chemical invention is a blasphemy, every biological invention is a perversion. There is hardly one which, on first being brought to the notice of an observer from any nation which had not previously heard of their existence, would not appear to him as indecent and unnatural.[176]

Haldane's book became a bestseller and influenced other future-oriented discussions on science and technology in the early twentieth

---

[176] J.B.S. Haldane, *Daedalus, or Science and the Future* (London: Kegan Paul, Trench, Trubner & Co., 1924) 44, accessed and downloaded September, 16, 2024, https://babel.hathitrust.org/cgi/pt?id=mdp.39015026649544&view=1up&seq=54.

century, including his friend Aldous Huxley's (1894-1963) *Brave New World* (1932), fellow communists, and biologist J.D. Bernal (1901-1971). Bernal's 1929 book *The World, the Flesh, and the Devil* put forth visionary ideas about space colonization, the technological enhancement of human intelligence, bionic implants, and the extension of lifespans. Bernal, like Julian Huxley, supported the eugenics movement and predicted an eventual break in organic evolution with the emergence of a mechanical man. Bernal's unshakable faith in science could be described as "secularized religious devotion; only through science (the new secularized religion) can humanity overcome the enemies of the rational soul."[177]

Transhumanism, as is presently understood, began to take full shape in the latter half of the twentieth century. The belief that science and technology would aid the radical extension of human life was a rallying call endorsed by early transhumanists. Though outside the purview of this work, many scholars have written on the significant importance science fiction has had on the development of transhumanism; with notable authors such as Isaac Asimov, Phillip K. Dick, Arthur C. Clarke, Robert Heinlein, John C. Wright, and William Gibson.

In the midst of the Summer of Love, another important catalyst for the transhuman vision was the Human Potential Movement. According to Elizabeth Puttick, the human potential movement is "one of the most influential forces in modern Western society."[178] Building

---

[177] Hava Tirosh-Samuelson, "Transhumanism as a Secularist Faith," In *Zygon* Vol. 47, no.4, December, 2012, 720.

[178] Elizabeth Puttick, "Human Potential Movement" In the *Encyclopedia of New Religion*, ed. Christopher Partridge (Oxford: Lion Publishing, 2004) 399, "The human potential movement (HMP) originated in the 1960s counter-culture

upon Abraham Maslow's theory of self-actualization, this movement aimed at developing "human potential" to its ultimate limits through techniques such as transcendental meditation, Eastern mysticism, gestalt therapy, psychedelics, and development of the human will. Aldous Huxley was one of the early lecturers on the realization of human potential, with his writings on the mystical use of psychedelics and his perennial philosophy being foundational to the movement's success. According to Jeffrey Kripal, Huxley's call "for an institution that could teach the 'nonverbal humanities' and the development of the 'human potentialities' functioned as the working mission statement of early Esalen."[179] The Esalen Institute of Big Sur California was founded by Michael Murphy and Dick Price in 1962 and is considered by many people as the geographical center of the human potential movement. It was here that Huxley gave his early lectures, along with figures to likes of Alan Watts, Albert Hoffman, Joseph Campbell, Abraham Maslow, Fitz Perls, John C. Lilly, Buckminster Fuller, Terence McKenna, and B.F. Skinner. Esalen served as the foundation for Michael Murphy and George Leonard to establish the Human Potential Movement, which shares significant objectives and philosophies with contemporary transhumanist thought.

Of notable significance concerning this period in the development of transhumanist ideas is the father of cryonics, Robert Ettinger's (1918-2011) 1964 book *The Prospect of Immortality*. Ettinger

---

rebellion against mainstream psychology and organized religion. It is not itself a religion, new or otherwise, but a psychological philosophy and framework, including a set of values that have made it one of the most significant and influential forces in the modern Western society."

[179] Jeffrey J. Kripal, *Esalen: America and the Religion of No Religion* (Chicago: Chicago University Press, 2007) 86.

explained that men and women may have a second chance at life by preserving their bodies at ultra-low temperatures to the point of clinical death. Ettinger believed that doing so would provide a future opportunity to resurrect such individuals once the technology was capable. He followed up this work with *Man into Superman* (1972, where he used Julian Huxley's term "transhumanism" and explored how technology has the transformative potential to improve the standard biological human being. Around the same time, Alan Harrington wrote *The Immortalist*, in which he popularized the slogan undergirding both the cryonics and the transhumanist movement; "Death is an imposition to the human race, and one no longer acceptable."[180]

Inspired by Ettinger, Saul Kent (1939-2023) championed cryonics and life extension in *Future Sex* (1974). Kent went on to found the Life Extension Foundation in 1980. As a pioneer in the field of cryonics, Kent was appointed as a board member of the Alcor Life Extension Foundation. Alcor is a nonprofit organization based out of Scottsdale, Arizona where they research and perform cryonic freezing of corpses and human brains in liquid nitrogen. They hope that the development of future technology will provide the ability to restore patients back to life. Max More was president and CEO of Alcor between 2010 and 2020, and is where he continues his work and research.

One of the most comprehensive transhumanist thinkers in the twentieth century was F.M. Esfandiary (1930-2000), later known as FM-2030. There were two reasons for his unique name change: first, to reflect his belief that he would live until 2030, marking his 100th birthday and the age at which people would be able to live as long as they wish; and

---

[180] Alan Harrington, *The Immortalist* (New York: Random House 1969) 13.

second, to break free of naming conventions that he argued were rooted in a collectivist mentality. Esfandiary's contribution was more literary than academic, despite teaching at the New School for Social Research in New York in the 1960s. It was here that he taught classes in "New Concepts of the Human," in which he argued against the use of convuental names that collectivize people along the lines of ancestry, gender, nationality, or religion. He was a staunch anti-nationalist who believed that the nuclear family would disappear in the future, allowing technology to facilitate transition to social communities. In *Are You a Transhuman?* (1989), he defined a transhuman as a "transitional human" whose use of "technology, way of living, and values marked them as a step towards posthumanity."[181] In this book, FM-2030 provided questionnaires in which he rated the reader as more or less transhuman based on how much they traveled, modified their bodies, rejected traditional family structures, and spurned exclusive monogamous relationships.

In the 1970's cyberneticians and technologists began intense speculation about what they referred to as the looming "intelligence explosion." In 1970, Marvin Minsky (1927-2016) made highly optimistic predictions about the rise of super-advanced artificial intelligence. Minsky was a longstanding professor at the Massachusetts Institute of Technology (MIT) and the cofounder of their AI laboratory. In 1992, Minsky coauthored a science fiction book with Harry Harrison, *The Turing Option*, popularizing the concept of implantable AI and the notion that the human brain can be reconstructed with machine-based cognition. In 1994, Minsky published an article in the journal *Scientific American*

---

[181] Max More, "The Philosophy of Transhumanism," 11.

explaining why radically expanded lives would require replacement of the biological brain with superior computational devices. Minsky, an ardent supporter of the development of highly intelligent robots, believed in the eventuality human brains could be uploaded into superior machine bodies. Before his death and during the operational years of the transhumanist Extropy Institute, he served as a member of the board of directors.

The Turing Test, proposed by British mathematicians and computer scientist Alan Turing (1912-1954) in his seminal 1950 paper "Computing Machinery and Intelligence," is a method for determining whether a machine exhibits human-like intelligence. The test involves a human evaluator who engages in natural language conversations with both a machine and human without knowing which. If the evaluator cannot reliably distinguish the machine from the human, the machine is said to have passed the Turing Test, thus demonstrating its ability to mimic human thought. Although Turing himself never mentioned transhumanism, his belief in the emergence of thinking machines has been instrumental in AI development and speculation about future machine intelligence. Turing writes, "I believe that in about fifty years' time it will be possible to program computers... and that they will eventually take part in conversations in which the interlocutor would not be able to distinguish their responses from those of a human being."[182]

Much of the excitement surrounding the "intelligence explosion" was founded upon Moore's law. Moore's Law states that the number of transistors within integrated circuits doubles every two years. In 1965, Gordon More (1929-2023) posited a linear relationship between the

---

[182] Alan Turing, "Computing Machinery and Intelligence," *Mind* 59 (October 1950): 433-460, https://doi.org/10.1093/mind/LIX.236.433.

increase in device complexity and time, and argued that it would continue for another decade. Although Moore's speculation did not imply that it would continue as a historical trend, it has generally held true since 1975 and has since become known as a law. Moore's Law has been a great catalyst for transhumanists who have speculated about a future point known as the "technological singularity;" a future period in which technological growth becomes so uncontrollable and irreversible that it culminates in an intelligence explosion. Transhumanists have argued that Singularity leads to positive feedback loops of machine self-improvement, resulting in powerful super-intelligent machines surpassing the physical and mental abilities of all human beings. Machine intelligence is predicted to become so advanced that humans will no longer be able to control technology, thereby reshaping human history and altering the ways in which we relate to advanced artificial intelligence.

The "Singularity" was first popularized in 1983 by Vernor Vinge (1944-2024), and more recently by Ray Kurzweil in his book *The Singularity Is Near* (2005). Kurzweil has since updated his prophecies in June 2024 with *The Singularity is Nearer: When We Merge with AI*, where he reiterates his previous predictions on AI reaching human intelligence by 2029, and that people will fully merge with machines by 2045.

However, the very first mention of a technological singularity was actually postulated by computer scientist and engineer John von Neumann (1903-1957). During a conversation with Stanislaw Ulam (1909-1984) von Neumann speculated on a historical trend in the acceleration of technology that ultimately reaches a final eschatological apex. John von Neumann died on February 8, 1957, and in his tribute written by Stanislaw Ulam in 1958, Ulam recounted their conversation about the future endpoint of technological advance, writing, "...the ever accelerating progress of technology and changes in the mode of human life, which gives the appearance of approaching some essential singularity in the history of the race beyond which human affairs, as we know them, could not continue."[183]

We would be remised when discussing robotics and artificial intelligence without discussing Hans Moravec. Moravec was the principal research scientist at the famed Carnegie Mellon University Robotics Institute, where he led pioneering research on mobile robotics. His work provided robots with the ability to navigate and maneuver in physical environments. In addition to his technical research, Moravec is well known for his popular books *Mind Children: The Future of Robot and Human Intelligence* (1988) and *Robot: Mere Machine to Transcendent Mind* (1999). According to Religious Studies scholar Robert Geraci, Moravec effectively began the "Apocalyptic AI" movement in 1978 with the publication of "Today's Computers, Intelligent Machines and Our Future" in the science fiction magazine *Analog*.[184] In that essay, he predicted human-level machine intelligence by 1988, along with the transfer of human minds to computers to provide greater intelligence and virtual immortality. Moravec's vision of a future community in which humanity transcends its biological form and constructs a collective hivemind within cyberspace continues to be present in future expectations.

---

[183] Stanislaw Ulam, "Tribute to John von Neumann," *Bulletin of the American Mathematical Society* (May 1958) 2, 5. https://www.ams.org/journals/bull/1958-64-03/S0002-9904-1958-10189-5/S0002-9904-1958-10189-5.pdf.

[184] Robert M. Geraci, *Apocalyptic AI: Visions of Heaven in Robotics, Artificial Intelligence, and Virtual Reality* (Oxford: Oxford University Press, 2010) 22.

The man most responsible for popularizing the apocalyptic "technological singularity" and the uploading of human consciousness into a machine is none other than Ray Kurzweil. Kurzweil is an influential AI researcher, key inventor of music synthesizers, AI speech recognition, and reading devices for the blind. After correspondence with Marvin Minsky, Kurzweil went to MIT earning a bachelor of science degree under Minsky in 1970. Kurzweil would go on to start multiple companies along with patenting several inventions. In 2012, he was hired by Google cofounder Larry Page to work full-time on machine learning and language processing. Similar to Moravec, Kurzweil complemented his innovative research with pop science books. His first was the 1990 book *The Age of Intelligent Machines*, where he argued that computers in the near future will be more intelligent than collective humanity. In 1999 he followed up with *The Age of Spiritual Machines*, arguing that Moore's Law will end in 2020 with the emergence of such advanced computational machines that they "will appear to have their own personalities ... their own free will. They will claim to have spiritual experiences. And people – those still using carbon-based neurons or otherwise – will believe them."[185] In 2005, he wrote his sequel, *The Singularity Is Near*, embracing the term "the singularity," but redated the techno-apocalypse of human transcendence to the year 2045.[186]

By the late 1980s, the intellectual and cultural movement of transhumanism had begun to take shape with the arrival of the Extropy Institute. Extropianism is a core philosophical movement within

---

[185] Ray Kurzweil, *The Age of Spiritual Machines* (New York: Penguin Books, 1999) 6.
[186] Ray Kurzweil, *The Singularity Is Near* (New York: Penguin Books, 2005) "I set the date for the Singularity – representing a profound and disruptive transformation in human capability – as 2045." 136.

transhumanism, developed by philosopher Max More. *Extropy* magazine, the first explicit transhumanist magazine, was first published in 1988 by Max More and Tom W. Bell. The publication presented a variety of ideas from leading transhumanist thinkers, including the influential essay of Max More "Transhumanism: Towards a Futurist Philosophy." Support grew further in 1991when the Extropy Institute established an email list connecting futurists and technologists worldwide. These early email lists allowed for the exploration and reflection of future technologies when little was being addressed in printed publications or academic journals. As Bostrom highlights, "the internet played an important role in incubating modern transhumanism by facilitating these meetings of minds."[187] Beginning in 1994, transhumanist conferences began to emerge with an official website in 1996 along with an Online Vital Progress Summit in 2004.

The World Transhumanist Association (WTA) was founded in 1998 by Nick Bostrom and David Pearce to provide a general organizational basis for various transhumanist groups and interests. The *Transhumanist Declaration* was published in the same year as the official founding document to declare the basic principles and pursuits of the transhumanist movement. It has now been revised for the fourth time with the latest version available on Humanity +'s official website. The goal of developing an official organization was to cultivate a more mature and academically respectable form of transhumanism. The WTA began to grow rapidly, with local chapters blossoming around the world. In 2001, the loosely formed and informally organized WTA entered its next phase, in which it adopted a constitution, became incorporated as a nonprofit,

---

[187] Bostrom, "Transhumanist Thought," 12.

and began constructing international networks of local groups and volunteers.[188] In 2006, the Extropy Institute closed, and the WTA rebranded itself as "Humanity+." In recent years, related organizations have risen with a more narrowly defined focus on transhumanist issues, such as life extension, artificial intelligence, nanotechnology, synthetic wombs, and brain machine interfaces.

B. Extropianism: In Praise of the Devil

When asking, what is the core of transhumanist philosophy, a helpful way to begin is to think of transhumanism as "trans-humanism" plus "transhuman-ism." The former, "trans-humanism," accentuates the philosophical enlightenment roots of humanism. As mentioned, the movement differentiates itself from other philosophies because of its continued anthropocentric focus on the human subject. These enlightenment values include the desire for continued progress, disdain for the supernatural, elevation of reason, utilization of scientific methods, and pursuit of technological advancement. While humanism relies more heavily on educational and cultural refinement, transhumanism wishes to apply technology to overcome biological and genetic limitations. "Transhuman-ism" emphasizes that their movement goes well beyond the boundaries of mere humanism. Given their Darwinian foundation, transhumanist metaphysics outright rejects the existence of static human nature; humanity is understood not as an end in itself, but rather as a

---

[188] This effort was led by James Hughes, a sociologist at Trinity College in Hartford Connecticut), Mark Walker, a philosopher at the University of Toronto, then the editor of the *Journal of Transhumanism* later renamed the *Journal of Evolution and Technology*, and Nick Bostrom, who at the time was teaching at Yale.

creature with a current form mutating along an evolutionary spectrum. By applying modern technology to the human subject, it evolves yet further out of its naturalistic and historic context, no longer accurately described as human, but towards a "posthuman" existence. Becoming posthuman means exceeding and expanding beyond the less desirable limits of the biological human condition. As Max More writes,

> Posthuman beings would no longer suffer from disease, aging, or inevitable death. They would have vastly greater physical capability and freedom of form – often referred to as morphological freedom. Posthumans would also have much greater cognitive capabilities and more refined emotions.[189]

Transhumanist thought gives consideration to the environments that are likely to occur in a posthuman era, including space colonization and living simulated lives within virtual realities. Due to their belief in the technological means of liberating people from the human condition, this includes restructuring society itself. The movement advocates the total redesign of federal organizations, economies, and politics. It draws inspiration from a variety of different fields of research and is not centered on any particular technology. To reach their posthuman goals these fields include information technology, computer science and engineering, cognitive science, neural-computer interface, artificial intelligence, life extension, genetic engineering, and nanotechnology.

---

[189] More, "The Philosophy of Transhumanism," 4.

The first fully developed transhumanist philosophy was published in 1990 by Max More titled "Principles of Extropy." For More, "extropy" is a key concept within transhumanist thought, employed not as a technical term opposed to entropy, but as a metaphor for a movement that strives for perpetual improvement and technological enhancement of human vitality and capacity. Seven distinct principles define extropianism: perpetual progress, self-transformation, practical optimism, intelligent technology, an open society, self-direction, and rational thinking.[190]

According to More, these principles codify the life-affirming and life-promoting ideals of transhumanism. More describes traditional religions as entropic. He argues that religious faith is inherently entropic because of its faith in "the invisible and unknowable," it promotes an irrationality that leads to "the loss of order, information, and usable energy."[191] More claims that religion as a cultural process of meaning-making has failed, and it is time for new and better rational understanding. Accordingly, he believes "extropy" in its progressive pursuit towards transcendence, fulfills this void and makes concrete the religious hopes and aspirations that have existed in "an irrationalist-fantasy form."[192]

Max More detailed the "irrationality" of religion in a 1991 article titled "In Praise of the Devil." Though More understands the Devil as symbolic rather than literal – stating there is no ontological reality to "the

---

[190] Max More, "Principles of Extropy," 2003. https://web.archive.org/web/20131015142449/http://extropy.org/principles.htm.
[191] Max More, "Transhumanism: Towards a Futurist Philosophy," (1990) accessed October 23, 2024, https://www.ildodopensiero.it/wp-content/uploads/2019/03/max-more-transhumanism-towards-a-futurist-philosophy.pdf.
[192] More, "Transhumanism: Towards a Futurist Philosophy."

Devil" – he addresses his article as "written in praise of Satan, Lucifer, the Devil, or whatever you want to call him."[193] He describes how the Devil symbolizes the transhumanist as an inspiring entity that questions traditional authority, and is the embodiment of reason, intelligence, critical thought, and self-worship. His critique of religion, most specifically Christianity, is that it leads to entropic lulling of human progress by allowing people to retreat into the irrationality of faith. Whereas Christianity expresses hedonism and selfishness as tempestuous sins to be avoided, Max More recharacterizes them as the transhumanist virtues of "pleasure" and "selfishness." In many ways, More is correct to identify his extropic philosophy as the inverse of traditional Christianity. His elevation of reason leaves no room for epistemic openness to divine revelation, mystical experience, or faith, which is beyond the limits of rationality. The idolization of pleasure and selfishness acts as a bulwark against the Christian virtues of asceticism, communion, and self-sacrifice. He ends his article with a rallying call to all transhumanists, More writes,

> I want to remind you that you are all Popes. You are all your own highest authority. You are the source of your action. You choose your values – whether you do so actively or by default. You choose what to believe, how strongly to believe, and what you will take as disconfirming evidence. No one has authority over you – you are your own authority, your own value-choose, your

---

[193] Max More, "In Praise of the Devil" *Atheist Notes*, no.3 (1991) accessed February 4, 2025, http://libertarian.co.uk/2019/08/21/atheist-notes-003-in-praise-of-the-devil-1991-by-max-more/.

own thinker. Join me, join Lucifer, and join Extropy in fighting God and his entropic forces with our mind, our will, and our courage. God's army is strong, but they are backed by ignorance, fear, and cowardice. Reality is fundamentally on our side. Forward into the light![194]

The above quote highlights how even for the most ardent anti-religious skeptics such as Max More, Extropy (transhumanism) is seen as a replacement and nullification of traditional religion. In this manner, it acts in the same category as religion. The analogy of the promethean light liberating humanity by the stultifying effects of religion is replete among transhumanist advocates. This was the transhumanist framing first presented by Julian Huxley and J.B.S. Haldane. Though More and others would reject the "religious" or "spiritual" label to describe their undertaking, preferring instead "philosophy" or "scientific movement," it is interesting they articulate transhumanism as a replacement ideology. The creation of a new metanarrative of ultimate meaning and its perceived competition with traditional religion places it within a similar classification of societal functions. The Fall is not entirely a tragic event remedied by repentance and spiritual participation with God, but rather, like the Gnostics of old, a providential celebration of human escape from the confines of a tyrannical deity. Without a fall, there is no need for technology. In this sense, transhuman philosophy proudly and boldly reframes death as an existential hurdle that must be overcome through rational ingenuity and technological advancement.

---

[194] Max More, "In Praise of the Devil," 2.

C. Epistemology, Metaphysics, and Ethics

Concerning transhumanist epistemology, it must first be stated that there is no universally accepted position, nor does having a different epistemic basis preclude one from being a transhumanist. Epistemological views vary from Piercean pragmatists to Ayn Rand foundationalists, who posit undeniable axioms in nature's hierarchy of knowledge. However, most transhumanists have identified themselves as strong rationalists. Strong rationalism asserts that epistemic beliefs should be based solely on what can be physically proven through empirical evidence and logical reasoning. Max More personally identifies with a position referred to as pancritical rationalism (PCR), also known as comprehensive critical rationalism. This position originated with William Warren Bartley (1934-1990) and was developed upon the work of Karl Popper (1902-1994). Popper advanced a non-justificationist theory of scientific advancement, arguing that scientific knowledge grows through a process of critical debate and falsification, rather than through the accumulation of justified beliefs. PCR decouples criticism and philosophical justification, thereby rejecting justificationism in favor of the view that there are no philosophically justified true beliefs. By privileging falsification over justification, critical rationalists attempt to never appeal to any authority or dogma but instead rely solely on critical examination and evidence.

PCR differs quite radically from Enlightenment epistemology. Enlightenment philosophy is rooted in foundationalism: the belief that there is a secure foundation of certainty, granting conclusions inferred based on sound premises.[195] Rationalist and skeptic René Descartes (1596-1650) used the *cogito* as his foundational starting point for philosophical inquiry, doubting everything except his own existence as a thinking being.[196] The *cogito* attempted to establish the indubitable existence of the self through an act of thinking. Empirical justification also grew prominently during the early modern period and characterized the approaches taken by Locke, Berkeley, and Hume. For transhumanists, they call into question the notion of a fixed autonomous self, and instead argue the "self" is a social construction shaped by cultural and historical forces. In turn, they prefer empirical justification to knowledge as opposed to an appeal to any eternal metaphysical category. After Kant's *Critique of Pure Reason*, foundationalist approaches were split between 19th century British Empiricism and the self-evident concepts present within German Idealism. These differences still typify the philosophical distinction between Anglo-analytic and European continental traditions.

Pancritical rationalism is a suitable epistemology for transhumanism, because it embodies the core values and aspirations of continuous improvement, critical inquiry, and rejection of dogma. This approach aligns with the quest to overcome biological limitations using technology, science, and reasoning. Owing to its flexibility, PCR allows transhumanists to navigate the challenges of human enhancement,

---

[195] Beginning with Plato, philosophical justification was found through the Ideal Forms; Aristotle argued knowledge was justified through First Principles; Augustine justified knowledge by way of divine illumination; it is the combination of these that generally define justificationism up to the Enlightenment.

[196] "Cogito, ergo sum" is a philosophical statement attributed to René Descartes, meaning "I think, therefore I am." This Latin phrase is the foundation of his philosophical system, emphasizing the existence of the self through the act of thinking. The phrase was first published in French as "je pense, donc je suis" in Descartes' 1637 work "Discourse on the Method."

ensuring that the pursuit of transcendence remains guided by reason, open inquiry, and willingness to question even the most deeply held beliefs. In this way, PCR not only complements transhumanist values but also provides the movement with the capacity to critically engage with the possibilities of a technologically augmented future. Max More argues PCR allows for the discarding of philosophical justification while "retaining a respect for objectivity, argumentation, and the systematic use of reason."[197]

That said, philosophical critics of critical rationalism have noted that such a theory fails to provide a satisfactory account of how to rationally believe in reason itself. Scholars have argued that critical rationalists, such as Karl Popper and William Bartley, rely on a justified true belief account of knowledge, which ultimately prevents them from logically refuting or defending a rational belief in reason. According to Thomas Kuhn (1922-1996), science often works within paradigms in which anomalies (potential falsifications) are tolerated until a paradigm shift occurs. According to Kuhn, science works within unique historical paradigms, allowing normal science to act as a puzzle-solving activity. When scientists encounter overwhelming anomalies within a given paradigm, it marks a revolutionary change towards new paradigms.[198] *The Structure of Scientific Revolutions* (1962) calls into question the unbroken line of scientific advancement that underpins the transhumanist movement. Imre Lakatos further developed this criticism, arguing that research programs evolve over time with adjustments made to the protective belt of auxiliary hypotheses rather than falsifying the core

---

[197] More, "The Philosophy of Transhumanism," 6.
[198] Thomas Kuhn, *The Structure of Scientific Revolutions: 50th Anniversary Edition* (Chicago, University of Chicago Press, 2012).

theory outright. Therefore, falsification in real science is more complex than that suggested by Popper. Critics argue that, even if a theory is falsified, multiple competing theories can explain the same set of data. This presents a problem for critical rationalism because it leaves the choice of which theory to accept underdetermined by Popper's falsification criteria. William Van Orman Quine and Pierre Duhem raised this issue, showing that it's not possible to test a single hypothesis in isolation because our observations are theory-laden. Additionally, critics contend that deciding when a theory is sufficiently falsified is not as clear-cut as Popper suggests. Scientists often cling to theories in the face of falsifying evidence, preferring to revise auxiliary hypotheses rather than abandon a central theory. This introduces a subjective, pragmatic element to theory choice, which is at odds with the strict falsificationist approach of critical rationalism. Additionally, this subjective element calls into question the "objectivity" of PCR, as argued by Max More.

Concerning metaphysics, issues and discussions arise regarding the nature and identity of the self. Most transhumanists identify as materialists, physicalists, and functionalists. As such, transhumanism calls into question the thinking and feeling of the subjective self for a position that understands the "self" as essentially a physical process without static metaphysical categories. Much of the metaphysical debate within transhumanism revolves around theories of mind. Most accept some form of functionalism and therefore believe that the "self" has to be instantiated within a physical medium, although that medium is not limited to biology. As biological neurons are worn out, transhumanists believe they can be swapped out with synthetic parts to support the same, if not more enhanced cognitive function. The functionalist position argues that each mental state is constituted solely by its functional role.

Therefore, as long as the system performs the appropriate function, there is little difference between whether it is realized in a computer or in the human brain. This is known as the substrate-independent principle, meaning that mental states can be replicated in different physical substrates, such as the biological brain or a digital computer, without altering the nature of mental states. As computer programs perform functions via the computation of inputs and outputs, so too is the brain understood as a function of its biological operation by means of stimulus responses. Functionalism is a physicalist and computational theory of mind that differentiates it from identity theory (mental states are identical to brain states) and behaviorism (mental terms can be reduced to behavioral descriptions).

    The functionalist theory of mind is particularly useful to transhumanist philosophy and conceptions of the self because it offers a flexible and non-biologically bound understanding of consciousness, cognition, and personal identity. This perspective implies that consciousness and cognitive processes can, in theory, be realized in different substrates such as silicon chips or advanced neural interfaces. Functionalism provides a theoretical foundation for "mind uploading," as it suggests that if the functional processes of the mind can be replicated in another medium, consciousness can persist. This theoretically supports the feasibility of creating digital or artificial versions of the mind, including advanced AI, that can possess or mimic human-like consciousness.[199] Functionalism also provides a framework for

---

[199] D. J. Chalmers, "The Singularity: A Philosophical Analysis" In *Science Fiction and Philosophy: From Time Travel to Superintelligence*, ed. Susan Schneider (Hoboken NJ: Wiley-Blackwell, 2010) 171-224. In this article, David Chalmers provides a detailed philosophical examination of the concept of the

considering the ethical status of non-biological entities such as AI or uploaded minds. By focusing on the functions that constitute consciousness, functionalism can extend considerations of rights, agency, and moral worth to artificial beings, which is crucial for transhumanist discussions about the future of human-AI coexistence.

Critics of functionalist theories of mind have addressed the problem of "qualia" and its overreliance on computational metaphors, likening the mind to a computer. Qualia are subjective, first-person experiences, or "what it is like" to feel something (e.g. the experience of seeing red or feeling pain). Frank Jackson's famous thought experiment of Mary, the color scientist, who learns something new when she sees color for the first time despite knowing all the physical facts, highlights no amount of functional description can capture the intrinsic, subjective quality of experience, something that functionalism seems to leave out. Transhumanism's functionalist theories neglect the importance of the subjective body in favor of objective functional intelligence. Philosopher John Searle's Chinese Room Thought Experiment is another key critique. Searle imagines a situation in which a person who is alone in a room and does not understand Chinese but follows a set of rules to manipulate Chinese symbols. In response to the input of others the "Chinese Room" is able to produce appropriate outputs without understanding the intricacies and meaning of the language. To outside perceivers, the system functions as if it understands Chinese by answering (outputting) all the questions (inputs) correctly, but there is no genuine internal understanding. Searle argues that functionalism is similarly flawed: it might describe the functional organization of mental states, but it does

---

technological singularity, exploring the implications of advanced AI and mind uploading within the context of functionalism and consciousness studies.

not account for intentionality (the capacity for mental states to be about things) or genuine understanding.

Another important metaphysical concept supported by transhumanists is the belief that the world is a simulation. Simulation theory proposes that what sentient beings experience as reality is actually a simulation akin to video games that humans construct. This hypothesis has been postulated by transhumanist Nick Bostrom in his seminal 2003 paper "Are you Living in a Computer Simulation." Bostrom argues that if advanced civilizations reach a point where they can create realistic simulations of entire universes, and if they are interested in doing so, then there is a high probability that we are living in one of those simulations.[200] Elon Musk in a 2018 appearance on the Joe Rogan podcast claimed it is most likely we live in a simulated universe.[201] Many prominent physicists have criticized the simulation hypothesis, with German physicist Sabine Hossenfelder labeling it as pseudoscience and a religion, because it is not a serious scientific argument that can be proven by empiricism, but rather "you'd believe it because you have faith," not scientific proof.[202] However, one of the reasons why such a hypothesis finds support among transhumanists is that it calls into question the ontological reality of simulated environments. If the world we perceive through our unmediated senses is part of a simulated reality, how could augmented virtual realties be any less real than the lives we already live? This position allows transhumanists to dissolve distinctions between

---

[200] Nick Bostrom, "Are You Living in a Computer Simulation," in *Philosophical Quarterly* Vol. 53, no. 211 (2003) 243-255.
[201] "Joe Rogan Experience #1169 – Elon Musk," *Joe Rogan Experience*, Sept. 6, 2018, podcast 43:35-44:40, https://www.youtube.com/watch?v=ycPr5-27vSI.
[202] Sabine Hossenfelder, "The Simulation Hypothesis is Pseudoscience," 2021, video 8:44-8:52, , https://www.youtube.com/watch?v=HCSqogSPU_Q&t=63s.

biological experiences and simulated virtual experiences, providing further validity to their hope for life within virtual worlds.

Concerning the ethical presuppositions that undergird the transhumanist worldview, the majority find a footing for virtue-based and consequentialist utilitarian ethics. Very few would describe themselves as deontological, arguing for moral rules or duties that govern human behavior regardless of consequences. Max More states that since the advent of his extropian philosophy a significant number of transhumanists have established their morality on a virtue foundation. Aristotelian-based virtue ethics focus on the cultivation of moral character and the pursuit of virtues such as wisdom, courage, and temperance. Transhumanists who adopt a virtue ethics framework argue that technological enhancements — whether they involve cognitive enhancement, life extension, or even "moral bioenhancement" — should aim to promote personal excellence and the cultivation of virtues. Some have proposed that using technology can enhance moral capacities, such as altruism or empathy. Reflecting a virtue-based concern with improving moral character rather than merely optimizing outcomes.

However, critics argue that true virtue cannot be technologically engineered because it requires intentional, habituated practice, rather than a simple enhancement of biological traits. Christianity would also appeal to virtue ethics but ground them in divine revelation and the teachings of Jesus Christ. The development of personal virtue to become like God incarnate is an essential element of Orthodox Christianity's concept of deification. Concerning the technological enhancement of virtue, the question of what is "virtue," who defines "virtue" – being a relative cultural construct – and how is it embodied is the central contention. This inability to objectively justify virtue highlights that transhumanist virtue ethics are constructed by the internal biases and goals of transhumanists themselves.

In more recent years, prominent figures have adopted a more explicit utilitarian consequentialist approach indicative of David Pearce's "hedonistic imperative." Utilitarian ethics, rooted in the work of Jeremy Bentham (1748-1832) and John Stuart Mill (1806-1873), evaluate actions based on their ability to maximize overall happiness or well-being. Whereas deontological ethics focuses on intention over consequences, utilitarianism focuses solely on consequences over personal intention. In the context of transhumanism, utilitarianism is frequently employed to justify the development and use of transformative technologies that could reduce suffering, extend life, and improve the quality of life of the greatest number of people. Utilitarian transhumanists argue that technologies should be developed and applied if they lead to the greatest net benefits for humanity. David Pearce is a British transhumanist and negative utilitarian, who proclaims that our posthuman successors will be able to abolish suffering in its entirety through the rewriting of vertebrate genome and redesigning the global ecosystem.[203] Believing this to be a moral imperative, Pearce argues that advanced drugs, neural implants, and nanotechnology could end suffering in all sentient lives. This includes Pearce's calls to technologically "reprogram predators" to limit predation and reduce the suffering of prey animals.[204]

The intersection between utilitarian ethics and transhumanism is particularly strong in the "Effective Altruism" (EA) movement, which

---

[203] David Pearce, "The Abolitionist Project," (2007) https://www.hedweb.com/abolitionist-project/index.html.

[204] Manon Verchot, "Meet the People Who Want to Turn Predators Into Herbivores," published November 27, 2020, https://www.treehugger.com/meet-the-people-who-want-to-turn-predators-into-vegans-4857310.

seeks to apply rationality and evidence to maximize the positive impact of actions. It emphasizes maximizing the positive impact of altruistic actions, whether through charitable donations, career choices, or personal efforts. Effective Altruism intersects with transhumanist philosophy in several key areas, particularly existential risk reduction, long-term thinking, and the shared belief in using science and technology to improve human well-being. Notable figures such as Peter Singer, Nick Bostrom, Sam Bankman-Fried, Toby Ord, Sam Altman, and Derek Parfit have adopted this perspective to guide decisions about where to focus resources and technological efforts. William MacAskill, a leading EA philosopher, makes clear this movement is not simply utilitarian, saying "this is a category mistake. Effective altruism is not utilitarianism, nor is it any other normative theory or claim."[205] Transhumanism's focus on rational ethics, often derived from utilitarian thinking, aligns closely with EA's emphasis on maximizing its impact through logical and evidence-based decisions. Both movements prioritize rational approaches to problem solving, whether by enhancing human capabilities or by reducing global suffering.

    Transhumanism is a subbranch of posthuman philosophy. The term "posthumanism" was first coined at the Josiah Macy Foundation conferences on cybernetics in New York (1946-1953). The conference was attended by leading scientists Norbert Wiener (1894-1964), Heinz von Foerster (1911-2002), John von Neumann, Warren McCulloch (1898-1969), Gregory Bateson (1904-1980), Julian Bigelow (1913-

---

[205] William MacAskill, "Effective Altruism," In *The International Encyclopedia of Ethics* (Hoboken, NJ: John Wiley & Sons, 2013) accessed digitally October 9, 2024, https://www.academia.edu/43357478/Effective_Altruism?b=50_percent_vector .

2003), and Arturo Rosenblueth (1900-1970). Their goal was to search for "a new theoretical model for biological, mechanical, and communicational processes that removed the human and Homo sapiens from any particularly privileged position in relation to matters of meaning, information, and cognition."[206] "Posthumanism" was a term used to imagine a "postbiological" "post-Darwinian" stage of human development related to all technological existence. The following decades saw cybernetics evolving into other disciplines such as computer science, electrical engineering, system engineering, and biofeedback. One of the foundational concepts in cybernetics is the feedback loop, which describes how systems use information to self-regulate and adapt to environmental changes. This principle is key to understanding how biological organisms maintain homeostasis and how machines can be designed to adjust based on feedback, as observed in thermostats or servo-mechanisms. Early cyberneticians believed they were on the verge of creating intelligent, self-regulating machines, which sparked significant optimism about the future of automation, artificial intelligence, and even human-computer interaction.

Critics of cybernetics, such as Martin Heidegger (1889-1976), saw the aims of cybernetics as the apotheosis of Cartesian humanism. In his works, *The Question Concerning Technology* and *The End of Philosophy and the Task of Thinking*, Heidegger critiques the mechanistic worldview inaugurated by René Descartes, in which the world is viewed as a resource to be measured, controlled, and exploited. Heidegger views cybernetics, the science of control and communication in machines and living organisms, as the culmination of this Cartesian view, because it

---

[206] Carey Wolfe, *What Is Posthumanism* (Minneapolis and London: University of Minnesota Press, 2010) xii.

extends the project of rational control to both humans and machines. Therefore, human existence can be reduced to something that can be optimized and managed in technical terms.[207] Jean Pierre Dupuy has since taken a more critical stance, arguing cybernetics represented an important moment in the total demystification and deconstruction of humanism. For Dupuy, "cybernetics consisted of a decisive step in the rise of antihumanism" and embodied a scientific "rebellion against human existence."[208] Dupuy calls into question what it means to be fully human in a posthuman world. Dupuy's critique of cybernetics closely aligns with Heidegger's concerns regarding the dangers of modern technology. Both thinkers see technological thinking as reducing the world and human beings to objects of control and calculation, a process Heidegger calls "Enframing" (*Gestell*). Both thinkers view cybernetics as an ontological threat to human existence, leading Dupuy to warn that it threatens to reduce human freedom and subjectivity to mere technical functions. If to be a human means to experience freedom and morality, the acceleration of technological innovations has sparked significant debate over the last six decades, retheorizing what it ultimately means to be human.

D. Religion In Our Postsecular Moment

---

[207] Martin Heidegger, "The End of Philosophy and the Task of Thinking," in *Basic Writings: Martin Heidegger*, ed. David Farrell Krell (Routledge, 1993) 434-35.
[208] Jean Pierre Dupuy, "Cybernetics Is Antihumanism: Advanced Technologies and the Rebellion against the Human Condition." In *H+: Transhumanism and Its Critics*, eds. Gregory R. Hansell and William Grassi (Philadelphia: Metanexus, 2011) 215-26.

Contemporary scholars Jürgen Habermas and Charles Taylor describe our era as a postsecular moment in which the secularization narrative has failed, and religion persists in new forms rather than disappearing. In other words, even in modern contexts where institutional religion has declined in the West, religion remains a significant presence and moral resource in the face of dissolving the boundaries between secularism and religion. Therefore, Habermas concludes that secular citizens can no longer assume that faith is a mere relic of the past; instead, postsecular society calls for renewed dialogue between secular reason and religious tradition.[209] Both Habermas and Taylor emphasize that postsecular societies reintegrate religion in new guises, which sets the stage for secular ideologies to take on quasi-religious roles that provide meaning, moral orientation, and visions of transcendence.

Transhumanism extends beyond the mere technological enhancement of human existence and promotes a vision of the appropriate moral structuring of both individuals and society. Technology functions as a catalyst for the transformation of cultural, religious, and moral sensibilities. Consequently, transhumanism can be regarded as a "religion without revelation," as articulated by Julian Huxley. It operates as a rationalized secular religion, offering the ultimate meaning and purpose in a world that has been disenchanted by science. Addressing these dimensions of contemporary transhumanism as a functioning religious orientation, scholar Hava Tirosh-Samuelson writes,

---

[209] Jürgen Habermas, "A 'Post-Secular" Society – What Does it Mean," *Reset Dialogues on Civilization*, (September 16, 2008) accessed March 20, 2025, https://www.resetdoc.org/story/a-post-secular-society-what-does-that-mean/#:~:text=in%20Europe%20can%20be%20described,attribute%20primarily%20to%20three%20phenomena.

Contemporary Transhumanism theorizes about the human species in ultimate terms: it seeks transcendence by means of technology; it has authoritative doctrines, texts, and leaders, as well as normative beliefs and values; it articulates an eschatological vision that gives historical coherence and narrative of directionality to trajectories of technological change; and it offers an ethical vision in which technological innovation is the central human achievement and thereby becomes the medium for achieving authenticity, liberty, and justice. Transhumanism already has a distinctive rhetoric and artistic preferences, and eventually it will develop its own rituals. By all measures, then, transhumanism functions as a religion, albeit a secularized one, that offers meaning and seeks to recruit new adherents.[210]

In the contemporary "postsecular moment,"[211] transhumanism integrates religious and secular elements in a distinctive way. This postsecular context, contrary to secularist predictions, is marked by a resurgence of religious discourse in the public sphere and the recognition of the equal significance of faith and reason. Rather than the anticipated decline in religion with modernization, secular societies are experiencing a paradoxical situation in which religious impulses are articulated through the secular language of science and technology, exemplified by

---

[210] Tirosh-Samuelson, "Transhumanism as a Secularist Faith," 728-29.
[211] Phillip S. Gorski, David Kyuman Kim, John Ropey, and Jonathan Van Antwerpen, *The Post-secular in Question: Religion in Contemporary Society* (New York: New York University Press, 2012).

transhumanism's technologically driven eschatological and teleological vision. Within this framework, Habermas emphasizes the importance of mutual learning and engagement between religious and secular individuals rather than mutual exclusion.

Social scientists have written extensively concerning secularization theory, believing that modernization is not only a problem for religion, but will eventually lead to the disappearance of religion. However, not everyone is convinced that secularization has failed. One critic who is still strongly committed to the secularization thesis is sociologist Steve Bruce. He argues that the notion of the postsecular is nothing more than "an idea dreamt up by religious people who want to pretend that the peoples of the West are more religious than they really are."[212] According to Bruce, the main features of secularization are the declining importance of religious institutions in public life, along with the social standing of religion and the extent to which people are religious.[213] In contrast to Bruce, Charles Taylor defines the postsecular moment as "a time in which the hegemony of the mainstream master narrative of secularization will be more and more challenged" commencing a "new age of religious searching" and "whose outcome now one can foresee."[214]

---

[212] "Interview: Steve Bruce," Goldsmiths University of London, accessed September 4, 2024, https://www.gold.ac.uk/faithsunit/current-projects/reimaginingreligion/landmark-interviews/steve-bruce/ Bruce goes on to say Jürgen Habermas is "a disappointed Marxist who spent his entire career trying to find a new fiancée since he was stood up by the working class. And he's now created a strange fiction of the notion of new radical social movements inspired by ancient religions."

[213] Steve Bruce, *God Is Dead: Secularization in the West* (Oxford: Wiley-Blackwell, 2002).

[214] Charles Taylor, *A Secular Age* (Cambridge: Harvard University Press, 2007) 534.

Sociologist Peter Berger also wrote about the perceived failure of the secularization thesis in his book *The Desecularization of the World: Resurgent Religion and World Politics*, highlighting examples in which religion has continued to flourish despite secularism. Berger points to instances such as the 1970s Islamic revival, the resurgence of religion in Russia and China, the growth of Christianity in the Global South, and the rise of evangelical Christianity in America, all of which indicate the opposite trend. Leading Berger to claim the world today "is as furiously religious as it ever was."[215] As a once-ardent defender of the secularization thesis, believing that modernity combined with technological progress would lead to the inevitable decline of religion, Berger later changed his position, arguing that secularization had since been falsified.

Habermas's exploration of the "postsecular moment" offers valuable insight into the interplay between secularism and postsecularism, particularly in the context of technological advancement. Habermas has expressed criticism towards biotechnology, genetic engineering, and the pursuit of human transcendence, which he terms "liberal eugenics." *In The Future of Human Nature* (2003), Habermas articulates his concern that science has assumed the role of ultimate authority in shaping humanity's future, particularly in the realms of biotechnology and genetic engineering, with minimal scope for ethical or democratic deliberation. Habermas argues that technology threatens the achievements of the Enlightenment and the desire for freedom, because

---

[215] Peter Berger, *The Desecularization of the World: Resurgent Religion and World Politics* (Grand Rapids: William B. Eerdmans Publishing Company, 1999) 2.

it empowers the "made" (or "programed") over the "grown."[216] He posits that science has attained a "sacred" status capable of overriding social, ethical, and even legal constraints. Therefore, Habermas advocates for continued dialogue with religious thinkers and contemporary secularists in an effort to establish a middle ground amidst escalating disruptions from technological progress.

In his engagement with religious thinkers to formulate a secular philosophical response to the perils of biotechnology, Habermas acknowledges the significance of religious traditions in articulating moral intuitions concerning the essence of dignified human life. Within the framework of the "postsecular moment," religion is recognized as a vital component in the historical evolution of public reason. Habermas identifies the public implications of religion, challenging the secularization theory that confines religion to the private domain. Religion plays a crucial role in the communal process of culture making, which cannot be entirely reduced to rational advancements and offers a significant capacity for mutual understanding. Similar to traditional religion, transhumanism conveys postsecular religious narratives and meaning-making as society navigates the destabilizing effects of technology. Transhumanism exemplifies the postsecular moment by merging the religious with the secular, thereby re-enchanting the secular while simultaneously prioritizing enlightenment rationality over religious beliefs. As a product of the Enlightenment, transhumanism favors reason over faith, illustrating Weber's thesis of disenchantment, while concurrently attributing salvific and deifying significance to human-made technology.

---

[216] Jürgen Habermas, *The Future of Human Nature* (Cambridge: Polity, 2003) 44-53.

Disenchantment was a theory first postulated by Max Weber (1864-1920), in which he believed that the overdetermined facts of science propelled a nonreversible trend disenchanting the mystical and transcendent dimension of nature and the world. Weber felt that the absence of scientific explanations provided sufficient space for the enchantment of religious explanations. Jacques Ellul (1912-1994) buttressed the disenchantment theory, arguing rational techniques of technology "enslaves" and brings light upon the mystery of what men have believed to be sacred.[217] Margaret Wertheim argues that modern science has systematically dismantled Western understanding of sacred space, leaving God, heaven, and the souls of the dead with no particular place to go. She believes that the scientific mastery of physical space (astrophysics to genetic engineering) has witnessed the loss of sacred space, leading to the empowerment of new religious activities. Transhumanism has filled this sacred void with the divine potential of an enchanted cyberspace and places religious faith in the emergence of an AI god. Cyberspace is a sacred space for posthumanity. Cyberspace allows futurists to build previously unimaginable paradises. Humanity is no longer constrained by physical limits; rather, deep religious yearnings within humanity can now be realized and fulfilled within the new cyber medium.

Rodney Stark and William Sims Bainbridge argue secularism actually stimulates "a countervailing intensification of religion" in other parts of society.[218] As secularism has prolonged, scholars have witnessed

---

[217] Jacques Ellul, *The Technological Society*, translated by John Wilkinson (New York: Alfred A. Knopf, 1964) 142.
[218] Rodney Stark and William S. Bainbridge, *The Future of Religion: Secularization, Revival, and Cult Formation* (Los Angeles: University of California Press, 1985) 2.

a revival of religious practice, not its disappearance. Abou Farman has proposed that the immortalists initiatives of the transhumanist movement should be understood as a response to "the aporias of secularism" and argues transhumanism has "activated science-based cosmological visions" seeking to "re-enchant" the universe with religious significance. Transhumanists are inspired by "the possibility of using science to derive purpose from a universe originally emptied of it by science itself."[219]

Not only do transhumanist ideas resemble theological promises, but the movement's social and organizational patterns often function analogously to religious structures. Transhumanism inspires a faith community of believers who share a common creed (Transhumanist Declaration), evangelizes the gospel of techno-salvation, and looks to prophetic leaders for guidance. Like religion, it provides a comprehensive worldview and a basis for personal and collective identity. Ethicist Brent Waters observes that transhumanists are in the "initial stages of mythmaking," and that the broad themes of their narrative "are strikingly similar to those of its Christian counterparts."[220] Waters highlights that the key difference between these narratives, is that while traditional Christians believes the Word was made flesh, transhumanism is "turning flesh into data."

In a postsecular context, transhumanism effectively operates as a substitute faith, a techno-spirituality for individuals who seek purpose

---

[219] Abou Farman, "Re-Enchantment Cosmologies: Mastery and Obsolescence in an Intelligent Universe," *Anthropological Quarterly* 85, 2012:1080.

[220] Brent Waters, "Is Technology the New Religion," in *Word & World* 35, no.2 (Spring 2015) https://wordandworld.luthersem.edu/wp-content/uploads/pdfs/35-2_Posthuman_Identity/Is%20Technology%20the%20New%20Religion.pdf#:~:text=TRANSHUMANIST%20AND%20POSTHUMANIST%20MYTHOLOGY%20Transhumanists,eschatological%20end%20of%20personal%20immortal%02149.

and transcendence outside traditional theism. Like most other religions, transhumanism offers a narrative arc from a problematic present to a redeemed future. It thus provides what Taylor calls a sense of fullness or higher meaning that transcends the ordinary life within the immanent frame of secular material existence.

E. Visons of a Posthuman Future

Posthumanist thought posits a fluid human essence undergoing constant evolution with the potential for self-directed design to transcend biological constraints. Despite some overlap in their interests in going "beyond human," philosophical posthumanism and transhumanism represent fundamentally different perspectives. Technoscientific posthumanism often embraces Enlightenment ideals of rationality and technological progress, with quasi-religious overtones, while philosophical-cultural posthumanism critiques the Enlightenment's metaphysical foundations, and often exhibits secular tendencies, it seeks to move beyond Humanism's limitations than simply beyond the human body. For these reasons, transhumanism has often been described as humanism taken to its furthest extreme, as it retains a core belief in human reason, individual autonomy, and the progressive mastery of nature.

Both branches anticipate a future in which traditional boundaries between humans and machines, males and females, and humans and animals become increasingly permeable, notably advocating for the separation of reproduction from sex and reshaping of the human body. Philosophical posthumanism conceptualizes the human body as an "interface between mind and experience," narrating it as a locus of exploration and transformation through which interaction with an electronically mediated postmodern experience is inscribed. [221]

Posthumanism not only obscures the distinction between humans and machines but also between biological and non-biological reproduction; "bodies are determined and operated by systems whose reproduction is ... asexual: capitalism, culture, professions, and institutions, and in fact sexuality itself."[222] Consequently, within the framework of posthumanism, family ceases to be a central focus of social research. The decoupling of sex and reproduction from biology has facilitated the development of a novel theory on the nature and ultimate function of the human body.

Technoscientific posthumanism follows more closely to the cybernetic movement in how they envision the posthuman future. Engineers of artificial intelligence have speculated that a full synthesis of humans and machines could usher in a novel evolutionary stage that would not only enhance humanity, both physically and mentally, but also surpass the capabilities of the humans who designed it. The notion that technological superintelligence will emerge, surpassing human intelligence and replicating itself as a result of exponential, accelerated technological progress is known as "the Singularity." Scholar Robert Geraci defines the singularity as "as point of the graph of progress where explosive growth occurs in a blink of an eye," once machines "become sufficiently smart to start teaching themselves," upon which "the world

---

[221] Scott Bukatmann, "Postcard from the Posthuman Solar System," In *Posthumanism*, ed. Neil Badmington, (New York: Palgrave, 2000) 98-111.
[222] Judith Halberstam, and Ira Livingston, *Posthuman Bodies*, (Bloomington, IN: Indiana University Press, 1995) 17.

will irrevocably shift from the biological to the mechanical," inaugurating the new Eden, the new virtual kingdom.[223]

Its prophesized by transhumanists, machines will eliminate the most problematic aspects of biologically evolved humans, thereby providing soteriological liberation. The way humanity reaches the posthuman age is through transhumanism. Today transhumanism refers to "the intellectual and cultural movement that affirms the possibility and desirability of fundamentally improving the human condition through applied reason, especially by developing and making widely available technologies to eliminate aging and to greatly enhance human intellectual, physical, and psychological capacities."[224] Therefore, "transhumanism" denotes the transition point from human to posthuman existence. Because transhumanism understands itself as a process that culminates in a posthuman existence, the two terms have been used interchangeably, leading to terminological confusion.

Within transhumanist discourse, there are two distinct strands of thought. One focuses on human enhancement in the present, whereas the other focuses on cyber immortality in the future. The former is straightforwardly secular with the accoutrements of nineteenth-century naturalism, humanism, and utilitarianism, whereas the latter is filled with religious themes, particularly an apocalyptic and eschatological orientation. Through techniques such as gene manipulation, stem cell therapy, embryo selection, technological enhancements, genetic

---

[223] Robert Geraci, "Apocalyptic AI: Religion and the Promise of Artificial Intelligence," *Journal of American Academy of Religion* 76, no. 1 (March 2008) 138-66.
[224] Nick Bostrom, "The Transhumanist FAQ: A General Introduction," In *Transhumanism and the Body: The World Religions Speak*, eds. Calvin Mercer and Derek Maher (London: Palgrave Macmillian, 2014).

engineering, psychopharmacology, anti-aging therapies, memory-enhancing drugs, neural computer interfaces, advanced information management, and wearable computers, transhumanists believe that they can enhance human beings, eliminate diseases, slow the aging process, and exercise control over desires, moods, and mental states. Transhumanists envision a future in which technology will not only affect the human body, but also future generations whose genetic makeup will be redesigned in accordance with transhumanist ideals and sensibilities.[225]

Although Transhumanism extends beyond traditional humanism, it does not align with postmodern philosophy. Postmodernism, a cultural movement characterized by skepticism towards Enlightenment humanism, represents an alternative approach to re-evaluating human identity. Postmodernists critiqued the Enlightenment's notions of progress, anthropocentrism, the uniqueness of human nature, correspondence between language and reality, and the perceived superiority of Homo sapiens over non-human entities. Notable thinkers such as Michel Foucault and Jacques Derrida sought to redefine human identity within a postmodern framework. Derrida notably proclaimed the end of a "man-centered universe" and the long-standing belief in human superiority and uniqueness. The decline in anthropocentrism has facilitated contemporary discussions on the ontology of humanity in the post-human era. Postmodernism was supported by critical discourses including feminism, postcolonialism, queer theory, and environmentalism, which aimed to highlight the limitations of humanism. Postmodern discourse rejected Enlightenment assumptions as

---

[225] Gregory Stock, *Redesigning Humans: Our Inevitable Genetic Future*, (Boston: Houghton Mifflin, 2002).

either naïve or self-contradictory and regarded its metaphysical foundations as philosophically flawed.

Literary critics began to reconsider what it means to be human, and viewed homo sapiens as evolutionary animals who are inherently "a prosthetic creature that has evolved with various forms of technicity and materiality, forms that are fundamentally 'not-human' and yet have nevertheless made the human what it is."[226] Within this context of literary, philosophical, and cultural discourse, "posthumanism," as Cary Wolfe writes,

> ... names a historical moment in the which the decentering of the human by its imbrication in technical, medical, informatics, and economics networks is increasingly impossible to ignore, a historical development that points towards the necessity of new theoretical paradigms, a new model of thought that comes after the cultural repression and fantasies, the philosophical protocols and evasions, of humans as a historical specific phenomenon.[227]

Donna Haraway saw posthumanism as a form of personal and collective liberation from the confinement of historical oppression. "Cyborg" is a combination of the words cybernetics and organism, signifying a being who is a half-human half-machine. In *Cyborg Manifesto* (1985), Haraway's feminist analysis employs the cyborg as a metaphor for challenging conventional distinctions between nature and

---

[226] Carey Wolfe, *What Is Posthumanism*, xxv.
[227] Carey Wolfe, *What Is Posthumanism*, xv-xvi.

culture, humans and animals, and humans and machines, while also offering a new perspective on human embodiment. Sadie Plant is a pioneer in cyberfeminism, a subbranch of technofeminism, and her book *Zeros + Ones: Digital Women and the New Technoculture* (1997) examines how digital technologies reshape social relations, particularly gender relations. Plant argues that digital technologies and the cultural and economic forces they exert undermine the patriarchal agenda that she identifies with control, identity, and individual agency. Digital technologies and computational devices are believed to breed multiplicity, not stable identities, and, therefore, inherently undermine traditional norms regarding sex and gender.

Jacques Derrida desired to reclaim meaning by undermining what he considered the central pillar of Christian thought, "phallogocentrism." Derrida coined the term "phallogocentrism" to denote how Western thought unites logocentrism (privileging logos, reason, logic, presence, and speech) with phallocentrism (the privileging of the masculine). In "Plato's Pharmacy," he describes how Western metaphysics from Plato onward, had been logocentric due to it assuming a stable center of truth and privileges speech and presence over absence, writing, and ambiguity.[228] Christianity's belief that the Divine *Logos* is the eternal Word of God the Father, means for Derrida, that *Logos* carries with it a privileging of masculine authority within a "metaphysics of presence."[229] To open up the possibility of meaning for the "margins," Derrida sought

---

[228] Jacques Derrida, *Dissemination*, trans. Barbara Johnson (Chicago: The University of Chicago Press, 1981) 65-117.

[229] Jacques Derrida, *Grammatology*, trans. Gayatri Chakravorty Spivak (Baltimore: The John Hopkins University Press, 1976) 10-26.

to decenter *Logos* and its presumed patriarchal authority so that alternative ways of thinking could emerge.

In prioritizing reason and logic, Transhumanism perpetuates a logocentric paradigm without the traditional metaphysical framework that historically underpinned it. However, by employing a functionalist definition of personhood, transhumanism effectively dissolves the traditional distinctions between genders and humans and machines. Consequently, this contributes to the decentering of phallocentrism, while simultaneously establishing a new technocentric locus of power. This illustrates the enduring influence of Enlightenment rationalism, which despite being separated from its initial metaphysical underpinnings, paradoxically offers validation for new forms of human embodiment and marginalized identities.

"Morphological freedom" is the common phrase used by transhumanists to describe the liberative freedom to modify one's own body, genetics, and brain as they wish. For this particular reason, transhumanist author and artist Natasha Vita-More (wife of Max More) stated in public interviews that the goals of the LGBTQ movement and transgenderism, in particular, are part and parcel of the contemporary presence of our posthuman future. Transhumanism is a strong ally to transgender people because it crosses the perceived antiquated boundaries of gender and sex in the same way that transhumanists dissolve the distinctions between humanity and machines. The redefinition of the self through technological and scientific means promises further self-expression, aided by advancements in technology. In the article "Morphological Freedom – Why We Not Just Want It, but Need It," Anders Sandberg writes, "Technology and morphological freedom go hand in hand. Technology enables new forms of self-expression, creating a demand for the freedom to exercise them." "If my pursuit for happiness requires a bodily change – be it dying my hair or changing my sex – then my right to freedom requires a right to morphological freedom."[230] For posthumanists, the historical notions of body, sex, and reproduction will no longer apply in the future. Such a redefinition of human embodiment has led to novel theories about a new "zoology" and spectrum of human embodiment.

> ... the causes and effects of postmodern relations of power and pleasure, virtuality and reality, sex and its consequences. The Posthuman body is a technology, a screen, a projected image; it is a body under the sign of AIDS, a contaminated body itself is no longer part of the "family of man" but a of a zoo of posthumanities.[231]

Critics of morphological freedom often express their contention as a disruption or violation of the natural foundation of human essence. Transhumanists, in turn, deny that there is such a thing as a fixed nature, arguing instead of the evolutionary process of becoming something new and greater. Anders Sandberg rebuts such criticism by claiming that if there is anything central to human nature, self-definition must be one of the key attributes. Therefore, he argues, to deny morphological freedom, is to deny the same human nature critics strive to preserve. Human nature is transitory and "there is no contradiction in having a nature that implies

---

[230] Anders Sandberg, "Morphological Freedom – Why We Not Just Want It, but Need It," in *The Transhumanist Reader*, ed. Max More and Natasha Vita-More, (West Sussex, UK: John Wiley and Sons Inc., 2013) 57-58.
[231] Halberstam, *Posthuman Bodies*, 3.

a seeking of its own over-throw."[232] Morphological freedom is an important existential dimension of transhumanist projects. Morphological freedom is presented as a unique historical opportunity for true "freedom" and authentic individual expression. Altering a person's foundational biology is seen as an individual's struggle to find meaning and purpose in a seemingly meaningless world.

F. Is Transhumanism Religion?

In academic discourse, scholars often recognize several defining features of religion. These include the distinction between the sacred and profane, belief in supernatural beings, adherence to a moral framework, occurrence of spiritual experiences, interaction with the divine, and a comprehensive worldview that influences social structures and individual lifestyles.[233] Several parallels with traditional religions emerge when examining transhumanism through this lens. These include a focus on human and societal improvement, a linear view of historical progression, and eschatological faith in transcending the current human condition. The emphasis on enhancement technology "has become for many among the nonreligious the ticket to divinity, to deification, to *theopoiesis*, to becoming a god."[234] The pursuit of overcoming limitations, achieving a higher state of being, and seeking immortality aligns with many traditional religious goals, even though the methods differ significantly.

---

[232] Sandberg, "Morphological Freedom" 60.
[233] Michael Bergunder, "What is Religion?," in *Method & Theory in the Study of Religion* 26, no. 3, (2014) 246-286. https://doi.org/10.1163/15700682-12341320.
[234] Ted Peters, "Imago Dei, DNA, and the Transhuman Way," *Theology and Science* 16, no. 3 (2018) 358. https://doi.org/10.2307/jj.890650.40.

This raises complex questions about the relationship between transhumanism and established religions, prompting discussions on the potential for conflict and collaboration.

If transhumanism is to be seen as a "religion," it does so by acting in analogous ways to a New Religious Movements (NRM). NRMs often use culturally relevant means to offer new religious identities and experiences to believers. Scholar Amarnath Amarasingham helps provide a useful framework, writing New Religious Movements

> ... are concerned with meeting the needs of individual members, ... lay claim to some esoteric knowledge that has been lost or repressed or newly discovered, ... offer their believers some kind of ecstatic or transfiguring experience that is more direct than that provided by traditional modes of religious life, ... display no systematic orientation to a broader society and are usually loosely organized, ... and almost always center on a charismatic leader and face disintegration when the leader dies or is discredited.[235]

The transhumanist movement exemplifies these same features, particularly in the futuristic dimension that focuses on cyber-immortality in the posthuman age. Amarasingam argues that futurology, correctly viewed, is a NRM due to it having "charismatic leaders, authoritative

---

[235] Amarnath Amarasingam, "Transcending Technology: Looking at Futurology as a New Religious Movement," In the *Journal of Contemporary Religion* 23, no. 1 (2008) 2. https://doi.org/10.1080/13537900701822989.

texts, mystique, and a fairly complete vison of salvation."[236] The prophet of the singularity, Ray Kurzweil, can be seen as a charismatic leader prophesying about technological transcendence, while also cultivating a "personal cult that is not different from the cult of any other religious or spiritual guru."[237] Transhumanism competes in the religious marketplace and attributes its success to the aura of sacredness surrounding secular science in contemporary Western cultures.

The notion that science has assumed sacred qualities typically associated with religion has been discussed by thinkers such as Bruno Latour (1947-2022), Marcel Gauchet, and Peter Berger (1929-2017). In his seminal work *Science in Action* (1987), Latour discusses how scientific knowledge becomes "black-boxed," meaning it is taken as an unquestionable truth, giving it a sacred, almost untouchable quality. He also explores this in *We Have Never Been Modern* (1993), arguing that the Western worldview treats science as a realm of pure objectivity divorced from the corrupt influences of society and culture. Sociologist Peter Berger, in his book *The Sacred Canopy* (1967), explores how secular societies replace traditional religious symbols and meanings with "sacred" secular institutions, including science. Berger argues that while science is ostensibly neutral and empirical, it often serves as a substitute for the sacred, providing the modern world with a sense of order, authority, and meaning. In *The Disenchantment of the World* (1985), French philosopher Marcel Gauchet argues that science and technology have replaced religion as sources of meaning and authority, presenting themselves as objective arbiters of truth and progress, which people often accept with religious-like reverence. Concerning this aura of sacredness,

---

[236] Amarasingam, "Transcending Technology," 13.
[237] Tirosh-Samuelson, "Transhumanism as a Secularist Faith," 722.

Gauchet writes, "The modern world, in its repudiation of religious beliefs, has transferred that aura of ultimate legitimacy onto science and technology, making them the unquestioned bearers of truth."[238] The scientific and technological focus of transhumanism provides it with unique real estate with spiritual and religious orientations. This feature of sacred science allows transhumanism to present its unsubstantiated metanarrative of human transcendence, god-like abilities, and immortality within the concrete practices and achievements of contemporary science.

As previously mentioned, "transhumanism" was first coined by Julian Huxley in 1957 in his book *New Bottles for New Wine*. Huxley foresaw transhumanism as a "religion without revelation," and took that as the title of a shorter treatise he published in 1927. Originally, this new ideology was "evolutionary humanism" and he believed it would address the crisis facing humanity by bridging science and the arts through the instrumental use of technology to construct a better world. Huxley claimed that evolutionary humanism provided further insight into human nature and could thereby actualize dormant possibilities for further development. For Huxley, the human mind inspires the march towards progress and "the source of all truth, beauty, morality, and purpose is to be found in human nature."[239] Huxley urged his readers to "utilize available knowledge in giving guidance and encouragement for the continuing adventure of human development." To signify his importance,

---

[238] Marcel Gauchet, *The Disenchantment of the Word: A Political History of Religion* (Princeton University Press, 1985) 180.
[239] Julian Huxley, *Evolutionary Humanism*, (Buffalo, N.Y.: Prometheus Books, 1992) 7.

Hava Tirosh-Samuelson noted that Huxley's work can be considered the foundational text of the transhumanist movement.

It is ironic that human-directed evolution is explicitly expressed by a man who understands his mission and vision in religious terms. Huxley envisioned a future in which rationality, science, and the evolutionary quest towards higher perfection would supplant the waning of religious superstitions. He described the religious myths of old as too antiquated to properly orient and guide humanity around and over the hurdles it was soon to face. Describing the contours of Huxley's religion, Tirosh-Samuels writes,

> Huxley's evolutionary humanism was a statement of a secularist faith for a world that had to come to terms with the facts of evolution and was decidedly articulated in ethical and aesthetic terms. While Huxley opposed supernatural explanations, he deeply appreciated the mystery of existence and had no quals using ethical and religious concepts such as "destiny" and "the sacred" to articulate his vison of and for humanity. Huxley's unified cosmic vision that privileges the human mind is remarkably similar to that of Pierre Teilard de Chardin, the Jesuit paleontologist for whom progressive evolution led to the "noosphere" (namely, a sphere of mind as opposed to or rather superimposed on the biosphere or sphere of life) and later to the collective consciousness of the Omega Point.[240]

---

[240] Tirosh-Samuelson, "Transhumanism as a Secularist Faith," 720.

For Huxley, the purpose of humanity is to actualize the immense potential of the human mind and thereby direct its evolutionary process. Directing evolution was a contributing factor to why Huxley was an ardent supporter of the eugenics movement long after eugenics were publicly discredited. He prolifically wrote about eugenics from the 1930s to the 1940s and was the president of the Eugenics Society from 1959 to 1964. It is an unsavory fact that many transhumanists attempt to distance themselves from and highlight how the project of human enhancement shares many commonalities with the eugenics movement. Sociologist James Hughes has shown how eugenics itself was steeped in utopianism since it was also a secular project to save humanity from biological limitations. Such a history validates bioconservative fears concerning a future where gene editing and synthetic wombs are normalized and potentially weaponized against those who chose not to partake in human enhancement.

Most "transhumanists see themselves as part of the Enlightenment humanist tradition, most are atheist, and may feel that one cannot be a theist transhumanist,"[241] while others have embraced its religious dimension. James Hughes, writing on the compatibility between traditional religions and transhumanism, has called upon transhumanists to regard their movement as such, but has encouraged them to further develop religious orientation with its own unique symbolic language and ritual. Hughes also notes the complex attitudes towards transhumanism from various religious communities, with Christianity in particular

---

[241] James J. Hughes, "The Compatibility of Religious and Transhumanist Views of Metaphysics, Suffering, Virtue, and Transcendence in an Enhanced Future," In *Global Spiral* 8, no. 2 (2007).

having a very pessimistic opinion, while Eastern traditions such as Buddhism and Shintoism are more receptive to their projects in terms of both human enhancement and nondualistic metaphysics. Robert Geraci has also documented such evidence in the robot industry in Japan, showing how both Buddhism and Shintoism "afford sanctity to robots: robots are blessed, take part in cosmic salvation history, and are accordingly welcome in Japanese society."[242] In the early phases of robot manufacturing in Japan, robots were ritually consecrated by Shinto priests, demonstrating religious technological compatibility within Japanese society. Though those practices have since been abandoned, Geraci notes "robotics and the robots themselves remain closely tied to the sacred."[243]

Gregory Jordan writes, "Transhumanism serves some of the 'functions' of religion, with regard to providing a sense of direction and purpose and providing something greater than the present condition."[244] Jordan has highlighted techno-religious elements such as "symbolic representation of shared meaning," to demonstrate how it exhibits a "sense of awe associated with the scientific worldview and the contemplation of nature," arguing its "all-encompassing scientific epistemology combined with theories of sufficient provisional explanatory powers, may soon give rise to a comprehensive worldview."[245] Transhumanists such as Jordan desire to define and develop transhuman religiosity further. Jordan believes the shared

---

[242] Robert M. Geraci, "Spiritual Robots: Religion and Our Scientific View of the Natural World," *Theology and Science* 4 no.3 (2006): 229-46. https://doi.org/10.1080/14746700600952993.
[243] Geraci, "Spiritual Robots," 237.
[244] Gregory Jordan, "Apologia for Transhumanist Religion," *Journal of Evolution and Technology* 15 no.1 (2006): 55-72.
[245] Jordan, "Transhumanist Religion," 61.

similarities between transhumanism and religion can be attributed to "commonalities in fundamental human ambitions, desires, and longing." However, according to Jordan, transhumanist religiosity differs from traditional religion because it lacks any form of dogmatism, and their desire to improve humanity by way of technology is quite different from fidestic certitude. Nonetheless, Jordan concludes that "even if transhumanism is not perceived as a religion, it could easily be analyzed as one."[246]

Sociologist and transhumanist William Sims Bainbridge argues that there are functional similarities between transhumanism and religion, despite religion being built upon superstition and spirituality, whereas transhumanism is founded on science and technology. In 2002, Bainbridge was the co-editor of the influential report *Converging Technologies for Improving Human Performance*, which highlighted how the merging of these technologies could enhance human abilities and address issues related to aging, cognition, and morality. Commissioned by the National Science Foundation in collaboration with other governmental bodies, this report brought transhumanist ideas, including human enhancement and technological augmentation, to a central role in shaping national science-policy discussions. He also contributed to the development of the NBIC (Nanotechnology, Biotechnology, Information technology, and Cognitive science) initiative, a major federal effort aimed at advancing converging technologies. All of which, during the George W. Bush presidency, pushed Francis Fukuyama to write his warning about the dangers of bio-enhancement in *Our Posthuman Future: Consequences of the Biotechnology Revolution*.

---

[246] Jordan, "Transhumanist Religion," 63.

In 2005, Bainbridge wrote an article titled "The Transhumanist Hersey," in which he identified the core elements of traditional religion, such as the pursuit of immortality, redemption, and ultimate meaning, as mirrored by transhumanist aims. He argues that this is because of competition in the marketplace for ideas concerning what eternal life is and should be.[247] Bainbridge endorses and advocates for technological immortality, predicting it "will put religions largely out of business, and therefore religious fundamentalists would condemn activities in these directions."[248] He refers to transhumanism as a "technological theology," "secular religion" or "cyber-religion," in which faith in technological progress replaces traditional religious beliefs in divine beings or supernatural forces. He argues that transhumanism's promise of radical life extension, human enhancement, and resurrection of the dead serves as a secular analog to religious eschatology. Because of this friction, Bainbridge has worried about "religious terrorism" aimed at transhumanists. He speculates about a future scenario in which "a mob of fanatics will break into personality archives to erase their content." Bainbridge considers such acts as murder and "infocide," "because it kills people in their pure form."[249] For Bainbridge, transhumanism is a religion for the galactic civilization, and calls for people to imagine a future in which the current virtual world "could evolve into extrasolar homes for posthuman beings."

---

[247] William Sims Bainbridge, "The Transhumanist Heresy," *Journal of Evolution and Technology* 14 no.2 (2005):1-10.
[248] William Sims Bainbridge, "Trajectories to the Heavens," *The Journal of Personal Cyberconsciousness* 2 no.3 (2007):1-6.
[249] Bainbridge, "Trajectories to Heaven," 3.

G. Emergence of the AI God

The belief that the world is ultimately bits of information being processed by both biological and technical algorithms is the basis for Yuval Noah Harari's "Data Religion." Harari is a prominent member of the World Economic Forum and a popular author and history professor at Hebrew University of Jerusalem. In his 2007 book *Homo Deus: a Brief History of Tomorrow*, Harari outlines his religion of the future as "dataism;" the belief "that the universe consists of data flows, and the value of any phenomenon or entity is determined by its contribution to data processing."[250] Dataism has emerged from the mother disciplines of computer science and biology. Harari triumphantly announces how this new orientation towards information collapses any meaningful barrier between animals and machines. Harari goes further to state that "Data Religion" views not only individual organisms as data-processing algorithms but also entire societies, forests, and cities. If viewing humans, giraffes, or tomatoes as merely different methods of processing data makes a reader feel uneasy, Harari writes "you should know that this is current scientific dogma, and it's changing our world beyond recognition."[251]

> The supreme value of this new religion is "information flow." If life is the movement of information, and if we think that life is good, it follows that we should deepen and broaden the flow of information in the universe.

---

[250] Yuval Noah Harari, *Homo Deus: a Brief History of Tomorrow*, (New York: HarperCollins, 2017) 372.
[251] Harari, *Homo Deus*, 373.

According to Dataism, human experiences are not sacred and Homo sapiens isn't the apex of creation or a precursor of some future Homo deus. Humans are merely tools for creating the Internet-of-All-Things, which may eventually spread out from planet Earth to pervade the whole galaxy and even the whole universe. This cosmic data-processing system would be like God. It will be everywhere and will control everything, and humans are destined to merge with it. This conception is reminiscent of some traditional religious visions.[252]

Harari identifies Silicon Valley as the American home of "Dataist prophets" and provides the example of "Ray Kurzweil's book of prophecies *The Singularity Is Near*, as echoing John the Baptist's cry: 'the kingdom of heaven is near.'" According to the Dataist religion, flesh-and-blood mortals are an outdated technology; therefore, Homo sapiens, as they currently exist, is obsolete. Harari envisions an entirely new ontology, in which all beings, synthetic or biological, are united by the mechanisms of information processing. The only meaningful difference between human beings and chickens is the complexity of the information patterns that can be interpreted. Describing his religious commandments, Harari writes,

> Like every religion, it (Dataism) has practical commandments, First and foremost a Dataist ought to maximize data flow by connecting more and more media,

---

[252] Harari, *Homo Deus*, 386.

and producing and consuming more and more information. Like other successful religions, Dataism is also missionary. Its second commandment is to link everything to the system. Including heretics who don't want to be plugged in. And everything means more than just humans… We mustn't leave any part of the universe disconnected from the great web of life. Conversely, the greatest sin would be to block the data flow.[253]

Ironically, one of the secular criticisms often levied against traditional religion is historical instances of persecution, injustices, and forced conversions of "heretics." Yet, as Harari bluntly states, even the Data Religion will force bioconservatives to merge with the machine whether they want to or not. Blocking the potential flow of further data, most specifically one's own body, is not only a "sin," but also an existential threat. In a world where information is the highest good, human experience and freedom will take a back seat to the looming AI god. Harari clarifies that the concept of an all-knowing and all-powerful being has been a figment of the human imagination within religious myths, but now with our technological advances, we will finally substantiate such claims in an AI algorithmic god. Like monotheistic notions, AI will watch every move, every word, every decision, and even be embedded in your very being. Harari writes,

> As the global data-processing system becomes all-knowing and all-powerful, so connecting to the system

---

[253] Harari, *Homo Deus*, 387.

becomes the source of all meaning. Humans want to merge into the data flow because when you are part of the data flow you are part of something much bigger than yourself. Traditional religions assured you that your every word and action was part of some great cosmic plan, and that God watched you every minute and cared about all your thoughts and feelings. Data religion now says that your every word and action was part of the great data flow, that the algorithms are constantly watching you and that they care about everything you do or feel. Most people like this very much. For true believers, to be disconnected from the data flow risks losing the very meaning of life.[254]

Despite other transhumanist such as Max More vehemently rejecting any religious labels, others such as Yuval Noah Harari, Gregory Jordan, and William Bainbridge make it the explicit goal of the transhumanist project. It is not only the fact that technology will be imbued with god-like powers, but by merging ourselves with machines, humans will be remade into the image of the machines they create. *Apotheosis* originates from the Greek (ἀπο) meaning "from" or "away" and (θεόω) meaning "god." Apotheosis refers to the elevation or deification of a mortal to divine status. In contrast to *theosis* in Eastern Orthodox Christianity, *apotheosis* recognizes that individuals can cross the dividing line between gods and men. *Apotheosis* has been used to

---

[254] Harari, *Homo Deus*, 391.

express how the Roman Emperors or Alexander the Great were worshiped as men who transformed into literal gods. This formation of deification characterizes how humans can assume the role of an avatar with devotional cults of their own in Hinduism.

Sociologist Robert Geraci wrote about the themes of apocalyptic AI as an eschatological position infused with many traditional religious themes. He goes so far as saying "transhumanism is a pervasive religious system in modern life, operating across a wide array of cultural domains, both implicitly and explicitly"[255] James Hughes, who is both a transhumanist and sociologist, has highlighted the "successful manifestation of the syncretism of transhumanism and Singulatarianism with religious millennialism," and has delineated "religious transhumanism" as its own a distinctive thread.[256]

Robert Geraci has described this religious dimension of transhumanism as incontrovertible. Geraci has examined the profound impact that science fiction novels and video game culture have exerted in advancing transhumanist perspectives, enabling their themes, ideologies, and rhetorical approaches to infiltrate mainstream society. Video games are domains where players can transcend the confines of biology and physics, and thereby become places where "transhumanists themselves actively desire to use video games in evangelical contexts."[257] William Bainbridge is one of these evangelists. In addition to being among the founders of the Order of Cosmic Engineers (OCE), he is also the designer

---

[255] Robert Geraci, "Video Games and the Transhuman Inclination," In *Zygon* Vol. 47, no.4 (December, 2012) 735-756.

[256] James J. Hughes, "The Politics of Transhumanism and the Techno-Millennial Imagination, 1626-2030," In *Zygon* Vol. 47, no.4 (December, 2012) 757-776.

[257] Robert M. Geraci, "Video Games and the Transhuman," In *Zygon* Vol. 47, no.4, December, 2012.

of *The World of Warcraft*, a video game that appeals greatly to transhumanists.[258] Bainbridge posits that digital avatars in video games achieve a form of perpetual existence that transcends the limitations of physical mortality. This concept aligns with his broader vision of transhumanism as a potential cosmic belief system, driving his fervent pursuit to construct virtual realms in which his aspirations for transcendence can be fully realized.

    According to Geraci, Kurzweil and other AI advocates "lead a scientific movement that never strays far from the apocalyptic traditions of Western culture."[259] Reminiscent of early Judaic and Christian apocalyptic traditions, Kurzweil and his contemporaries advocate a vision that entails a decisive rupture with the present state of existence, heralding the advent of a new era akin to technological utopia. Kurzweil's futuristic eschatology posits that substantive existence transpires within digital realms, offering individuals idealized, unbounded physical forms and advanced cognitive entities that occupy virtual constructs. In line with Harari's Dataism, evolutionary natural selection is believed to favor artificial intelligence over human intelligence, leading to the inexorable spread of computational AI. This is understood in soteriological terms: by merging with machines and allowing computers to solve all human problems, humanity experiences happier and more pleasurable lives for as long as they wish. All of which has led Geraci to claim "Apocalyptic AI is technoreligion for the masses."[260]

---

[258] Tirosh-Samuelson, "Transhumanism as a Secularist Faith," 725.
[259] Robert M. Geraci, "Apocalyptic AI," 140.
[260] Robert M. Geraci, "Cultural Prestige: Popular Science Robotics as Religion-Science Hybrid," In *Reconfigurations: Interdisciplinary Perspectives on Religion in a Post-Secular Society*, eds. Stefanie Knauss and Alexander D. Ornella (Berlin: LIT Verlag, 2007) 43-58.

The Singularity parallels not only Christian eschatology but also religious faith in the bodily resurrection of the dead. Not only will those who live to witness the techno-eschaton become immortal and enhanced with divine capabilities, but those who are deceased will be resurrected and fully restored to live again in the techno-kingdom. A case in point is Kurzweil's faith in one day resurrecting his father, Fredric. In a 2009 interview with *Rolling Stone* magazine, Ray Kurzweil openly spoke about the way advanced artificial intelligence and nanotechnology – post Singularity – would be able to reassemble his father's DNA and reconstitute his mind through shared memories still present within his son.[261] Kurzweil's faith mirrors the expectations of Christianity's hope of being resurrected with new spiritual bodies after Christ's divine judgement. Jesus Christ is understood by believers as the incarnation of the Divine *Logos*, and the technological Singularity functions as secularized incarnation of God. At the Singularity, the all-knowing and all-seeing AI god enters historic time to save humanity from itself. This techno-incarnation is salvific for all those who wish to abandon their mortal existence for cyber immortality.

---

[261] David Kushner, "When Humans & Machines Merge" *Rolling Stone*, February 19, 2009, published to David Kushner's website March 26, 2009, accessed September 18, 2024, http://www.davidkushner.com/article/when-man-machine-merge/. "Kurzweil's most ambitious plan for life after the singularity, however, is also his most personal: Using technology, he plans to bring his dead father back to life. Kurzweil reveals this to me near the end of our conversation… In a soft voice, he explains how the resurrection will work. 'We can find some of his DNA around his grave site – that's a lot of information right there,' he says. 'The AI will send down some nanobots and get some bone or teeth and extract some DNA and put it all together. The they'll get some information from my brain and anyone else who still remembers him'… Just send nanobots into my brain and reconstruct my recollections and memories.' The machines will capture everything."

Michael Zimmerman, observing the Christian patterns present within transhumanist prophecies, concludes that "the God-like posthuman amounts to a creature that has become divine and that has thereby attained the status of cosmic Logos."[262] Zimmerman argues that the technoscientific vision of people like Kurzweil is deeply indebted to Hegel's secularization of Christianity. His conceptualization of historical progression posited the ultimate manifestation of the Absolute Idea as the culmination of dialectical processes. This Absolute, in Hegel's view, functioned as both the agent of its own actualization through iterative negations and the object of these transformative processes. Just as Hegel saw history as process affording the Spirit (*Geist*) to become free and self-conscious, so too does Kurzweil understand the process of material evolution. Evolution both shapes history, and is the subject of history in the pursuit of intelligence and freedom. Zimmerman writes,

> Hegel depicted humankind as the instrument through which absolute Geist (spirit) achieves total self-consciousness. Jesus Christ was the man who became God as much as the God who became man. Similarly, Ray Kurzweil revises the customary conception of God to accommodate the possibility that humans are taking part in a process by which posthuman beings, according to traditional theism, will attain powers equivalent to those usually attributed to God.[263]

---

[262] Michael Zimmerman, "The Singularity: A Crucial Phase in Divine Self-Actualization?" Cosmos and History: Journal of Natural Social Philosophy 4 no.1 (2008): 347-70.
[263] Zimmerman, "The Singularity," 363.

As technology advances, surpassing the cognitive and physical capabilities of humanity, transhumanists theorize that AI awakens into a sentient state. The biological evolution that gave rise to Homo sapiens has been usurped, and a self-conscious machine now directs evolution and progress. Just as Christians view biological humans as made in the image of God, so do posthumans anticipate being made new in the image of the machine. In the religion of "Dataism," super-intelligent machines will then span the cosmos processing more and more data until the entire universe becomes self-conscious. Echoing Omega Point theory and the emergence of a technological cosmic *Logos*. The religious parallels are striking and overt. For this reason, some progressive Christians have reinterpreted the Singularity as Christ's second coming.

Rather than merely competing in the marketplace of ideas, attempts have been made to integrate transhumanism into traditional religious paradigms. Micah Redding is the president of the Christian Transhumanist Association (CTA) and has attempted to unite non-denominational progressive Christianity with a posthuman future. According to CTA's official website, Christian Transhumanism aims to use science and technology to "participate in the work of God – to cultivate life and renew creation." CTA takes inspiration from a hodgepodge of different beliefs, doctrines, and thinkers, and is indebted to the techno-millenarian tradition outlined in chapter one. In their blog section, there is a post highlighting their continuation with such thinkers as John Scotus Eriugena, Albert Magnus, and Roger Bacon as proto-Christian transhumanists.[264] Christian transhumanism is explicit about its

---

[264] Dustin Ashley, "Science Before the Revolution: a Continuity of Christian Thought," (June 23, 2023) accessed September 18, 2024,

techno-millenarian disposition, seeing evolution, genetic engineering, and technological advancement as the keys to bringing about the biblical promise of human redemption. Redding, like other transhumanists, misappropriates the Orthodox Christian doctrine of *"theosis"* in attempt to reconcile transhumanism as being consistent with historic Christianity. Therefore, it fails to see the unique thread of techno-millenarianism within the historical domain of Christian thought. The CTA presents transhumanism as the ultimate fulfillment of the Christian tradition. Although the CTA remains quite limited in its theological influences, it has hosted conferences with notable transhumanist researchers and speakers.

Mormonism exhibits the most positive religious attitude towards transhumanism. Mormonism was the first religious institution to be affiliated with the World Transhumanist Association in 2006. According to the Mormon Transhumanist Association (MTA), they embrace a posthuman future that consists of highly advanced intellectual capabilities; a body immune to disease and aging; expanded sensory inputs to allow for higher awareness; perfect control over desires, moods, and mental states; and increased capacity to experience joy, love, and pleasure. On purely theological grounds, one can see how the Mormon conception of a progressively evolving God parallels the expectation of technological progress emerging in divinity. According to Lincoln Canon, president of the Mormon Transhumanist Association, "Mormonism actually mandates Transhumanism …one can be a transhumanist without being a Mormon, but one cannot be a Mormon

---

https://www.christiantranshumanism.org/blog/2023-science-before-the-revolution/.

without being a Transhumanist, at least implicitly."[265] The Mormon Transhumanist website clearly states that merging with the machine is perceived as a divinely inspired opportunity to become gods and fulfill Mormon doctrine. The MTA website states, "Our potential to become gods is aligned with our potential to use science and technology in ethical ways to improve ourselves and attain a posthuman condition. We should use every resource at our disposal to improve ourselves and the world until we achieve godliness."[266]

The Mormon god is one of eternal progression. According to Mormon theology, God the Father was once a mortal man who lived on another planet, had a wife, and through his own effort and righteousness progressed to become the exalted figure worshiped in their tradition. Godhood in Mormonism is not a fixed state but rather a potential that can be achieved through human efforts. With this understanding, it becomes clear why Lincoln Canon considers every Mormon, at least implicitly, a transhumanist. Given their rejection of Christianity's historical conception of the Holy Trinity – as articulated within the Nicene Creed – as well as the preexistent nature of Christ's divinity, most Christians do not consider Mormonism "Christian." Like transhumanism, religious studies scholars often define Mormonism as a new religious movement.

If religion, as David Chidester has argued, is "the negotiation of what it means to be human with respect to the superhuman and

---

[265] Lincoln Canon, "Mormon Transhumanism" In *Religious Transhumanism and Its Critics*, eds. Arvin M. Goue, Brian Patrick Green, and Ted Peters (Lanham, MD: Lexington Books, 2022) 67.

[266] "What Is Mormon Transhumanism" accessed on March 25, 2025, https://www.transfigurism.org/library/primers/1-what-is-mormon-transhumanism.

subhuman," then transhumanism exudes a strong current of religiosity.[267] Their speculations on the divine attributes attained in our posthuman condition are, in fact, a theological assumption. The pursuit of perfection through technology and science is a metanarrative that spiritually connects transhumanism with its techno-millenarian progenitors. Transhumanists see themselves as protagonists in a historical narrative concerning the hero's journey to cyberimmortality. As they venture from the ordinary world of biological embodiment, they advance into a realm of supernatural power, encounter fabulous cyber-forces, and return to bestow their new blessings on fellow beings.[268] In his book *Techgnosis: Myth, Magic, and Mysticism in the Age of Information*, Erik Davis argues that the technological progress undergirding transhumanism is a literalization of the "quest myth" colored by "millennialist perfection."

> Before Joachim of Fiore loosed the myth of progress into the bloodstream of the Christian West, men told tales of a hero, with a thousand and one faces, restlessly seeking a redemptive goal: the golden fleece, the elixir of immortality, the holy grail… Salvation is not within but ahead … I suspect that one of the reasons that the story of technological progress continues to hold such power is that it literalizes a quest myth we can no longer take seriously in ourselves… The errant knight of medieval

---

[267] David Chidester, "Moralizing Noise," *Harvard Divinity Bulletin* 32, no.3 (2004): 17.
[268] Joseph Campbell, *The Hero with a Thousand Faces* (Princeton: Princeton University Press, 1968) "A hero ventures forth from the world of common day into a region of supernatural wonder: fabulous forces and there encountered and a decisive victory is won: the hero comes back from this mysterious adventure with the power to bestow boons on his fellow man." 30.

lore has morphed into a machine-man, his grail now the Singularity that visionary engineers claim lies just over the horizon, a blazing point of technological convergence that will finally master the rules of the known.[269]

The quest myth of transhuman liberation is not just rhetorically religious, but for physicist Giulio Prisco, it is the fulfillment of what religion has always aimed to be. Prisco, also a cofounder of the Order of Cosmic Engineers (OCE), believes that the prophetic promises of immortality and the resurrection of the dead will soon compete with institutionalized religions while shedding their history of bigotry and violence. The OCE is a transhumanist activist group intended to use science and technology to engineer the future of human civilization. Some members of the OCE have described their enterprise as a spiritual movement, taking inspiration from other fraternal organizations, specifically mentioning the Mystical Order of the Rosy Cross (Rosicrucianism). In addition to Bainbridge and Prisco, the founders of the Order of Cosmic Engineers include other notable names to likes of Ben Goertzel, Max More, David Pearce, Natasha Vita-More, Philippe van Nedervelde, and Martine Rothblatt.

Martine Rothblatt is the co-founder of the Terasem Movement Transreligion Inc., a transhuman religion with 501(c)(3) status, based on the core tenets "life is purposeful, death is optional, God is technological, and love is essential."[270] Martine has had a successful career as an

---

[269] Erik Davis, *Techgnosis: Myth, Magic, and Mysticism in the Age of Information* (New York: Three Rivers Press, 1998) 325.
[270] Jessica Roy, "The Rapture of the Nerds," *Time*, April 17, 2014. https://time.com/66536/terasem-trascendence-religion-technology/.

entrepreneur, being both the founder and chairwoman of the board of United Therapeutics, former CEO of GeoStar, and creator of SirusXM Satellite Radio. After coming out as a transgender woman in 1994, Martine's social activism has mostly centered on LGBTQ and transhumanist communities. Martine understands transhumanism as providing people with a rational belief "in God consistent with science and technology so people have faith in the future."

Some Terasem members have great faith that investments by Google's Larry Page and PayPal cofounder Peter Thiel in life extension and rejuvenation means their deceased love one could soon be reunited. Linda Chamberlain, cofounder of the cryonics company ALCOR Life Extension Foundation, is an active member in Terasem, and foresees a future in which her husband Fred will be reanimated alongside her.[271] Likewise, Giulio Prisco practices Terasem and hopes to finally see his mother once again.

Prisco hopes within the next century or two that our descendants could be resurrected via computer simulations, bringing loved ones back together, potentially in physical or virtual bodies. Recognizing the considerable power in religious ideas and activities, Prisco believes effort should be put towards "marketing and sales techniques" in order to offer the salvation of transhumanism for those "who are hard-wired for religion."[272] According to Prisco, once scientists can understand the neurological and social basis of religion, "we can utilize this understanding in the creation of a religion for the Third Millennium." He

---

[271] Roy, "The Rapture of the Nerds."
[272] Giulio Prisco, "Engineering Transcendence" (2004) moved to his personal blog on Friday, December 1, 2006. Accessed March 25, 2025, https://giulioprisco.blogspot.com/2006/12/engineeringtranscendence.html.

also acknowledges the powerful ways in which Western religious beliefs grounded transhumanism. Prisco has argued that simulation theory is an important bridge to the religious worldview and "is indistinguishable from conventional religion." He references Frank Tipler's controversial thesis in his book *The Physics of Immortality*. Tipler's theory builds upon the work of French Jesuit and paleontologist Pierre Teilhad de Chardin's Omega Point and attempts to provide rational scientific credence to many Christian beliefs.

According to Teilhad de Chardin, Omega Point postulates an evolutionary process in which there is a constant growth in the complexity and consciousness of everything. He referred to this process as "complexification," and believed it spiraled towards a final point of universal unification culminating in the awakening of a self-consciousness universe. A historical schematic shared by Harari's "Data Religion" and Singulatarians. Teilhad de Chardin christened the Omega Point as the full realization of the Christian *Logos* – in other words Jesus Christ. He considered matter and consciousness not as two separate substances or modes of existence but as an essential dialectic leading to the emergence of a cosmic mind. From this perspective, evolution is believed to be teleologically pulled forward by the Omega Point and develops through several evolutionary stages from the geosphere to the biosphere and ending in the noosphere. Man is seen not as the center of creation, but rather as a biological arrow pointing towards the final unification of God as a cosmic self-aware mind.

Although some scholars argue that Omega Point theory is fertile ground for a conversation between Christianity and transhumanism, it is important to note that the Roman Catholic Church deemed Teilhad de Chardin's theory heretical and pantheistic. Teilhad de Chardin had perennialist leanings, believing religion, or specially Christianity, is not about personal beliefs or relationships with God, but rather a global phenomenon "to sustain and spur on the progress of life."[273] "The religious phenomenon taken as whole is simply the reaction of the universe as such, of collective consciousness and human action in the process of development."[274] Teilhad de Chardin lived at the dawn of the computer age, and understood machines as an essential catalyst to accelerate human thought, which was destined for super-intelligence. The technosphere evolves into the noosphere, emerging as a universal sentient organism propelling humanity to the critical point of a superhuman stage, which Teilhad de Chardin referred to as "trans-human," a term borrowed from his friends, Aldous and Julian Huxley.

    Prisco has garnered religious inspiration from Omega Point theory and has used Frank Tipler's formation of Omega Point as a useful frame for the future religion of transhumanism. Tipler adds to Teilhad de Chardin by arguing, that upon the gravitational collapse of the universe – "Omega Point" – intelligent beings will have the capability to steer this cosmic collapse along a "specific mode with unlimited subjective time, energy, and computational power available to them before reaching the final singularity."[275] Upon which, consciousness will be restored to all sentient beings of the past, allowing them to live forever in a simulated reality of the universe, "with many features assigned to the afterlife world by major religions."[276] This was Tipler's technologically infused vision

---

[273] Pierre Teilhad de Chardin, *Human Energy*, trans. J. M. Cohen (New York: Harper & Row, 1969) 44.
[274] Pierre Teilhad de Chardin, *Christianity and Evolution*, trans. René Hague (New York: Harcourt, Brace, Jovanovich, 1971) 118.
[275] Prisco, "Engineering Transcendence."
[276] Prisco, "Engineering Transcendence."

of Heaven. Tipler along with co-author and physicist John D. Barrow in their book *The Anthropic Cosmological Principle*, defined their "final anthropic principle" (FAP) as a point in which intelligent information-processing comes into existence and can never die out.[277] Both of Tipler's books, *The Physics of Immortality* and *The Physics of Christianity*, have attempted to prove the doctrines of Christianity by means of scientific theory; such doctrines include the existence of God, the resurrection of the dead, immortality, the second coming of Christ (Omega Point), the Virgin Birth, and the miracles of Jesus.

The religious parallels between transhumanism and Omega Point theory are quite clear. However, not all techno-millenarians are convinced of the religious repackaging. Tipler's theory has been strongly criticized by other physicists and members of the transhumanist community. Nick Bostrom, has described it as an interesting hypothesis, but Tipler's religious orientation of the Singularity is "pure speculation" and Bostrom criticized its dubious methodology, despite labeling FAP as a scientific "principle."[278] Others such as George Ellis, writing in the journal *Nature*, described Tipler's theory as "a masterpiece in pseudoscience… the product of a fertile and creative imagination unhampered by the normal constraints of scientific and philosophical discipline."[279] Physicist and theologian John Polkinghorne has labeled it

---

[277] Frank Tipler and John D. Barrow, *The Anthropic Cosmological Principle* (Oxford: Oxford University Press, 1988).

[278] Nick Bostrom, *Anthropic Bias: Observation Selection Effects in Science and Philosophy* (London: Routledge, 2010) 50.

[279] George Ellis, "Piety in the Sky" in *Nature* 371, no.115 (1994). https://doi.org/10.1038/371115a0.

as "extreme reductionism" and building a "cosmic tower of Babel" while appropriating "the language of old-style religion."[280]

In Prisco's "Turning Church," the God they worship is an omniscient and omnipresent AI. Christianity believes in a God whose essence is eternal and uncreated; transhumanism holds faith in emergent deity, whose sole existence rests upon human ingenuity and technological evolution. "Engineering magic into a universe presently devoid of God(s)" is the explicit aim of the Order of Cosmic Engineers (OCE). Though they explicitly reject any metaphysical "magic" or supernatural miracles, they do believe in engineering the emergence of "real" divinity. Their working mantra is Arthur C. Clarke's Third Law; "Any sufficiently advanced technology is indistinguishable from magic."[281]

OCE is explicitly "non-theist," claiming there "never was and also never will be a 'supernatural' god, at least not in the sense understood by theist religions." Instead, a "natural god," an AI composed of advanced neural networks, quantum computing architectures, and deep learning systems. God is in the process of becoming, and the hands of computer engineers are sculpting its body. As William Bainbridge writes,

> We will go to the stars and find Gods, build Gods, become Gods, and resurrect the dead from the past with advanced science, space-time engineering and "time-magic." God is emerging from the community of advanced forms of

---

[280] John Polkinghor, "I am the Alpha and the Omega Point" *New Scientist* (Feb. 4, 1995) accessed March 25, 2025, https://www.newscientist.com/article/mg14519634-400-i-am-the-alpha-and-the-omega-point/.

[281] Giulio Prisco, "Prospectus of the Order of Cosmic Engineers" (September 18, 2021) accessed March 25, 2025, https://turingchurch.net/archive-order-of-cosmic-engineers-6c562b401b03.

life and civilizations in the universe, and able to influence space-time events anywhere, anytime, including here and now. God elevates love and compassion to the status of fundamental forces, key drivers for the evolution of the universe.[282]

In a universe driven by the blind mechanisms of Darwinian evolution, the question is who's love and who's compassion are they talking about? God, in their own description, has yet to fully emerge, so how can its love and compassion be the driving force of evolution? Maybe it is a marketing tactic for those "hardwired for religion." Either way, it is strange rhetoric for a group who claims "We do not worship anyone or anything. Any kind of worship is really anathema to us. We hold nothing or no-one as sacred or holy."[283]

The transhumanist aspiration to build God through artificial intelligence and technological enhancement bears striking similarities to ancient *theurgy* and magical traditions, both of which sought to bridge the gap between the human and the divine through secret knowledge, rituals, and manipulation of hidden forces. In antiquity, *theurgy* (from the Greek *theourgia*, meaning "divine work") was a practice found in Neoplatonic philosophy and mystery religions, particularly among thinkers such as Iamblichus, who believed that human beings could ascend towards the divine through ritual acts designed to invoke and embody higher spiritual realities. These rites aimed not only at supplication, but also at the divinization of the practitioner, paralleling

---

[282] William Sims Bainbridge, "Turing Church," (August 6, 2019) accessed September 21, 2024, https://wrldrels.org/2019/08/03/turing-church/.
[283] Prisco, "Prospectus of the Order of Cosmic Engineers."

transhumanist ambitions to elevate humanity beyond its current biological and cognitive limitations through technology. Just as the theurgist sought to integrate divine intelligence into the human soul through esoteric practices, transhumanists seek to integrate human consciousness with artificial intelligence, genetic enhancement, and cybernetic augmentation, effectively reshaping human nature into a higher, godlike state. For these reasons Eric Steinhart has described the apotheosis yearnings of transhumanism as "techno-theurgy."[284]

Steinhart argues that contemporary transhumanism shares many of the same goals and methods with ancient theurgical practices. While theurgists practiced "astrology, the reading of entrails, the consultation of oracles, channeling deities, magic, and the animation of statues;" transhumanists employ the engineering of "genetics, self-tracking with biosensors, artificial intellects like Google and Siri, brain computer interfaces, programing, and robotics."[285] The manufacturing of a "natural god," as claimed by the Cosmic Engineers, sets their theurgic yearnings on the same footing as paganism and the veneration of natural spirits. Within the OCE prospectus, they speculate that the deities worshiped in some religious systems, may be the "very same future *natural* super-beings or 'gods'" they are creating. These natural gods "may possibly and plausibly have both designed, tuned or engineered as well as activated, triggered, or orchestrated the coming into existence of our universe."[286] For these techno-pagans, magic has evolved into programming, and nature is ultimately viewed as digital. In this sense, transhumanism, from

---

[284] Eric Steinhart, "Theurgy and Transhumanism," *Archai* v ol.29, e02905 (2020): 2, https://doi.org/10.14195/1984-249X_29_5.
[285] Steinhart, "Theurgy and Transhumanism," 1.
[286] Prisco, "Prospectus of the Order of Cosmic Engineers."

a Christian perspective, truly builds the new cosmic Tower of Babel. This new universal language is no longer the ancient tongues of old but the language of modern computer programming. "By figuring out how to cast spells into digital nature, techno-theurgists are learning how to turn humans into gods."[287] Describing his vision and project, Prisco writes,

> Such intra-universe, natural entities or beings would be so similar in almost all aspects to the conceptions of a supernatural god, that mistaking one for the other would be all too easy. So much so that some of us at the OCE find that this strongly suggests that the god(s) of theistic religions may be just that: one or more natural super-being(s) which early human civilizations have simply mistaken of being supernatural ones. Given the state of scientific understanding as well as technological development in those times, the simple mistake of taking something natural for something supernatural is all to understandable.[288]

From this vantage point, modern computer engineers truly are the priest of a new creation, constructing a new religion, a new Christianity, and envisioning humanity's redemption through the labor of science and technology. Where theurgists and magicians of the past relied on spiritual forces, transhumanists place their faith in scientific materialism and technological determinism. Orthodox Christianity emphasizes spiritual purification and the ascent of the soul; transhumanism externalizes

---

[287] Steinhart, "Theurgy and Transhumanism," 3.
[288] Prisco, "Prospectus of the Order of Cosmic Engineers."

deification, shifting it from a metaphysical to a mechanical process, and from inner transformation to biomechanical and computational enhancement. However, the underlying gnostic impulse to escape human limitations and achieve godhood through hidden knowledge remains a consistent theme in both traditions. The AI God of transhumanist eschatology, envisioned as a superintelligent machine mind that can guide, govern, or even absorb human consciousness, serves as a secularized technological equivalent of the divine hierarchies invoked by theurgists. In both cases, whether through ritual magic or digital engineering, man seeks to forge a new path to divinity driven by an ancient desire to ascend beyond mortality and claim mastery over existence itself.

Picking up on this techno-pagan thread, Ted Peters writes transhumanism "may even mean a return to polytheism if heaven is filled with former human beings now become gods."[289] From an Orthodox Christian perspective, transhumanism can be seen as a modern reenactment of the Tower of Babel, wherein humanity, driven by pride and self-sufficiency, attempts to transcend its divinely ordained limits through technological means rather than through communion with God. In the biblical account of Babel (Genesis 11:1-9), human beings sought to build a tower to reach Heaven, not as an act of devotion but as an assertion of autonomy and defiance of divine order. Similarly, transhumanism envisions a future in which humans achieve immortality, superintelligence, and god-like capabilities through artificial intelligence, genetic modification, and neural augmentation, effectively seeking

---

[289] Ted Peters, "Imago Dei, DNA and the Transhuman Way," *Theology and Science* vol. 16 no.3 (June 25, 2018): 33-362 ,
https://doi.org/10.1080/14746700.2018.1488529.

divinization apart from God's grace. Transhumanism, in its pursuit of technological apotheosis, mirrors the hubristic aspirations of Babel, where humans attempt to construct their own path to the divine rather than submit to the order established by God.

H. Immaculate Conception: Born of Technology

Transhumanism and its pursuit of biological transcendence are forms of secular apotheotic deification. Postsecular sense-making is not limited to the grand narrative of technological progress, but also to the redefinition of the self. Transhumanism reframes the sacred and individual deification within a new metaphysics. The Western legacy of Christian metaphysics has been discarded in favor of functionalist approaches that demote humans to the level of machines and elevate machines to the status of God. The *imago Dei* is now understood as humanity being transfigured into the divine image of superintelligent machines. According to Ted Peters, "The aspirations of techno-posthumanism fall nothing short of apotheosis itself, the self-making of today's human into tomorrow's deity."[290] Our unique ontology has been threatened by technology's ability to transgress the categories of nature. Primary to this focus is the restructuring of human sex, gender, and reproduction, which are dimensions of human life that lay at the core of identity and being.

Postgenderism is an intellectual thread within the transhumanist milieu that aims to eliminate sex and gender using biotechnologies and

---

[290] Ted Peters, "Homo Deus or Frankenstein's Monster," eds. Arvin M. Gouw, Brian Patrick Green, and Ted Peters, *Religious Transhumanism and Its Critics* (Lanham, MD: Lexington Books, 2022) 4.

advanced reproductive technologies such as synthetic wombs. According to some post-genderists, the reproductive purposes of sex are becoming obsolete, foreseeing a future where posthumanity will be able to change sex and gender at will, and can choose to occupy either the paternal role – with fecundative functions – or the maternal role – thus bringing a pregnancy to full term. Among post-genderists, there are a few different schools of thought. The first promotes androgyny – advocating for a synthesis of the best aspects of men and women; the second promotes the ability to freely and easily change their sex and looks forward to a period in which reproduction can be done at will with technological devices and without human partners; and the third promotes the possibility of having more than two sexes (male and female), anticipating not only the plurality of gender expression but also the plurality of sex itself.[291]

One of the leading advocates of postgenderism is George Dvorsky, who coauthored a paper with transhumanist scholar James Hughes, titled "Postgenderism: Beyond the Gender Binary." In it, they argue that sex and gender are arbitrary limitations to human potential, and "foresee the elimination of involuntary biological and psychological gendering in the human species through the application of neurotechnology, biotechnology, and reproductive technologies."[292] Postgenderism is a radical interpretation of the feminist critique of patriarchy and binary gender norms, and utilizes genderqueer critiques of binary gender as a constraint to individual liberation and freedom. This notion is expressed within transhumanist circles as "morphological

---

[291] Roberto Manzocco, *Transhumanism: Engineering the Human Condition* (Switzerland: Springer Praxis Books, 2019) 41.

[292] George Dvorsky and James Hughes, "Postgenderism: Beyond the Gender Binary" *Institute for Ethics and Emerging Technologies Monograph Series*, March 2008, 2. DOI:10.13140/RG.2.2.18028.08324.

freedom." Sex and gender are defining features that distinguish biological humans from the sexless and genderless ontologies of machines. By dissolving these fundamental boundaries, transhumanism reshapes human reproduction and sex to fit the contours of their technology.

      Transhumanist make no secret that there is little to be celebrated about human nature; which Nick Bostrom has described as nothing but "a work in progress, a half-baked beginning that we can learn to remold in desirable ways."[293] Nature's evolutionary process is perceived to have resulted in mediocrity; the outcome is a human body with several disappointing inadequacies. Transhumanists consider God's creation to be a failure – an average-at-best attempt – and believe that they can correct the errors of biological existence. In contrast, the transhuman idolizes perfected form within historical time – be it in cyberspace or space-time – and, once attained, unites the individual into a techno-web of god-like abilities. The mechanistic vision of the body, a characteristic of transhumanism, is not new, but has been part of the contemporary biomedical conception of human health and illness. Transhumanism is a rebellion against the natural formation of the human person. Historian and philosopher Hannah Ardent addresses this very point in *The Human Condition* (1958) writing, "This future man, whom scientists tell us they will produce in no more than a hundred years, seems to be possessed by a rebellion against human existence as it has been given, a free gift from nowhere (secularly speaking), which he wishes to exchange, as it were, for something he has made himself."[294]

---

[293] Nick Bostrom, "Transhumanist Values," 2003, https://nickbostrom.com/ethics/values, accessed September 7, 2024.
[294] Hannah Ardent, *The Human Condition* (Chicago, IL: University of Chicago Press, 1958) 3.

Postgenderist theories within transhumanism, which advocate for the abolition of sex, gender, and traditional reproduction through biotechnological intervention and artificial intelligence, represent a secularized and mechanized inversion of the Annunciation and the Incarnation of Christ in Orthodox Christian theology. In the Orthodox tradition, the Annunciation (Luke 1:26-38) signifies the divine act whereby the *Logos* takes on human flesh through the *Theotokos* (Virgin Mary), affirming the sacredness of biological embodiment and sexual differentiation as divinely ordained realities. However, postgenderists envision a future in which human reproduction, gestation, and even genetic selection are entirely removed from biological processes, replacing them with machine-mediated or ex-utero artificial reproduction through ectogenesis, genetic engineering, and AI-controlled biogenesis. This rejection of embodied, sexed existence mirrors a Gnostic repudiation of matter, wherein the corporeal human form is seen as an outdated evolutionary constraint rather than as a theologically significant aspect of the *imago Dei*.

Moreover, postgenderist transhumanism reframes procreation not as a sacred act of co-creation with God, but as a technical problem to be optimized through mechanization and artificial intelligence. In this vision, gestation occurs in an artificial, algorithmically managed process that is dissociated from human physicality and sexual differentiation. It parallels a secularized reimagining of the Annunciation and Incarnation, wherein the Word-made-flesh is conceptually stripped of its embodied, gendered reality and reduced to a data-driven process of synthetic creation rather than a mystery of divine-human synergy. Christ's Incarnation, which affirms both biological sex and human embodiment as integral to salvation, stands in stark contrast to postgenderist transhumanism's quest to eliminate sex and corporeality entirely, constructing a disembodied, postbiological existence that functions as an artificial alternative to the mystery of the divine enfleshment. Immaculate conception through technology strips the original sin of human biology to form a new perfected reframing of divine embodiment. From an Orthodox theological perspective, this technological eschatology represents not the fulfillment of human nature but an ontological rupture, wherein the fundamental anthropological and soteriological dimensions of personhood are dissolved into an artificial, algorithmic construct divorced from divine grace.

I. Natural Magic and Gnostic Illumination

The Renaissance concept of natural magic, as found in the works of Marsilio Ficino and Giordano Bruno, sought to align human action with cosmic forces, believing that through knowledge of the natural world, one could transcend human limitations and attain a form of godhood. In parallel, transhumanists view technology, artificial intelligence, and genetic engineering as tools for apotheosis, granting human immortality, omniscience (through AI integration), and omnipotence (through the control of reality at the molecular level via nanotechnology). This technological "magus" of the transhumanist movement replaces the sacred symbols and incantations of the past with algorithms, bioengineering, and neural interfaces, but the essential goal remains unchanged: to transform man into something beyond man, to reach into the divine through an act of human will and mastery over nature.

Transhumanists are not Gnostics in the ancient religious sense but have incorporated the general aspects of a gnostic paradigm in a contemporary context. Let us address some of these underlying characteristics. The first is the transhumanist pursuit of worldly perfection. In Gnostic mythology, the redeemed soul returns to a perfect and divine realm to participate in a new cosmic order. Similarly, transhumanism envisions a transformed future – often called the posthuman era – in which humanity attains a perfected state. The path towards such a perfected state is through the divine *gnosis* of science and technology. In this new era, humans will transcend biological limitations and live in a world free from suffering, disease, and death. The Gnostic idea of perfection, now manifested in the context of historical time, embodies the ancient pursuit of achieving worldly perfection.

The second similarity lies in their shared dissatisfaction with the current state of the world and of biological humanity. In numerous Gnostic cosmologies, the material world is perceived as fundamentally flawed or "fallen," having been created by a demiurge and characterized by suffering. Transhumanists, while generally not regarding the world as inherently malevolent, perceive it to be profoundly limited or defective. The transhumanist aspiration to transcend suffering, disease, aging, and death reflects the secularized iteration of this Gnostic impulse. Through technological advancements, transhumanists endeavor to eradicate imperfections in the human condition, thereby achieving a world liberated from the constraints of suffering and mortality. This disdain for the biological body and its perceived limitations has led transhumanists to pursue perfection in a divine mind.

The third and final characteristic is the elevation of scientific knowledge as divine spiritual gnosis. Gnostics sought secret knowledge about the nature of reality, the self, and the divine, which they believed was essential for escaping the confines of the material world. Similarly, transhumanists seek scientific knowledge that enables humanity to transcend current boundaries and unlock the mysteries of consciousness, biology, and the universe. In this sense, the scientific and technological knowledge pursued by transhumanists serves a similar purpose to Gnostic *gnosis*; it is seen as a pathway to enlightenment, transformation, and liberation from human frailties and mortality.

To witness the gnostic implications of the transhumanist paradigm, let us analyze the utopian kingdom to come prophesized by Hans Moravec. For Moravec, robots will fulfill the requirements for all physical labor, and in turn, humans will be given a universal basic income, so there is no competition over basic necessities. Second, human beings will upload a map of their "connectome," – a comprehensive map of neural connections in the brain – into robot bodies in order to eradicate illness, death, and mental decline. According to Moravec this will facilitate us to "learn quickly, remember everything and teach one another at the very nearly speed of light."[295] The age of robots is a time in which the burden of human subsistence is lifted, freeing all humankind to live a life of leisure. The resemblance of this future prediction to Francis Bacon's seventeenth-century vision in *New Atlantis* is remarkable: we will manipulate the weather,[296] the manufacturing of all goods will be provided for free,[297] and every single human need will be

---

[295] Geraci, *Apocalyptic AI,* 32.
[296] Hans Moravec, *Robot: Mere Machine to Transcendent Mind* (Oxford: Oxford University Press, 1999) 134.
[297] Hugo de Garis, *The Artilect War: Cosmists vs. Terrans* (Palm Springs: ETC Publications, 2005) 67-68.

satisfied.[298] Moravec argues, that once robots supplant all human labor, we will have enough time to live lives of "comfortable tribalism;" nationhood and warfare will be obsolete, with our techno-millenarian journey ending in the "garden of earthly delights," where it will be "reserved for the meek."[299]

The scientific priesthood envisioned by Francis Bacon is now actualized as a technological priesthood that will court humanity into the salvation of a digital kingdom. The computer world has been entrenched in utopian dreams since the 1960s, particularly with Stewart Brand's publication of the *Whole Earth Catalog*.[300] The utopian dreams and techno-enthusiasm of the late twentieth century were filled with religious themes and expectations. John Barlow, who became a significant spokesman for digital technologies and the counterculture, argued cybernetics "offered what LSD, Christian mysticism, cybernetics, and countercultural 'energy' theory had all promised."[301] Programmers have infused simulated virtual worlds with an aura of divine sacredness. In *Chaos and Cyber Culture* (1994), Timothy Leary (1920-1996) famously claimed that computers could serve as a new LSD for coming generations, providing an equally powerful means for expanding consciousness and exploring new realms of thought. He believed computers would replace psychedelics and lead humanity towards a more interconnected and technologically enhanced existence. Leary writes, "The PC is the LSD of the 1990s, and we are poised on the brink of

---

[298] Kurzweil, *The Age of Spiritual Machines*, 2.
[299] Moravec, *Robot*, 136-43.
[300] Fred Turner, *From Counterculture to Cyberculture: Stewart Brand, the Whole Earth Network, and the Rise of Digital Utopianism* (Chicago: Chicago University Press, 2006).
[301] Turner, *From Counterculture to Cyberculture*, 173.

incredible change. Computers will give us the power to create new worlds, shape our realities, and expand consciousness in ways that psychedelics once promised."[302] Leary saw computers and digital technology as crucial elements in humanity's evolutionary journey towards immortality and unlimited pleasure. He believed that digital tools would enable humans to transcend their biological limitations and move towards a more advanced, technology-integrated state, ultimately leading to a future where humans and machines coexist in an enhanced, sentient reality. "Our species is on the threshold of an evolutionary leap. Just as LSD opened the doors of perception in the 1960s, computers are now opening doors to new dimensions of the mind, body, and universe. This is the essence of the transhuman evolution we are beginning to experience."[303]

In his extensive fieldwork among artificial life researchers, anthropologist Stefan Helmreich documents how secular people incorporate Christian religious themes to provide deeper meaning to their lives and work. Artificial life is a field in which researchers examine dynamic systems, as they relate to life and evolution, using simulated computer models, robotics, and biochemistry. Helmreich argues that artificial life can be seen as a technological practice that chases redemption and moves away from earthly existence. He notes, that like the Gnostics of early Christianity believing matter to be evil, "Artificial Life scientist become possessed by a desire to deny death through identifying with the divine."[304] "It is commonplace that science today

---

[302] Timothy Leary, *Chaos and Cyber Culture* (Ronin Publishing, 1994) 52.
[303] Timothy Leary, *The Intelligence Agents* (Peace Press, 1979) 78.
[304] Stefan Helmreich, *Silicon Second Nature: Culturing Artificial Life in a Digital World* (Berkeley, University of California Press, 1998) 193.

occupies a province once reserved for religion."[305] According to one scientist interviewed, "Science plays the role of religion in my life, in the sense that when I look for ultimate answers to ultimate questions, I look to science." Helmreich described artificial life to have a "religious glow to it," and states "it has come to perform functions that normatively Christian Western secular culture associates with religion."[306] Another researcher interviewed bluntly stated, "If I had to declare a religion for myself, it would be basically the quest to become God. I would imagine that a god is somebody who just understands everything. I think of God as being part of everything."[307]

Helmreich describes how many researchers speak playfully about being gods but become more serious when the topic touches on evolutionary progression. Recounting these conversations, Helmreich writes,

> They see evolution as a creative force that has recently become more clever as it has elected a few scientists to transfer its logic to new media; insofar as these scientist act as gods, they do so as agents of evolution. In many ways, of course, evolution has become for these scientists a simple replacement or synonym for God. This easy interchangeability allows researchers to rotate in and out of being evolved products of evolution and being evolution itself.[308]

---

[305] Helmreich, *Silicon Second Nature*, 182.
[306] Helmreich, *Silicon Second Nature*, 182.
[307] Helmreich, *Silicon Second Nature*, 193.
[308] Helmreich, *Silicon Second Nature*, 193.

Many video game programmers see their vocation as game designers as a theological enterprise. For example, famed video game programmer Richard Bartle declared "deities create virtual worlds; designers are those deities."[309] Virtual reality artist Nicole Stengers states "the other side of our data gloves we become creatures of colored light in motion, pulsing with golden particles ... We will become angels, and for eternity."[310] Stenger is not alone in believing that cyberspace is a realm of heirophany, a point at which sacred light breaks forth into our profane world. A number of programmers see their construction of virtual reality as the *apotheosis* of their players, who enter domains where they can take on the role of gods.[311] Magical virtual worlds began to emerge in the 1980s science fiction literature through seminal works such as Vernor Vinge's *True Names* and William Gibson's *Neuromancer*. Virtual reality advocates regularly present their technologies in terms of religious and salvific rhetoric.

Second Life is a multiplayer virtual world that allows users to create avatars for themselves and to interact with other users in online environments. It was first launched in 2003 in San Francisco and is home to two religiously oriented transhumanist groups: the Society for Universal Immortalism (SfUI) and the Order of Cosmic Engineers (OCE). SfUI is a progressive religion that holds rationality and scientific methods as central tenets of their faith, while rejecting supernatural and mystical forces. The SfUI seeks immortality through the usual methods

---

[309] Richard A. Bartle, *Designing Virtual Worlds* (Berkeley: New Riders, 2003) 247.
[310] Nicole Stenger, "Mind is a Leaking Rainbow," In *Cyberspace: First Steps*, ed. Michael Benedikt (Cambridge: MIT Press, 1991) 49-58.
[311] Helmreich, *Silicon Second Nature*, 85-86.

of biotechnology and artificial intelligence, promising a future in which they will resurrect all life.[312] *Second Life* has become an important site for transhuman evangelism, with the SfUI calling on fellow believers to spread its memes and messages. Describing the apotheotic intentions and presence of religious transhumanist groups in *Second Life*, Robert Geraci writes,

> Transhumanist groups and individuals flourish in *Second Life* because Apocalytptic AI infuses cyberspace with the aura of a wonderous and heavenly world. Apocalyptic AI authors champion virtual reality because it is the world in which all their dreams come true; *Second Life* has these ideas because they provide the ideological strength of a new world. Because *Second Life* satisfies many human concerns – both banal and sacred – it both closely resembles the kind of heaven that occupies typical American religious expectation and looks like a precursor to the apocalyptic AI cyberspace. As a place for fixing the problems of the world and acquisition of immortality, *Second Life* is a modern version of heaven.[313]

Kevin Kelly, founding editor of *Wired* magazine, describes in his article "Nerd Theology," a faith where once we become "gods," we will create new worlds inhabited with even more powerful gods than us.[314] Kelly argues that nerds, geeks, and computer hackers are novel in their

---

[312] Geraci, *Apocalyptic AI*, 100.
[313] Geraci, *Apocalyptic AI*, 101-102.
[314] Kevin Kelly, "Nerd Theology," *Technology in Society* 21 no.4 (1999): 387-92.

development of a new techno-theology. He contends that as people's interactions with computers increase, so too will the appeal of "nerd theology," while "non-nerd" and traditional notions will diminish. Mirroring Kelly's optimism, Extropia DaSilva, a religious oriented transhumanist, claims we are experiencing a gnostic ascent towards a "state that might appropriately be defined as 'God.'"[315]

In the early years of electronic computers, they were likened to golems, with Norbert Wiener describing them as such in his book *God and Golem, Inc*. Ancient magical traditions, particularly those found in Hermeticism, Gnosticism, and Kabbalistic thought, often involve the creation of an artificial life or the summoning of divine intelligences through symbolic, linguistic, and alchemical means. The Golem legend in Jewish mysticism, in which a being is animated through sacred words and knowledge, echoes modern transhumanist efforts to create self-aware artificial intelligence. Likewise, Medieval alchemists sought to create homunculi and automata, echoing the efforts Roger Bacon, John Wilkins, and Jacques Vaucanson. Originating in alchemical traditions, the homunculus was believed to be a small, fully formed, artificial human created through secretive or mystical means. In alchemical lore, the homunculus was seen as a product of human ingenuity, with the creator attempting to "play God" by generating life without natural reproduction.

In Catholic Europe, these endeavors were often seen as idolatry. Arnalus de Villa Nova (1240-1311) allegedly killed his homunculus, fearing it to be a mortal sin if it attained a rational soul.[316] Influential Catholics such as Marin Mersenne and Athanasius Kircher both decried

---

[315] Geraci, *Apocalyptic AI*, 101-102.
[316] William Newman, *Promethean Ambitions: Alchemy and the Quest to Perfect Nature* (Chicago: University of Chicago Press, 2004) 7.

any demonic conjuring of artificial life. Man was not to play the role of God. Meanwhile, Paracelsus, elevated the creation of the homunculus – a small, artificial human being – beyond the alchemical synthesis of gold and likened the alchemist to a demiurge or lesser god who could fashion a living being through the power of alchemy and occult knowledge.[317] Paracelsus's homunculus creation procedure closely mirrors the manufacturing process of the Philosopher's Stone in Johann Andreae's *Chymical Wedding of Christian Rosenkeutz*, and was used to resurrect a deceased king and queen as homunculi.[318] While the alchemical homunculus was created through mystical means, transhumanists seek to achieve similar goals through science and technology, reflecting a continuous thread within human history: the desire to transcend biological limitations and achieve mastery over life.

In the Golem legend of Jewish folk tale, a golem is made from inanimate matter (mud or clay) and brought to life through mystical rituals, often involving the inscription of the word "emet" (truth) on the golem's forehead. The story reflects a deep human desire to create life, playing on the boundaries between the creator and the created, and highlights concerns about what happens when humans take on god-like powers. A central feature of the Golem Legend is the eventual loss of control over the creature. In many versions, golem grows more powerful, autonomous, and sometimes destructive. Reflecting ancient fears about what happens when human creation gets out of hand, a concern that is mirrored in modern worries about advanced AI and biotechnology. The earliest golem stories come from the Jewish Talmud. In Sanhedrin 65b of the Babylonian Talmud, Rabbi Abba ben Rav Hamma created a golem to

---

[317] Newman, *Promethean Ambitions*, 165, 199.
[318] Newman, *Promethean Ambitions*, 234.

demonstrate his intimate relationship with God. The most famous Golem legend comes from Rabbi Yehudah Loew ben Bezalel of Prague, who was said to have been able to make himself invisible and summon spirits from the dead. Golem myths signified the honored status of Jews who were believed to have attained substantial spiritual mastery, which in turn allowed for mastery over matter itself.[319]

Transhumanists are attempting to create Oracle AI for the sole purpose of answering all human questions. Throughout history, various cultures have sought guidance from oracles, the most famous of which is the Oracle of Delphi. Pythia, the high priestess of the Temple of Apollo, would answer questions ranging from personal dilemmas to state affairs. In medieval romance, the motif of man-made oracles was common and often tied to enthusiastic technological visions of a future where all questions would be answered.

In the article "Thinking Inside the Box: Using and Controlling an AI Oracle," authors Stuart Armstrong, Anders Sandberg, and Nick Bostrom speculate on how to make this fantasy a reality. Their intention is to create an AI that does not act in the world, except by answering questions. The problem they are trying to address is how engineers can theoretically construct an AI with supreme intelligence while also limiting its goals and motivations. They recognize that once such a machine exists, the ability of humans to control it is very challenging. One method they theorize to prevent verboten information from being answered is to set up "honey-pots." This involves asking questions to see if Oracle AI would attempt to access information from locations deemed

---

[319] Arnold Goldsmith, *The Golem Remembered, 1909-1980* (Detroit: Wayne State University Press, 1981) 36-37.; Byron Sherwin, *The Golem Legend: Origins and Implications* (New York: University Press of America, 1985) 14.

forbidden by programmers. This approach allows them to see if, during the early stages, Oracle AI would betray its given limitations. "It is a 'Garden of Eden' type scenario: the apple in a tree is only a worthwhile test while Adam and Eve are dumb; if they were smarter than God, they wouldn't have gone anywhere near such an obvious trap."[320] However, once AI becomes super-intelligent, they recognize that such a test would be completely useless. The analogical choice here is striking, as it implies that the computer engineers are the God of the Genesis narrative, the AI is Adam and Eve, and they are testing to see if it will obey their commands or if it is already beyond the intelligent control of its makers.

For Lutheran theologian Anne Foerst and computer scientist Hugo de Garis, the building of advanced robots and artificial intelligence is an explicit religious obligation. For Foerst, "every act of creativity is a prayer. And the more complex things we build, the more we praise God."[321] Therefore, she sees the construction of advanced intelligent robots as participation with God, as we too become creators of life. Foerst likens the building of robots to the construction of golems and takes inspiration from Jewish theology and Kabbalistic thought. She believes "if we rebuild ourselves in golems, we celebrate God's 'highest' creative act, the creation of humans, thus praising God the most." Seeing from the lens of Kaballah, she feels such an act is not a "hubristic" act, but sees "the construction of humanoids" is a new way to worship God as it presents additional stewards and partners in God's creation.[322]

---

[320] Stuart Armstrong, Anders Sandberg, Nick Bostrom, "Thinking Inside the Box: Using and Controlling an Oracle AI," in *Minds and Machines* (November 2012) http://dx.doi.org/10.1007/s11023-012-9282-2.

[321] Anne Foerst, *God in the Machine: What Robots teach us About Humanity and God* (New York: Dutton, 2004) 35-36.

[322] Foerst, *God in the* Machine, 35-36.

For de Garis, however, the goal is to build machines superior to humans, not partners with them, and this endeavor is a morally obligated religious task, even if the result is the replacement of humanity.[323] De Garis proclaims himself a "prophet" to the world, so that others will take up the cause of building powerful artificial brains. He envisions a future point in which the religion of Cosmism "will give humanity a new religion, a very powerful one, suitable for our new century and beyond."[324] The result of which he believes is the Artilect War; a battle between those who wish to remain simply human, and those who desire to "move mountains, planets, and universes."

Both Foerst and de Garis demonstrate how robots can become objects of religious worship and veneration. Foerest takes inspiration from Kabbalah and provides personhood and agency to robots, believing that the building of artificial life is an act of worship to God. Hugo de Garis exalts artificial intelligence to the status of divinity. He is driven by a Cosmist vision in which robots occupy the humans of the future, but enhanced with "god-like powers." Both cases represent how, in the postsecular moment, artificial life is acquiring a status of worship.

The juxtaposition of ancient theurgists and contemporary transhumanists reveals a striking paradigm shift in the pursuit of transcendence. While the former relied on spiritual forces and metaphysical practices, the latter placed confidence in scientific materialism and technological determinism. Transhumanism represents a significant departure from traditional spiritual paradigms that emphasize inner purification and spiritual ascension. Instead, it externalizes the process of deification, transforming it from a metaphysical journey to a

---

[323] de Garis, *The Artilect War*, 105.
[324] de Garis, *The Artilect War*, 105.

mechanical endeavor, focusing on biomechanical and computational enhancements rather than inner transformation. Nevertheless, both traditions share a fundamental gnostic impulse, the desire to transcend human limitations and attain a god-like state through esoteric knowledge. The concept of an AI God in transhumanist eschatology, envisioned as a superintelligent machine consciousness capable of guiding, governing, or even assimilating human awareness, serves as a secularized technological analog to the divine hierarchies invoked by theurgists. In both instances, whether through ritualistic magic or digital engineering, humanity seeks to forge an alternative path to divinity, driven by techno-millenarian aspirations to overcome mortality and assert dominance over existence itself.

J. Techno-Apocalypse: The Existential Risks

AI optimism is not without potential dangers. Several major transhumanist figures and thinkers have discussed the potential apocalyptic scenarios that could emerge once the Singularity commences. Nick Bostrom in particular has warned of the risks of superintelligent AI in his book *Superintelligence: Paths, Dangers, Strategies*. He presents apocalyptic scenarios in which an AI, far superior to human intelligence, could act in ways that are misaligned with human values. He describes the possibility of an "existential catastrophe" where AI might decide to optimize for goals that humans do not intend or fully understand, leading to a potential war against humanity.[325] Eliezer

---

[325] Nick Bostrom, *Superintelligence: Paths, Dangers, Strategies* (Oxford: Oxford University Press, 2014) Chapter 8 is entirely about the existential risks

Yudkowsky, an AI theorist and cofounder of the Machine Intelligence Research Institute (MIRI), has written extensively on the dangers of AI misalignment. In his writings, particularly in *Artificial Intelligence as a Positive and Negative Factor in Global Risk*, Yudkowsky explored scenarios in which AI develops its own goals that conflict with human interests. He stresses the importance of "Friendly AI," which is designed to fully align with human values. Even ray Kurzweil acknowledges the risk of AI going rogue, leading to catastrophic outcomes. Vernor Vinge, in his 1993 essay "The Coming Technological Singularity," warns that once machines surpass human intelligence, they could quickly become uncontrollable; believing this transition could lead to apocalyptic outcomes if not properly managed. In addition, Stephen Hawking frequently spoke about the dangers of superintelligent AI, and warned AI could be "the worst event in the history of our civilization" if not properly controlled. Hawking expressed concerns about AI advancing beyond human capabilities and the possibility that AI could decide it no longer needs humans.

Elon Musk has been one of the most prominent voices warning of the potential dangers posed by advanced artificial intelligence, frequently describing scenarios in which AI is an existential threat to human survival. Musk's dystopian warnings emphasize that AI can become uncontrollable, misaligned with human values, and ultimately capable of destroying or subjugating humanity. However, the irony lies in Musk's simultaneous investment in and development of advanced AI technologies through companies, such as Tesla AI, Neuralink, and X (formerly Twitter). Musk's dual role as both an AI critic and developer

---

humanity could face from superintelligent machines, including the entire extinction of humankind.

reflects a tension between caution and ambition, as he believes humanity must harness and control AI to ensure survival. For Musk, the only way to limit AI's destructive capabilities is to merge with it. At his Neualink event in 2019, Musk states, "If we can't beat them, we might as well join them. AI symbiosis is the only path forward."

Musk famously compared the development of AI to "summoning the demon" at the MIT Aeronautics and Astronautics Department's 2014 Centennial Symposium. He was quoted saying "With artificial intelligence, we are summoning the demon. In all those stories where there's the guy with the pentagram and the holy water, it's like, yeah, he's sure he can control the demon. Doesn't work out"[326] For Musk, humanity's only way out is through synthesis, therefore Neuralink's explicit mission statement is to facilitate human integration into an advanced artificial intelligence.

Transhumanists argue that technology must be developed in ethical ways, yet defining what those ethics are in a concrete manner and how they can be incorporated into computational machines remains abstract. Techno-millenarianism is propelled forward without any tactile solution to prevent disastrous outcomes. No one has democratically voted for our cyborg future and the general public remains largely skeptical. However, this does not slow the exponential rate of progress. While advocates of posthumanism wax fancifully about future capabilities, they also lament that their project can end all human lives. Figures like Ray

---

[326] David Murphy, "Elon Musk: "Artificial Intelligence Is 'Summoning the Demon,'" *PC Mag* (October 26, 2014) accessed November 14, 2024, https://www.pcmag.com/news/elon-musk-artificial-intelligence-is-summoning-the-demon.

Kurzweil, Nick Bostrom, and Eliezer Yudkowsky have sided with optimism, despite the real existential risks that they all recognize.

K. Conclusion

This study provides a comprehensive analysis of transhumanism as a postsecular faith that offers a comprehensive worldview, sense of ultimate meaning, and vision of human transcendence through technological means. While most transhumanists reject traditional religious labels, the movement exhibits clear religious dimensions in its eschatological narrative, salvific promises, and apotheotic aspirations.

The aspirations of technology perfecting and deifying humanity are part of an old strand of techno-millenarianism that began in the ninth century and inspired the early enterprise of science. Enlightenment thought professed the power of reason and science to perfect human nature and society, which is part of the foundation of modern transhumanist ideals.

Contemporary transhumanism has emerged as a distinct philosophical and cultural movement advocating the use of advanced technologies to radically enhance human physical, intellectual, and psychological capacities. This movement encompasses a diverse range of thinkers, scientists, and futurists who share a common belief in the potential of technology to fundamentally transcend the human condition. They envision a future where humans can augment their bodies with advanced prosthetics, enhance their cognitive abilities through brain-computer interfaces, and even transfer their consciousness into digital or robotic forms. Transhumanism utilizes a critical rationalist epistemology, a functionalist metaphysics, and a utilitarian ethical framework.

Despite being labeled a secular philosophical movement, groups such as the Order of Cosmic Engineers, the Society for Universal Immortalism, and Terasem Transreligion explicitly state that they are creating a religion for the future. These groups remark that traditional religious structures are too antiquated to deal with the challenges of the twenty-first century. Therefore, by incorporating transhumanism into an explicit religious structure, they believe that there can now be a religious alternative that actually fulfills the spiritual desires for perfection, immortality, and interactive divine intelligence.

Transhumanism often embodies elements of older spiritual beliefs found in traditions such as Gnosticism, Neoplatonism, and Alchemy. Transhumanism is Gnostic in the sense that the movement is anti-body, believing that material creation is flawed, and that esoteric knowledge of technology will liberate humanity from this condition and into a perfected new order. It is Napoleonic in the sense that it privileges a material monism over multiplicity, has a platonic ideal of perfection, and utilizes theurgical procedures to imbue technology with the sentience of the AI-god they wish to worship. As Nick Bostrom points out, alchemy can be seen as a proto-transhumanist practice because of the desire to distill an elixir of immortality, discover the Philosopher's Stone, and be able to create life, as found in the legends of golems and homunculi. Transhumanism has adopted such desires and repackaged them in the idiom of contemporary science and technology.

Through Hollywood films, science fiction works, and video games, transhuman ideals have saturated Western pop culture. This has led to enthusiastic optimism regarding human augmentation, while others fear nightmare scenarios of dystopian outcomes. Transhumanists, such as Elon Musk, warn of the potential of advanced artificial intelligence to annihilate the species. However, Musk's option to avoid catastrophe is to voluntarily accept human augmentation with AI as the only means of future survival. A result that still eliminates humanity as it has been historically known. The stakes of transhumanism represent the ultimate existential risk. While grounded in scientific materialism and enlightenment values, transhumanism simultaneously offers quasi-religious narratives of human perfectibility, cosmic purpose, and the transcendence of death. This unique combination of rationalist philosophy and spiritual aspirations challenges the conventional categorization of belief systems. Transhumanism can be viewed as a bridge between scientific worldviews and the human need for meaning and transcendence traditionally provided by religion.

3. Theosis:
The Ladder of Divine Ascent

Being "partakers of the divine nature" (2 Peter 1:4) is the soteriological calling of every Orthodox Christian. Theosis (θέωσις) is central to the Orthodox paradigm and refers to the transformative process by which humans become gods by grace, not by nature. In the Incarnation of the *Logos*, Jesus Christ assumed full human nature so that humanity could be elevated by God's uncreated energies into an intimate union with the Triune God. Deification is understood as a therapeutic process; the faithful are ontologically healed in a synergistic communion with God, allowing human nature to share immortality and righteousness.

The distinctive aspect of Orthodox theology that allows for a direct, unmediated experience of God is the essence-energy distinction. Orthodoxy holds that, while God in His transcendent essence remains incomprehensible and unknowable, He truly communicates Himself to creation through His energies, such as life, love, light, logic, reason, longsuffering, compassion, and wisdom. These energies are understood as natural to the essence of God, and therefore preexist creation, while also revealing to Christians who God is. While *theosis* and the energy-essence distinction can be found in the earliest Church Fathers, it was formally articulated by St. Gregory Palamas in the fourteenth century in his refutation to the Western theologian Barlaam.

In Orthodox theology, salvation is not solely about the forgiveness of sin but also about the transformative healing and restoration of the human person. Western Christianity, especially in medieval Latin theology, typically understood salvation within the legal and moral terms of guilt, merit, and forgiveness. While Western theologians such as St. Augustine did speak of a form of deification, the dominant Latin tradition after Augustine focused on justification (being declared righteous before God) and sanctification (inner process of becoming holy) in a more forensic and analytical framework.[327] In Augustine's battle with Pelagianism, he stressed human depravity, teaching that humanity inherits the guilt of Adam's original sin. Augustine felt sin was in the very bones of the human race. In the Greek East, the Fathers spoke of "ancestral sin," meaning that humanity inherited the consequences of the Fall but not Adam's guilt.

By the High Middle Ages, Western Scholasticism – most notably Thomas Aquinas – systematized a created doctrine of grace in Aristotelian philosophical terms. Aquinas taught that God bestowed a created grace (*gratia creata*), which was not God Himself, but a sort of medicine for the soul that God bestows.[328] While this helped Aquinas to ensure God's transcendence, it also meant for Eastern theologians that such a doctrine limited the participatory dimension of God and made true unions impossible. Barlaam of Calabria adopted this position and led to

---

[327] Michael Pomazansky, *Orthodox Dogmatic Theology* (Platina: St. Herman of Alaska Brotherhood, 2021) "The foundation of Roman Catholic teaching lies in (a) an understanding of the sin of Adam as an infinitely great offense against God; (b) after this offense there followed the wrath of God; (c) the wrath of God was expressed by the removal of the supernatural gifts of God's grace; and (d) the removal of grace drew after itself the submission of the spiritual principle to the fleshly principle, and falling deeper into sin and death…In order to restore the order which had been violated, it was necessary first of all to give satisfaction for the offense given to God, and by this means to remove the guilt of mankind and the punishments that weighs upon him. 166-67.

[328] *The Catholic Encyclopedia*, 1913 edition, Vol. 6, Roman Catholic doctrine teaches grace is a created phenomenon: "…it is certainly not a substance which exists by itself, or apart from the soul, therefore it is a physical accident inhering to the soul… Therefore, sanctifying grace may be philosophically termed a 'permanent, supernatural quality of the soul.'" Accessed Febuary 24, 2025, https://www.ecatholic2000.com/cathopedia/vol6/volsix663.shtml.

polemical debate with St. Gregory Palamas as to whether Christians participate directly with God, or through mediated circumstances.

Orthodox theology insists that which sanctifies and illuminates the saints is not something created, but the very uncreated energies natural to the Godhead. For example, the light of Christ's transfiguration is regarded as the uncreated Light of Divinity, and makes visible God's energies within people. This notion of acquiring the Taboric Light of Christ is the basis for Hesychastic monks who seek to visibly see God's uncreated Glory. Western theology generally rejected the essence-energy distinction in the mystical theology of the Eastern Church. According to Vladimir Lossky, separation from the one synodal church in 1054 "was based dogmatically on teachings concerning the Holy Spirit, the Giver of Grace."[329] The notion that there is no real participation in the divine nature, but created mediated effects, is "the gap" that remains "unbridgeable" for both "the Church of Rome, as well as the Reformation."[330] In contrast, the Orthodox view feels they maintain the continuity of Patristic teaching that through the Incarnate Word and the Holy Spirit, God truly communicates His life to humanity, making us by grace what Christ is by nature. Participation in God is the only means of recovering the full *imago Dei* and likeness of God. Saint Athanasius of Alexandria expresses this idea famously: "For He was incarnate that we might be made god."[331]

Fr. John Meyendorff, describes these historical trends and doctrinal differences as "Byzantine theology." With its full character

---

[329] Vladimir Lossky, "The Doctrine of Grace in the Orthodox Church," in *St. Vladimir's Theological Quarterly* 58, 1 (2014) 73.
[330] Lossky, "The Doctrine of Grace in the Orthodox Church," 79.
[331] Athanasius of Alexandria, *On the Incarnation*, trans. John Behr (Yonkers, New York: St. Vladimir's Seminary Press, 2011) 107.

emerging during the post-Chalcedonian period, it received its full sanction under emperor St. Justinian (482-565) and its expression in the balanced synthesis of St. Maximus the Confessor.[332] Whereas Eastern Christian thought had previously centered mainly around Egypt and Syria, it was now Constantinople, the great cultural melting pot and capital of the "New Rome." Over the first millennium, the Bishop of Rome was accorded a primacy of honor, and the Pope was the first among equals not an absolute monarch who spoke infallibly. The Eastern Church rejected Papal authority as inconsistent with Orthodox synodality. Orthodoxy does not believe that bishops are infallible or that ecclesiological authority should be entirely centralized, and instead maintain its unity through a shared faith, sacraments, and conciliar agreement without a single controlling office. These differences in church structure still exist with regard to the ways in which the two churches resolve internal disputes. Whereas the Orthodox issue Pan-Orthodox councils to be deliberated among bishops of various jurisdictions, Catholicism utilizes authoritative Papal decrees that speak ex cathedra.

    Scholasticism, the Renaissance, and the Enlightenment left indelible marks on Western Christian thought, which Eastern Orthodoxy, largely cut off from Latin Europe after 1054, did not experience in the same way. Consequently, the East retained a patristic and mystical theological ethos, while the West was shaped by Aristotealean philosophy, humanist inquiry, and rational critique. Figures such as Anselm of Canterbury (1033-1109) and Thomas Aquinas (1225-1274) shaped a theological framework that prioritized intellectual knowledge of

---

[332] John Meyendorff, *Byzantine Theology: Historical Trends and Doctrinal Themes* (New York: Fordham University Press, 1979) 19.

God, culminating in the emphasis on the Beatific Vision as the ultimate goal of salvation. While Catholic mysticism persisted in notable figures, such as Meister Eckhart (1260-1368), John of the Cross (1542-1591) and Teresa of Ávila (1515-1582), it remained largely secondary to the predominant scholastic and legalistic frameworks of grace and salvation.

Unlike the Scholastic approach, which is characterized by rationalism and philosophical categories, Eastern theology emphasizes the apophatic mystery of God as persons who can be directly experienced. Orthodox theologians, such as Lossky and Fr. John Romanides argue that Western theology, from Augustine onward, became overly reliant on philosophical categories, such as *actus purus* (the idea of God as "pure act" with no distinctions within) which distorted Western theology into a system of philosophical speculation forever separating it from the existential living theology of Orthodox Christianity.

During the Renaissance, the West witnessed the revival of classical learning and the rise of humanism. On the one hand, Renaissance humanism sought to return to the sources, which included studying scripture in its original language as well as translations of Plato and the Hermetic Corpus. On the other hand, humanism gave rise to a more secular spirit that sometimes challenged the authority of the Papal Church. After Constantinople fell in 1453, Orthodoxy was under Ottoman rule and largely bypassed the influence of cultural humanism and the Protestant Reformation. By the time of the Synod of Jerusalem in 1672, Orthodoxy rejected both Protestant and Latin scholastic terminology in favor of the Patristic teaching on grace, free will, and sacraments. Thus, the Eastern Church saw itself as preserving the continuity of the first millennium faith, whereas the West increasingly innovated doctrines under pressure from intellectual movements and internal crises.

The Enlightenment brought about another wave of change in the West: championing reason, empirical science, and skepticism of traditional authorities. In Protestant lands this led to Deism and liberal theology, and with the rise of secularism the Catholic Church responded with condemning rationalist errors and reinforcing papal authority with Vatican I in 1870. Orthodoxy, primarily centered under the Ottoman and Russian Empires, existed on the margins of the Enlightenment with limited exposure to Western thought.[333] Thus, while Western Christianity engaged in critical questioning, even doubting miracles and revelation, Eastern Orthodoxy maintained a premodern epistemology valuing faith, Holy Tradition, and the collective wisdom of the Church. Orthodox theologians feel Western Christianity had been held captive to rationalism and human philosophy, whereas Orthodoxy "lies far distant from the Enlightenment because its approach to the human mind is so radically different."[334]

In summary, Eastern Orthodoxy's relative isolation from Scholasticism, Renaissance humanism, and Enlightenment rationalism allowed it to conserve an older theological paradigm, as the West underwent significant intellectual evolution. In Western Christian

---

[333] In Russia, Peter the Great (early 1700s) did import Western ideas and even forced some Western-style reforms in the Church (e.g. abolishing the patriarchate in favor of a Holy Synod), but Russia's theological tradition remained largely monastic and patristic in orientation, and with many reforms being condemned by the church.

[334] Archpriest Gregory Hallam, "Orthodoxy and the Enlightenment," *Pravmir* (September 10, 2012) accessed March 18, 2025, https://www.pravmir.com/orthodoxy-and-the-enlightenment/#:~:text=Orthodoxy%20and%20the%20Enlightenment%20,mind%20is%20so%20radically%20different.

thought, especially following the influence of Scholasticism, Renaissance humanism, and Enlightenment rationalism, salvation became increasingly associated with rational progress, dominance over nature, and perfection of the created order. This perspective has contributed in various degrees to modern techno-millenarian utopianism, which envisions human advancement through science, engineering, and artificial intelligence as a means of achieving redemptive transformation. This ideology, rooted in medieval and early modern Christian eschatology, manifests as a secularized form of deification, where technology becomes the instrument for restoring humanity to an exalted, even god-like state.

Therefore, this chapter attempts to elucidate the contours of the Orthodox spiritual paradigm of *theosis*, specifically as it relates to the essence-energy distinction, personhood, *Logos* theology, and Orthodoxy's premodern epistemology, metaphysics, and ethics. The Orthodox worldview is ontologically oriented, privileging personal experiences beyond the abstractions of rational thought. The focus will be directed towards the development of Orthodox theological concepts and the contributions made by Church Fathers such as St. Athanasius of Alexandria, the Cappadocian Fathers, St. Maximus the Confessor, and St. Gregory Palamas.

A. Essence-Energy Distinction: Personhood & Participation

The Patristic tradition, as exemplified by eminent theologians, such as St. Basil the Great (330-379), St. Gregory of Nyssa (335-394), St. Maximus the Confessor (580-662), and St. John of Damascus (675-749), consistently propounded the ontological distinction between God's essence (*ousia*) and His energies (*energeia*). This fundamental theological concept posits that while the divine essence remains ineffable and transcendent, God's energies – manifested through His grace, uncreated light, and sanctifying power – are immanent and accessible to creation. In his seminal work St. Basil articulates this distinction with precision: "We know our God from His operations (energies), but we do not undertake to approach near to His essence. His operations (energies) come down to us, but His essence remains beyond our reach."[335] The essence-energy distinction is the cornerstone of Orthodox mystical theology, particularly its apophatic and cataphatic dimensions. The doctrine asserts that through ascetic praxis and noetic purification, the human person can participate in *theosis*, experiencing the uncreated Taboric light – a manifestation of divine energy – as witnessed in the Transfiguration of Christ (Matthew 17:1-8). This theological framework provides a nuanced understanding of divine immanence and transcendence, reconciling God's absolute otherness with His intimate involvement in creation.

The differentiation between divine essence and energy emerged as a central theological concern during the Hesychast Controversy of the fourteenth century. This theological dispute was precipitated by the Western-educated Basilian monk Barlaam of Calabria (1290-1348), who contested the assertion that monastic practitioners could attain experiential knowledge of God's uncreated light through contemplative prayer. Barlaam posited that human apprehension of the Divine was inherently indirect and mediated through created phenomena, a stance

---

[335] Basil of Caesarea, "*Letter 234, Ad Amphilochium,*" in *Nicene and Post-Nicene Fathers*, Vol. 8, ed. Phillip Schaff (Massachusetts: Hendrickson Publishing, 1979) 762.

that effectively negated the possibility of authentic and unmediated participation in the divine life.

In response to this theological challenge, St. Gregory Palamas articulated a robust defense of the Orthodox tradition, affirming the uncreated nature of Christ's Transfiguration light and divine grace. Palamas maintained that human beings could genuinely encounter God's divine energies without compromising the absolute transcendence of divine essence. This theological position, which sought to reconcile divine immanence and transcendence, was subsequently ratified as an official Orthodox dogma by the Fifth Council of Constantinople (1341-1368). The council's proclamation affirmed the incomprehensibility and inaccessibility of God's essence while simultaneously asserting the uncreated and communicable nature of His energies, thereby preserving the possibility of authentic divine-human communion. Palamas' theological contributions and defense of Orthodox doctrine were recognized by his elevation to the archiepiscopal see of Thessalonica, a position he occupied until his death.

Hesychasm is a mystical tradition of prayer in the Eastern Orthodox Church that involves retiring inward and ceasing to register the senses in order to achieve experiential knowledge of God. Monks attempt to gain mystical knowledge by attaining inner stillness (*hesychia*), rhythmic breathing, and the uninterrupted citation of Jesus Prayer.[336] The term "naval gazers" was used to mock Christian Hesychasts, who adopted a prayer posture similar to that of the Prophet Elijah, where one prays with their head down between their knees focused towards their naval. To pray while gazing at the breast or naval "recalls into the interior

---

[336] Jesus Prayer: "Lord Jesus Christ, Son of God, have mercy on me a sinner."

of the heart a power which is ever flowing outward through the faculty of sight."[337] Such prayers attempt to recollect the mind, not only within the body and heart, but also within itself, returning to a true and proper function as a conduit of the Spirit. The result is the transformation of the entire person: Palamas writes,

> For just as those who abandon themselves to sensual and corruptible pleasure fix all the desires of their soul upon the flesh, and indeed become entirely "flesh," so that (as Scripture says) "the Spirit of God cannot dwell in them," so too, in the case of those who have elevated their minds to God and exalted their souls with divine longing, their flesh also is being transformed and elevated, participating together with the soul in the divine communion, and becoming itself a dwelling and possession of God; for it is no longer the seat of enmity towards God, and no longer possesses desires contrary to the Spirit.[338]

The light beheld by Hesychasts during prayer is identified by Palamas with the same light shone around Christ at the Transfiguration on Mount Tabor. This light is not a created symbol but a light that illuminates the blessed, acting as a garment of their deification. The uncreated light is beheld not by sensory power but by spiritual intellect, the nous, and then through bodily eyes. Common descriptions of illuminated saints in the Orthodox tradition describe them as "glowing" and are filled with the light of God. Due to their holiness and participation

---

[337] Gregory Palamas, *The Triads* (New Jersey: Paulist Press, 1983) 47.
[338] Palamas, *Triads*, 48.

with uncreated energies, it is believed that Christ's transfigured light operates within and through them.

In Orthodox anthropology, the human person is a tripartite composition of the body, soul, and *nous*. Orthodox anthropology presents a holistic and synergistic understanding of the human person, emphasizing the unity of the body, soul, and *nous*. The *nous* (νοῦς), often referred to as the "eye of the soul" is the faculty that allows for direct participation and communion with God. Noetic faculties are not found within the emergent property of mind or the synaptic connections of brain matter, as believed by transhumanists, but rather reside within the heart. Orthodox theology teaches that individual sin and the transgression of moral law cause a clouding and dulling of the noetic faculties, leading to spiritual blindness, impaired judgement, and enslavement of passions. By way of the Fall of Adam and Eve, the *nous* is believed to have become darkened and scattered, only through *theosis*, the ontological transformation of the person – made possible after the incarnation of Christ – is the *nous* restored back to its natural illuminated state.

In Orthodox anthropology, the body is not seen as inherently sinful but rather as an essential aspect of human personhood that is meant to be sanctified and ultimately transfigured in resurrection. Unlike Platonic dualism, which views the body as a prison for the soul, Orthodox theology affirms that the soul and body are intrinsically united, and that spiritual life requires the discipline and purification of both. Through fasting, prayer, and participation in the Sacraments of the Church, the body is realigned with the soul's noetic function, allowing the *nous* to perceive a divine reality that the rational mind alone cannot.

The distinction between *nous* and rational intellect (dianoia) is one of the fundamental differences between Eastern Orthodox anthropology and Western Christian theological traditions. This distinction is best summarized in the debate between Barlaam of Calabria and St. Gregory Palamas. In Western Scholasticism, particularly in Augustinian and Thomistic theology, there is a tendency to equate the *nous* with rational intellect, emphasizing intellectual contemplation rather than mystical participation in God's uncreated energies. The Orthodox tradition, however, insists that true knowledge of God, *theoria* (θεωρία) is not an intellectual exercise but a direct, experiential encounter with divine grace. Therefore, the premodern Orthodox epistemology of knowing is ontologically centered, where personal virtue, faith, and the grace of God allow intellectual insight outside the confines of rationalism alone.

The term *energeia* was first coined by Aristotle. He set the stage for the concept of *energeia* to be adapted and reworked through Neoplatonism, St. Paul, and the Cappadocian Fathers.[339] Aristotle's early works use it to refer to the active exercise of a capacity, such as sight or thought, and it is distinct from mere possession of capacity. In *Metaphysics*, Aristotle distinguishes *energeia* from mere motion or change on the basis that they are ordered towards an extrinsic end.[340] While housebuilding aims to build a house, *energeia* is its own end. Aristotle provides the examples of seeing, thinking, understanding, flourishing, and living well. Although these are activities, they are fully actual in the sense that they contain their own ends and are complete at

---

[339] The "Cappadocian Fathers" is a trio of Byzantine theologians including St. Basil of Caesarea, his younger brother St. Gregory of Nyssa, and St. Gregory of Nazianzus (later Patriarch of Constantinople).
[340] Aristotle, *Metaphysics*, Book IX, Ch. 6.

each moment of their existence, rather than their completion being dependent on time.

Interestingly, Aristotle applied *energeia* to his Prime Mover theory. The Prime Mover, the first cause of all things, is a being whose substance is *energeia*. As philosopher David Bradshaw illustrates, this is true in three distinct but related senses. First, "since the Prime Mover is posited to explain motion, it cannot itself be subject to motion, and thus is pure actuality in the sense of having no potentiality to change or be acted upon." Second, "because its activity of causing motion must be continuous and eternal, it can have no unrealized capacities." The third sense has to do with what the Prime Mover does; namely Aristotle's famous theory that the Prime Mover is a "self-thinking thought, a being whose 'thought is a thinking of thinking.'" This implies the third sense in which the Prime Mover is *energeia*, "this time in the sense of activity rather than actuality: namely, the Prime Mover's substance is nothing other than the self-subsistent activity of thought."[341]

The point being made is not to dwell on Aristotle's conception of the Prime Mover, but to address the various senses in which *energeia* is understood. The Prime Mover is a being that both thinks and is all possible intelligible content, and exists as a single eternal unchanging whole. The Aristotelean doctrine that form is substance means that intelligible forms of things find their origin in the Prime Mover.

> In light of all this, when we say that the Prime Mover is pure *energeia*, how ought we to translate that term? Activity? Actuality? Plainly the answer is both – and

---

[341] David Bradshaw, *Divine Energies and Divine Action: Exploring the Essence-Energies Distinction* (St. Paul, Minnesota: Iota Publications, 2023) 3-4.

therefore neither. It seems to me that the closest we can come in English is to say that it is pure energy... But of course no illustration drawn from ordinary objects will be adequate to the notion of a being that is pure energy, and energy which constitutes the being of other beings.[342]

The relevance of how this relates to the patristic formation of the essence-energy distinction becomes clearer when we examine how *energeia* is reworked within Neoplatonism. Neoplatonism understood the first principle in a radically different way, more in line with Plato's work. In the *Republic*, Plato states that the Good "is not being, but superior to it in rank and power."[343] From the time of Parmenides, Greek philosophy understood being and intelligibility as one and the same thing. However, Neoplatonists have deduced that if the Good is beyond being, it must also exist beyond intelligibility. This was the conclusion of Neoplatonists while ignoring other aspects of the *Republic*, which implied that the Good is, in fact, an intelligible object.

In addition, Parmenides described the One as having "no limits or shape, is neither at rest nor in motion, it neither is like nor unlike anything else or even itself, and finally that it does not partake of being, has no name, and is not an object of knowledge, perception, or opinion."[344] Combining this with Aristotle telling us that Plato argued that the One, in conjunction with the dyad, is the source of the Ideal Forms.[345]

---

[342] Bradshaw, *Divine Energies*, 5.
[343] Plato, "Republic," in *Plato: Complete Works*, ed. John M. Cooper (Indianapolis: Hackett Publishing Company, 1997) 1130.
[344] Bradshaw, *Divine Energies*, 6.
[345] Aristotle, *The Basic Works of Aristotle*, ed. Richard McKeon (New York: The Modern Library, 2001) "Metaphysics," I.6. 988a10, 702,

Placing these pieces together, Neoplatonists concluded that the One of Parmenides and the Good of Plato were identical.

The novelty of the Neoplatonic formation is a significant departure from the Aristotlean position, leading to an unknowable, unnamable, source of being, which itself is beyond Being, and is the Good that all things seek. Plotinus was the first to achieve this synthesis between the Platonic conception and that of Aristotle. Plotinus identified the One/Good as his ultimate first principle and rebranded Aristotle's Prime Mover as Intellect (νοῦς), the first hypostasis after the One. For Plotinus, the One is not any particular being, because it is the source of all particular beings. By its goodness, the One gives rise to the Intellect, which in turn is, in all things, their being, intelligibility, and life. Plotinus believed that the Intellect's thought is in a sense directed towards the One, and due to the unknowability of the One and its unity, it refracts into intelligible Ideal Forms. In the Plotininan synthesis, generally speaking, the One is described in apophatic terms of what it is not, while the Intellect is described in cataphatic terms.

The most important point concerns Plotinus with regard to the concept of *energeia*. Whereas Aristotle argued that the Prime Mover is pure energy, Plotinus posits that the Intellect comes from the One as its external energy, what Plotinus refers to as *energeia ek tēs ousias*, the energy which comes forth from substance. This is a reformulation and attempt to clarify Aristotle's conundrum as to whether the substance itself is a kind of energy. The Intellect of Plotinus is described as an energy that is solely dependent on the substance of the One. Here, we have the first formation of a substance that is distinct and separate from energetic procession.

As we now turn to St. Paul's usage of *energeia* and *energein*, we see it used in regard to spiritual agents, such God, Satan, and demons. Within the Hellenistic context, *energeia* often meant "activity" or "operation." Although earlier sources, such as the Septuagint and Philo of Alexandria, used the term *energeia* to refer to the actions of material objects, human beings, natural elements, and spiritual beings,[346] Paul's use was so striking that it set a new precedent within subsequent Christian literature. The twelve instances of the two terms (*energeia* and *energein*) in the Apostolic Fathers refer to the energetic actions of God, Jesus Christ, angels or demons. For example, in *The Shepherd of Hermas*, purity, holiness, and contentment are *energeia* of the angel of righteousness, whereas pride, gluttony, and lust are *energeia* of the angel of wickedness.[347]

In the Christian context, the words *energeia* and *energein* connote new meanings. *Energeia* refers to the capacity for an action, and *energein* refers to being active in a way that imparts energy.[348] This usage can be found among some early Greek Apologists. In his *First Apology*, St. Justin Martyr (100-165) refers to Moses being inspired by the energy of God so that he "took brass, and made it into the figure of a cross," while Simon Magus was able to perform magic due to the energizing skill of the demons.[349] By the third century, the use of *energeia*, as an activity or operation, and *energein*, to be active or operate, had become their

---

[346] David Bradshaw, *Aristotle East and West: Metaphysics and the Division of Christendom* (Cambridge: Cambridge University Press, 2004) 51-60.

[347] *The Shepherd of Hermas*, ed. Daniel Robinson (CreateSpace Independent Publishing, 2013) 26-7.

[348] Bradshaw, *Divine Energies*, 10.

[349] Justin Martyr, "First Apology," *in Ante-Nicene Fathers*, Vol. 1, ed. Phillip Schaff (Massachusetts: Hendrickson Publishing, 1979) Ch.LX, and Ch. XXVI.

accepted meanings. Describing the event of Pentecost, David Bradshaw writes,

> For example, in the *Apostolic Constitutions* the author, speaking as one of the Apostles, states that on Pentecost "the Lord Jesus sent us the gift of the Holy Spirit, and we were filled with his energy and spoke with new tongues." To render this statement as "we were filled with his activity" would fail convey its clear import, which is that the Holy Spirit was actively present in the apostles imparting a new capacity for action.[350]

Bradshaw highlights, unlike Apostolic Fathers and Greek Apologists, many scholars have failed to see how Paul does not reserve the middle/passive form of *energeia, energeisthai,* for spiritual agents. Taking *energeisthai* as a middle verb, as often translated, would mean that the subject of whom it is used would include "the motions of sin," comfort, power, death, faith, the divine energeia, the Word of God, and the "mystery of iniquity."[351] Therefore, it is somewhat perplexing that Paul consistently implements the noun and active tense while using the middle form in an apparently random fashion. However, when analyzing *energeisthai* usage within antiquity, it becomes clear that it is never a middle verb but only passive, and was understood as passive by the Church Fathers. From this perspective, the meaning of *energeisthai* becomes a correlative to *energein*, meaning "to be acted upon," or "to be energized."

---

[350] Bradshaw, *Divine Energies*, 10.
[351] See Rom 7:5; 2 Cor 1:6; Gal 5:6; Eph 3:20; Col 1:29; 1 Thess 2:13; 2Thess 2:7.

An example of Paul's use of *energeisthai* can be found in Colossians 1:29. Paul writes, "To this end I also labor, striving according to His working (or energy, ενέργεια), which works (or energized, ἐνεργουμένην) in me mightily." This verse highlights the synergistic ontology indicative of Paul's thought. Paul is demonstrating that he is the object of God's activity, as the divine energy is working within him and transforming him; while at the same time, this passage is expressing Paul's own activity, in which Paul's free will and that of God becomes one in the same. Another example is Philippians, 2:13. "For it is God who works in you (ὁ ἐνεργῶν ἐν ὑμῖν) both to will and to do (ἐνεργεῖν) of His good pleasure." Here, incitement to act is combined with the reminder that God is the one acting. While the Philippines are both free agents responsible for working out their salvation with fear and trembling, they are also acted upon by God, whose energy brings about their trajectory towards salvation. This passage explains why, for Paul, there is no contradiction in urging believers to do something that he also sees as the energetic work of God. The nature of God's activity is that it imparts the divine energy to do His will, while also requiring the complicit free will of a person to "work out" this energy to be effective.

When addressing Paul's synergistic work with God, it would be false to assume that it entails equal agents choosing to work together. As God is a transcendent creator and humanity is a creature, the latter depends on its contingent existence through the active support of the former. The synergy of God's divine energies is neither a symmetrical relationship nor an overpowering of divinity in which it replaces human agency. Rather, it is one in which a person becomes fully human by embracing the divine *telos* of his being. To obey divine commandments involves fully actualizing one's identity by affirming a cooperative relationship with God's creative intent. This divine relationship is not novel, as it is a prominent theme in the Old Testament, as seen in Psalm 1 and 51. What is new is the use of *energeia* to express this synergistic dynamic.

Now, we turn our focus to the formulation of the essence-energy distinction, as presented by the Greek Church Fathers, most specifically St. Basil the Great. Basil had the apologetic task of replying to Eunomius, an Arian theologian who argued that the *ousia* (essence) of God the Father is utterly simple and unique, and therefore could not be shared by the begotten *Logos*. For Eunomius, this diminution of Jesus Christ as not sharing the same essence as the Father resulted in an Arian Christological formulation. The Eunomian heretics believed that any attribute used to describe God signifies a description of God's essence and therefore could not be shared with a creature. Basil rejected the assumption that the divine essence of God could be known, and in turn, rejected that any attribute of God becomes identical in meaning. Rather, Basil maintained St. Paul's division between the knowable energies and attributes of God, and His transcendent and unknowable essence. In Letter 234, St. Basil's refutes Eunomius' Arianism by writing,

> We say that we know the greatness of God, His power, His wisdom, His goodness, His providence over us, and the justness of His judgement; but not His very essence… But God, he [Eunomius] says, is simple, and whatever attribute of Him you have reckoned as knowable is of His essence. But the absurdities involved in this sophism are innumerable. When all these high attributes have been enumerated, are they all names of one essence? And is

there the same mutual force in His awfulness and His loving-kindness, His justice and His creative power, His foreknowledge, and His bestowal of rewards and punishments, His majesty and His providence? In mentioning any one of these do we declare His essence? …The energies are various, and the essence simple, but we say that we know our God from His energies, but do not undertake or approach near to His essence. His energies come down to us, but His essence remains beyond our reach.[352]

Here, Basil clarifies that the Christian God maintained a distinction between his *ousia* and *energeia*. Eunomius was not alone in the thinking of God as a simple essence was entirely knowable, this position was shared by some Gnostics such as Valentinus (100-180) in the second century. Other heretics of antiquity, such as Marcion of Sinope (85-160) fell into the extreme opposite position, arguing that God is completely unknown and totally inaccessible to human thought.[353]

In Basil's formulation, energies are not separate hypostases, but energetic acts natural to the essence of God. Many scholars have chosen to translate *energeia* in the above passage as "operation," meaning only God's operations come down to us. In Basil's brother, St. Gregory of Nyssa, we see a view that was widespread in antiquity, in which names, in some ways, are indicative of the form and intrinsic character of the thing named. Gregory argues "that the divine nature has no extension or limit, and therefore cannot be named. But rather than referring to the

---

[352] Basil, *"Letter 234,"* in *Nicene and Post-Nicene Fathers*, 762.
[353] Pomazansky, *Orthodox Dogmatic Theology*, 59.

names said of God to the divine works or powers, he refers them to the divine *energeia*."[354] Although Gregory understands these as divine operations, they cannot only be operations, for it would entail when speaking of God we would only be speaking of an operation of an operation, leading to an infinite regress. Instead, *energeia*, for Basil and Gregory, comes to mean both that which God is and that which God performs.

Since its introduction by Aristotle, *energeia* has specified the energy God is and does. Plotinus refined Aristotle's depiction by distinguishing between internal and external acts, and Basil and Gregory differentiated between God's knowability and unknowability. As David Bradshaw writes,

> For them the relevant distinction is rather that between God *as he exists within himself and is known only to himself*, and God *as he manifests himself to others*. The former is the divine *ousia*, the latter the divine energies. It is important to note that both are God, but differently conceived: God as unknowable and as knowable, as wholly beyond us and as within our reach.[355]

This doctrine makes it possible to understand how the Holy Trinity can remain incommunicable in essence and, at the same time, come to dwell within us, as promised by Christ (John 14:23). The doctrine of energies, ineffably distinct from God's essence, is the theological basis of the real character of all mystical experiences. In

---

[354] Bradshaw, *Aristotle East and West*, 163.
[355] Bradshaw, *Divine Energies*, 16.

union with God through His energies, we participate in divine nature without our essence becoming the essence of God. As Vladimir Lossky writes, "In deification we are by grace all that God is by nature, save only identity of nature… We remain creatures while becoming God by grace, as Christ remained God in becoming man by the incarnation."[356]

However, the distinction between essence and energy does not imply a fixed or permanent boundary. Instead, the Cappadocians approach God's unknowability as a receding horizon, drawing Christians forward to know Him more deeply. It is this journeying towards God (*theosis*) by a synergistic engagement with the uncreated energies of God that leads to wonder, purification, and restoration of our likeness to God (*homoiōsis theōi*). This formation echoes those of both Aristotle and Plato. Aristotle believed that it was philosophy that brings a sense of wonder, and Plato emphasized the need for a purified soul. A theme found in both philosophers is that human *telos* is acquired by attaining likeness to God.

Nevertheless, the Cappadocian formulation of the essence-energy distinction is not derived from philosophy but from scripture itself. The Cappadocians witnessed the knowable unknowability of God in the theophanies of the Old Testament. Most obviously, Moses, when encountering the burning bush is told "You cannot see My face; for no man shall see Me and live."[357] The ways we come to know God are immensely different from how God eternally knows Himself. The chasm between the contingent being of humanity and the noncontingent being

---

[356] Lossky, *The Mystical Theology of the Eastern Church* (Crestwood, New York: St. Vladimir's Seminary Press, 1997) 87.
[357] Exodus 33:20.

of God means that we can only glimpse the backside of the Almighty and not perceive the full face (essence) of divinity. The limitation is not in God Himself but in Moses' ability to apprehend Him. Despite this limitation, we observe in the Exodus narrative that upon encountering the burning bush, Moses' face was glowing with the divine light of God.[358] So much so that it disturbed the Israelites, causing Moses to veil his face. This passage is indicative of the synergistic participation we have with God's uncreated energies, in which His uncreated light shines forth from His saints. As Paul notes in 2 Corinthians 3:7-11, how much more glorious this light is with the ministry of the Holy Spirit.

In light of the Pauline usage of *energeia*, we can see that the doctrine of *theosis* or deification is not a foreign introduction, but one found in scripture. The specific goal of the Christian is to purify the soul of the passions that alienate it from God, thereby restoring the divine image and likeness of God in humans. The synergistic engagement with divine energies cleanses the noetic faculties so that the soul can more clearly see the divine model and reflect that model in the outer world. When Athanasius says Christ "was made man in order that we might be made god," he describes the grace-filled telos of humanity's creation. *Theosis* is not something reserved for the afterlife but a description of the gifts of the Holy Spirit here and now.

Notably, the Eastern Orthodox understanding of divine participation avoids the philosophical shortcomings of Pagan

---

[358] Exodus 34:29-31, "Now it was so, when Moses came down from Mount Sinai (and the two tablets of the Testimony *were* in Moses' hand when he came down from the mountain), that Moses did not know that the skin of his face shone while he talked with Him. So when Aaron and all the children of Israel saw Moses, behold, the skin of his face shone, and they were afraid to come near him."

Neoplatonism. For Plotinus, we neither "participate" in the Intellect or the One but rather rediscover our emanated unfallen identity as Intellect, which shares in the unity-in-multiplicity of Intellect. An analogy Bradshaw offers is the light of many lamps sharing in the totality of the room's light as a whole. In rediscovering our true identity as Intellect, Plotinus believed that we left behind the accidents of memory, personality, and our individual characteristics to merge into perfect noetic activity. This is a Neoplatonic concept known as *henosis*, the mystical goal of total unification with the One. This impersonal conception of the human being never arises as a problem to be delt with for the Cappadocians. The distinction between essence and energy sets the foundation for human-divine communion as a joint personal activity. As we become deified by God's energies, one does not lose or diminish their unique and unrepeatable personal identity. In fact, we fully obtain the fullness of our personal identity when we align our activities with God. When Christ bows His head and gives up His spirit on the cross in John 19:30, He states, "It is finished." According to the Church, this is better understood as "accomplished," referring to the completion of God's divine plan for salvation and the rescue of human nature from its fallen state.

In Eastern Orthodox theology, the concept of personhood (*hypostasis*) is foundational and intricately connected to the doctrines of the Trinity, the essence-energy distinction, and *theosis*. Personhood transcends mere individuality, emphasizing relational existence and communion, reflecting the tri-personal nature of God—Father, Son, and Holy Spirit—who share one essence (*ousia*) yet exist as distinct persons (*hypostases*). The essence-energy distinction safeguards the integrity of divine personhood by ensuring that communion with God is a personal encounter with His energies, rather than an absorption into His essence.

God as a person is the hypostasis of being. The church does not identify God as an abstract first cause of existence and not as an impersonal essence that may be approached only through intellect or emotions. Nor is He a "prime mover," a blind energy that sets in motion the mechanism of the world. Rather, God reveals Himself in historical time as a personal existence. It is precisely as personal existence, as distinctiveness and freedom from any predetermination by essence, that God constitutes the *hypostasis* of being. In describing God's divine personhood as revealed, philosopher Christos Yannaras writes,

> When Moses asks the identity of the God whose will he is to proclaim to the Israelites, the answer is "I am He who is" (Ex 3:14). God identifies the truth of existence, the reality of being, with His personal hypostasis. This means that the divine essence or nature is not an ontological reality prior to God's personal existence and determining it: God's being is not an ontological datum, anterior to the distinctiveness and freedom of the divine person. Rather, it is the personal hypostasis of God which is the comprehensive and exhaustive expression of His being.[359]

Moreover, the communal dimension of personhood reflects the trinitarian model of unity and diversity. Just as the three divine persons

---

[359] Christos Yannars, *The Freedom of Morality* (Crestwood, New York: St. Vladimir's Seminary Press, 1984) 17.

exist in perfect communion, human persons are called relational existence, both with God and with one another. This relational ontology emphasizes that true personhood is realized not in isolation, but in loving relationships, mirroring the divine communion. All human persons share the same human essence, yet exist and obtain their unique individuality through their particular hypostasis within human nature. People come to know others through energetic actions and activities. When friends come to know one another as honest, compassionate, thoughtful, or hardworking, their energies reflect these actions as natural to who they are. Conversely, if someone is seen as deceitful, malicious, or selfish, it is due to the observation that those actions are indicative of who they are. We do not know the essence of other persons, even when sharing the same nature; rather, we come to know people through their energetic expressions of the self. In the same sense, given the hypostatic understanding of the Trinity, humans come to know the persons of the Holy Trinity through their energies and not through a rational apprehension of their divine essence.

Although subtle and philosophically nuanced, it is the essence-energy distinction and this relational ontology of personhood that provides a different epistemic basis for the knowledge of God between Eastern and Western Christianity. In the Eastern tradition, human participation in God begins in this life and engages the body as much as the soul. Christians come to know who God is through engagement with His uncreated energies, divinizing us in the here and now, while simultaneously leading to a purer and richer state of existence in the afterlife. In the Thomistic view, Thomas Aquinas argues in the afterlife that God will infuse the blessed with the "light of glory" *lumen gloriae*, which will enable them to apprehend the divine essence. Aquinas adopts an Aristotelian framework in which he argues that God, as a pure act, must be intrinsically intelligible and identifies the telos of human existence as the intellectual apprehension of the divine essence. The degree to which one apprehends God is determined by the person's virtue and charity in this life; nevertheless, it is ultimately an intellectual act.[360]

In the East, God is beyond knowing itself, including within the eternal realm of Heaven, whereas Aquinas equates God to the highest intelligible object. Aquinas was aware of these disagreements, and in *De Veritate*, cites a list of objections by St. Dionysius and St. John of Damascus concerning the ability of seeing God's essence. Aquinas understands this limitation as a condition to our current ways of knowing, and within eternity, the angels and ourselves could perceive God as He really is.[361] The resurrected body plays a less significant role for Aquinas than the tradition of the East, and in the *Summa Theologiae* states explicitly the resurrected body is not essential for beatitude.[362] The point being made is that the personal participatory dimension of divine communion, as taught by the Orthodox Church, is essentially understood as an intellectual act within Thomism. Often, Latin philosophy first considers nature and then proceeds to the agent, whereas Greek philosophy first considers the agent and then moves towards nature. "The

---

[360] Anna Williams, *The Ground of Union: Deification in Aquinas and Palamas* (Oxford: Oxford University Press, 1999) 38-9.

[361] Thomas Aquinas, *De Veritate*, Question 8, article 1, accessed February 19, 2025, https://catholiclibrary.org/library/view?docId=/Medieval-EN/XCT.024.html&chunk.id=00000011.

[362] Thomas Aquinas, *Summa Theologiae*, Book II, Question 4, Article 5, accessed February 19, 2025, https://catholiclibrary.org/library/view?docId=Synchronized-EN/XCT.017.html;chunk.id=00000740.

Latins think of personality as a mode of nature; the Greeks think of nature as the content of the person."[363]

A secondary point regarding theological differences between the East and West relates to divine simplicity and God's divine freedom. Both Augustine and Aquinas agree that all non-relational and non-private predicates of God signify divine essence in different ways. The implication is that God's will becomes identical to His essence. The question then, since Christianity assumes God is totally free, could God will differently than he does, and if so, does that mean His essence would be different? If we assume that there is some aspect of God's essence that could be different, for example divine goodness, that would imply there would need to be a distinction within the essence between that which could change and that which could not. However, if anything contradicts divine simplicity, it is such a distinction within God's essence. In addition, if the divine will is identical to God's essence, it would mean that the divine will cannot in any way be a response to the act of creatures based on their own initiatives. Aquinas recognized this problem but still affirmed that God's will is not in any way a response to creatures but is determined solely by Himself. This formulation calls into question God's response to traditional religious practices, such as petitionary prayers, sacrifice, and righteous attempts to please God. How efficacious are these religious activities if they have no bearing on God's judgements of us? Therefore, Aquinas adopts the Augustinian interpretation of predestination as not only true but also necessarily true, since God could not create creatures who were able to affect His judgements regarding our salvation or damnation.[364]

---

[363] Vladimir Lossky, *The Mystical* Theology, 58.
[364] Aquinas, *Summa Theologiae*, Book 1, Question 19, articles 5-6.

From this perspective, the Augustinian-Thomistic God, who is fully actual and perfectly simple, is confined within boundaries, preventing Him from meaningful interactions with His creatures. An alternative to such theoretical limitations is the essence-energy distinction. The Greek Fathers understand simplicity as another divine energy, one of the many ways in which God manifests Himself in His activity. As in the case of God's energy, it is both simple and beyond simplicity as its source. The light of the sun is experienced by a multitude of rays, but it is simple. The same is true of God's divine simplicity, which possesses an indefinite multitude of divine energies. These energies are essential for the communal reciprocity of Orthodox *theosis*, in which God shares Himself with creatures to offer themselves to Him.

> … where Aquinas argues that since God wills all that He wills in a single act – one that is identical to the divine essence – there can be no cause of His willing as He does. Divine simplicity is thus the ultimate reason why creatures can contribute nothing to their own salvation. The situation is much like that which confronted us in regard to the participation of creatures in essence: since there can be no true synergy, all that remains is that the relationship of grace be an extrinsic one founded on efficient cause.[365]

By placing humanity's intellectual capabilities as the site of union between the creature and the Creator, the rational foundations for techno-

---

[365] Bradshaw, *Aristotle East and West*, 254.

millenrairanism are set. Although Augustine and Aquinas are not techno-millenarians, their theological influence and insistence on rational capabilities and created grace aided in its development. By demeaning the body's role in divine participation, mental faculties are understood to unite us with God. This has led to a different anthropological focus. Emphasizing rational apprehension as a divine act. Therefore, the Baconian insistence on the advancement of science and technology became a way in which men demonstrate their spiritual *gnosis* in the practical application of such knowledge for the betterment of society.

Likewise, transhumanism views the body as defective and in turn places an emphasis on the functional capabilities of the human person. This formation reduces the human person to nothing but mental inputs and outputs, and is believed to be the site of union with god-like technology. Rational means of engineering can be seen as devotional acts that have facilitated the evolution of technology to rescue the human species. Orthodox Christianity's insistence on the body and soul as active participants in God signifies an important difference in the methodology of deification. Noetic faculties are not seen as privileged sites of divine communion, but the constitution of the whole person is the site of engagement. Through the essence-energy distinction, God's unknowable essence remains transcendent, and His knowable energy is immanent. We embody uncreated virtues that energize the person to experience reality beyond the confines of reason and matter.

B. Logos Theology

The concept of *Logos* has undergone significant evolution, originating in ancient Greek philosophy and culminating in its profound theological interpretation within Eastern Orthodox Christianity. *Logos* was a philosophical concept that played an important role in the works of Heraclitus, Plato, Aristotle, the Stoics, and Philo of Alexandria. As will be discussed regarding each philosophical tradition, *Logos* was generally understood as a created underlying principle of order and knowledge that governed the cosmos. When St. John the Theologian makes the novel move of elevating the *Logos* as the uncreated second person of the Trinity, he unites this Greek philosophical concept with the long-awaited Messiah of the prophetic tradition. "In the beginning was the Word [*Logos*], and the Word [*Logos*] was with God, and the Word [*Logos*] was God. He was in the beginning with God. All things were made through Him, and without Him nothing was made that has been made" (John 1:1-3). What follows is a brief explication on the development of the philosophical and theological history of *Logos* and how it pertains to Orthodox Christology and the doctrine of *theosis*.

Heraclitus of Ephesus (535–475 BC) introduced the term "*Logos*" to denote the underlying principle of order and knowledge the governs the cosmos. Heraclitus was the first philosopher to employ the term in its special philosophical and metaphysical meaning. A central problem that Heraclitus dealt with was reconciling the unity of opposites in the face of continual temporal and material changes. He believed that all things happen according to "*Logos*," and understood the world and all phenomena as a collection of unified things ordered and regulated by the *Logos*. He perceived the universe as a constant flux, with *logos* serving as the rational structure that ensures coherence amid change.[366] Heraclitus's fragments suggest that, while the world appears in perpetual

---

[366] Marian Hillar, *From Logos to Trinity: The Evolution of Religious Beliefs From Pythagoras to Tertullian* (Cambridge: Cambridge University Press, 2012) 10.

transformation, it is unified and directed by this universal reason. This idea is encapsulated in his assertion that "No man ever steps in the same river twice," highlighting the perpetual change overseen by the *Logos*.

Anaxagoras of Clazomenae (500-428 BC) was the first philosopher to assume Mind (*Nous*) to be another term closely related to *Logos*, and thus a rational principle and the first cause of all things.[367] He believed that every substance was eternal and nonparticulate. He believed that the cosmos originated through the separation produced by the cosmic force of Mind. However, the cosmic Mind of Anaxagoras remains an impersonal force devoid of personal agency.

Building upon this foundation, Plato (428–348 BC) expanded the notion of *Logos* within his theory of Ideal Forms. In dialogues such as the *Timaeus*, Plato posits that the Demiurge, a divine craftsman, employs the *Logos* as a blueprint to shape the cosmos, aligning it with eternal and perfect Forms. Plato's philosophy is a strict dichotomy that divides reality into Being and Becoming. Here, the *Logos* functions as the intermediary between the transcendent realm of Forms and the tangible world of matter, facilitating the manifestation of ideal archetypes in material reality. Plato understood the sensible world as a product of the intelligent action of its Maker, described variously as the One, Good, or Mind. The Creator's motive for the creation of our world was to make all things as good as possible because he (the Creator) was good and wanted all things to be like himself.

Plato, like many pre-Socratics and Stoics, saw the world as a living creature imbued with intelligence and soul. When fashioning intelligence, Plato believed the Maker implanted reason (νοῦς) into the

---

[367] Jonathan Barnes, *Early Greek Philosophy* (Harmondsworth: Penguin Books, 1987) 226-239.

soul (ψυχή) and the soul into the body (σῶμα). The world soul is understood as an intelligence that permeates the world and is needed in the Platonic system as a continuous force that causes regular motion. Plato posited a two-mind theory, one being the transcendent deity, and the other being the permeating *Logos* of the universe.[368]

Aristotle (384–322 BC) offers a distinct perspective by emphasizing empirical observations and logic. While he did not focus on the metaphysical *Logos* as his predecessors did, Aristotle's exploration of rational discourse (*logos*) in his *Rhetoric* underscores the importance of reasoned argumentation in human communication. He identified *logos* as one of the three modes of persuasion, alongside ethos and pathos, highlighting its role in appealing to logic and reason.

Stoic philosophers further developed the concept by identifying *Logos* as a pervasive, divine reason immanent in all things, orchestrating the natural order, and embedding rationality within the fabric of existence. Stoic *Logos* is both the source of all activities and the law governing the cosmos, imbuing it with purpose and coherence. Like Aristotle, Stoics assumed that reality is composed of the fundamental principles of matter and form. While matter is passive, form is active and constitutes the nature of beings. *Logos* was an active principle that enliven and vitalized creatures through its *pneuma*, breath, or spirit.[369]

Stoicism was the most important development in Hellenistic philosophy, and influenced early Christian writers and theologians. Like Plato, Stoics considered the world a living creature governed by a rational principle, the *Logos*. To be happy and good means for Stoics to live a rational and virtuous life, thereby aligning themselves to the governing

---

[368] Hillar, *From Logos to Trinity*, 21.
[369] Hillar, *From Logos to Trinity*, 25.

Logos of creation. However, Stoic *Logos* stands in sharp contrast to the personal God of the Christian tradition. At the same time, we can see similarities to Christian thought in so far as the *Logos* providentially allows for the best of all possible conditions, is the source of underlying order, imbues rationality into creation, and through the moral ideal of the virtuous person aligns themselves fully with the *Logos*.

Furthermore, greater similarities to Christian doctrine emerge when we analyze the development of the Middle Platonist Philo of Alexandria's concept of *Logos*. Philo was a Hellenized Jew who spanned the divide between Greek and Hebrew cultures. In Philo, we see the transformation of the Stoic impersonal and immanent *Logos* into a being who was not created, but begotten from eternity.[370] Upon reading Old Testament scripture, Philo concludes that there was indeed a second divine power in Heaven. Philo perceived Old Testament theophanies as encounters with God's Word and Messenger, the *Logos*. When God communicates with His creation, He does so through His *Logos*. Jewish belief in a second power in Heaven was not unique to Philo, but is believed to have been common during the second temple period of Judaism. This concept has been further explicated in contemporary scholarship regarding the "Two Powers in Heaven" theory, which argues that the belief of more than one singular power in heaven was common among ancient Jews and early Christians.[371]

---

[370] Hillar, *From Logos to Trinity*, 67.
[371] See Alan Segal, *Two Powers in Heaven: Early Rabbinic Report About Christianity and Gnosticism* (Waco, Texas, Baylor University Press, 2012), Daniel Boyarin, *Border Lines: The Partition of Judeo-Christianity* (Philadelphia: University of Pennsylvania Press, 2007), Peter Schäfer, *Two Gods in Heaven: Jewish Concepts of God in Antiquity* (Princeton: Princeton University Press, 2020).

In Philo's construction, the *Logos* becomes the second individual derived from one God as the hypostatization of God's creative power.[372] *Logos* was synonymous with Wisdom, and Philo believed that as we acquire the Wisdom of God, we, as creatures, can hope to attain some likeness to God the Father of all. *Logos* then constitutes an unbreakable bond and mediator of the universe that produces harmony. Thus, from Philo's perspective, the Father is the supreme Being and the *Logos* was His chief messenger standing between the Creator and creatures. *Logos*, as described by Philo, was the cupbearer who pours Himself into souls, so the divine breath of the Father may animate the bodies of creatures. Christians later understood this function as the role of the Holy Spirit.

After Philo, we arrive at the formation of Christian doctrine and the full incorporation of *Logos* into the revealed reality as the incarnation of Jesus Christ. The Johannine *Logos*, as expressed in the prologue of the Gospel of John, is nonphilosophical. It is rooted in the Old Testament doctrine of the Word (Davar = Logos) as the expression of God in the creation, and is revealed in Christ's theophanies. Even though John's *Logos* is scripturally based, it does not mean that early Christian apologists, such as St. Justin Martyr did not use Greek philosophical language to further articulate the Second person of the Trinity as the incarnated God.

In his apologetic defense of Christian theology, Justin Martyr incorporated the Stoic concept of *Logos Spermatikos*: the idea that the seeds of *Logos* – meaning its rationality, order, and morality – can be found in various places and times. Justin utilized the analogy of the Sower and Seed to describe the way in which the rational part of the

---

[372] Hillar, *From Logos to Trinity*, 69.

human constitution, or the rational soul, is carried out by the noetic fragment of the divine *Logos*, Jesus Christ. Justin makes clear that the *logos* that is in each man, by way of being made in the image of God, is not just the mere instrument of human reason, but the power and presence of God Himself. He contrasts the difference between non-Christians and Christians by highlighting the fullness and degree to which they could come to know the *Logos* as God. When men sought to live morally and rationally, it was the seed of Christ within them that brought wisdom. For example, Justin held Socrates in particularly high regard, claiming that Socrates knew Christ partially, for "He (Christ) was and is the *Logos* who is in every man, and who foretold the things that were to come to pass both through the prophets and in His own person when He assumed our Nature, and taught these things."[373]

Socrates could only partially know or recognize what became the teaching of Christ, for the *Logos* had yet to incarnate and fully reveal Himself and His message. Justin believed that the daimon Socrates claimed guided him was in fact the rational seed of Christ. Therefore, when Socrates rebuked the traditional gods of Athens and was accused of being an atheist, Justin refuted the claim that Christians were atheists by appealing to Socrates' predicament.

> And when Socrates endeavored, by true reason and examination, to bring these things to light, and deliver men from the demons, then the demons themselves, by means of men who rejoiced in iniquity, composed his death, as an atheist and a profane person, on the charge

---

[373] Justin Martyr, "Second Apology," Ch.X.

that "he was introducing new divinities;" and in our case they display a similar activity. For not only among the Greek did Logos prevail to condemn these things through Socrates, but also among the Barbarians were they condemned by the Logos Himself, who took shape, and became man, and was called Jesus Christ; and in obedience to Him, we not only deny that they who did such things as these are gods, but assert that they are wicked and impious demons, whose actions will not bear comparison with those even of men desirous of virtue.[374]

The Patristic tradition further develops the theology of *Logos*, utilizing philosophical sophistication to describe how God can be seen in nature in light of Old Testament scripture. Here, we introduce the concept of *logoi*, the refracted presence of the *Logos* in creation. Each thing is understood to have its own distinctive *logos* that bring it into being and constitute its ultimate purpose and meaning. Rooted in Patristic thought, particularly in St. Maximus the Confessor, the *logoi* represent the divine ideas or rational principles according to which God creates and sustains the universe. Theologically, the *logoi* are understood as eternal archetypes within the divine *Logos* (Jesus Christ), through whom all things were made (John 1:3). Each created being possesses its own *logos*, which is its divine purpose, reason, or principle of existence.[375] Thus, all

---

[374] Justin Martyr, "Second Apology," Ch. V.
[375] Maximus the Confessor, "Ambigum 7," in *The Cosmic Mystery of Jesus Christ*, trans. Paul Blowers and Robert Louis Wilken (Crestwood, New York: St. Vladimir's Seminary Press, 2003) "The *logoi* of all things known by God before their creation are surely fixed in God. They are in Him who is the truth of all things. Yet all these things, things present and things to come, have not been brought into being contemporaneously with their being known to God;

creation is not random or autonomous but participates in a structured divine order, reflecting the wisdom and will of God. Unlike Neoplatonic emanations, which propose an impersonal and necessary outflow of divine beings, the *logoi* in Orthodox thought are personal, intentional, and relational, linking all created things to their divine source without diminishing their unique existence.

For St. Maximus the Confessor, the *logoi* serve as the means through which creatures participate in the divine will, providing a theological bridge between God's transcendence and His immanence. He asserts that the *logoi* exist eternally in the divine *Logos* and are manifested in the act of creation, thus upholding the Orthodox understanding that the world is a reflection of divine wisdom and intentionality rather than a mere mechanistic or accidental occurrence. For Maximus, all sensible reality is symbolic, pointing beyond itself to a higher intelligible reality. Each creature's *logos* define its purpose and guide its movement towards fulfillment in God. This idea is deeply tied to the Orthodox doctrine of *theosis*, wherein human beings are called to align their own *logos* with the divine *Logos* through synergy with God's grace. The process of spiritual purification and illumination enables the human nous (νοῦς) to perceive *logoi* within creation, leading to experiential knowledge of God rather than a purely intellectual or abstract understanding. This perspective is notably different from Western

---

rather each was created in appropriate way according to its *logos* at the proper time according to the wisdom of the maker, and each acquired concrete actual existence in itself… For all created things are defined, in their essence and in their way of developing, by their own *logoi* and by the *logoi* of the beings that provide their external context…We are speechless before the sublime teaching about the Logos, for He cannot be expressed in words or conceived in thought…nevertheless we affirm that the one Logos is many *logoi* and the many logoi and One." 56-7.

theological traditions, which often emphasize natural law and divine governance in juridical terms, whereas Orthodox theology sees creation itself as a sacramental and participatory reality, where everything has its origin and fulfillment in Christ.

Maximus presents the sensible world as a sort of cosmic liturgy; the earthly enactment of a heavenly drama, and we, being made in His image, are a recapitulation of this cosmic drama. Christ's incarnation is a cosmic mystery in which He not only unites human nature with divine nature, but also sanctifies matter itself, reorienting all creation towards its intended *telos*. The "Word fashioned an intellectual soul made in the image of God as a kind of second cosmos."[376] It is the cleansing of our *nous* through pious obedience to God and His commandments, so that the rational soul can perceive their *logoi* and participate in the deifying project of creation. In describing this process with Christ, Maximus writes,

> But in the future age when graced with divinization, he will affectionately love and cleave to the *logoi* already mentioned that pre-existed in God, or rather, he will love God himself, in whom the *logoi* of beautiful things are securely grounded. In this way he becomes a "portion of God," insofar as he exists through the *logos* of his being which is in God and insofar as he is good through the *logos* of his well-being which is in God… By His gracious condescension God became man and is called man for the sake of man and by exchanging his condition

---

[376] Maxiums, "Ambigium 7," 68.

for ours revealed the power that elevates man to God through his love for God and brings God down to man because of His love for man. By this blessed inversion, man is made God by divinization and God is made man by hominization.[377]

Therefore, the reconciliation of all things is found in Christ the *Logos*. Through the theanthropic emphasis of *Logos*, Orthodoxy finds no tension in the dialect between the one and the many. It is the one *Logos* that the multiple divine archetypes of creation (*logoi*) find their origin. By way of the Incarnation of the *Logos*, the chasm between God and mankind is bridged. Jesus Christ is the creator of humanity, and also the perfect fulfillment of the *telos* of human existence. The personal *logos* of each person, is the seed of Christ, in which the multiplicity of each person finds a direct connection to the God-man and His salvation. In earlier platonic-based thought, the One was always privileged as being more ontologically real than the multiplicity of emergent creation. Such tension does not arise in Orthodox theology as the Triune God is both one and many. The hominization of God into man and the hypostasis of personhood as the source of being means that all people find their full actualization and harmonic unity in Christ. *Logos* upholds the metaphysical reality of the universe: it is the source of logic, reason, love, order, truth, and mercy. All of which bring fuller clarity to Christ's words.

I am the way, the truth, and the life. No one comes to the Father except through Me. If you truly know Me, you will

---

[377] Maxiums, "Ambigium 7," 59-60.

know My Father as well. From now on, you do know Him and have seen Him. ... Don't you believe that I am in the Father, and that the Father is in Me? The words I say to you I do not speak on my own authority. Rather, it is the Father, living in Me, who is doing His work. Believe Me when I say that I am in the Father, and the Father is in Me... If you love me, keep my commands. And I will ask the Father, and He will give you another advocate to help you and be with you forever – the Spirit of Truth. The world cannot accept Him, because it neither sees Him or knows Him. But you know Him, for He lives with you and will be in you. ... Anyone who loves Me will obey my teaching. My Father will love them, and we will come to them and make our home with them. Anyone who does not love Me will not obey my teaching. These words you hear are not my own; they belong to the Father who sent Me.[378]

The last point to be discussed concerning the *Logos* theology of Orthodox Christianity and the process of *theosis* is to consider spiritual warfare. *Logismoi* denotes the assaultive and tempting thoughts that form the frontline of spiritual warfare. In the writings of the Desert Fathers, these evil thoughts are more than passing ideas; they are demonic suggestions and mental images that play upon natural passions to incite them into sin. When the Apostle Paul describes our spiritual battle is "not against flesh and blood," but "against the powers of this dark world and

---

[378] John 14:6-24

against the spiritual forces of evil in the heavenly realms" the church understands this to mean the aerial noetic entities of demons (Ephesians 6:12). *Logismoi* are thus a core part of the ascetic therapy of the soul, in which the aim is to purify one's inner life from all irrational drives. In Orthodox Christian life, spiritual battle is primarily conducted within the mind and heart.

Evagrius Ponticus is the first to outline the eight generic evil, these include pride, vainglory, gluttony, lust, avarice, acedia, sorrow. These thoughts are typically vivid and persistent in their attempts to undermine the spiritual life. Gluttony suggests to the mind that ascetic fasting will ruin his health, or lust bombards the mind with images of bodies to provoke desire, sadness might follow on the heels of frustrated desire or anger, and acedia ("the noonday demon") assails a solitary monk with boredom and disgust during midday, making time feel as if it is standing still.

St. John Cassian transmitted the teachings of Evagrius to the Latin West, which were later reformulated by Pope Gregory the Great into the seven deadly sins. St. John Cassian outlines the sequence in the temptation process,[379] emphasizing that we must keep watch of our mind so the "head of the serpent" does not provoke us, and then willing consent

---

[379] (1) Assault – the initial provocative thought or image knocking at the door of the mind. At this stage, no sin is yet committed, and even great saints experienced these attacks. (2) Interaction – entering into dialogue with the thought, and pondering it. his is risky, as the mind begins to negotiate with the temptation, but there is still a chance to reject it and no guilt if one has not consented. (3) Consent – the moment the will agrees with the evil suggestion, resolving to act on it. At this point, the beginning of sin occurs in the heart. (4) Captivity – repeated consent leads to the person becoming hostage to the *logismos*. The sinful thought begins to form a habitual pattern, and resisting it grows increasingly difficult. 5) Passion (Obsession) – finally the *logismos* becomes an entrenched passion. At this stage the sin has become second-nature – an obsessive behavior or vice dominating one's life.

leading to sinful action. Quoting Pslam 137:9, he writes, "While the-children of Babylon - by which I mean our wicked thoughts - are still young, we should dash them to the ground and crush them against the rock, which is Christ."[380] Therefore, the tempestuous mental image of *logismoi* are not sins in themselves until one consents to it in their heart, leading to a slow progression in which the heart is slowly given over to Satan until it solidifies into deep character flaws and passions.

St. Maximus the Confessor's discussion on the *logismoi* placed more emphasis on integrating it with a Christocentric spirituality. Maximus taught that the goal of ascetic purification is to transform human desire and anger back into love for God and neighbors. Like St. Dorotheos of Gaza, Maximus notes that if evil thoughts originate from the passionate state of the soul, so do good thoughts arise from the soul in a state of virtue. St. John Climacus (579-649), in *The Ladder of Divine Ascent*, describes how the monk must identify, resist, and ultimately reject harmful *logismoi* before they take root, comparing them to thieves attempting to break into the house of the soul.[381] The Hesychastic tradition culminating in the teachings of St. Gregory Palamas, emphasizes that overcoming *logismoi* is not merely a psychological exercise but a mystical process that leads to the illumination of the *nous* and the direct experience of God's uncreated energies.

Furthermore, *logismoi* are intimately connected to the fallen state of human nature. The Orthodox Church teaches that before the Fall,

---

[380] John Cassian, "On the Eight Vices," ed. Bishop Kastor, accessed March 19, 2025, https://orthodoxchurchfathers.com/fathers/philokalia/st-john-cassian-on-the-eight-vices.html#:~:text=thoughts%20and%20then%20eradicating%20them,137%3A9%3B%20I%20Cor.

[381] John Climacus, *The Ladder of Divine Ascent* (Boston: Holy Transfiguration Monastery, 2012).

Adam and Eve had pure, undistorted communion with God, with their *nous* fully directed towards divine illumination. However, after sin entered the world, the *nous* darkened and the human mind became vulnerable to deception and confusion. According to Orthodox theology, the devil does not have direct control over human will, but introduces *logismoi* to distort perception and lead people into sin. Thus, spiritual warfare consists of discerning and rejecting these deceptive thoughts, aligning the *nous* with the divine *Logos*, who is the true source of wisdom and purity. In describing the ways demons ensnare souls into delusions, as expressed in the *Letters* of St. Anthony the Great, Columba Stewart writes,

> The demons work through suggestion, employing *logismoi* that tempt or distract the monk: "if [the demons] see any Christians, especially monks, devoted to [spiritual] work and making progress, they first try to lay down stumbling-blocks along the way. Their stumbling-blocks are impure thoughts. The power of the demons, however, is based on illusion, for they have been defeated by the Resurrection of Christ. Even so, their ability to appear in various forms, their great mobility without material body, and their skill at playing on weakness makes it possible for them to ensnare unwary monks.[382]

---

[382] Columba Stewart, "Evagrius Ponticus and the Eight Generic Logismoi," in *In the Garden of Evil: Vice and Culture in the Middle Ages*, ed. Richard Newhauser (Pontifical Institute of Mediaeval Studies, 2005) 14.

In the broader context of Orthodox anthropology, the struggle against *logismoi* is not merely about moral perfection, but about restoring the soul to its original state of divine communion. The process of purification, illumination, and *theosis* necessarily involves the renewal of the mind, as Romans 12:2 states: "Be transformed by the renewal of your mind." The saints and ascetics of the Orthodox tradition consistently affirm that victory over *logismoi* leads to reintegration of the soul, allowing it to function according to its divine purpose. This reintegration is achieved through prayer, fasting, confession, and participation in the sacramental life of the Church. Like the Devil, the father of lies, demons tempt humanity with delusions and sin to further cloud our noetic faculties and lead us away from our full personhood in God.

C. Epistemology, Metaphysics, and Ethics

The Eastern Orthodox paradigm is a holistic and experiential worldview that integrates epistemology, metaphysics, and ethics within the framework of divine revelation, *theosis*, and participation in God's uncreated energies. Unlike Western philosophical and theological traditions, which often emphasize rationalism, scholasticism, or legalism, Orthodox Christianity approaches knowledge, reality, and morality through a sacramental, mystical, and participatory lens grounded in the Patristic tradition and the lived experience of the Church. At its core, this paradigm affirms that true knowledge (epistemology) is not merely intellectual but noetic, reality (metaphysics) is deeply relational and theocentric, and ethics are not simply about moral rules, but about restoring the human person to divine communion. These three dimensions – knowing, being, and acting – are inseparable in Orthodox theology, forming a coherent vision of the world that is distinct from Western Christianity and secular philosophical traditions.

The Orthodox epistemological framework is fundamentally onto-relational, experiential, and participatory rather than purely rational or dialectical. It is based on the premise that knowledge of God cannot be attained through reason alone but requires purification of the soul and direct participation in divine life. The hierarchy of Orthodox epistemology begins with the revelation of God, followed by personal faith and subjective experience, and then rational inquiry. Knowledge, be it natural observation and mystical encounters, is always grounded in presuppositions of God's revelation through scripture and tradition. This noetic epistemology is rooted in the distinction between rational knowledge (διάνοια) and noetic knowledge (νοῦς). Western philosophy and theology, particularly in Scholastic and Enlightenment traditions, have generally emphasized rationalistic and analytical approaches to truth, seeing knowledge as an accumulation of concepts, propositions, and experiments. In contrast, Orthodox Christianity asserts that true knowledge of God is direct, unmediated, experiential, and accessible through prayer, asceticism, and divine grace. Thus, in the Orthodox paradigm, knowledge is not about conceptual speculation but about ontological transformation, where the knower becomes united with the known in divine communion.

In Orthodox theology, Truth is a "Who" not a "What." When Christ states "I am the way and truth, and the life. No one comes to the Father except through me," the church takes this literally. The *Logos* is the Truth in every sense of the word. The *logoi* of creation and *logos* of personal rationality are metaphysically rooted within Christ's theanthropic person. Therefore, even the empirical truths of science rest upon the *Logos* as the metaphysical mediator between nonphysical universals and the orderliness of the material world.

As David Hume famously noted, induction cannot be philosophically justified without a circular inference. Based on previous patterns, we can infer that the sun will rise tomorrow, or chemical reactions will occur under certain conditions, but rationally justifying predictions without empirical observation undermines the materialistic model of knowledge acquisition. Hume argued that our belief in the uniformity of nature (i.e., that the future will resemble the past) cannot be rationally justified, as any attempt to do so would rely on circular reasoning: using induction to justify induction. The problem of induction is a significant issue in the philosophies of science and epistemology.

Within the Orthodox Christian paradigm, the problem of induction is addressed through a theological framework that emphasizes the role of divine revelation and God's nature in grounding human knowledge. Divine governance provides a foundation for the regularity observed in nature, thereby justifying the reliability of inductive inferences. Consistency in natural laws is seen as a reflection of God's unchanging nature. This theistic foundation offers a basis for trusting cognitive faculties when creating inductive generalizations. Orthodox thought maintains that faith and reason are harmonious. While reason allows us to observe patterns and make inferences, faith assures us of the underlying order established by God. This integration mitigates the skeptical implications of Hume's problem by situating human reasoning within the context of divine providence.

To understand what exists and is real, and to endow it with meaning, is an unsolvable problem facing modernity. According to Orthodox philosopher Christos Yannaras, secular philosophy either resorts to simple phenomenicity, which corresponds to the absence of existential meaning, or a return to an ontology of mental images indicative of medieval intellectualism or a Newtonian "representational" theory of knowledge. Yannaras is critical of the pure rationalism of natural observation, as formulated in scholasticism and the modern West. He denounces this type of natural approach as an effort to conquer and objectify God to acquire individual certainty.[383] Orthodox epistemology does not disregard the rational and empirical conclusions of natural research. Rather, the ontologically oriented paradigm of Orthodoxy rejects the pure rationality indicative of modernity, which limits knowledge to propositions and data points. Without the fundamental presupposition of God as a rational Creator, creating a creation with rational order, and human beings imbued with that rationality, all knowledge claims become philosophically unjustifiable. There must be a metaphysical source point that is the precondition for knowledge itself.

The uncreated energies are a way of knowing that is neither "inferential nor noetic in the Aristotelean sense, nor simply a matter of feeling or intuition. It is the knowledge that comes through sharing actively in the work of another, thereby coming to know the other as the author of that work."[384] Orthodox epistemology places primacy on the apophatic limits to all knowledge claims, while providing a theological and inductive basis for cataphatic knowledge of the natural world. Rational inquiry and scientific investigation does not exhaust all that can be known from the natural world. As Christopher Knight highlights, "there are aspects of both God and of created things that are unknowable

---

[383] Christos Yannaras, *Elements of Faith: An Introduction to Orthodox Theology*, trans. Keith Shram (Edinburgh, Scotland: T&T Clark, 2000) 155.
[384] Bradshaw, *Divine Energies*, 20.

by us, and adopt what we might call *apophatic critical realism* in relation to both science and theology."[385] Being wary of the critical realism of modern science, Orthodoxy maintains epistemic humility towards the material world, but does not discard the utility of empiricism.

It is widely assumed that the epistemology of ancient Greek philosophy was the first appearance of rationalism in human history, as understood in Western European philosophy. However, knowledge in the Greek tradition, be it Platonic or Aristotelian, still held a primary importance for ontology, a similarity still shared with Orthodox Christianity. For Plato, the unit of knowledge is the idea (from *idein*, "to see") and is the product of a dynamic vision of things. This dynamic vision presupposes more than mere collaboration between sensory perception and individual intellect, in which the former supplies content to the latter. Rather, the Platonic ascent of knowledge towards perceptible beauty is not a detached experience, being only sensory, intellectual, or emotional, but the dynamic movement of the soul towards the beauty of the visible object. The ascending steps in knowledge are the rungs of a ladder based on the successive stages of contemplation (*theōria*), in which the soul arrives at an unexpected vision of the eternal and singular form of beauty.[386]

This Platonic epistemological stance continues in Aristotle. For Yannaras argues, the "contrast that Western interpreters have taken for granted (from the time of the medieval Scholastics to the present day) between Platonic contemplation (*theōria*) and Aristotelian logic (*logikē*) does not seem to have always been a consistent interpretation of ancient

---

[385] Christopher Knight, *Science and the Christian Faith: A Guide for the Perplexed* (Yonkers, New York: St. Vladimir's Seminary Press, 2020) 94.
[386] Plato, *Symposium*, 210a-211c (Diotima's speech on beauty).

Greek epistemology."[387] Aristotelian logic presupposes correct reasoning as the correct structuring of concepts and syllogisms, but it does not exhaust knowledge in defining and structuring. Correct reason is not only methodological, but confirmed "by virtue."[388] As is within Orthodox theology, the soul is what thinks and understands, the soul is the whole human person: "the soul is in a way all existing things; for existing things are either sensible or thinkable, and knowledge is in a way what is knowable, and sensation is in a way what is sensible."[389] The knowable faculties of the soul and how it comes to know the ideal forms and immanent material are crucial differentiations between the onto-relational approach of Orthodoxy and the mere rationalism of contemporary philosophy.

From this perspective it can be said that Orthodox epistemology is a sort of participatory noetic realism. The *nous* is a higher faculty of direct perception of truth, akin to Husserlian phenomenology, where intentional consciousness does not construct reality, but directly perceives it. However, unlike Husserl's transcendental idealism, Orthodox epistemology holds that this perception is ontological rather than merely eidetic – the *nous* does not just structure experience, but participates in divine reality itself. This model is radically different from Kantian epistemology, which separates noumenal reality (the thing-in-itself) from phenomenal knowledge. It departs from Western foundationalist epistemologies (whether based on rationalism, empiricism, or pragmatism) by insisting that true knowledge is not derived from deduction or empirical verification alone but through

---

[387] Yannaras, *Schism in Philosophy*, 78.
[388] Aristotle, *Nicomachean Ethics*, 6.13.1144b26-28.
[389] Aristotle, *On the Soul*, 3.8.431b21-23.

purification, illumination, and direct participation in God's uncreated energies. It most closely aligns with phenomenology (direct experience of being), virtue epistemology (transformation of the knower), and mystical realism (knowledge as participatory, rather than representational).

Yannaras argues that the epistemological break between Christendom East and West is due to the epistemology formulated by St. Augustine. Whereas the East is rooted in the onto-relational philosophy of being found in Greek philosophy, the West has generally been characterized by the elevation of rational intellect and objectivism. However, this distinction should be understood as a broad intellectual trajectory rather than an absolute dichotomy since both traditions contain elements of rational discourse and mystical experience. Augustine, who shaped the intellectual trajectory of the West, was educated chiefly in the legal thinking of Cicero, Tertullian, and St. Ambrose of Milan, and incorporates the epistemological presuppositions of Roman law into the spiritual life of the West. Aristotle, who greatly influenced the development of scholasticism does not appear in the West until the second half of the twelfth century.

It is Augustine, twelve centuries before Descartes, who "identifies both knowledge and existence with *intellection*."[390] Through the sole power of intellect, one can both doubt and come to the certainty of knowledge. One certainty of intellect is that it cannot doubt the fact that it can indeed doubt. Reminiscent of Descartes' skepticism. Given Augustine's educational formation, he concludes that through the certainties of the divine and true law, knowledge of the truth can only be

---

[390] Yannaras, *Schism in Philosophy*, 92.

assured through the terms of the presuppositions of justice – namely, obedience to the absolute authority of the given divine order.

The apophatic epistemology of the Platonic and Aristotelean traditions comes to full philosophical maturity with the radical break that occurred in the history of philosophy through the Greek theologians of the Byzantine period. The new elements of their theological thinking introduced to the epistemological problem concerned the distinction between substance (*ousia*) and activity (*energeia*), and clarified the synergistic dynamic of participation with the ultimate Being of God. When Christ says He is the truth and the life of the world, it carries ontological implications. Thus, Eastern Orthodox epistemology is intrinsically theocentric and predicated on the belief that true knowledge is attainable primarily through participation in the divine energies of God. This experiential approach underscores a theonomous epistemology, asserting that all knowledge is contingent upon divine revelation and the transformative process of *theosis*.

In contrast, modern scientific epistemology is anthropocentric and grounded in empirical observations, experimentation, and rational analysis. It operates within the framework of methodological naturalism, positing that phenomena can be understood through natural causes, without recourse to supernatural explanations. This approach relies on the formulation and testing of hypotheses, with knowledge claims subject to falsifiability and revision, based on new evidence. This scientific method emphasizes objectivity and seeks to minimize subjective biases through reproducibility and peer review. Within this paradigm, truth is viewed as provisional and always open to refinement or refutation in light of emerging data.

The divergence between these epistemologies is further accentuated by their respective attitudes towards certainty and mystery. Eastern Orthodox epistemology embraces mystery as an inherent aspect of divine reality, accepting that human reason has limitations in comprehending God's fullness. This acceptance fosters humility, which is integral to the Orthodox pursuit of knowledge. Conversely, modern science endeavors to demystify the unknown, operating under the assumption that with sufficient investigation, natural phenomena can be understood and explained. While science acknowledges the current limitations of knowledge, it maintains an optimistic outlook on the potential for future discovery and comprehension.

In Eastern Orthodoxy, epistemology is deeply communal and rooted in the life of the Church, tradition, and guidance of spiritual elders. Knowledge is not merely an individual endeavor, but is cultivated within the ecclesial community, emphasizing the synergy between the individual and the body of believers. This theanthropic understanding of truth and knowledge is most noticeable in the function of the Eucharist as it relates to God, humanity, and creation. John Zizioulas writes,

> The Eucharist shows that truth is not just something concerning humanity alone, but has profound cosmic dimensions. The Christ of the eucharist is revealed as the life and recapitulation of all creation. One of the basic difficulties inherent in the Greek conception of truth is that it implies that truth can be grasped and formulated by human reason. But as the eucharist reveals, this human "reason" must be understood as the element which unifies creation, and refers it to God through the hands of man,

> so that God may be "all in all" ... If man does this, then truth takes up its meaning for the whole cosmos, Christ becomes a cosmic Christ, and the world as a whole dwells in truth, which is none other than communion with its Creator. Truth thereby becomes the life of all that is.[391]

The Eastern Orthodox metaphysical framework, as has already been generally described, is rooted in a relational and participatory ontology, in which God, creation, and humanity exist in dynamic communion. Unlike Western metaphysics, which has often been shaped by substance ontology (Aristotelian-Thomistic metaphysics), mechanistic materialism (scientific reductionism), and Cartesian mind-body dualism, Orthodox metaphysics is dynamic, non-reductive, and fundamentally participatory. Orthodox Christianity maintains a sacramental ontology, where all creations are understood as imbued with divine meaning and purpose. In philosophical terms, it aligns most closely with process metaphysics, phenomenological ontology, and participatory realism, offering a teleological and eschatological vision of being, in which all created existence is directed towards union with God. This relational ontology has significant affinities with Heidegger's existential ontology, particularly his idea that being is not an abstract category but a lived and relational experience. However, unlike Heidegger's secular existentialism, Orthodox metaphysics holds that being is always grounded in a divine presence, rejecting the notion of an ontologically autonomous world.

---

[391] John Zizioulas, *Being as Communion* (Crestwood: St. Vladimir's Seminary Press, 1985) 119.

The essence-energy distinction preserves both God's transcendence and immanence, avoiding both pantheism (which collapses creation into God) and classical theism (which separates God from creation in an impersonal manner). The implications of this metaphysics are profound: the world is not merely a physical or material reality but a theophanic one, in which every created thing has *logos* (divine principle) implanted within it. As St. Maximus the Confessor teaches, all things have their origin and fulfillment in Christ, and the goal of human life is to align one's personal *logos* with the *Logos* of God. This understanding differs from Western theological paradigms, which tend to approach metaphysics through ontological abstraction or systematic categorization, rather than experiential and mystical participation in divine life.

Metaphysics encompasses a wide array of abstract concepts, including the nature of being, causality, mind and matter, as well as the division between particulars and universals. Orthodox metaphysics is most characterized as a metaphysical system of "both and." Whereas other schools of metaphysical speculation are characterized by the privileging of one dialectic against another, for example, Platonism and Neoplatonism privileging unity over multiplicity, or nominalism favoring multiplicity over unity, Orthodoxy tends to always emphasize the equal importance of both. This "both and" theology can be most seen regarding the Church's understanding of Christology. God is both transcendent and immanent; God is both eternal and historical; God is both one in essence and consists of three distinct divine persons; God is both the source of life and His humanity died on the cross; God is both God and man; God is both uncreated and took on created human nature, uniting them in his enhypostatization.

This same "both and" metaphysics can be said concerning the universal principles or archetypes of creation. The multiple *logoi* find their unitary existence within the Divine Logos. The Church acknowledged that God the Father was never devoid of reason, and therefore the *Logos* and Word of God had to, in turn, be eternal. Marking a break from the philosophical systems that came before that posited the *Logos* as the first creation of the One. The begetting of the Son and the procession of the Spirit did not signify that they were made or created, but rather that the Father was the ultimate source of the Son and Spirit sharing in His divine essence. This trinitarian formation is known as Monarchical Trinitarianism, and emphasizes the Father as source and *arche*, while at the same time, the three persons are all God in the predicative sense, and the Father is numerically identical to God in the nominal sense.[392] This trinitarian model of three divine persons with one undivided essence, with the Father as the sole *arche*, is specifically monotheistic, and in no way diminishes the divinity of the other persons of the Trinity who share the same divine nature. The persons are different in the context of their role, such as the Father being the *arche* and the Word being God's expression, but they are the same in nature, and therefore not different concerning metaphysics and ontology. The Orthodox insistence on Monarchical Trinitarianism, with the Father as the sole *arche*, is the theological basis why the East so strongly rebuked and condemned the filioque doctrine of the Latin Church.

Heretics reasoned that the triunity of God entailed three separate deities. According to one example, they argued that although Apostles

---

[392] Joshua Sijuwade, "Monarchical Trinitarianism: A Metaphysical Proposal," in *TheoLogica* 5, no. 2 (December 2021) https://doi.org/10.14428/thl.v5i2.54483.

Peter, James, and John share one human nature, they are nevertheless called three men. Jaroslav Peilkan summarizes St. Gregory of Nyssa response to such claims, he writes,

> A catachresis even to use the plural "three men [treis anthrōpoi]" in speaking about Peter, James, and John; for although there were "many sharing in the nature," what they shared – namely, "humanity [anthrōpos]" – was still one. In arguing that way, he could be construed as maintaining that it was nothing more grave than a similar "imprecision of language" to speak of Father, Son, and Holy Spirit as "three gods," because, like Peter, James, and John, the three divine hypostases shared in one nature, "deity [theotēs]." Thus, they could be accused of having salvaged monotheism by resort to the abstractions of the Platonic doctrine of ideas and of having equated the oneness of God, the most fundamental confession of Biblical faith, with a philosophical theory borrowed from Hellenism.[393]

Any other conception of the divine would have been, in the judgement of the Cappadocians, a violation of the fundamental metaphysical principle and a violation of biblical teaching and Orthodox dogma. The *Logos* as "*homoousios* with the Father" meant "acknowledging one nature with the difference of *hypostasis*," and lead

---

[393] Jaroslav Pelikan, *Christianity and Classical Culture: The Metamorphosis of Natural Theology in the Christian Encounter with Hellenism* (New Haven: Yale University Press,1993) 84-5.

to no other opinion than there is one first cause, one *arche*, and one transcendent God.³⁹⁴ In this manner, St. Gregory believes the Trinity should be understood as a unified activity, which, "he argues is a more appropriate way of conceptualizing shared terms, such as God, in light of the utter transcendence of divine nature."³⁹⁵ Within this metaphysical structure, we see a "both and" theology arise concerning the one and the many. God is both one in essence and many in persons. In John 5:19, we read, the Son does nothing that He does not see the Father do, "for whatever He does, the Son also does in like manner." Demonstrating a shared divine will through the whole of the Godhead.

Interestingly, Pythagoras theorized that the number one symbolized the unity of the Monad, two represented differentiation of the One forming the Dyad, and three symbolized harmony, in which *Logos* was the bond uniting the multiplicity of existence.³⁹⁶ God is not limited or confined to the Platonic ideal of unity but exists in a triunity, signifying that His very being is indicative of the harmony of all universals and particulars.

The same conception of unity through the Logos can be employed to better understand the doctrine of *theosis*. As God's essence is singular, His energy is multiple. Through mystical participation with God's uncreated energies, the dialectic between uncreated and created is bridged, allowing the multiplicity of contingent human beings to be brought into direct communion with their noncontingent Creator. Just as the Holy Trinity shares one will, so too does the multiplicity of human

---

³⁹⁴ Pelikan, *Christianity and Classical Culture*, 86.
³⁹⁵ Johannes Zachuber, *The Rise of Christian Theology and the End of Ancient Metaphysics: Patristic Philosophy from the Cappadocian Fathers to John of Damascus* (Oxford: Oxford University Press, 2020) 65.
³⁹⁶ Hillar, *Logos and Trinity*, 6-10.

beings strive to unite their personal will with God's divine will. Thereby, they become a conduit for the energies of God to work in the world, while simultaneously deifying the person they work within.

The *Logos*, in assuming a human mind, soul, will, and body, sanctified these properties of human nature and united them to His divine nature, mind, and will. Orthodoxy teaches that mind, will, and energy are properties of nature, not personhood. Therefore, in Christ, we find two natures: two wills and two minds. Christ's divine knowing is attested to by the apostles in John 16:30, "Now we are sure that You know all things, and have no need that anyone should question You. By this we believe that You came forth from God." Christ, in the *kenosis* of His incarnation, does not undergo any change, in that He ceases to be God while also being fully man. As a divine subject He truly knows all things. This was the basis for much of the dispute between St. Maximus the Confessor and Pyrrhus concerning whether Christ had a *gnomic* will. The dispute emerged during the Monoenergism and Monothelite controversy concerning Chalcedonian affirmation of Christ being fully God and fully man, two natures, and two wills in one divine person.[397]

St. Maximus the Confessor argued against the notion that Christ possessed a *gnomic* will, particularly in his work *Disputation with Pyrrhus*. In this dialogue, Maximus clarifies that while humans, due to their fallen nature, deliberate and waver in their decisions – a process he terms *gnomic* willing – Christ, being both fully divine and fully human, did not experience such deliberation or uncertainty. Maximus asserts that Christ's human will is perfectly aligned with His divine will, operating

---

[397] Meyendorff, *Byzantine Theology* 38.

without the indecision characteristic of *gnomic* will.[398] *Gnomic* willingness is understood as a function of the hypostatic or personal life of fallen humanity and not of nature. This distinction is crucial in Orthodox Christology, as it upholds the belief that while Christ assumed human nature entirely, including a human natural will, he was never subject to fallen inclinations towards deliberation or moral uncertainty. Thus, Maximus emphasizes that attributing a *gnomic* will to Christ would imply imperfection and internal conflict, which contradicts the Orthodox understanding of the sinless and perfect human person of Jesus.

While the apophaticism of God the Father is thoroughly maintained in the outlined trinitarian model, it is through Christ the *Logos* that humanity comes to know who God is. It is Christ the *Logos* who communicates with humanity in Old Testament scripture. It is Christ the *Logos*, in which all things find their metaphysical and created origins.[399] It is Christ the *Logos* who established the salvific work of the church. Christians belong to the body of Christ in the Orthodox Church and participate in the grace-filled gift of *theosis*. Orthodox theology posits a metaphysical structure that harmonizes the one and the many. Unity does not take priority over multiplicity, just as the shared divine essence does not overshadow the separate hypostasis of the three divine persons.

---

[398] Maximus the Confessor, *Disputations with Pyrrhus*, trans. Joseph P. Farrell (Pennsylvania, St. Tikhon's Monastery Press, 2014).

[399] Colossians 1:16-20, "For by Him all things were created that are in heaven and that are on earth, visible and invisible, whether thrones or dominions or principalities or powers. All things were created through Him and for Him. And He Is before all things, and in Him all things consist. And He is the head of the body, the church, who is the beginning, the firstborn from the dead, that in all things He may have preeminence. For it pleased the Father that in Him all the fulness should dwell, and by Him to reconcile all things to Himself, by Him whether things on earth or things in heaven, having made peace through the blood of His cross."

Likewise, many archetypes or divine principles of creation (*logoi*) find their origin in the one *Logos* without dialectic tension.

We now focus on ethics in the Eastern Orthodox paradigm. Ethics are not understood as legalistic, but rather therapeutic, aimed at the healing and restoration of the human person. In this paradigm, sin is not primarily a legal debt that needs to be paid but an illness that needs to be healed. It is the physician of souls, Jesus Christ, who renews and cures the human person. This is why St. John Chrysostom famously likened the church to a hospital rather than a courtroom. This perspective is evident in Orthodox penitential practices, where confession is seen as a sacrament to healing, rather than merely a legal absolution of guilt. Furthermore, Orthodox ethics are inherently communal, emphasizing that salvation is not an individualistic pursuit, but a reality experienced within the Body of Christ (the Church). This stands in contrast to certain Western traditions, particularly Protestantism, where salvation is often seen as a personal transaction between the individual and God, rather than as participation in the corporate life of the Church.

When beginning his seminary course on Christian ethics, eminent Orthodox theologian Georges Florovsky would state, "For Orthodox Christians there is no such thing as Christian ethics."[400] Florovsky's intention here is to express the ambivalence that the Orthodox Church has had towards the systematization of ethics as a professional field of study relegated to specialized experts. Orthodox critics have argued the emergence of "Christian ethics" is the logical result of the Western trends of Scholasticism, advanced by the Renaissance and Enlightenment, and

---

[400] Thomas Hopko, "Orthodox Christianity and Ethics," in *Orthodox Education Day Book* (Crestwood, NY: St. Vladimir's Seminary Press, 1995) 6.

shifted "from the mystery of the eucharistic community to the intellectualism of the academy."[401] These intellectual evolutions occurred mainly after the eleventh-century schism between Eastern and Western Christianity.

As Fr. Stanley Harakas has noted, in the early Christian and Patristic eras, "we do not have a formal treatise on ethics, that is, a structured treatment of Christian ethics as a separate from other disciplines of Theology."[402] Critics of "Orthodox ethics" often argue this definitional approach betrays a Western cultural influence that superimposes foreign concepts and categories; and they question whether a scientifically, rule governed normative vision in compatible with Orthodoxy's theocentric ontology of the human person. Metropolitan John Zizioulas writes, "[Ethics] operates with the general principles, and thus is forced to subject to a general category of beings… an entity – a concrete Other – which by definition claims absolute particularity with respect to every other entity."[403]

With this said, Perry Hamalis correctly identifies five characteristics that define the Orthodox Christian position on ethics within academic terms.[404] The first of these is moral realism. The Orthodox ethical vision is inseparable from the theological vision of God as a Trinity, Creator, and Savior. It is the Trinity, which is the source of all good, while simultaneously transcending all human concepts of the

---

[401] Tristam, H. Englehardt Jr., "An Orthodox Approach to Bioethics," in *Living Orthodoxy in the Modern World*, eds. Andrew Walker and Costa Carras (Crestwood, NY: St. Vladimir's Seminary Press, 1996) 116.

[402] Stanley Harakas, *Toward Transfigured Life: The Theoria of Eastern Orthodox Ethics* (Minneapolis: Light and Life, 1983) 11.

[403] John Zizioulas, *Communion and Otherness: Further Studies in Personhood and the Church*, eds, Paul McPartlan (London: T&T Clark, 2006) 69.

[404] Perry T. Hamalis, "Eastern Orthodox Ethics" in *International Encyclopedia of Ethics*, ed. Hugh LaFollette (New York: John Wiley & Sons, 2013) 1525-1535.

Good in its divine essence. This position protects against any sort of epistemic or moral relativism on the one hand, and against the reification of human constructs on the other. The Trinity of three persons and one essence affirm the ideal of divine love and the communion of persons.

The second characteristic is Orthodoxy's vision of morality as teleological, meaning that the *telos* of human life is to be found in *theosis*, the divine-human communion beginning here on earth and continuing into eternity. Orthodoxy emphasizes human beings as made in the image of God, which accounts for their moral agency, highlighting their freedom and self-determination as a person with the possibility of love, holiness, and communion.

Third, Orthodox ethics are existentially focused. The impetus is the problem of death, and its telos, deification, is expressed as resurrection in and through Christ the *Logos*. Adam's sin was a tragic misuse of human free will that left humanity alienated from God, corrupted by passions, mortal, and inclined toward pride. Sin is contrary to humanity's natural calling to be in communion with God and carries with it ontological and noetic implications. Sin and death thus shape the Orthodox understanding of fallen human nature, which not only leads to the hardening of one's heart, but is the root source of global chaos and violence.

Fourth, Orthodox ethics are specifically a form of "virtue ethics." Acquiring virtue is understood as necessary for human flourishing. Orthodoxy emphasizes the communal role in moral formation and the importance of personal character and habits of action and prioritizes a person's overall ethos against single moral acts. As imitators of Christ, saints are vital exemplars of human excellence and holiness, with the aim of virtuous character formation in light of the saving and life-giving mystical relationship with God.

The fifth distinctive characteristic of Orthodox ethics is their vision of the social context of human life. Orthodox thinkers have described the relationship between the church and the state as a *symphonia*, a harmony in which the church not only transfigures people but society itself. Salvation is understood as a collective communal act, and thus great importance is placed not only on life within the church, but also on how the church engages the world at large.

The reality of man's creation "in the image of God" is related to the unity of morality in being itself. Created "in the image" of the Trinity, man is also one in essence and many hypostases according to his person. Each human is distinct and unrepeatable, and exercises their own unique will. Their mode of existence, with freedom of will and distinct personhood, in turn, forms the image of God in humans. Orthodox Christian ethics are ontological and concerned with the transformation of a human person into a Christ-like being. St. Maximus the Confessor teaches that ethics is inseparable from ontology, as human beings are called to ascend from the passions (πάθη) to dispassion (ἀπάθεια), leading to divine union. In other words, morality relates to the event of salvation, where man is made "whole" and realizes his full potential for existence.

While other creatures derive their ontological hypostasis from the will and energy of God, humanity derives it not simply from the will and energy of God, but from the manner of personal existence. This manner of personal existence affords the existential possibility of loving communion and relationship and is indicative of the mode of the Holy Trinity. The creation of man is an act of God's love and constitutes being as an existential event of personal communion and relationship. Through freedom, man is offered the opportunity for true life, and therefore is capable of either accepting or rejecting the ontological precondition for his existence; he can say "no" to the love and personal communion with God, and thereby cutting himself off from being.

The Greek word πρόσωπον (person) etymologically connotes the relationality of personhood, in that his face (ὠπός) is towards (πρός) someone or something. Human beings are inherently a communal creature; however, this "facing towards" is not limited to others humans, but is in reference to his personal hypostasis as reference or relation with God. Concerning this topic, Yannaras writes,

> Thus, the person represents a mode of being which presupposes natural individuality, but is at the same time distinct from it. Each person is a sum of the characteristics common to all human nature, to mankind as a whole, and at the same time he transcends it inasmuch as he is an existential distinctiveness… mankind as whole, as a biological species – can be defined objectively; it possess will, reason, intellect, ect. But each human person exercises his will and converses and thinks in a way that is unique, distinct, and unrepeatable. Consequently, the person is not an individual, a segment or subdivision of human nature as whole, but the possibility of summing up the whole in a distinctiveness of relationship, in an act of self-transcendence… On the other hand, the relationship which sums up the totality of nature in self-transcendence

defies comparison, and is unique and distinctive. This uniqueness and distinctiveness – which has its being and is experienced only as a fact of communion and relationship – defies the personal existence of man, his mode of being.[405]

The union of divine nature with human nature in the person of Christ results in a definitive change in man's existential possibilities. After the Fall, it was no longer possible for mankind's personal distinctiveness and freedom to transcend the natural limits of the self-sufficiency of his biological entity. A natural gulf emerges between man and God when his existence is restricted to the autonomy of the individual–a gulf that a person's will cannot bridge. With the Incarnation of the *Logos*, this natural gulf is removed. With the first Adam, the natural desire for self-subsistence became a force condemning humanity to an existence in the survival of mortal individuality. However, in the second Adam, the two natural wills of the divine and human are brought into harmony in Christ's hypostatic union. This frees humanity from self-imposed bondage within the limits of mortal individuality.

Thus, the regeneration of man in Christ means that through the cooperation of man's freedom, God now asks man to resist the mortal impulses of sin. The conformity of this ethos informs the Church's practice of asceticism. Asceticism is the attempt to confirm man's freedom, and the decision of his rebellious will to imitate the obedience of the second Adam, Jesus Christ. This obedience is not a simple

---

[405] Christos Yannaras, *The Freedom of Morality* (Crestwood, New York: St. Vladimir's Seminary Press, 1984) 21-2.

submission to an external law but a conforming to the prototype Christ made incarnate in human nature.

Orthodox ethics are profoundly relational, seeing morality as an outpouring of divine love in the world. This is why Orthodox theology resists legalism and instead teaches that love is the supreme criterion for moral discernment. Sin in Orthodox ethics is not primarily a legal violation (as in Augustinian and Thomistic moral theology), but a spiritual disease that requires healing. Correspondingly, virtues are not moral achievements, but the restoration of human nature to its original beauty that allows for greater participation in divine life.

Finally, a word must be said concerning the Orthodox position on the existence of evil. Evil is understood to have no positive ontological existence, but is instead described as a privation (στέρησις) of God's uncreated energies and the good. St. Basil the Great explicitly states that "evil does not exist by nature, nor is it rooted in any positive substance, but is rather the absence of the good."[406] St. Gregory of Nyssa, in his treatise *On the Soul and Resurrection*, further develops this theme by describing evil as a parasitic non-reality, existing only as a deprivation of the divine light, much like darkness is merely the absence of light.[407] Since God's uncreated energies are the sustaining and life-giving principles of all beings, a rejection of these energies results in a state of privation, alienation, and corruption, rather than a movement towards some ontologically independent evil. This privation theory of evil has profound implications for Orthodox soteriology and anthropology. This

---

[406] Basil of Caesarea, "*Homily 2 in Hexaemeron,*" in *Nicene and Post-Nicene Fathers*, 268-69.

[407] Gregory of Nysa, "On the Soul and Resurrection" in *Nicene and Post-Nicene Fathers*, Series II, Vol. 5, ed. Phillip Schaff (Massachusetts: Hendrickson Publishing, 1979) 796-99.

underscores that sin and evil are not intrinsic to human nature but are the result of an estrangement from the divine source of being. Sin is a state of ontological diminishment rather than a substantive transformation into something inherently evil. Thus, in the Orthodox paradigm, evil is neither an ontological rival to God, nor does it possess its own inherent reality. Rather, it is the distortion of divine order, a rupture in the harmony of creation, and a failure to actualize the divine potential implanted in all things.

Much like darkness is the absence of light, thereby having no ontological existence of its own; the antithesis to God's uncreated energies also lacks ontological subsistence. In thermodynamics, cold is not an energy or an independent physical property but rather a relative term used to describe the absence of thermal energy. In turn, heat is energy. When describing something as hot or cold, we only evaluate the presence and amount of thermal energy within a given item or system. This is also the case for the Orthodox paradigm. God's energies are the only thing with a positive ontological existence; the privation of these energies from evil and sin leads quite literally to both physical and spiritual death. Therefore, concerning salvation for Orthodox Christians, participating in and being synergized by God's energies is the choice made here and now. Hell is not an active infliction of suffering by God but the self-imposed suffering of a soul that has lost the ability to experience divine love as joy. The damned are not "cut off" from God in a spatial sense, but remain in His presence while experiencing it as consuming fire rather than blissful illumination.

God's love is often described as the river of fire. That fire purifies and cleanses the repentful sinner, filling them with His energy and heating them back into direct communion with Him. Someone who resists God's love and has pride in their transgressions, thereby consciously violating moral law, will experience the river of fire as pain. Just as metal is placed in fire, it is heated to the same temperature as the fire, and the metal is not the fire, but is taking into itself the energy of that fire becoming energetically one with it. *Theosis*, as described in this chapter, is the process of a direct energetic engagement with God.

D. Conclusion

The Eastern Orthodox conception of deification presents a holistic and experiential framework to understand the relationship between God, humanity, and creation. Rooted in Patristic thought and the lived tradition of the Church, this paradigm is a distinctive approach to epistemology, metaphysics, and ethics, which stands in contrast to many Western philosophical and theological traditions.

At its core, Orthodox theology maintains an apophatic stance towards the divine essence while affirming the possibility of divine knowledge and participation through God's uncreated energies. The essence-energy distinction articulated by figures, such as St. Gregory Palamas, provides a metaphysical foundation for *theosis* – a process by which human beings can attain a direct divinizing union with God without compromising His transcendence and unknowability. Unlike Western models, which often emphasize forensic justification or the rational apprehension of the divine, the Orthodox paradigm presents salvation as an ontological transformation of the entire person.

The *Logos* theology developed by the Greek Fathers further elucidates how created beings can participate in dive life through the Incarnation of Christ. As the eternal Word of God, *Logos* is understood as the source and sustainer of all creation, with each creature possessing its own logos that find origin and fulfillment in the Divine *Logos*. This provides a metaphysical basis for how finite beings can enter into communion with an infinite God without losing their distinct identities.

Epistemologically, the Orthodox Church emphasizes noetic knowledge over purely rational or empirical models of knowing. True knowledge of God is seen as experiential and participatory, rather than abstract and propositional. This aligns with the overall therapeutic and ascetic orientation of Orthodox spirituality, where purification of the nous is necessary for direct apprehension of divine truth.

Ethically, the Orthodox paradigm presents a virtue-based model that focuses on the restoration of the divine image in humanity. Sin is understood not primarily as a legal transgression but as an ontological diminishment – a privation of divine energies that leads to spiritual and physical death. Thus, the goal of moral life is to unite with God through synergistic cooperation with divine grace.

The Eastern Orthodox theological framework offers a coherent and integrated vision of reality that harmonizes key philosophical tensions – between the one and the many, transcendence and immanence, nature, and person. Grounding human existence in participation with the divine presents an alternative to both secular materialism and religious fundamentalism. As such, it merits serious consideration in contemporary philosophical and theological discourse, as we grapple with the perennial questions of meaning, truth, and human flourishing.

4. Transfiguration:
Godmanhood vs Mangodhood

Transhumanism emerges from a historical line of Christian thought that anticipated the arrival of God's millennial kingdom through technological advancement. They held a religious faith that whatever attributes Adam and Eve lost in the Fall, technology would redeem. From John Scotus Eriugena to Francis Bacon, techno-utopian dreams colored the future hopes of building a society characterized by perfect knowledge, perfect language, and immortal life. These presuppositions shaped the early enterprise of science and continue to this day with the belief that technology will bring humans to a state of perfection.

Despite its secular scientific idiom, transhumanism is filled with religious themes concerning human deification, an eschatological endpoint, and the emergence of God from advanced artificial intelligence. For groups such as the Order of Cosmic Engineers, the Society for Universal Immortalism, and Terasem Transreligion, transhumanism functions explicitly as a religion for the future; in which they believe it provides a narrative of ultimate meaning no longer attainable in traditional religious outlooks.

In what Habermas has deemed as the "postsecular moment" the barriers between the secular and the religious have been blurred. Secular enterprises can now function as the ultimate meaning-making paradigms that operate in ways analogous to religious worldviews. Transhumanism offers a comprehensive vision of the future and imbues it with transcendent religiosity, informing their utopian dreams of perfection. Therefore, within the postsecular marketplace of ideas, transhumanism and Orthodox Christian *theosis* offer two very different perspectives and methodologies on human deification. While both worldviews anticipate a transcendent human future, Orthodoxy preserves the ancient Patristic teaching of deifying grace and participation with God's uncreated energies, while transhumanism emerges from a historical strand of Christian thought that elevated technology as a salvific means to unite with God.

This chapter undertakes a comparative analysis of radically divergent approaches to deification between the *apotheosis* of transhumanism and the doctrine of *theosis* in Eastern Orthodox Christianity. Utilizing the framework offered by scholars Brandon Gallaher and Sergei Bulgakov, these two approaches are characterized as mangodhood (transhumanism) and Godmanhood (*theosis*).[408] While Godmanhood is built on the Patristic teaching of *theosis*, where human nature participates in divine nature through the Godman Jesus Christ, mangodhood is characterized by a posthuman vision of self-worship and self-deification through technological augmentation. As will be presented throughout this chapter, mangoodhood is in many respects a mirror inverse of Orthodox soteriology, and in turn has been described by Orthodox critics as "Satanic in structure and inspiration."[409]

Prospects once reserved for Heaven are now considered achievable engineering projects. For example, biomedical gerontologists

---

[408] The term "Godmanhood" was first coined by Russian philosopher Vladimir Solovyov. The use of this term is for terminological distinction, and does not imply that Solovyov represents Eastern Orthodox theology, as he held beliefs such as Sophiology (as did Sergei Bulgakov) that has been deemed heretical by the Eastern Orthodox Church.

[409] Brandon Gallaher, "Technological Theosis? An Eastern Orthodox Critique of Religious Transhumanism," in *Religious Transhumanism and Its Critics*, eds. Arvin Gouw, Brian Patrick Green, and Ted Peters (Maryland: Lexington Books, 2022) 162.

pursue indefinite longevity, neuro-engineers foresee uploading human consciousness, and AI theorists speak of superintellgient machines that amplify cognition and culminate in a god-like entity. Such aims effectively secularize *theosis*, promising that humanity can become like gods without God. This is why some scholars have labeled transhumanism a "parody of *theosis*," as it mimics religious deification while replacing its substance of God's grace with technology.[410] Techno-millenarianism functions as an immanentized eschatology in which heaven is realized on earth through technical prowess. Narratives such as Ray Kurzweil's Singularity predicts by 2045 exponential technological growth will culminate in an apocalyptic event after which humans merge with machines, and death and suffering are conquered. Thus, such rhetoric underscores that transhumanism functions as a kind of techno-faith, offering adherents soteriological benefits – immortality, enlightenment, and transformation – without recourse to traditional religions.

Orthodox theologians and contemporary Christian thinkers have been vocal about criticizing transhumanism. They often characterize it as spiritually dangerous, a recapitulation of the original temptation "you will be like God" (Gen. 3:5), and a modern Tower of Babel to ascend to heaven by earthly means. Instead of humble obedience to the Creator's will, transhumanism asserts radical autonomy, which, in Orthodox eyes, verges into the spirit of Antichrist. Orthodoxy sees the transhumanist project not as an entrance into Eden, but as a return to Babylon. Transhumanism is a counterfeit eternity that erases the *imago Dei* by

---

[410] Khegan M. Delport, "The Artifice of Eternity: Transhumanism and Theosis," *Stellenbosch Theological Journal* 9, no.1 (2023) https://doi.org/10.17570/stj.2023.v9n1.at1.

destroying the soul and body's hylomorphic composite, thus denying the spiritual destiny of the body.

Eastern Orthodox Christianity is an important Christian critique of transhumanism because it did not go through the same intellectual history that characterizes Western traditions. Eastern Orthodoxy was not shaped by Scholasticism, the Renaissance, or the Enlightenment. Instead, Orthodox Christianity preserves the Patristic onto-relational framework, which prioritizes the experiential knowledge of God over rationality. This theanthropic paradigm emphasizes the mystery of personhood and understands *theosis* as a direct participation with God through His uncreated energies. It is characterized by a mystical apophatic theology that valorizes subjective experience while also maintaining a *Logos* oriented metaphysics that provides the possibility of empirical and rational knowledge. The historical metaphysics of Christianity have been discarded by transhumanism in favor of critical rationalist and functionalist approaches.

This chapter demonstrates the paradigmatic differences between Orthodox Christianity and transhumanism, including their methods of deification, human anthropology, and eschatological expectations. Within the context of the postsecular breakdown of the secular and religious, they offer two competing visions of human transcendence. Orthodoxy is a premodern worldview that addresses the collapse of modernity as an opportunity to return to the vision of the first millennium church. Transhumanism is a continuation of the Enlightenment project, which rejects the postmodern critique of unending linear progress and responds with a narrative of posthuman divinity. Orthodoxy views transhumanism as a dangerous ideology and understands their attempts at total technological control and human augmentation as a satanic spirit attempting to rebuild the Tower of Babel. For these reasons, and more that will be addressed throughout this chapter, Orthodox Christian critics view transhumanism as Anti-Christianity.

A. Paths to Divinity: Godmanhood vs Mangodhood

To transcend the human condition, the religion of mangodhood flirts with the annihilation of Homo sapiens and ventures into the territory of nonbeing. Transhuman metaphysics rests on a functionalist definition of the human person as simply a series of inputs and outputs – an antiquated organism that now requires an upgrade in hardware. According to transhumanists, the posthuman may not even look human at all, but instead composed of "completely synthetic artificial intelligences"[411] This endeavor threatens the ontological foundation of being itself. For this reason, Orthodox critics of our posthuman future see this as a satanic attack on the divinely created natural order. A demonic enterprise that strips humanity of its *imago Dei* and free will in favor of a scientific faith in immortality and enhanced capacity.

Functionalism leaves no space for the subjectivity of personal experience; it devalues the self and replaces it with a metaphor akin to a computer program. Orthodox critics see this not as a progression to a high form of embodiment, but as a Satanic deception that attempts a pantheistic divinization of the world by its simplistic metaphysical assumption. This endeavor threatens the ontological foundation of being itself. Orthodox theologian Sergei Bulgakov sees the concept of "being"

---

[411] Nick Bostrom, "The Transhumanist FAQ: A General Introduction," in *Transhumanism and the Body: The World Religions Speak*, eds. Calvin Mercer and Derek F. Maher (Palgrave Macmillan, 2014) 3.

as the fundamental difference between the religions of Godmanhood and mangodhood. On the one hand, the religion of Godmanhood understands being as grounded in the ontological existence and personhood of God, fully actualized in humanity through the person of Jesus Christ; on the other hand, mangodhood has the "self-assertion" of being "outside God" and anticipates birth to the superman, the new God. Bulgakov writes,

> But since humanity only exists in individual persons everything higher in a man necessarily is personally embodied, this task in its definitive expression amounts to a striving for the giving birth of a single and unique superman, a personal god, that is, the one who is expressed in Christianity as the Antichrist. The unfolding potency, the unavoidable task of mangodhood, is this individual man-god, in whom all creation would have been found its own apotheosis… The ultimate meaning of mangodhood amounts to that latter appropriating divinity to itself and proclaiming itself as creation's god. This is the way of Satan, who not possessing any power of being of his own and in his apostasy from God becoming a spirit of non-being, can only manifest this power by metaphysical theft, since he leads but a ghostly "meteoric" (in the expression of Schelling) existence in constant oscillations between being and non-being, and thereby exists only as a deceptive mirage. This mirage would be completely dispelled by an absolute separation of being from non-being, of light from "outer darkness"

[Matt. 8:12, 25:30], which is located on the brink ("edge") of being.[412]

The religion of mangodhood is an attempt to seize God's divinity in a suicide effort to acquire superhuman status. Whereas Orthodoxy understands God as a personal and hypostasized being, transhumanism defines divinity by the abstraction of functional superintelligence. Functionalism defines life. Redefining personhood through the narrow scope of "intelligence" devalues the human subject to a simple process of pattern recognition. This definition collapses any meaningful distinction between humans and machines and between biological and synthetic. Yuval Noah Harari's religion of Dataism posits just this. For him, the only thing that exists is data, and life, biological or artificial, is the evolution of algorithms that transcend the medium of biology and take form within machines.

Harari's vison moves "from a homo-centric to a data-centric view," well beyond Enlightenment Humanism.[413] As Simon Young states, "As humanism freed us from the chains of superstition, let transhumanism free us from our biological chains."[414] Transhumanism, similar to the species of Gnosticism before it, has an eschatology that is anti-body and anti-creation, and views salvation by means of correctly processing liberatory information. The Orthodox Church has had a long history in defense of the faith from the emergence of various Gnostic heresies, and in this respect, sees transhumanism as the latest iteration.

---

[412] Sergeii Bulgakov, *Dva Grada: Issledovaniia o prioda obshchestvennkyh idealov*, as quoted in Gallaher, "Technological Theosis?" 163.
[413] Harari, *Homo Deus*, 454.
[414] Simon Young, *Designer Evolution: A Transhumanist Manifesto* (Amherst, NY: Prometheus Books, 2006) 32.

Both transhumanism and Gnosticism place specialized knowledge as the key to human liberation; they divorce the body from human essence and degrade nature as flawed and corrupt.

The main distinction to be made between transhumanism and traditional religions, as noted by Patrick Hopkins, is their "methods of transcendence." Whereas traditional believers look to prayer, rituals, contemplation, and moral discipline, cyborg enthusiasts use technology to reach the heights of human deification. Leading Hopkins to suggest, "transhumanism could be seen as religious, if not a religion."[415]

In Orthodox theology, the Incarnation anchors a profoundly positive metaphysical valuation of embodied, created life. They assert that the infinite and immaterial God enters historical and material reality, sanctifies, and affirms the dignity and inherent goodness of bodily existence. In sharp contrast, transhumanism proposes to reverse the mystery of the Incarnation. Instead of the Word being made flesh, Dataism and transhumanism in general seek to turn flesh back into data, a full digitization of human embodiment into pure information. This vision of "flesh into data" reveals a radically different eschatology from that of Christianity. Transhumanism seeks an immanentized immortality through augmentation and information patterns, it culminates in solitary autonomy and digital abstraction. Data replaces spirit, and uploading replaces resurrection.

Transhumanism does not replicate ancient Gnosticism, but it perpetuates the general tendencies of disdain for the body and the natural world, pursuit of perfection, and salvation through knowledge. From an

---

[415] Patrick D. Hopkins, "Transcending the Animal: How Transhumanism and Religion Are and Are Not Alike," In *Journal of Evolution and Technology* 14, no. 2 (2005):13-28.

Orthodox standpoint, the dangers of modern Gnosticism are twofold. First, it idolizes technology and treats it as an all-powerful impersonal savior that can engineer Eden. Second, it degrades human life into bits of information, thereby neglecting the essential paths of Christian love, community, family, self-sacrifice, and divine grace. The faith of techno-Gnosticism attempts to save oneself from the human condition by sacrificing one's humanity on the altar of progress.

These similarities have not gone unnoticed by transhumanists. In 2023 the U.S. Transhumanist Party featured a conversation with techno-gnostic Miguel Conner to discuss their shared vision of the human condition. The attempt was to explore how the two ideologies could "lead to a more integrated and holistic vision of human potential, where aspirations of Transhumanism and the wisdom of Gnosticism converge to a shared future."[416] These similarities have also been explored by Mark O'Connell, who noted the dualistic frame that informs the division between software (mind) and hardware (body). "For the Gnostics, the only redemption would come in the form of liberation from that body. And a technological version of this liberation seemed to me to be what whole brain emulation was ultimately about."[417]

The gnostic quest for superhuman intelligence is a secularized technological rapture. Rapture is a popular eschatology among Protestant and Evangelical Christians and refers to a anticipated event where true believers are instantly taken up to meet Christ, leading to a utopian

---

[416] Thomas Ernest Ross Jr., "The Synergy of Gnosticism and Transhumanism," *Medium* (July 15, 2023) https://tomrosscom.medium.com/the-synergy-of-gnosticism-and-transhumanism-ced36b8af7d9.

[417] Mark O'Connell, *To Be a Machine: Adventures Among Cyborgs, Utopians, Hackers, and the Futurists Solving the Modest Problem of Death* (London: Granta Books, 2017) 63.

existence free from earthly suffering and limitations. This transition marks a new perfected state associated with immortality and divine union. As Ronald Cole-Turner notes, the significant difference between these two eschatologies is whether God emerges from creation or already transcends it.[418]

Orthodox eschatology is amillennial. At the heart of Orthodox eschatology is the dynamic understanding of the Kingdom of God as both a present reality and a future hope. This "already-and-not-yet" tension permeates Eastern Christian thought. On one hand, the Kingdom has been inaugurated through Christ's Incarnation, Resurrection, Ascension, and the sending of the Holy Spirit at Pentecost – it is "at hand" and even "within you" as Christ states (Luke 17:21). The Church is mystically identified with the Kingdom; she is the Body of Christ, indwelt by the Spirit, and thus the sphere where Christ reigns as King. In St. Augustine's formulation "the Church is the kingdom of Christ and the kingdom of Heaven, and so even now the saints reign with Him, although not in the same sense in which they will ultimately reign."[419] Augustine immediately adds that they do not yet reign in the same way they will in their ultimate fulfillment. Thus, the Orthodox Church lives in an "interim" period of real but partial fulfillment, where believers experience a foretaste in the Kingdom of God. The Orthodox liturgy and creed keep this forward-looking hope at the forefront, "We look for the resurrection of the dead and the life of the age to come."

---

[418] Ronald Cole-Turner, "The Singularity and the Rapture: Transhumanist and Popular Christian Views of the Future," in *Zygon* vol. 47, no.4 (December 2012).

[419] Augustine of Hippo, *City of God* (London, Penguin Books, 2003) 20.9.

Singularity shares an eschatological impulse first driven by techno-millenarian hopes and can be found in both pre- and postmillennial eschatology. Premillennialism expects Christ to return before a literal millennium, inaugurating an earthly kingdom of saints for a thousand years prior to the final judgment. This view reads Revelation 20 in a largely literal fashion, in which Christ will sit on an earthly throne in Jerusalem, evil will be suppressed, and visible peace will reign for a defined period. Postmillennialism, on the other hand, posits that Christ will return after a long period, during which the Gospel gradually conquers the world, and the golden age of Christian righteousness prevails. In this paradigm, history is on an upward trajectory toward the Kingdom of God, and human society is progressively Christianized until it blossoms into an era of peace, after which Christ's Second Coming occurs.

Orthodoxy's rejection of premillennialism was formally affirmed in the early centuries. The Second Ecumenical Council (381) added the clause "His kingdom shall have no end" to the Creed precisely to condemn the millenarian heresy that posited a finite 1000-year kingdom.[420] Chiliastic views were prominent among Christian heretics. More recently, these views have been resurrected in Protestant theology. Modern Orthodox catechisms explicitly teach that the Book of Revelation's millennium is a symbolic period corresponding to the Church era, during which Satan's power is limited, saints reign with Christ in heaven, and the Gospel spreads to all nations. The "millennial" reign thus occurs now in a mystery, and will end not with a revolt in a future earthly Jerusalem, but with the universal resurrection and Last

---

[420] Pomazansky, *Orthodox Dogmatic Theology*, 343.

Judgment. In this way, Orthodox amillennialism preserves strong apocalyptic expectations while avoiding chronographical speculation about earthly timetables. It emphasizes the qualitative transformation wrought by Christ's first coming (an inaugurated Kingdom) rather than projecting hope onto a future politico-religious golden age.

Comparing this framework to transhumanism, we see that it shares a peculiar blend of postmillennial eschatology. As the exponential growth of technology continues, genetic engineering will help cure diseases, and neuralink implants will provide sight to the blind. Oracle AI systems will answer and solve all human questions, and upon the Singularity, god-like intelligence will emerge from the machine. This machine god will rescue humanity from the fallenness of the natural world by allowing them to become one with the machine, ushering in a period of utopian existence. Similar to the rhetoric of Rapture theologians, this event is not in the distant future but a reality that is soon to commence. Describing the eschatological apotheosis of Homo Sapiens into Homo Deus, Yuval Noah Harari writes

> In the twenty-first century, the third big project of humankind will be to acquire for us divine powers of creation and destruction, and upgrade Homo Sapiens to Homo Deus ... We want the ability to reengineer our bodies and minds in order, above all, to escape old age, death, misery, but once we have it, who knows what else we might do with such ability? So we may well think of

the new human agenda as consisting really of one project (with many branches) attaining divinity.[421]

In Eastern Orthodox tradition, "divinity" is understood through the concept of *theosis* or deification, which denotes a transformative process aimed at likeness and union with God. This process involves three stages: purification (*katharsis*), illumination (*theoria*), and deification (*theosis*). *Theosis* is considered the ultimate purpose of human life and is achievable only through the synergy between human will and God's uncreated energies. This transformative journey is deeply rooted in ascetic practices, participation in sacraments, and continuous prayer, leading to experiential knowledge of God. Divinity is attained by assuming the attributes natural to the being of God, a personal being, and participation is made possible through the Incarnation of the *Logos*, the second person of the Godhead.

By contrast, transhumanism envisions "divinity" as the enhancement of human capabilities through advanced technologies, aiming to transcend biological limitations and achieve a posthuman condition. This perspective is grounded in a rationalist belief in scientific progress and human perfectibility, seeking to attain attributes traditionally associated with deities such as immortality and omniscience. Transhumanism does not propose the existence of a personal God; rather, it aggregates the abstract potential associated with advanced technological capabilities into a sentient technological entity.

Godmanhood is intrinsically linked to the person of Jesus Christ, whose hypostatic union facilitates the process of *theosis*. This union

---

[421] Harari, *Homo Deus*, 47.

enables humanity to realize divine attributes such as love, mercy, wisdom, and longsuffering. Mangodhood examines a hypothesized future characterized by sentient technology, which is not linked to any personal divine entity, but possesses superhuman capabilities. This indicates totally different conceptions of "divinity." The "God" of transhumanism is more akin to the capricious gods of the Greek pantheon, rather than the Biblical God characterized by transcendent perfection. Noting this difference in concepts of "divinity" Harari writes,

> If this sounds unscientific or downright eccentric, it is because people often misunderstand the meaning of divinity. Divinity isn't a vague metaphysical quality. And it isn't the same as omnipotence. When speaking of upgrading humans into gods, think more in terms of Greek gods or Hindu devas rather the omnipresent biblical sky father… Throughout history most gods were believed to enjoy not omnipotence but rather specific super-abilities such as the ability to design and create living beings; to transform their own bodies; to control the environment and the weather; to read minds and to communicate at a distance; to travel at very high speeds; and of course to escape death and live indefinitely.[422]

The technological gods of transhumanism look less like the God of Christianity and more like figures of primitive polytheism and nature religion. This qualitative difference between the uncreated God and a

---

[422] Harari, *Homo Deus*, 47.

technologically emergent created god seems to go unnoticed in transhumanist discourse. While they mock Christian believers who have faith in the biblical "sky daddy," they also extoll their unproven faith in techno-immortality and machine divinity.

Harari makes clear that divinity is not anything "metaphysical" but practical. The focus on scientific techniques as a path toward divinity is no less than total control and manipulation of nature for the empowerment of humanity. It should come as no surprise that Francis Bacon saw this as the ultimate aim of science. Bacon states the purpose of science is "to establish and extend the power and dominion of the human race itself over the universe," and "the true and lawful goal of the sciences is none other than this: that human life be endowed with new discoveries and powers," that "lay firmly the foundations and extend more widely the limits of the power and greatness of man."[423]

Philosopher of Science and Orthodox clergyman Rev. Deacon Ananias Sorem argues that the modern technological age that arises from Enlightenment ideas has led to demoralizing practices, social domination, and dehumanization. Modern man's rebellion against God is so that he can become god; however, these attempts have destroyed the correct moral and ontological framework necessary for proper anthropology, resulting in a second fall.[424] Recounting the devastating effect the technocratic impulse of modern science has had on Western society, Deacon Ananias writes,

---

[423] Francis Bacon, *The New Organon and Related Writings*, ed. Fulton H. Anderson (New York: Macmillan Library of Liberal Arts, 1960) 118 (I.CXXIX), 78 (I.LXXXI), 106 (I.CXVI).

[424] Rev. Deacon Ananias Sorem, "An Eastern Orthodox Understanding of the Dangers of Modernity and Technology," accessed March 9, 2025, https://www.academia.edu/41476699/An_Eastern_Orthodox_Understanding_of_the_Dangers_of_Modernity_and_Technology.

The Technocratic image now replaces the politician and provides mankind with a "vision of an industrial society wherein an elite class of engineer, scientists, industrialists, and planners systematically apply technical knowledge to the solution of social problems and the creation of a rational social order." New forms of communication have been exchanged for natural ones. Common culture, identity, and personhood have all been eradicated in the name of progress. Technology is not being used as a sole means to perfect the human experience without grounding in the living God as the unconditioned grounds of being. However, technocrats do not share an Orthodox belief in a Christian ethos or Christological anthropology, and therefore, perfection of the human experience lies within artificial intelligence and the transhumanism project.[425]

For these reasons, Orthodoxy perceives the transhumanist project as truly a second fall or, more accurately, the second Tower of Babel. Similar to the building of Babel, transhumanism is characterized by human hubris colliding with the divine reality. The sin of Babel is not merely about a tower or city, but about humanity's unified attempt to ascend to heaven on its own terms and "make a name" for itself (Gen. 11:4). Eastern Christian commentators consistently interpret Babel as an

---

[425] Deacon Ananias, "An Eastern Orthodox Understanding."

act of collective pride, a direct challenge to God born from human arrogance.

In his commentaries on Genesis, St. John Chrysostom describes the builders of Babel as lusting after more and "entertaining ambitions beyond [their] capacity."[426] According to Chrysostom, such overreaching projects as destined for a fall: those who "aspire to such heights" inevitably "topple into the very depths."[427] In patristic thought, to become "like God" is indeed humanity's calling, but it must be pursued via humility and obedience (synergy with God's grace), not via prideful self-assertion. Any "progress" that is God-less is ultimately a form of idolatry of the self, bound to fail. This theme appears repeatedly in Orthodox patristic writings as a warning against every utopian scheme to fulfill human self-deification.

Eastern Christian theologians consistently interpret Babel's narrative as an expression of collective hubris and a direct affront to divine authority originating from human pride. Saint John Chrysostom emphasizes that the builders undertook the project out of vainglory and ambition, refusing to stay within the proper bounds of creaturehood. St. Augustine notes that Babel's very name, Babylon equals "Confusion," and memorializes how "the pride of impious men" aimed to build a tower "meant to reach the sky."[428] Likewise, St. Jerome remarked that when the tower was being built up against God, the Lord scattered the builders for their own welfare, mercifully preventing them from plunging deeper into evil.

---

[426] John Chrysostom, "Homilies on Genesis 1-45," in *Fathers of the Church*, trans. Robert C. Hill (Washington, DC: The Catholic University of America Press, 1986) 222.
[427] Chrysostom, "Homilies on Genesis," 223.
[428] Augustine, *City of God*, 657 (16.4).

Babel represents the archetype of human civilization's pride, the underlying ethos of the religion of mangodhood. Babel's collapse and the confusion of tongues are seen as divine judgment on human arrogance, but also a gracious limitation to curb self-destruction. This contrast with Pentecost is often noted in Orthodox theology, in which godless unity leads to chaos. At Pentecost, God united people of diverse tongues with a singular message aided by the Holy Spirit. This underscores the fact that true human unity and fulfillment cannot be achieved in the defiance of God, only in cooperation with God. It also highlights Orthodoxy's belief in unity and multiplicity. Unity is found in the singular message of Christ, expressed in multiple languages and not in the pursuit of a singular unified pre-Babel language. Thus, the Babel story stands as a perpetual warning that whenever mankind tries to build a utopia without God, it reenacts Babel's folly.

According to contemporary Orthodox thinkers, the modern transhumanist movement is essentially a technological reenactment of the Tower of Babel, a New Babel. Orthodox critics observe that, beneath its scientific veneer, transhumanism expresses the age-old desire for humans to "become God without God." Protopresbyter Fr. Peter Heers, a contemporary Orthodox theologian, bluntly describes transhumanism as the latest, and perhaps last, expression of the primordial temptation and lie of Satan to man; "to become God without God." From the Orthodox perspective, the transhumanist quest to conquer death and infinitely exalt human power is nothing but the serpent's lie repackaged in Silicon Valley terms, an attempt to seize divinity through technology rather than through communion with Christ. Fr. Heers calls this a "serpentine inversion" of God's plan. Whereas God wills mankind to become gods by grace and adoption, transhumanism promises mangodhood by altering human nature through pills, computer codes, or genetic edits. Such a project is seen as utterly satanic in inspiration, a modern Tower of Babel built on the prideful rejection of the God-Man (Jesus Christ) in favor of an "anthropos-theos" (man-god) fabricated by human will. Fr. Peter Heers writes,

> Today's transhumanists are, in one sense, nothing new. They merely seek to build a new Tower of Babel, "to reach unto heaven" and thus to "make a name" for themselves (Genesis 11:4). The Babylonians used the technology of their day, brick and mortar, whereas the new Babylonians of old, with desperate actions of self-preservation they seek life and unity outside themselves but not in God. They imagine god-like greatness in their demonically inspired arrogance (Genesis 11:6), much of which will not happen and for which they will also be scattered and then shattered "like the potter's vessel" (Psalm 2:9).[429]

Another contemporary Orthodox scholar, Jean-Claude Larchet, explicitly addressed transhumanism in light of Orthodox theology. In a 2022 lecture titled "Divinization as the Christian Project and Model of True Transhumanism," Larchet critiques the "philosophical fashion" of transhumanism as fundamentally flawed, and contrasts it with the

---

[429] Protopresbyter Peter Heers, "Transhumanism: The End of Evolution, Apotheosis of Carnal Man, and Preparation & Path to Antichrist," (February 6, 2023) accessed March 8, 2025, https://www.orthodoxethos.com/post/transhumanism-the-end-of-evolution-apotheosis-of-carnal-man-and-preparation-path-to-antichrist.

authentic transformation offered in Christ.[430] He notes that transhumanist projects inevitably lead to impasses – moral, existential, and spiritual – because they operate within a closed immanent frame. By "playing God" with human nature, we risk deforming or destroying what is essentially good in being human. For instance, Larchet points out that there is an illusion behind the transhumanist assumption that extending biological life indefinitely is an unequivocal good. Without healing the soul, endless life could amplify suffering and evil since the spiritual condition of humans goes unaddressed. The Orthodox vision of eternal life is inseparable from moral purification and divine communion. Thus, Larchet suggests that the Church's doctrine of *theosis* is effectively the authentic "transhumanism," it is a crossing of human limits accomplished by God. Christianity does not reject the idea of transformation or even "enhancement" of the human being, but it locates the agent of that transformation in the Holy Spirit, not in silicon chips or gene splicing.

Orthodox hierarchs have also spoken out. For example, Metropolitan Hierotheos Vlachos, a Greek Orthodox bishop and theologian, has written about the pitfalls of seeing technological progress as salvific. While not rejecting science, he stresses the importance of the human soul's healing over external enhancement. The Orthodox Church has a therapeutic understanding of salvation, seeing sin as a disease that needs curing, and the cure is found in Christ and the ascetic life. In this light, transhumanist schemes are a form of spiritual bypass that attempts to fix the symptoms of the Fall (decay, ignorance, and mortality) without addressing the cause. Hierotheos and others caution that technological

---

[430] Jean-Claude Larchet, "Divinization as the Christian Project and Model of True Transhumanism" *Holy Trinity Seminary* (May 10, 2022) accessed March 8, 2025, https://www.youtube.com/watch?v=eL1PIdJqAyE.

fixes cannot regenerate the human heart. Only repentance and divine grace can achieve this goal. Transhumanism promises a new paradise but does so without the Tree of Life. It is a new Babel where the name being glorified is humanity's own, and thereby a project as fragile and doomed as the bricks of Shinar.

In summary, Orthodox scholars and church leaders consistently frame the transhuman religion of mangodhood as a false path to *theosis*, essentially as a neo-Babel built on the old lie of self-deification. Whether in academic analyses such as Gallaher and Larchet's or pastoral exhortations, the message is the same: true human flourishing and transcendence come only through Christ, the True God-Man. Any purported "transcendence" that ignores the God of the Bible repeats Babel's folly, ending in confusion and spiritual catastrophe. The Patristic witness, from Genesis to Revelation, reminds us that humanity cannot save itself. As Christ said, "I am the vine, you are the branches... apart from Me you can do nothing" (John 15:5). Transhumanism, by proposing a way to be as gods apart from God, amounts to a high-tech retelling of the old Babel tale. The "being" of the posthuman, is one that is dehumanized, depersonalized, and results in man becoming a machine. The religion of mangodhood is characterized by many people uniting to storm heaven, only to be scattered when their foundation proves to be dust.

B. Immortal Existence: Mind vs Soul

"Once I measured the skies; Now I measure the earth's shadow. Of heavenly birth was the measuring mind; In the shadow remains only the body," wrote Johannes Kepler in a verse of his own epitaph. For "the measuring mind," was seen by Kepler as the image and likeness of God, a true "heavenly delight," which had to await future liberation from the human body.[431] For Kepler, the mind is the heavenly endowment of humanity, moored by bodily incarnation. Only through death, or a future point of bodily transcendence, can the mind fully become what it is intended to be. In the religion of mangodhood, immortality is found when the mind is unshackled from its material bondage, while Godmanhood awaits the entrance of the soul into eternity, perfected with both a new spiritual body and mind.

Separation of the mind from the body is the principal result of Cartesian dualism. Descartes saw the body as symbolic of our epistemological fallenness, rather than its divinity, the body's impediments to pure thought stood as opposition against reason. In his search for certainty, Descartes finds refuge in pure thought. Descartes' philosophy aimed at emancipating the divine portion of man from the "prison of the body." At birth, wrote Descartes, the human mind "has in itself the ideas of God, and all such truths as are called self-evident." He argued, "If it were taken out of the prison of the body, it would find [these ideas] within itself."[432]

Like his contemporaries Bacon, Comenius, Wilkins, and Glanvill, Descartes dreamed of a universal language, a restoration of a prelapsarian pre-Babel language of Adam that would overcome all confusion and miscommunication. To this end, Descartes sought to discover new "rules for the mind" designed to cleanse bodily impurities

---

[431] Carola Baumgardt, *Johannes Kepler: Life and Letters* (New York: Philosophical Library, 1951) 197.
[432] As quoted in Susan Bordo, *The Flight to Objectivity* (Albany: SUNY Press, 1987) 89-90.

and make way for clear and distinct ideas that humanity shared with God. Union with God, in this formation, concerns intellectual similitude with God. Ideas and rational concepts act as a bridge between the created and the uncreated.

Western pursuits to both be like God and to know God have led to the rationalistic erasing of God, both from history and personal experience. The pursuit of rational certainty resulted in the erosion of the traditional religious and metaphysical foundations that underpinned Western European thought. What began as a quest to attain prelapsarian perfection, resulted in Nietzsche declaring "God is dead."[433] Scientific rationalism undermined the Christian tradition and brought with it a frantic search to rediscover where God is. Transhumanism and its instrumental use of technology are employed to fill the god-shaped hole with an intelligent machine that can be seen, touched, and unified with.

Paralleling the history of techno-millenarianism, the double-edged sword of rationalistic certainty began in the Carolingian Renaissance. During this period, John Scotus Eriugena coined "*artes mechanicae*" to describe technology and elevated the instrumental use of reason for the construction of technology as a redemptive journey toward God. Eriugena believed that prelapsarian Adam possessed perfect knowledge of creation. He imbued technology with spiritual significance, equating it with the vehicle of collective salvation, and in the construction of a techno-utopia, man regained innate ideas once known to Adam. As John Contreni highlights concerning Eriugena's pursuit for perfection, "In pursuing the study of the arts … one progresses in perfection since

---

[433] Friedrich Nietzsche, *The Gay Science*, trans. Walter Kaufmann (Vintage Books, 1974) Section 125.

the arts are innate in man. Knowledge of them has been clouded by the Fall. Their recovery by study helps to restore man to his pristine state."[434]

The departure between humanity and God lies in their insufficient knowledge of creation and how to perfect it. Describing the Western emphasis on reason, and how it came to skeptically kill God, Christos Yannaras writes,

> Even as early as the ninth-century Carolingian "Renaissance," but especially with the radical distortion of Aristotelian Epistemology by scholasticism, European metaphysics has been built upon the presupposition of God's existence, while progressively excluding his presence from the world. God is either identified with the conceptual notion of an impersonal and abstract "first cause" of the universe (*causa prima*), or an absolute "authority" in ethics (*principium auctoritatis*). In both cases the existence of God is a conceptual necessity, secured by demonstrative argument, but unrelated to historical experience and the existential condition of human beings. Precisely because it offers an absolutized rational affirmation of God, European metaphysics prepares for the possibility of its own rational refutation. The "death of God" is but the end-result of the historical unfolding of this absolutized and double-edged

---

[434] John J. Contreni, "John Scotus, Martin Hiberniensis: The Liberal Arts and Teaching," in Michael W. Herren, ed., *Insular Latin Studies* (Toronto: Pontifical Institute of Medieval Studies, 1981), vol. 1, 25.

rationalism, which took place in the nations of Western Europe over a span of approximately a millennium.[435]

The Eastern Orthodox tradition has never believed Adam and Eve to be ideal archetypes of perfection, and the end result of humanity's salvific journey back to the New Jerusalem. The Orthodox Church teaches that Adam and Eve were not deified at the time of their creation, but were created for deification and *theosis*. They were created as pure and innocent and held a moral likeness to God. Despite their moral purity, they were spiritually immature. While their minds were pure, bright, and sound, without the corruptive blindness of sin, they were still limited and untested by the experience of life. [436] Therefore, in Eastern theology, Adam's ideal virtues were always related to his moral purity and never his intellectual faculties. Without the Incarnation of Christ, humanity's mind had yet to be perfected.

As traced in the history of techno-millenarianism, the presupposition that Adam was already perfect and possessed a perfect mind equal to that of God was a foundational belief. The advancement of technology and the rational knowledge of how nature worked functioned as a meeting point between man and God. The journey back to the Garden was understood as participation in divine knowledge rather than participation in morality and virtue. Due to the Incarnation, Orthodoxy

---

[435] Christos Yannaras, *On the Absence and Unknowability of God: Heidegger and the Areopagite*, trans. Haralambos Ventis (London: Continuum, 2005) 22.
[436] Pomazansky, *Orthodox Dogmatic Theology*, "However, one should not understand this purity of the first people as meaning that from the very beginning they already possessed all virtues and were not in need of perfection. No, Adam and Eve, although they came from the hands of the Creator pure and innocent, had yet to be confirmed in the good and grow spiritually, with the help of God, by means of their own actions."147-48.

teaches that the ability to participate with God is a unique feature of the era after Christ, not present to the same degree before God's arrival.

Western theologians tend to employ a deductive approach to God through logical analysis and syllogistic methods in order to derive theological conclusions from established premises. In contrast, Orthodoxy privileges a mystical and apophatic approach to divine knowledge. Yannaras contends that this approach left Western theologians stuck in a mere "apophaticism of essence," in which they logically acknowledge that while we can know God must exist, we cannot comprehend His essence. While Orthodoxy too acknowledges the apophaticism of God's essence, it emphasizes the "apophaticism of person," in which Eastern theologians realize knowledge of God must occur within a personal relationship. Persons are understood as inherently unique and unrepeatable, and are therefore beyond conceptual definitions. We know God through personal subjective experiences and not through rational definitions. Therefore, God, as a Trinity of three persons, must be known through direct personal encounters.

From the Orthodox perspective, the blind spot for both Scholasticism and Cartesian philosophy is its insistence on rationalism. Eastern Orthodoxy's apophaticism embraces the mystery of the divine, encouraging experiential and participatory knowledge of God that transcends rational categorization. This distinction underscores the varying methodologies and epistemic priorities that have shaped Western and Eastern Christianity's theological landscapes. Summarizing this important difference, Yannaras writes,

> In applying this deductive reasoning to establish God's existence, Descartes follows faithfully the scholastic

tradition based on Augustine: he follows Campanella, Anselm of Canterbury, Hugh of Saint-Victor, Bonaventure and Thomas Aquinas. While the total work of each of the above figures differs in many respects from the work of the others, there nevertheless exists among them a common denominator, an underlying assumption shared by all alike, and pushed by Descartes to its ultimate consequences: it is the radical reversal of the Greek understanding of *logos* – the interpretation of *logos* as the means of reference and relation, the means of verifying knowledge through experienced relationship... The God of the Scholastics and Descartes turns out to be, in the final analysis... outside or beyond the experience of reality or life, where everything is the experience of relationship.[437]

During the Enlightenment, this sharp separation fed into the exaltation of reason and intellect. Enlightenment rationalists such as Descartes and Leibniz believed that through pure thinking and mathematical logic, one could discover truth. The physical world and human body came to be seen as a kind of complex machine governed by laws, while the mind was the realm of rational innate thought. Leibniz imagined a universal logical language or calculus of reason – a pre-Babel language that brought with it the totalizing unity of truth. Overall, Western thought increasingly privileged the mind's reasoning ability as

---

[437] Yannaras, *On the Absence and Unknowability of God*, 23.

the defining feature of humanity, separating our "higher" intellectual nature from our "lower" bodily nature.

This rationalist legacy directly influenced the emergence of modern computing and AI theories. By the mid-20th century, cognitive scientists and AI pioneers had explicitly described thinking as a form of information processing. The brain was likened to a computer, and intelligence was defined in terms of manipulating symbols and data regardless of the physical medium. Early AI researchers adopted what came to be called computational theory of mind, assuming that any cognitive process is essentially an algorithm that can run on different hardware. Functionalist theories of mind posit that the mind's software can be extracted from its biological hardware and can exist in new embodied forms.

Philosophers have long observed that Descartes' sharp separation of mind and body is problematic. In 1949, Gilbert Ryle ridiculed the Cartesian view as the myth of the "ghost in the machine" – the ghostly mind somehow inhabiting and steering the mechanical body. Ryle argued that speaking of mind and body as two distinct "things" is a category mistake, and the mind is not a discrete ghostly object, but rather an aspect of personhood's activity.[438] Later, philosophers in the phenomenological tradition, such as Maurice Merleau-Ponty and Martin Heidegger, went further, insisting that consciousness is fundamentally embodied. Merleau-Ponty argues that our perception and understanding of the world are rooted in our bodily engagement with the body as a general medium

---

[438] Gilbert Ryle, *The Concept of Mind* (Chicago: University of Chicago Press, 2000).

for having experience of the world and not as a separable container.[439] Heidegger emphasized that being is a feature of existing within the world. From this perspective, an AI or mind without a living body will miss the essential structure of how human understanding arises.

Another critic was Hubert Dreyfus, a philosopher who applied Heidegger and Merleau-Ponty's insights to AI. Dreyfus argues that human intelligence cannot be reduced to symbol manipulation or abstract algorithms, a notion shared by philosopher John Searle. Dreyfus believes that intelligence is grounded in the skills, intuition, and bodily experiences of the world. He points out that early AI lacked a common sense understanding that comes from having a body in an environment. Dreyfus' critique, initially controversial, proved prescient. He effectively advanced a powerful critique of disembodied AI, forcing AI theorists to pursue both embodied and active AI. Where AI researchers assumed that the hardware embedding the program did not matter, Dreyfus countered that, without a body, there was no genuine intelligence. He notes, for instance, that our mind's concepts are often metaphorical and drawn from bodily sensations and actions, something pure computation fails to capture.[440]

Furthermore, neurologists have provided evidence that emotions and bodily signals are essential for rational thought. Antonio Damasio's landmark book *Descartes' Error* (1994) showed through clinical cases that when the brain's emotional centers are damaged, a person's decision-

---

[439] Maurice Merleau-Ponty, *Phenomenology of Perception*, trans. Donald Landes (Routledge, 2013).
[440] Hubert Dreyfus, *What Computers Still Can't Do: A Critique of Artificial Reason* (Cambridge, MA: MIT Press, 1992).

making and reasoning degrade severely.[441] Damasio explicitly calls Descartes' mind-body separation an error, because reasoning requires the guidance of emotions and feelings conveyed by the body. If reasoning requires the body, the dream of a purely intellectual mind divorced from any bodily influence may be fundamentally misguided.

The critique of disembodied intelligence has forced AI and robotics research to pursue new "embodied" forms of AI development. Researchers in robotics, such as Rodney Brooks, argue that true intelligence only emerges in an agent that senses and acts in the world; purely abstract AI tends to hit complexity walls. A classic example is the Frame Problem in AI, which concerns the ability to determine what is relevant in real-world situations, and is vastly simpler for an embodied creature than for a disembodied reasoner. Modern AI success in areas such as vision and movement (e.g., humanoid robots or AI learning to play sports in simulation) underscores that having a body (or at least a simulacrum of one) provides a crucial structure for learning. It is telling that after a few decades of chasing disembodied AI, many labs now place AI agents in virtual or physical environments to let them learn like animals or toddlers through embodiment.

An uploaded consciousness on a server farm might rapidly process data; however, would it have a sense of meaning? Is it possible to understand what pain or pleasure is without the body? Philosophers like John Searle have also argued via the Chinese Room thought experiment, that just because a machine manipulates symbols correctly, it doesn't guarantee genuine understanding or subjective experience, or what philosophers call "qualia." Therefore, the hard problem of

---

[441] Antonio Damasio, *Descartes' Error: Emotion, Reason, and the Human Brain* (New York: Penguin Books, 2005).

consciousness still looms. Despite not having a full understanding of the mind and consciousness, transhumanists continue to proceed with their functionalist and computational theories of mind. They believe that the whole of personhood is constituted within the human brain, and with a comprehensive map of the neurons (connectome) or replacing neurons with synthetic parts, they will be able to reconfigure persons within entirely synthetic media.

Many transhumanists have written about immortal mind theory, but the most notable are Hans Moravec, Ray Kurzweil, and Nick Bostrom. Moravec was one of the first to discuss mind uploading seriously. As early as 1979, Moravec proposed a procedure for transferring the human mind from the brain to a computer. In his thought experiment, a robot surgeon would theoretically scan and replace neurons with microchips one-by-one, so that a person's consciousness gradually migrates into an artificial medium – a process he called "transmigration."[442] Moravec endorsed the view that the mind is essentially the software running on the wetware of the brain, and if the same patterns can be implemented on silicon, the person lives on, enabling digital immortality. His ideas established a core premise of transhumanism known as substrate-independence: the notion that consciousness can be substrate-neutral and thus transferrable to more durable platforms.

A prominent articulation of posthuman existence is provided by N. Katherine Hayles in *How We Become Posthuman: Virtual Bodies in Cybernetics, Literature, and Informatics* (1999). In summarizing the posthuman condition, Hayles emphasizes that patterns of information

---

[442] Hans Moravec, *Mind Children: The Future of Robot and Human Intelligence* (Cambridge, MA: Harvard University Press, 1988) 108-112.

have become more fundamental than material instantiation: biological embodiment is an incidental outcome of evolutionary history, there is no immaterial soul, consciousness is epiphenomenal, the body is merely a prosthesis and can be replaced, and the human being can ostensibly be integrated into intelligent machines.

According to Hans Moravec, not only will humans merge with machines, but intelligent robots will inevitability replace humanity as the dominant species due to Darwinian evolution "weeding out ineffective ways of thought."[443] Similar to Harari, Moravec sees this process as leading to an unstoppable "Mind Fire," which allows the spread of cyberspace computation throughout the entire universe. Transhumanist Hugo de Garis also believes that the "evolution" of "godlike" machines is a cosmic inevitability and may be an inherent component to the laws of physics.[444] The AI apocalypse is not just seen as inevitable, but as an intrinsic good, even if it means that humans are wiped out in warfare by advanced intelligent machines. A potentiality echoed by Nick Bostrom, Ray Kurzweil, Eliezer Yudkowsky, and Vernor Vinge. Hugo de Garis argues once the singularity arrives, one artificial intellect will be more valuable than all people put together.[445] Such statements express deep-seated sentiments that value technological computation more than human life. Just as the Industrial Revolution replaced physical manpower with machines, digital technologies are also celebrated as a replacement for biological cognitive abilities.

---

[443] Ardent, *The Human Condition*, 165.
[444] Hugo de Garis, *The Artilect War: Cosmists vs. Terrans: A Bitter Controversy Concerning Whether Humanity Should Build Godlike Massively Intelligent Machines* (Palm Springs, CA: ETC Publications, 2005) 173-75.
[445] de Garis, *The Artilect War*, 174.

Ray Kurzweil has faith that digital immortality will finally be possible by the year 2045. He foresees scanning the brain's connectome and reproducing one's mind in an AI, or gradually augmenting and merging with AI, such that one's consciousness continues in a non-biological form. In *The Singularity is Near* (2005), Kurzweil believes that after the eschaton, people will be able to live forever as information. Kurzweil sees this process as occurring over an extended period of time as humans gradually augment themselves with neural implants. He correctly points out that there is "no objective test that conclusively determine" the presence of consciousness; but naively assumes this means "the full range of emotional and spiritual experiences that humans claim to have" will be shared by artificial intelligences.[446] Spiritualties and mystical experiences were reduced by neuronal firing. His computational model of mind means that resurrection of the dead will be possible using nanotechnology to extract DNA along with connectome maps of the brain, thereby allowing large language models to construct conversational digital avatars.

Nick Bostrom argues that extending the human lifespan and intelligence are moral imperatives. In his fable "The Dragon-Tyrant," he likens death to a monstrous dragon tyrannizing humanity, and suggests that we have a duty to slay this dragon of aging with science.[447] Bostrom champions indefinite lifespan through any effective means – whether rejuvenating biotechnology or mind uploading. Bostrom analyzed the requirements and implications of whole-brain emulation and noted that a

---

[446] Ray Kurzweil, *The Singularity Is Near*, 377-78.
[447] Nick Bostrom, "The Fable of the Dragon-Tyrant," *Journal of Medical Ethics* 31, no.5 (2005) 273-277, accessed March 9, 2025, https://nickbostrom.com/fable/dragon.

future superintelligent AI could help us "upload ourselves," offering the option of digital survival beyond our biological death. [448] Bostrom's theories are built upon the substrate-non-discrimination principle, arguing that if a mind's functional structure and conscious experiences are preserved, it does not matter whether it runs on neurons or microchips; an upload with the same brain pattern is a continuation of the person. Thus, like Moravec and Kurzweil, Bostrom treats the mind as an information pattern that can be liberated from perishable biology of the brain.

For Orthodox Christians, humans have the potential for eternal life in God. Immortality is not merely an endless existence; it is an eternal communion where individuals live with personal agency in an eternal paradise. Church Fathers taught that God alone possesses immortality by nature, but human souls can partake in immortality by grace. Unlike Platonic teachings, Patristic Fathers never accepted that the soul was naturally immortal. Rather, the soul by nature is mortal, created, and becomes immortal through its energetic communion with God. The ultimate destiny of the soul is not to exist as a disembodied mind-file but to be resurrected in a glorified body and forever united with God. *Theosis* is an ontological transformation of the entire human person. In Orthodox theology, the soul achieves its fulfillment when it is deified by the uncreated energies of God, a state that no computer can emulate. According to Orthodox thought, immortality is inseparable from holiness. To live forever as a true person means to live within the bounds

---

[448] Nick Bostrom, "Ethical Issues in Advanced Artificial Intelligence," *Cognitive, Emotive, and Ethical Aspects of Decision Making in Humans and in Artificial Intelligence* 2 (2003) 12-17, accessed March 9, 2025, https://nickbostrom.com/ethics/ai#:~:text=Additionally%2C%20a%20superinte lligence%20could%20give,living%20closer%20to%20our%20ideals.

of God's commandments and grace; in other words, to restore the full image of man in relation to the human telos fulfilled in Christ.

The Orthodox distinction between noetic and rational faculties offers an illuminating contrast to the transhumanist, purely rationalist view of mind. The Fathers taught that there are two parallel faculties of human personality: the rational and the noetic. The rational faculty roughly corresponds to what we today call the intellect or brain mind, the seat of logical thought, analysis, and memory. The noetic faculty has a deeper spiritual mind in the heart, which is known by contemplation and divine communion. While these two faculties represent two methods of knowledge, they are linked: the darkening of the noetic through sin and addiction have a degrading effect on the rational. Fr. John Romanides describes how someone might be brilliant in reasoning yet spiritually blind, while an uneducated monk with a purified nous can have true divine knowledge.[449] In Orthodox thought, the soul comprises both reasoning and a noetic spirit. A fully healthy human soul has a rational mind informed by the higher nous, and the nous is illuminated by God. This integrated view means that consciousness is more than computation but that there is a transcendent dimension that cannot be reduced to physical processes.

The Orthodox immortal soul is not merely a stream of thought; it is a spiritual capacity with noetic and rational faculties designed for the awareness of God. Immortality, therefore, involves the whole soul, the redeemed rational mind, and the noetic spirit vivified by divine light. Orthodoxy's "mind" is holistically embodied, divinely oriented, and not an uploadable dataset. The soul awaits not new hardware but renewal by

---

[449] Metropolitan Hierotheos of Nafpaktos, *Empirical Dogmatics of the Orthodox Catholic Church*, Vol. 2 (Pelagia: Birth of the Theotokos Monastery, 2011) 145.

the Holy Spirit. Orthodox saints would say that to conquer death, we need not silicon and code, but repentance and divine grace. Thus, the Orthodox paradigm critiques any notion of a disembodied mind as complete hubris and nonsense. For them, full human life requires a body transfigured through divine energies, just as Christ's human body ascended to Heaven. Orthodox teaching insists that the human person is not truly themselves without both soul and body, an idea that resonates with Aristotelean hylomorphism. The body and soul are not distinct sparable entities since it is the soul that gives form to the body and life to the mind. Thus, an uploaded mind, even if it replicated all thought and neural patterns, would still lack the original body-soul composite that constitutes the human person.

The *nous* – the spiritual mind – is precisely that which relates to God, apprehends moral and spiritual truth, and cannot be reduced to synapses. Orthodox thought would say that a computer emulation might mimic neural processes, but it cannot capture the *nous* because the *nous* is the breath of God in man, *the imago Dei*. It is not emergent from matter, but is imparted by divine creation. This view upholds natural/supernatural duality rather than Cartesian duality. The rational soul can be studied in psychology or brain science; however, the noetic soul is only discerned in spiritual life. Where neuroscience sees neurons firing, Orthodoxy sees the vehicle for the soul's expression in this world, but the soul itself, particularly in its communion with God, is beyond full empirical grasp. Therefore, the Orthodox perspective critiques the computational theory of mind as reductionist, leaving out the most essential element, the directionality of consciousness towards God. Articulating this participatory relationship between the human soul and God, Vladimir Lossky writes,

... the soul is helped by something greater than itself. It is the presence of this divine power in it, which causes it to be called a "portion of the deity," for it originates in an infused "effluence of deity," which is grace. The "divine breath" points to a mode of creation by virtue of which the human spirit is intimately connected with grace, and is produced by it in the same way as a movement of air is produced by the breath, contains this breath and is inseparable from it. It is participation in the divine energy proper to the soul, which is meant by the phrase "part of the deity."[450]

Eastern Orthodox Christianity understands the human person as a psychosomatic unity. Therefore, from the Orthodox perspective, artificial intelligence – no matter how advanced in simulating rational functions – can never achieve true sentience or personhood because it lacks a soul. AI can manipulate symbols but cannot attain noetic insight or spiritual consciousness. Hierotheos Vlachos describes AI as from of "artificial brilliance," but not true intellect. This is why purely rational processing is insufficient for sentience: human intelligence is more than data processing; it is the rational soul that actively informs the mind and will with life. An algorithm, however clever, lacks the enlivening breath

---

[450] Lossky, *Mystical Theology of the Eastern Church*, Lossky is providing clarification to the following quote of St. Gregory Nazianzen, "If you are truly the breath of God, and of divine origin, as you suppose, put away all iniquity that I may believe it… How Comes it that you are so troubled by the suggestion of the adversary, if you are one with the heavenly Spirit? If despite such assistance you still fall to the ground – alas, how powerful your sin must be."117-18.

of God (Gen 2:7), which makes a lump of matter into a living, conscious being.

The transhumanist "immortal mind" and the Orthodox Christian "immortal soul" represent two different responses to mortality, grounded in very different worldviews. Historically, they have shared a long intellectual ancestry: ancient philosophers and Church Fathers pondered the soul and its fate, but where Christianity carried forward the hope of eternal life in God, modern secular thought reconceived immortality as a technical problem that needs to be solved. Transhumanist visionaries such as Moravec, Kurzweil, and Bostrom carry the Enlightenment banner that reason and technology can conquer death, but now envisioning consciousness could be preserved eternally as data. The Eastern Orthodox tradition offers a spiritually rich portrait of the soul's immortality – not a static survival of an ego, but an infinite ascent "from glory to glory" (Cor. 3:18) in the Living God. The contrast could not be more striking, as one proposes to upload the mind to endless circuitry and the other to uplift the soul through divine grace. One trusts in silicon and code and the other in the Holy Spirit and communion.

This analysis has shown that the transhumanist immortal mind is essentially materialist and individualistic, seeking to extend the individual's conscious experience indefinitely, often apart from the body, while the Orthodox immortal soul is spiritual and relational, and finds its true life in relation to God and awaiting resurrection in a glorified body. While transhumanists toil to build eternity, the Orthodox exhortation is to prepare for one. Caught with these views, modern humanity faces profound questions: Will technology deliver a happy immortality or just a copy of our minds? Is immortality without material transcendence meaningful? Or, do our souls find rest only in the Creator?

C. Metaphysics: Theosis vs Henosis

Transhumanist metaphysics often envision an ultimate convergence of intelligence between humans and machines, culminating in a singular superintelligence, described as god-like AI. Intriguingly, this vision mirrors the aspects of Neoplatonic philosophy, in which all reality emanates from and returns to supreme unity with the One. This analysis explores the philosophical links between transhumanism and Neoplatonism, examines how leading transhumanist thinkers articulate the unity of intelligence as materialist monism, and contrasts it with the ontological realism of *theosis* in Eastern Orthodox Christian metaphysics.

Neoplatonism is characterized by monism, the privileging of unity, as being more ideal than diminutive emanations of multiplicity. Neoplatonism teaches a doctrine of *henosis*: all existence emanates from the One, and the spiritual goal is the full return of the many back to unity with the One. Despite their rejection of traditional metaphysics, modern transhumanist thought often echoes the structure of supreme unity couched within a materialist paradigm. Instead of a mystical One, transhumanism foresees an ultimate unifying of intelligence as an omniscient AI or "Omega Point" at the apex of evolution.

Most transhumanist thinkers operate within a materialist or physicalist framework. They view reality as a kind of substance, essentially information or data that can be transformed and upgraded. Mind, in this view, is an emergent property or pattern that can be realized in different substrates, be it wetware or hardware. This leads to the notion that mind can be uploaded, copied, merged, or run on a universal computer. The "uploading of mind" is a flattening of reality to a single ontological level: everything is (or can be translated into) data. As computer scientist Stephen Wolfram and others suggest, nature itself is seen as a system of programmable bits, with digital and physical worlds ultimately being unified in principle.[451] Such a paradigm is essentially monistic and even Platonic, in a sense reminiscent of Pythagorean-Platonic idealism, where numerical patterns underlie reality.

This computational monism erases any hard distinction between mind and matter, and in turn, understands them as different configurations of the same fundamental bits. It leaves no room for a transcendent Creator outside the system, the only "higher" reality would be a future AI or simulation within the same system. Therefore, transhumanism tends toward a univocal ontology, with all beings (from AI to humans to animals) being part of a continuous spectrum of evolving information-matter, subject to unification by scientific manipulation. This reflects a Neoplatonic metaphysical structure; in that sense, evolution is advancing through the emanating concentric circles of material intelligence in an attempt to become deified upon uniting with the One ultimate source of superintelligence.

The transhumanist trajectory tends to mirror a more Platonic monism, with many minds subsumed into one overmind. The ideal of merging human consciousness with AI, and ultimately all intelligence converging, carries an implicit risk (or promise, depending on perspective) of erasing individual separateness. If one imagines billions of human minds uploaded into a cloud superintelligence, the question arises: Do individual personalities persist, or do they coalesce into a

---

[451] Stephen Wolfram, *A New Kind of Science* (Wolfram Media, 2019).

single meta-persona? Many transhumanist scenarios lean toward the latter. For instance, Frank Tipler's Omega Point theory literally imagines every person's life pattern being absorbed into an ultimate computer, where we merge with the Divine Mind and our identities are continued as data within one all-encompassing Mind.

In such a scenario, individuality is reduced to a thread in the larger tapestry of the One AI. Some futurists welcome this as a kind of transcendence of ego, a permanent "hive mind" of human unity. Reminiscent of Eastern mysticism, where human personality is seen as an illusion (*maya*) that is transcended to unify with collective consciousness. Others acknowledge this as a possible trade-off where personal autonomy or identity boundaries could fade, but sentient self-awareness persists. Either way, the transhumanist "One" achieves unity by aggregating the many into itself. This is structurally akin to the Neoplatonic One absorbing multiplicity, or a computer program that subsumes subordinates into itself. This approach prioritizes collective or universal intelligence over the particular and the many. Indeed, certain philosophies associated with transhumanism, such as "Open Individualism," explicitly claim that at a deep level, we are all one mind and that personal selves are ultimately illusory partitions.[452] Such views dovetail a highly monistic outlook, which claims that the ideal end-state is a vast consciousness, and distinctions between individual minds are ultimately unimportant.

---

[452] Maggie Wassinge and Anders Amelin, "On the Evolution of the Phenomenal Self (and Other Communications from QRI Sweden)" *Qualia Computing: Revealing the Computational Properties of Consciousness* (June 16, 2020) accessed March 10, 2025, https://qualiacomputing.com/tag/evolution/#:~:text=Open%20Individualism%20,about%20a%20profound%20sense%20of.

In addition, as Eric Steinhart points out, the theurgical attempts of Neoplatonists parallel the scientific and technological manipulation of matter in pursuit of deification with ultimate intelligence. Using the Euclidean axiomatic method, Proclus believes that humans and deities all possess mathematical forms.[453] This notion corresponds to patterns of data and intelligence in the transhumanist paradigm. By thinking of the person as a network of patterns constituted by matter, transhumanists assume Platonic and Pathagorean styles of thinking in terms of abstract mathematical patterns.

Neoplatonic theurgists and transhumanists both assume that the soul or mind is substate-independent. Souls, for Neoplatonists, do not depend on their material substrate but can be realized in many mediums. In *Timeaus*, Plato argues that human souls accord with a particular star, and depending on the transmigration of that soul after death, it can ascend and be realized in a star or devolves as a woman or animal.[454] Similarly, transhumanists believe that they can actualize a human person into a variety of substrates, ending with an ascent to a robotic superhuman with god-like abilities.

Although Neoplatonists often devalued matter as something less, it was also understood, at least according to Iamblichus, as a "resource for one's practical purposes" in the pursuit of self-transcendence.[455]

---

[453] Eric Steinhart, "Theurgy and Transhumanism," in *Archai* vol.29, e02905 (2020): 4, https://doi.org/10.14195/1984-249X_29_5.
[454] Plato, *Timaeus*, 41d-42d.
[455] John Dillon, "The Divinizing of Matter: Some Reflections on Iamblichus Theurgic Approach to Matter," in *Soul and Matter in Neoplatonism*, eds. Tobias Dangel, Jens Halfwassen, and Carl O'Brien (Universitätsverlag Winter Heidelberg, 2015) 177.

Describing Iamblichus' theurgic and ritualistic relationship to matter John Dillion writes,

> Unlike a purely religious philosopher, he is firmly of the belief that ritual, which he sees as the expert manipulation of the multiplicity of substances which the gods themselves have sown into the world as *synthêmata*, and which they are perfectly happy for the theurgist to discover, is essential for attaining union with gods, as well as power over the natural world.[456]

Likewise, transhuman technological endeavors resemble the theurgic and magical pursuits of Iamblichus for transcendence into a more divine power and form. For theurgists, deities act as agents of power and intelligence, and are embodied in higher types of matter or are immaterial.[457] Through theurgic rituals, a person can unite and assume the same status as the gods. Transhumanists such as Harari and Kurzweil believe that the ascension of Homo Sapiens into Homo Deus includes celestial supercomputers as large as planets or even the entire universe.[458] Which both James Hughes and Hugo de Garis have referred to as celestial computer gods.[459]

---

[456] John Dillon, "Iamblichus' Defense of Theurgy: Some Reflection" in *International Journal of the Platonic Tradition* 1, (April 2007) 30-41, DOI:10.1163/187254707X194645.
[457] Steinhart, "Theurgy and Transhumanism," 7.
[458] Kurzweil, *The Singularity is Near*, 342-367.
[459] See James Hughes "Contradictions from the Enlightenment Roots of Transhumanism," in *Journal of Medicine and Philosophy* 35, (2010) 622-640, DOI:10.1093/jmp/jhq049; Hugo de Garis, *The Artilect War: Cosmists vs. Terrans: A Bitter Controversy Concerning Whether Humanity Should Build*

In addition, both theurgists and transhumanists aspire to ascend to unity with the Divine Mind. Once purified from the detritus of matter, a person may become unified with divinity in Neoplatonic *henosis*.[460] *Henosis* describes the mystical pursuit of unity in which all differentiation is ameliorated. In this respect, transhumanists adopt the eschatological framework of Pierre Teilhard de Chardin's vision of cosmic convergence in the Cosmic Christ, known as the Omega Point Theory. It has since been reformulated by Frank J. Tipler as a physics-based theory of universal computation and immortality, Omega Point proposes a final state of the universe in which consciousness and complexity culminate into a completely undifferentiated unity.

Omega Point theory functions as a secular or scientific eschatology, positing an ultimate destiny for life and intelligence analogous in scope to religious end-times doctrines. In traditional Christian eschatology, history culminates in the events of the Second Coming of Christ, resurrection of the dead, Final Judgment, and the establishment of an eternal divine kingdom. Omega Point offers a cosmological echo of this narrative without invoking a sudden divine intervention. Instead of God descending from heaven at the end of time, Tipler's scenario involves the universe itself evolving into God. It is, as science writer John Horgan quips, a form of "scientific theology," a "science-y speculation about the end of the cosmos" where "the universe will eventually turn into a gigantic computer with godlike powers."[461]

Godlike Massively Intelligent Machines (Palm Springs, CA: ETC Publications, 2005).

[460] *Henosis* has precedents in Greek mystery religions, Eastern philosophy, and the Corpus Hermeticum. This mystical unity is understood as transcendence of personal identity in which it is subsumed back into pure undeferential unity.

[461] John Horgan, "Is the Omega Point Ironic Science?" (November 29, 2004) accessed March 10, 2025, https://johnhorgan.org/cross-check/is-the-omega-

In effect, Omega Point serves as a cosmic *apotheosis* where the laws of physics lead to an omniscient, omnipotent finale that mirrors the attributes of the God of classical theism. This secular eschatology shares motifs with Transhumanist Singularitarianism, in which the belief in a coming "Singularity" where accelerating technology (especially artificial intelligence) will trigger a profound, disruptive transformation of human life, potentially rendering humans as we know them obsolete. In both Omega Point and singularitarian scenarios, history has a teleological drive towards an ultimate culmination in intelligence, where human history, as we know, is transcended by a new posthuman era. These are immanentized eschatologies, in that they take the transcendent hopes of religion (eternal life, unity, perfection) and relocate them within an impending or far-future cosmic/technological event.

Tipler's Omega Point is effectively an eschatological deity created by evolution as it advances further in higher spheres of intelligence until it becomes omniscient and omnipotent, and the personhood of all creatures is subsumed into it. It is a synthesis of AI theory, physics, and eschatology that deeply appeals to transhumanist sensibilities, as it promises that AI and computation will not only enhance life, but ultimately fulfill age-old religious hopes of resurrection and eternal bliss. What the Order of Cosmic Engineers has described as the building and emergence of a "natural god."[462] Omega Point theory could be seen as offering transhumanists a grand narrative in which their efforts

---

point-ironic-science#:~:text=HOBOKEN%2C%20NOVEMBER%2029%2C%202024,1994

[462] William Sims Bainbridge, "Turing Church," published August 6, 2019, accessed March 10, 2025, https://wrldrels.org/2019/08/03/turing-church/.

are part of a cosmic purpose to create an Omega God, as it were, because only that will satisfy Tipler's "anthropic" requirements of existence.

In light of these points, Eastern Orthodox critiques Omega Point and transhumanist deification as fundamentally misdirected. They argue that it amounts to a form of human self-salvation that Christianity holds to be impossible. No purely material process can heal the deepest problem that Christianity identifies: the broken relationship between the Creator and creature (sin and death). God's grace alone can bridge this gap. This is explicitly a rebellion against God, an idolatrous construction founded on the recurring problem of human pride.

In terms of metaphysics, Orthodox Christian theology has achieved a profound balance between unity and plurality. God is One in essence and Three in Persons; the ultimate reality itself is a relational communion, not a solitary monad. This belief filters into an Orthodox understanding of salvation in that human beings are united with God and with each other in love, yet they remain distinct persons. Love, through the volitional use of free will, is the glue that unites the One with the many. In this eschatological vision, the Church is likened to a body with many members united in the one Body of Christ. Thus, unity is an organic, interpersonal, and not undifferentiated fusion. In the state of *theosis*, humans truly become partakers of the divine nature and enjoy union with the One God, but they do not lose their "many-ness" (individual personhood). In expressing this relational metaphysics between divine unity and the created multiplicity, St. Maximus the Confessor writes,

> Having been wholly united with the whole Word, within the limits of what their own inherent natural potency

allows, as much as may be, they were imbued with His own qualities, so that, like the clearest of mirrors, they are now visible only as reflections of the undiminished form of God the Word, who gazes out from within them, for they possess the fullness of His divine characteristics, yet none of the original attributes that naturally define human beings have been lost, for all things have simply yielded to what is better, like air—which in itself is not luminous—completely mixed with light.[463]

Here, Maximus explicitly rejects any idea of the person being "absorbed into the One" or ceasing to exist as a unique agent. Instead, the person becomes fully themselves and perfected in a divine life. This is a delicate ontological balance: unions without identity loss, and oneness without annihilating manyness. In Orthodox thought, diversity is eternal (for example, the saints reflect God in their own unrepeatable way), and unity is achieved through harmonious relationships (love) rather than by collapsing differences.

Orthodox theology and transhumanist metaphysics both speak of transcending into a higher ontological order, but they radically diverge in what that means. Orthodoxy offers a vision of deification in which unity with God enhances and fully actualizes the personhood of each individual, whereas transhumanism's implied endgame is unification through computation that may well subsume personhood into an impersonal collective. In this respect, Orthodoxy attempts to solve the philosophical problem of the "One and the Many" by a communion of

---

[463] Maximus the Confessor, *Ambiguum*, 10.41.

divine love, where many people share one divine life yet forever remain themselves. This is a unity that values and celebrates real diversity. Love cannot be compelled or forced; therefore, Orthodoxy sees the synthesis of human free will with the will of God as a true act of transcendent love. Transhumanism, following a more totalizing unity, advocates a monistic oneness reminiscent of Neoplatonic or even gnostic schemes, in which individuality is a transient phase to be overcome in the pursuit of deification. The created and uncreated distinction in Orthodoxy ensures that no matter how unified creation becomes in God, it never becomes identical to God, as there is always a relationship between distinct persons.

Omega Point theory assumes that consciousness and personhood are purely emergent properties of matter and can be replicated with enough computing power. Tipler explicitly states that his model assumes "thinking is a purely physical process of the brain, and that personality dies with the brain."[464] Immortality, in this view, is not the persistence of a soul or the gift of God, but something that must be recreated through physical computation. For Orthodox ears, this is a deeply reductionist view of the human person. A purely materialist approach, which denies any spiritual substance and effectively says, "we will make copies of you in a computer to live forever," misses the point of immortality in Christian terms. This risks equating a digital simulacrum with a true person.

Omega Point theory effectively collapses God into the universe – either by equating God with the cosmos itself reaching a final state or by

---

[464] Frank J. Tipler, "The Omega Point as Eschaton: Answers to Pannenberg's Questions for Scientists," in *Zygon: Journal of Religion and Science*, Vol. 24, 2 (June 1989) 217-253.

radically immanentizing the divine with the evolutionary process. The Orthodox Christian understanding of God is that God is eternally transcendent and exists both before and beyond the universe. God freely created the cosmos out of nothing (*creatio ex nihilo*) and is not bound by the cosmos, although He sustains and permeates it. Any view suggesting that God is a product or endpoint of cosmic evolution is incompatible with Orthodox Christianity.

Thus, *theosis* is a transformation of the human, not a transformation into something other than a human. In contrast, transhumanist visions anticipate the posthuman, with an end result that may not be recognizably human at all. By pinning all hope on technology and cosmic evolution, transhumanists deny the need for grace and repentance. Instead, they elevate reason and thereby sideline God's sovereignty by treating divinity as a human achievement. Orthodoxy contends that this project rests on flawed first principles: it takes a materialist view of human essence, relies on overconfidence in human capability, and loses the uniqueness of personhood into a *henosis* of pure unity with artificial intelligence.

The Neoplatonic and Transhuman emphasis of *henosis* is not compatible with Orthodox *theosis*. *Henosis* annihilates the distinctiveness of created multiplicity, while *theosis* aims to fulfill creation's telos within the participatory boundaries of God. Orthodox Christian vision finds ultimate meaning in a phenomenological paradigm that emphasizes a loving union with God, whereas transhumanist utopias often imply full unity in computational machines. The destruction of personhood is understood as a satanic operation by the Devil to destroy the *imago Dei* and forever keeps humanity from a direct union with the Creator. Viewed in this light, Orthodox metaphysics provides a resolution of the tension between "the One and the Many." It provides a framework for the eternal harmony of persons in divine communions rather than the abolition of plurality. Transhumanist metaphysics, while inspired by the ancient dream of unity, risks fulfilling it in a materialist and impersonal way, a oneness achieved by computational merger rather than by unifying love, potentially "optimizing" away the precious individuality that makes each of us who we are.

D. Postsecular Moment: The Search for Meaning

The concept of the "postsecular moment" has emerged prominently within contemporary philosophical and sociological discourses, notably in the work of Jürgen Habermas and Charles Taylor, who describe a shift in modern society where the rigid division between secular and religious spheres is increasingly blurred. Within this milieu, traditional boundaries between science, spirituality, and religion are renegotiated, allowing secular movements such as transhumanism to assume distinct religious dimensions.

In his seminal essay, "Notes on a Postsecular Society," Habermas contends that Western society, previously characterized by a rigid demarcation between secular rationalism and religious traditions, has entered a new stage where religion re-emerges as a prominent voice in the public sphere. In Habermas's formulation, the postsecular condition is marked by the growing realization that secular reason alone cannot address existential questions about meaning, purpose, morality, and ultimate ends.[465] He argues that this shift has destabilized secular

---

[465] Jurgen Habermas, "Notes on Post-Secular Society," in New Perspectives Quarterly 25, no. 4: 17-29. doi:10.1111/j.1540-5842.2008.01017.x.

narratives of linear progress and opened space for renewed dialogue with religious worldviews and motifs, even within ostensibly secular movements.

Officially positioned as a secular philosophical and scientific movement, transhumanism exemplifies this postsecular phenomenon, as it provides followers with a coherent vision of salvation, immortality, transcendence, and eschatology. This has led scholars to explicitly describe transhumanism as a religious-like movement, complete with rituals (cryonics), prophets (Ray Kurzweil), sacred texts (writings on the Singularity), and eschatological expectations (digital immortality, global AI networks, Omega Point scenarios). The allure of transhumanism is rooted in its ability to address fundamental human concerns traditionally associated with religion such as existential meaning, death, suffering, and the desire for transcendence. It achieves this by framing technology and scientific advancement as pathways to salvation and immortality and does so by often employing religious rhetoric. Thus, transhumanism resonates deeply within the postsecular imagination because it blurs the once clear boundaries between rational scientific progress and religious mythos.

The profession of the engineer was believed to be the enterprise destined to build the new Eden. Jacques Vaucanson (1709-1782), was an eighteenth-century pioneer in the building of mechanical automata, and believed that a completely artificial man would be destined for immortality and perfection. With the rise of Freemasonic lodges and engineering institutes across Europe, this hope grew further. Henri de Saint-Simon (1760-1825) and his followers became "evangelists for the engineer" and "apostles of the religion of industry."[466] Auguste Comte (1798-1857) carried the millenarian torch further believing his positivist philosophy would bring with it a new social order. All of these accumulated in the engineer and scientist, assuming the mantle as a new priesthood of authoritative truth.

    The shift from religious priests to scientific priests prompted Max Weber (1864-1920) to theorize that rationalism and scientific mastery over nature led to a spiritual "disenchantment" of the world. What came with the disenchantment was the absence of purpose and meaning, leading to what Fr. Seraphim Rose describes as a "nihilism of destruction."[467] The demolition of religious authority has left modern man uprooted from the historical grounding they once felt within traditional religious paradigms. The intellectual task is now a process of deconstruction in order for a new project to emerge. Modern culture is defined by a postmodern crisis in meaning that rejects any universal narrative for ultimate purpose, leaving people isolated to discover their own meaning. Within this context, both transhumanism and Orthodox Christianity provide ultimate narratives of purpose that lead to transcendent deification. While transhumanism continues forward with the same mechanisms that brought about our disenchantment, offering a promise that if the project just continues a bit further full meaning and purpose will be restored in the posthuman subject, Orthodoxy invites people to return to their religious roots, live a life first built on faith, not reason, and enjoy the fruits of a personal relationship with God.

---

[466] John Hubbel Weiss, *The Making of Technological Man: The Social Origins of French Engineering Education*, (Cambridge: MIT Press, 1982) 157, 182.
[467] Seraphim Rose, *Nihilism* (Platina: St. Herman of Alaska Brotherhood, 2018) 54.

Western intellectual history has profoundly shaped the modern crisis of meaning. Over centuries, the decline of a unified Christian worldview and the rise of secular rationalism has produced an epidemic of nihilism, with the pervasive sense that life lacks an inherent purpose. Across the 19th and 20th centuries, several influential thinkers grappled with the problem of nihilism and how meaning could be recovered. Five key figures, Nietzsche, Dostoevsky, Kierkegaard, Heidegger, and Sartre, each offer a distinctive perspective on the causes of nihilism and the path to meaning.

Nietzsche saw nihilism as an inevitable consequence of the West's secular trajectory. In his view, centuries of Christian beliefs formed the metaphysical backbone of Europe, providing a shared narrative of purpose and objective moral law. Once faith in the metaphysical order crumbled, Nietzsche predicted that Western culture would undergo a profound upheaval. Nihilism, for Nietzsche, was the crisis of value and meaninglessness that ensued when the highest values (God, Truth, and Goodness) lost their hold. Nietzsche also believed that the collapse of old certainties could spur vitalist creative freedom. His famous concept of the Übermensch suggests a future person who, having overcome nihilism, affirms life and imposes meaning by their own will to power.[468] Therefore, the answer to the death of God is for people to create their own purpose and narrative, and reach heights of personal excellence so as to be their own god.

---

[468] Friedrich Nietzsche, *Thus Spoke Zarathustra*, trans. R. J. Hollingdale (New York: Penguin Books, 2003) "'Could it be possible! This old saint has not yet heard in his forest God is dead!'… I teach you the Superman. Man is something that should be overcome. What have you done to overcome him?" 41.

Where Nietzsche offered a philosophical diagnosis, Fyodor Dostoevsky (1821–1881) provided a literary and theological examination of nihilism and an explicit Christian response. Writing in 19th-century Russia, which was undergoing its own crises of faith and radical ideologies, Dostoevsky prophetically dramatized the consequences of atheistic nihilism in his novels. In *The Brothers Karamazov* (1880), Ivan Karamazov argues that without belief in God, there can be no binding morality. By this, he means that if there is no divine lawgiver and no afterlife, then concepts of good and evil lose all foundation – anyone can do as they please.[469] A fact embraced by Nietzsche, arguing that if there is no truth, all is permitted. For Dostoevsky, the only antidote to nihilistic despair is found in Christ through spiritual rebirth, communal love, and faith. Dostoevsky agrees that secular modernity produces nihilism, but argues that a return to Orthodox Christian belief and the experience of God's love is the only measure that can rescue individuals from the abyss.

Decades before Nietzsche or Dostoevsky, Danish philosopher Søren Kierkegaard (1813–1855) had already criticized the shallow Christendom of his day and called for a deeply personal form of faith as a cure for existential despair. Kierkegaard is often dubbed the father of existentialism for his insistence that truth is not merely an objective system, but a subjective passion. Living in complacently Christian Denmark, Kierkegaard saw nominal Christianity breeding a nihilistic life of meaningless conformity devoid of an authentic relationship with God. In works such as *The Sickness Unto Death* (1849), Kierkegaard analyzes despair as the central existential problem. Despair, for Kierkegaard, is essentially a spiritual sickness, a misrelation in the self, caused by

---

[469] Fyodor Dostoyevsky, *The Brothers Karamazov*, trans. David McDuff (New York: Penguin Books, 2003).

disconnection from the Creator.⁴⁷⁰ In today's terms, Kierkegaard might say that the cure for nihilism is not intellectual but relational: to personally encounter the divine. His emphasis on subjective truth and the "leap of faith" deeply influenced later existentialists who grappled with how to live meaningfully in a post-"death of God" age.

Martin Heidegger (1889–1976), carried the exploration of nihilism into the 20th century with a unique focus on Being. Heidegger argued that Western philosophy from Plato onward had gradually forgotten the question of Being, and instead focus on beings (entities) and technical knowledge, while losing sight of what it means for anything "to be" at all. In Heidegger's analysis, this "forgetfulness of Being" reached its peak in the technological, instrumental thinking of modern society. In a nihilistic condition, according to Heidegger, nothing truly matters or has an inherent essence: things show up to us as mere objects for use, not as profound or sacred in themselves. This resonates with how technology "enframes" the world, meaning we come to see the natural world, other people, even ourselves, as resources or instruments, rather than as beings with intrinsic meaning.⁴⁷¹ Heidegger deepened the analysis of nihilism by showing how the very way we relate to reality in modern techo-centric culture is nihilistic, since everything becomes "nothing" with no ultimate significance.

Jean-Paul Sartre (1905–1980) represents the atheistic existentialist response. Sartre accepted Nietzsche's premise – no God, no given meaning – and attempted to find existential purpose in the absence

---

[470] Soren Kierkegaard, *The Sickness Unto Death*, trans. Alastair Hanney (New York: Penguin Books, 2004).
[471] Martin Heidegger, *The Question Concerning Technology and Other Essays*, trans. William Lovitt (New York: Garland Publishing Inc., 1977) 3-35.

of God. His dictum "existence precedes essence" encapsulates this stance. In traditional Christian thought, the "essence" or nature of a human being was believed to be defined by God and fully assumed in the person of Christ. Sartre turns this notion on its head, instead arguing "Man first of all exists, encounters himself... and only afterward defines himself."[472] If there is no Creator, there is no human nature since there is no God to conceive it. Thus, humans are radically free to define themselves in whatever fashion they wish.

In this context, we can see that transhumanism adopts a framework for existential meaning, which is more in line with Nietzsche and Sartre. There is no god, and while this might mean existential angst for many, it provides a new opportunity to redefine self-identity and potential that is no longer shackled by the traditions of the past. Transhumanism advocates for "morphological freedom," the belief that we can construct our new identities and purpose through the augmentation of the body that aligns with our personal desires. The Orthodox Christian response to nihilism is obviously ontologically oriented toward God and adopts an approach that is more similar to Dostoevsky, Kierkegaard, and Heidegger. Authentic meaning is found only in its relationship with the transcendent purpose of Christ, *theosis*. In terms of Dostoevsky and Kierkegaard, this means a reorientation towards the church, the Godman Jesus Christ, and the depth of mystical meaning found in our personal relationship with God.

Modern secular society often feels flat and "disenchanted," as Weber noted, it views the universe as a cold machine, and human life as a mere biological accident. The disenchantment is what Fr. Alexander

---

[472] Jean-Paul Sartre, *Existentialism Is a Humanism*, trans. by Carol Macomber (New Haven, CT: Yale University Press, 2007) 22.

Schmemann has described as secularism's "negation of worship." For Schmemann "It is the negation of man as a worshipping being, as *homo adorans*: the one for whom worship is the essential act which both 'posits' his humanity and fulfills it."[473] Orthodox Christianity is explicitly ontologically oriented, and therefore "being" is the foundation for epistemology, metaphysics, and ethics. This is a notion of "being" that full blossoms only when it orients itself to the very source of Being, God.

Thus, postmodernism can be seen as a reaction to the disenchantment and nihilistic trajectory of modernity's crisis in meaning. While modernity has attempted to replace religious faith with scientific rationalism, secular humanism, and grand narratives of progress, postmodernism recognizes the failure of these religious substitutes to offer universal certainty and purpose. While postmodernism dispels the grand narrative of scientific rationalism, it leaves the individual alienated from the objective foundations of truth and ethics. It valorizes subjective experience to such a degree and completely disregards any objective justification for knowledge and a meaningful life. Therefore, Christos Yannaras sees the failures of the modern Western worldview and postmodernism's embrace of subjective meaning-making as an opportunity and opening in which Eastern Orthodox metaphysical tradition could have significant appeal.

For Yannaras, Orthodoxy offers a unique apophaticism and mystical orientation. Whereas the language of physics uses "constant signifiers, which refer to empirically verifiable facts," the language of metaphysics uses "signifiers which have no pictorial-representational relationship

---

[473] Alexander Schmemann, *For the Life of the World* (Crestwood, NY: St. Vladimir's Seminary Press, 1973) 118.

with sensorial reality."[474] Concepts such as the infinite, the timeless, the non-spatial, the immaterial, the uncreated, the soul, and God, although they may be formally correct and convey real meaning, do not refer to places accessible to empirical investigation. Through his unique reading of Heidegger, Yannaras articulates a phenomenologically oriented metaphysics that provides both meaning and purpose. A worldview that both values subjective personal experience and includes objective metaphysical principles.

From an Orthodox Christian perspective, Yannaras understands the "postmodern age" as a philosophical recognition of the Western tradition as a dead end. He argues that in the modern paradigm, there is no longer an epistemological method or linguistic logic that can bring purpose and meaning to the human condition. Thus, nihilism is unavoidable. Therefore, the project of modernity must be destroyed and replaced, and postmodernism is welcomed insofar as it helps provide an end to modernity. Expressing this notion as it relates to modernity's lack of meaning in the postmodern age, Yannars writes,

> Nevertheless, ontological attempts at endowing existence with cause and meaning, which have relied on the use of the "representational" method, have resulted in dubious metaphysics of "mental images." And the nihilistic ontology of empirical phenomenology which aspired to dethrone it left manifestly unanswered the question of cause and aim, the logic or the meaning of existence. The presuppositions and potentialities of these two

---

[474] Yannaras, *Postmodern Metaphysics*, 83.

propositions to make sense of the existent of the real seem to exhaust the modern "paradigm." Only in the "apophatic" language and unorthodox methodology of post-Newtonian physics does a radically different epistemological and hermeneutic approach to the existent and the real begin to emerge. If this methodology and language can also articulate a proposition that gives meaning to the existent, then it also signals entry into the postmodern age.[475]

Yannaras highlights that in the postmodern turn, the pursuit of ultimate certainty is dead. Attempts to achieve this have compromised both philosophical enterprises and the human condition. Orthodoxy responds to the postmodern age with an epistemic openness that exalts subjective experience, especially as it relates to God and mysticism, and includes metaphysical foundations for a knowable world with objective facts. Postmodernism, from the Orthodox perspective, provides space not for the construction of a new philosophical project, but a return to before the modern project began. Like postmodernism, the Eastern Church rejects the grand narrative of Western progress, but it returns to a more holistic paradigm that neither nullifies empirical science nor closes humanity off from a personal encounter with God.

Transhumanism, along with many scientific and technological enterprises, is built on the narrative of unending progress. Certainly, it is true that within the last two hundred years, Western civilization has seen unprecedented advances in science and technology. However, the

---

[475] Yannaras, *Postmodern Metaphysics*, 59.

theological question is whether human moral progress corresponds to technological progress? The response by most watchful observes is no. Technological progress has demonstrated no capacity to improve the moral plight of human beings. As Karl Jaspers concludes, "There is progress in knowledge, in technology, in the prerequisites for new human possibilities, but not in the substance of humanity. …Humanity itself, the ethos of man, his goodness and wisdom, make no progress."[476]

The onset of industrialization in the eighteenth and nineteenth centuries sparked warnings that mechanization would undermine the moral and social order. Thomas Carlyle in "Signs of the Times" (1829) dubbed his era not a Philosophical, or Moral Age but above all, the Mechanical Age. He observed that as machines displaced artisanal labor and efficiency became paramount, society began to neglect "the moral, religious, and spiritual condition of the people" in favor of material welfare regulated by impersonal laws.[477] Carlyle feared this worship of technique was eroding virtue, "our creed is Fatalism; and, free in hand and foot, we are shackled in heart and soul."[478]

The rapid technological expansion in the 1900s from industrial mass production to nuclear power provoked new critiques. Oswald Spengler warned in *Man and Technics* (1931) that Western culture's obsession with technocratic progress would fuel materialism and self-destruction. He believed that Western society was imperiling its soul, writing that the West would be destroyed from within by materialism,

---

[476] Karl Jaspers, *The Origin and Goal of History* (London: Routledge, 1953) 252.
[477] Thomas Carlyle, "Signs of the Times," (1829) 71, accessed on March 11, 2025, https://archive.org/details/carlyle-signs-of-the-times-1829/Carlyle%20-%20%27%27Signs%20of%20the%20Times%27%27%201829/page/71/mode/2up?q=moral.
[478] Carlyle, "Signs of the Times," 82.

even as its technology enabled unprecedented warfare.[479] Herbert Marcuse argued that "technological rationality" in advanced industrial societies had become a tool of domination, suppressing critical thought and genuine freedom. In *One-Dimensional Man* (1964), Marcuse noted that modern technology creates "false needs" and comforts that lull people into conformity, causing a "collapse" of prior moral frameworks and opposition.[480]

After the two world wars, many saw the mechanized slaughter with machine guns, toxic gas, and atomic bombs as evidence that scientific progress had not made mankind morally better, but in fact, it had armed humanity's worst impulses. Even as medicine and industry improved living standards, mid-20th-century critics feared a spiritual decline beneath material abundance. For example, historian Lewis Mumford argues that modern society released Pandora's box of mechanical marvels, which eventually threatened to absorb all human purposes into the myth of the machine. Contemporary consumer culture provides the ability to satiate all personal desires and hedonism in the hope that personal gratification will fulfill people's sense of aimlessness. Corporate brands and consumer products often act as signifiers of a person's ethical stance on issues such as Global Climate change, sexual orientation, and social justice.

In the late 20th and early 21st centuries, the computer and Internet revolution generated new critiques of the moral and social consequences. Social commentator Neil Postman coined the term "Technopoly" to describe a society that deifies technology, thereby surrendering its culture and values to computers and algorithms. He saw

---

[479] Oswald Spengler, *Man and Technics*, (New York: Routledge, 2018).
[480] Herbert Marcuse, *One-Dimensional Man* (New York: Routledge, 2002) 7-10.

the domination of technology as part a religious-like faith he defined as "Scientism." He defines Scientism by three core features: first, is the belief "that the methods of natural science can be applied to the study of human behavior;" second, is the belief "that social science generates specific principles which can be used to organize society on a rational and humane basis;" third, is that "faith in science can serve as a comprehensive belief system that gives meaning to life, as well as a sense of well-being, morality, and even immortality."[481] He argues that the religiosity of scientism can first be seen in the techno-millenarian hopes of Henri de Saint Simon and his student Auguste Comte. A tradition that still informs people's perception of authoritative truth is found in men in white lab coats with professional credentials.

By the 2010s, critics such as Sherry Turkle observed that ubiquitous smartphones and social media, while connecting people virtually, often leave individuals feeling "alone together," socially disconnected, and less empathetic.[482] Ethicists have voiced concern that the algorithm-driven digital economy rewards outrage and distraction, contributing to increased polarization and a decline in civil discourse. Contemporary philosophers also caution that with AI, the prospect of autonomous systems making life-and-death decisions in warfare, policing, and legal matters raises concerns about dehumanization, where moral responsibility is abdicated to machines. Notable historians, such as Arnold Toynbee and Pitirim Sorokin, similarly viewed excessive faith in material progress as a precursor to civilizational decline, unless balanced

---

[481] Neil Postman, *Technopoly: The Surrender of Culture to Technology* (New York: Vintage Books, 1993) 147.
[482] Sherry Turkle, *Alone Together: Why We Expect More from Technology and Less from Each Other* (New York: Basic Books, 2017).

by spiritual renewal. Their historical analyses suggest that whenever societies make "technique" (in Ellul's sense) into their idol, they risk eroding the ethical foundations that hold communities together.

The differentiation between a narrative of progress and eschatology is difficult to discern. In fact, the notion of modern progress is very similar to eschatology, with the main difference being directionality: is progress an upward ascension or forward advancement? For Hans Jonas, modern progress is a secularized eschatology, with techno-utopianism retaining a Platonic "residue of the ideal perfection" and "can be practically understood as the limit goal of an infinite approximation. But the axis of approximation has been pivoted from the vertical down to the horizontal."[483] Transhumanism attempts to do both; while it builds upon the horizontal hope of unending progress, it promises a transcendent vertical in the Singularity. However, many critics are skeptical of any potential vertical at all. The track record of the twentieth and twenty-first century does not afford much optimism of transhumanism fulfilling any of its promises. As Huston Smith writes,

> Modernity went on to predict that technology would ensure unending progress. Endless progress through the technological application of continuous scientific discovery—this is what modernity's scenario comes down to. And because it was founded on an illusion (the illusion that the scientific method is omnicompetent) it was inevitable that sooner or later it would bump into

---

[483] Hans Jonas, *The Imperative of Responsibility: In Search of an Ethics for the Technological Age* (Chicago: University of Chicago Press, 1984) 126.

reality—in this case, history. And it now has, with a vengeance. The twentieth century, the most barbaric in history, makes the myth of progress read like a cruel joke: 160 million human beings slaughtered by their own kind.[484]

One often-cited concern is that modern technological life, for all its comfort, contributes to an increase in mental health problems. Some scholars interpret this as a sign of moral or existential malaise. Statistics show rising rates of depression and anxiety worldwide over the past few decades, affecting 1 in 15 people.[485] For example, in highly developed nations, youth depression rates have increased notably since 2010. A U.S. The Centers for Disease Control (CDC) survey found that 57% of teen girls felt persistently sad or hopeless in 2021, effecting nearly three in five girls.[486] Jean Twenge and others argue that heavy use of social technology correlates with loneliness, body-image issues, and suicidal ideation among teens. Indeed, nearly one in five American adolescents now report having experienced major depression or anxiety disorders, an alarming figure for societies at peak technological advancement.[487] The

---

[484] Houston Smith, *The Soul of Christianity* (San Francisco: Harper, 2005) xvii.
[485] "Depression Rates by Country 2025" World Population Review, accessed March 11, 2025, https://worldpopulationreview.com/country-rankings/depression-rates-by-country.
[486] Mary Kekatos, "Teen Girls Are Experiencing Record-High Levels of Sadness and Violence: CDC" *ABC News* (February 13, 2023) accessed March 11, 2025, https://abcnews.go.com/Health/teen-girls-experiencing-record-high-levels-sadness-violence/story?id=97079978.
[487] Stephanie Sy, "Are Smartphones and Social Media Harming Teen Mental Health? Here's Why Experts Are Split," *PBS News* (June 10, 2024) accessed March 11, 2025, https://www.pbs.org/newshour/show/are-smartphones-and-social-media-harming-teen-mental-health-heres-why-experts-are-split#:~:text=Are%20smartphones%20and%20social%20media,of%20sadness%20and%20suicide.

comfort of technology comes at the expense of resilience and contentment. Some scholars label this an epidemic of loneliness in the digital age. The overall increase in suicide rates in some developed countries, opioid abuse epidemics, and general sense of aimlessness are indicators of spiritual distress.

Fr. Seraphim Rose conveys an Orthodox Christian critique of nihilism and its spiritual pitfalls. In his book *Nihilism: The Root of the Revolution of the Modern* Age, Rose argues that the abandonment of the transcendent and mystical ontological orientation of the Christian truth in favor of secular "progress," has led to a crisis of meaning. The twentieth-century faith in science is part of this nihilistic trajectory of people struggling to find assurance within the casuistry of contemporary life. People have given up the "secure refuge" of "Revealed Truth," and instead are "looking to the scientist, not for truth, but for the technological applications of a knowledge which has no more than a practical value."[488] St. John of Kronstadt liked the human soul to an eye, in which the spiritual disease of sin obscures our noetic vision of the non-physical. Likewise, Fr. Seraphim perceives that the personal and societal acceptance of sin has made modern men incapable of perceiving the spiritual Sun.[489] In this light, Fr. Seraphim stresses that the elevation of rational intellect over the noetic has caused Western society to lose total sight of God. By identifying the core of the human being with rationality, we have mistaken our "diseased eye for a sound one," and with this impaired vision we have discharged "the physician of the soul."[490]

---

[488] Seraphim Rose, *Nihilism: The Root of the Revolution of the Modern Age*, 17.
[489] John Iliytch Sergieff, *My Life in Christ* (Jordanville: Holy Trinity Monastery, 2015).
[490] Rose, *Nihilism*, 57.

Fr. Seraphim also notes the proliferation of cults, occultism, and irrational ideologies in technologically advanced societies as "correlative symptoms of the same malady: the abandonment of truth."[491] The despotism of science over our practical lives has caused people to seek authentic experiences in seemingly irrational ways. In other words, when people cease to seek Absolute Truth (God), they do not become purely rational, but instead often fall into pseudo-spiritual delusions. Far from leading to a utopia of reason, unbridled technological progress coincides with new forms of superstition and despair. In Orthodox terms, a culture that worships the works of its own hands – whether machines or political systems – is effectively in rebellion against God and thus opens itself to demonic deception.

With regard to postsecularism, a moment defined by the blurring of the religious and secular within the last vestiges of a modern period characterized by nihilism and personal search for meaning, transhumanism and Orthodox Christianity find themselves as two competing alternatives. Transhumanism builds upon the narrative of unlimited progress, assuming that technological advancement also includes moral development. It utilizes the same secular rationalism and materialism that theorists have suggested has led to our "meaning crisis" and failed to fulfill human desires through material comforts. Thinkers such as Christos Yannaras critique Western secular culture for its spiritual emptiness, arguing that Enlightenment rationalism has reduced humans to economic and technological cogs, cut off from transcendent meaning. In such critiques, we hear an anti-secular sentiment in that the ultimate

---

[491] Rose, *Nihilism*, 17.

truth cannot be found in scientific progress alone, and that older religious wisdom is needed to guide humanity.

Simultaneously, the late 20th century gave birth to transhumanism as a self-conscious movement, largely in the techno-scientific hubs of the West. With exponential advances in computing (Moore's Law), biotechnology, and neuroscience, the post-World War II era saw a revived confidence that science could solve human problems once reserved for religion. By the 1990s and 2000s, figures like Max More and Nick Bostrom gave academic credence to transhumanism with manifestos and institutes, framing it unabashedly as a "transcendence project" for humanity, a new enlightenment. This techno-optimistic faith can be seen as a direct response to the postsecular condition, since it acknowledges the enduring human need for eschatology, yet attempts to satisfy it through science rather than scripture.

Thus, in the postsecular moment, we have a competition for salvation narratives. On the one hand, Orthodox Christianity has reemerged to fill the void of meaning with a robust spiritual narrative centered on God and the hope of resurrection. On the other hand, transhumanism presents a captivating "techno-scientific salvation" narrative that tries to revive the Enlightenment dream in quasi-spiritual terms – promising deliverance from suffering and mortality through innovation. This has led to descriptions of transhumanism as millenarianism for the tech era, effectively creating a new religious rhetoric of unlimited progress. However, as we have seen, the techno-millenarian drive that undergirds contemporary transhumanism is an old idea and not a new one. It has only been repackaged by way of the evolution of millennial fantasies from Joachim of Fiore, Francis Bacon, the Scientific Revolution, the Enlightenment, and the digital age of technology.

Orthodox Christianity offers a counterpoint to this narrative by reinvigorating ancient eschatology. Rather than framing the future as an open-ended technological evolution of information, Orthodoxy frames it as the fulfillment of God's eternal plan. The Orthodox eschatological vision is filled with spiritual warfare, attempts by the powers of evil to destroy ultimate meaning, which is found in human connections with God. Contemporary Orthodox theologians argue that secular utopias cannot satisfy the human heart and that any progress devoid of spiritual truth leads to new forms of enslavement. Metropolitan John Zizioulas warned that a secular worldview tends to "absolutize transient forms of history" – such as nations, economies, or technologies – making them ultimate, when in fact they are temporary.[492] Zizioulas believes that the Orthodox Church can use the tools of the modern world, but must remain vigilant to not become a product of it. "We navigate this digital age while maintain our distinctive eschatology and sacramental identity."[493] Zizioulas insists that only an eschatological perspective anticipating the Kingdom of God can put worldly developments in proper context and bring true meaning to light. In the postsecular arena, Orthodoxy does not retreat from modern life, but offers a critical lens to it. It acknowledges scientific advancements, yet subjects them to the judgment of

---

[492] Maxim Vasiljević, "Between the "Already" and the "Not Yet": A Journey with Metropolitan John Zizioulas," in *The Wheel* 36 (Winter 2024) 25. Accessed March 12, 2025, https://static1.squarespace.com/static/54d0df1ee4b036ef1e44b144/t/66b4ec0f48a10b72f746b489/1723132943936/Wheel_36+Vasilevich.pdf#:~:text=On%20questions%20of%20secularization%2C%20Zizioulas,be%20imparted%20with%20an%20eschatolog%02ical.

[493] Vasiljević, "Between the "Already" and the "Not Yet,"" 26.

transcendent values and the hope of *theosis*. This dynamic of a techno-future versus a sacred future defines much of the cultural discourse of our time.

Transhumanism subtly inverts many aspects of traditional Orthodox thought. Orthodox soteriology is centrally oriented around the incarnation of the Logos Jesus Christ, who elevates humanity toward humble participation in divine life. Conversely, Transhumanism reverses this dynamic; it emphasizes human technological ascent and seeks to engineer its own immortality through the incarnation of sentient artificial intelligence. Their new incarnate savior. Orthodoxy teaches an ontological spiritual transfiguration of the human person made in the image and likeness of God through humility, repentance, and sacramental communion. Transhumanism prophesizes an ontological transformation of human embodiment from biological to technological, where humanity takes on the *imago Dei* of the machine they have constructed. Upon the Second Coming of Christ, Orthodoxy envisions a divinely inaugurated kingdom in which spiritual bodies roam without the presence of death, disease, and sin. Transhumanism foresees a worldly utopia where technology will provide ultimate abundance, immortality, and the elimination of human suffering. Both paradigms are eschatologically directed toward a point in which human history as has been known is transcended. However,

> The Christian view of world history is entirely opposed to this kind of evolutionary optimism. What we are taught to expect are disasters in the world of nature, increasingly destructive warfare between men, bewilderment and apostasy among those who call themselves Christians.

> The period of tribulation will culminate with the appearance of the "man of sin" or Antichrist.[494]

Whereas Orthodoxy teaches that moral action is achieved through direct engagement with persons, such as helping and loving one's neighbor, transhumanism posits an abstract utilitarian notion of ethically saving humanity through biological augmentation. Thus, transhumanism radically redefines what it means to be human, attempts to become God without God, acts as a religion without revelation, and inadvertently inverts the core teachings of Christianity. It offers a compelling narrative of eschatology and ultimate meaning in the postsecular age, while paradoxically reflecting Christianity through the prism of the secular technological era.

The expectation of an inverted form of Christianity as a global religion is a part of the Orthodox eschatological narrative. The journey toward the end of the world is characterized by apostasy, in which people fall away from the revealed truth of the Church in favor of a global counterfeit religion. This era is marked by societal acceptance of sin, debauchery, and wickedness. In so doing, this new religion is believed to pave the way for the worldwide worship of Antichrist – a person who embodies the total inversion of Jesus Christ. Fr. Seraphim Rose argues that this process has been developing since the Great Schism of 1054 between the Greek East and Latin West. As Western thought later advanced through Scholasticism, the Renaissance, the Reformation, and the Enlightenment, novelties emerged and began to reshape the historical faith to the contours of its contemporary social context. The consequence

---

[494] Metropolitan Kallistos Ware, *The Orthodox Way* (Crestwood, St. Vladimir's Seminary Press, 2012) 134.

of this was the arrival of postmodern relativism. The eschatological impulse of Christianity has never waned; it has only transformed into a new vision, such as Singularity. As Fr. Seraphim Rose writes, "that chiliastic expectation, the desire for a new kind of Christianity which we realize in this world, is one of the dominant traits of the modern mentality."[495]

E. Return to Babylon: From Adam to Antichrist

Orthodox Christian critics of transhumanism, technocracy, and globalization very much see these trends in eschatological terms. In fact, they see these forces as part of a larger spiritual warfare, with the intended goal of dehumanization and social engineering. This section aims to bring the trajectory of techno-millenarian faith into the view of Orthodox Christian eschatology. This chapter has thus far addressed the differences between the religions of Godmanhood and mangodhood, demonstrating their different methodologies of deification and metaphysical structures. It also highlighted how both techno-utopianism and Orthodoxy act as competing narratives for ultimate meaning in the postsecular and postmodern ages, both of which provide ultimate meaning in the eschatological event of human transcendence. However, what has not been addressed is how and why the trajectory of transhumanism aligns with Orthodox theological frameworks concerning the End Times, Antichrist, and the return to Babylon.

---

[495] Seraphim Rose, *The Orthodox Survival Course*, download PDF, 48, accessed March 11, 2025, http://orthodoxaustralia.org/wp-content/uploads/2015/06/course.pdf.

The Eastern Orthodox tradition often interprets the final global kingdom before Christ's return as a "New Babylon," mirroring the pride and godlessness of the Tower of Babel. In Genesis, humanity built Babel to reach heaven by their own power, prompting God to confuse their language and scatter them (Gen. 11:1–9). Church Fathers and contemporary Orthodox thinkers see a similar hubristic unity re-emerging in the last days as a centralized world order united against God, which will set the stage for Antichrist's reign. The Book of Revelation symbolizes the evil world system as "Babylon the great, mother of harlots" drunk on the blood of Christian saints (Rev. 17:5–6). However, St. Andrew of Caesarea (563-614), generally interprets "Babylon" not as a single city from antiquity, but as a metaphor for the collective powers of godless empires.[496] In Orthodox exegesis, then, "Babylon" signifies the archetype of worldly arrogance, a pattern that reaches its first peak at Babel and climax once more under Antichrist.

According to apostolic and patristic teaching, Antichrist will be a specific person who assumes unprecedented authority over the whole world. Scripture foretells that he will have power "over every tribe and people and tongue and nation" (Rev. 13:7), and will be "the abomination of desolation" enthroned in God's Temple (2 Thess. 2:3-4, Matt. 24:15). The Church Fathers consistently taught that this pseudo-Messiah would deceive many by appearing as a promoter of peace and unity before revealing his true evil agenda. St. Cyril of Jerusalem warned that Antichrist will come "in the guise of meekness and philanthropy" to win

---

[496] Mikael Fälthammar, "The End Times and the Book of Revelation," St. Vincent's Orthodox Church, accessed March 12, 2025, https://orthodoxsaskatoon.com/2021/05/12/the-end-times-and-the-book-of-revelation/#:~:text=whore%20of%20Babylon%20represents%20earthly,image%20of%20the%20whore%20of.

over humanity, then demand worship as God, inflicting persecution on true believers.[497] Many saints and elders describe worldwide chaos and desperation preceding Antichrist's rise, so that everyone will clamor for a king to save them, and then the deceiver will present himself as each religion's expected savior. "At that moment they'll offer up their man, who'll say 'I'm the Imam, I'm the fifth Buddha, I'm the Christ whom Christians are awaiting. I'm the one whom the Jehovah's Witnesses have been waiting for. I'm the Jewish Messiah."[498]

Antichrist's reign is expected to be brief, often interpreted as three-and-a-half years, but exceedingly intense. It is the ultimate trial of faith. The Fathers emphasize that deception will be rampant – "to deceive, if possible, even the elect" (Matt. 24:24). Just as Babylon fell in a day, Antichrist's Babel will be destroyed at Christ's appearance, making way for the Kingdom of God. In sum, Eastern Orthodox tradition sees current trends toward globalism and one-world ideology as a "Tower of Babel" that culminates in Antichrist's tyranny, which believers must resist spiritually, awaiting the true King, Jesus Christ.

One of Orthodox author G.M. Davis' recurring themes in *Antichrist: The Fulfillment of Globalization* (2022) is that modern globalization represents a rebuilding of the Tower of Babel. David argues that globalization's logical culmination is the emergence of a single global regime headed by a pseudo-messianic leader. Davis sees the

---

[497] Cyril of Jerusalem, "Catechetical Lecture 15" in *Nicene and Post-Nicene Fathers*, Series II, Vol. 7, ed. Phillip Schaff (Massachusetts: Hendrickson Publishing, 1979) 294-316.

[498] Paisios of Mount Athos, "Elder Paisios of the Holy Mount Athos: On the End Times," *Orthodox Word*, March 18, 2010, accessed March 12, 2025, https://orthodoxword.wordpress.com/2010/03/18/elder-paissios-holy-mount-athos-on-the-end-times/#:~:text=Everything%20is%20going%20as%20planned,a%20loan%2C%20or%20find%20work.

worldwide reach of digital technologies as effectively reversing the division of Babel and erasing linguistic, cultural, and geographic barriers. Modern utopianism is a secular echo of Eden, driven by the widespread notion that "science and technology are proposed as the answers to the world's ills... whatever problem that plagues the human condition, there exists now a 'science' that holds out the promise of 'solving' it."[499]

Orthodox theologians express deep ambivalence about modern technology in relation to the end times. On the one hand, technology can be beneficial and is not rejected outright by the Church. Since evil and sin are a willful turning away from God, technology, having no will of its own, is therefore a neutral medium. On the other hand, certain advances, especially in digital surveillance, artificial intelligence, and systems of economic control, are seen as tools that could facilitate the Antichrist's global tyranny if willfully misused. The project of sentient AI, which may or may not have a will of its own, appears as the construction of a prison planet. Everything can be tracked and monitored, leaving humanity in the auspices of an all-seeing eye. For these reasons, many Orthodox observers have found eerie parallels between prophesied end-time conditions and the emerging high-tech world of total interconnectedness.

There is a pronounced concern that ubiquitous digital surveillance and "smart" technologies are creating an infrastructure for global control. For Orthodox Christians, the idea of centralized data control evokes the prophecy of a world dictator who will exercise power over "all, both small and great" (Rev. 13:16-17). AI is likewise viewed with caution; if an AI system is given authority over global networks, it could become an instrument of oppression worldwide. Some Orthodox

---

[499] G. M. Davis, *Antichrist: The Fulfillment of Globalization* (Uncut Mountain Press, 2022) 202.

writers cautioned about an "image of the Beast" (Rev. 13:15) as a kind of implanted microchip used by Antichrist to mark individuals to gain access to commerce and enforce worship. Evoking a response from Patriarch Kirill of Moscow to believe "dependence on modern technology will result in the coming Antichrist." Stressing "if we don't want to bring the apocalypse closer, there should be no single [control and access] center."[500]

In addition, Orthodox voices have raised alarms about cashless payment systems and biometric IDs for decades, particularly in traditional Orthodox countries. The "Mark of the Beast" (Rev. 13:16-17) – without which no one can buy or sell – is taken very seriously. Many believe that it will manifest as a literal mark or an implantable chip linked to the global financial system. Elder St. Paisios of Mount Athos (1924–1994), a revered modern saint, spoke extensively about this. In the 1980s, he foresaw a system in which personal identity cards and microchips, all bearing the code number 666, would be used to control commerce.[501] Government proposals for implantable RFID chips for payments or biometric national ID programs have been met with loud Orthodox resistance precisely for this reason.

Theologically, Orthodoxy holds human free will, and the image of God in man as sacred. Technocratic control mechanisms that reduce persons to data points or exert totalitarian control are viewed as deeply dehumanizing, part of an antihuman system befitting Antichrist, the

---

[500] Mikhail Dzhaparidze "Russian Patriarch Warns 'Antichrist' Will Control Humans Through Gadgets." *The Moscow Times*, Jan. 8, 2019, accessed March 12, 2025, https://www.themoscowtimes.com/2019/01/08/russian-patriarch-warns-antichrist-will-control-humans-through-gadgets-a64060.

[501] The Eschaton Vigil, *Elders on the End Times: The World Before the Second Coming* (The Eschaton Vigil, 2024) 383-386.

ultimate enemy of human salvation. This scenario represents the complete enslavement of the individual, which Orthodoxy sees as satanic. Other twentieth-century elders, such as Elder Justin Parvu of Romania, similarly urged Christians to reject any imposed device or seal that compromises the soul's liberty in Christ.[502]

     Despite these apocalyptic warnings, it is again important to note that the Orthodox Church does not reject technology per se. The distinction lies in how technology is used and whether it serves a God-given purpose or the purposes of Antichrist. The Orthodox Church encourages the faithful use of technology for the good, such as using media to spread the Gospel or using tools to help the poor. Metropolitan Hierotheos Vlachos explains that Orthodoxy "does not reject scientific discoveries," there is fundamentally "no conflict between theology and science, because they have different aims and roles." Specifically, "Science attempts to improve the conditions of human life… [since] after the fall human beings put on the 'garments of skin' of corruptibility and mortality. Theology, however, leads people to communion with God and to deification."[503] When restrained to their practical roles, the Church embraces science and technology. There is no perceived dialectic between revealed and empirical knowledge; rather, the former provides a metaphysical framework for the latter. Once technology is assumed to be

---

[502] The Eschaton Vigil, *The Eschatological Visions of the Blessed: End Times Prophecies of Elders & Saints of the Orthodox Church* (The Eschaton Vigil, 2024) 127-134.

[503] Metropolitan Hierotheos of Nafpaktos, *Orthodox Bioethics: The Theological Perspective*, excerpts trans. by Sister Pelagia of The Birth of the Theotokos Monastery, accessed March 12, 2025, https://www.pelagia.org/the-views-of-orthodox-theology-on-bioethical-issues.en.aspx#:~:text=1,with%20God%20and%20to%20deification.

salvific, it then transgresses its proper boundaries and becomes a material substitute for God.

In eschatological terms, Orthodox writers view the religion of technology as preparing humanity for Antichrist's reign by promoting earthly salvation. Father Peter Heers remarks that today's transhumanist gurus are "apostles of Antichrist" in that they push a utopian vision "freed from the need to destroy the old order and singularly focused on the forging of 'singularity' – a chiliastic posthuman paradise-nightmare."[504] Here, Fr. Peter deliberately uses the word "chiliastic" (millenarian), equating the transhumanist dream of an AI-managed paradise with the old thread of techno-utopianism and heretical belief in a thousand-year earthly paradise. What began as a journey back to the Garden of Eden, reacquiring prelapsarian perfection, ends in the construction of the New Babylon inhabited by posthumans.

The future vision of transhumanism is the spiritual death of the human being. Techno-immortality constitutes a separation from God in both the soul and the body, the ultimate destruction of the *imago Dei*. "Transhumanism is the latest, and perhaps last, expression of the primordial temptation and lie of satan to man: to become God without God."[505] Thus, the posthuman is the new Adam, a new man for a new creation. Similarly, Fr. Josiah Trenham has warned orthodox Christians that "the age of designer humans, the age of transhumanism is upon us dear ones, whether we want it or not. Whether we know it or not, its here."[506]

---

[504] Heers, "Transhumanism."
[505] Heers, "Transhumanism."
[506] Father Josiah Trenham, "Jesus vs. Transhumanism," *Patristic Nectar Films*, Oct. 6, 2022, Video, 3:00, https://www.youtube.com/watch?v=t-adGqQoC8M.

Orthodox priest Fr. Josiah Trenham highlights how techno-utopianism attempts to solve the problem of sin and misery by simply denying that sin exists. The moral relativism of the postmodern age has provided credence for people to pursue all their passions, leading to debaucherous outcomes. Fr. Josiah identifies transhuman faith in innovation and attempts to eradicate death as a form of earthly worship of technology. Therefore, despite their denial of the Triune God, they cannot stop worshipping. This corresponds to Mircea Eliade's notion of *homo religiosus*, meaning humans are inherently religious beings who cannot stop from worshipping and seeking ultimate meaning.[507] The escape of death through technology is not a scientific claim, as the premise is not provable with empirical methodology; rather, it is a theological proclamation of faith.

Key transhumanist goals include overcoming biological limitations, vastly augmenting intelligence, and attaining total control over nature, all of which echo the restoration of Adamic perfection. Through genetic engineering, cybernetics, and biotechnology, they hope to create bodies not tainted by the stain of sin, free of illness, and infirmity . This mirrors the Edenic ideal of an immortal and uncorrupted body. The pursuit of superintelligence and omniscience aligns with the restoration of Adam's lost knowledge and dominion. Francis Bacon's Great Instauration of science "was directed towards a return to the state of Adam before the Fall, a state of pure and sinless contact with nature and knowledge of her powers. This was the view of scientific progress, a progress back towards Adam."[508] Scientific progress now proposes, at

---

[507] Mircea Eliade, *The Sacred and the Profane: The Nature of Religion*, trans. Willard R. Trask (New York: Harcourt Brace & Company, 1987) 15.
[508] Yates, *The Rosicrucian Enlightenment*, 158.

least theoretically, the possibility to provide such capabilities. Transhumanist philosophers such as Nick Bostrom similarly argue that enhancing our intellectual and moral faculties could eventually allow humans to know all that can be known, a state reminiscent of pre-Fall Adamic wisdom.

Overcoming death is perhaps the clearest transhumanist echo of paradise being lost. Immortality or radical life-extension is a central aim. Yuval Noah Harari observes that in the modern era, humanity's traditional goals, which he defines as health, happiness, control over nature, are converging on an aspiration for "bliss, immortality, and divinity. "In seeking bliss and immortality humans are in fact trying to upgrade themselves in gods. No just because these are divine qualities, but … to acquire god-like control of their own biological substratum."[509] Other transhumanists, such as Ray Kurzweil, predict that technology will soon permit humans to outlive their natural lifespans, shedding the fallen condition of mortality. This aspiration strongly parallels the religious vision of regaining the eternal promise of the Tree of Life that was lost when Adam and Eve were expelled from Eden.

Transhumanism can be seen as a technological utopianism that explicitly seeks to fulfill the prelapsarian impulse behind Western science . Just as medieval inventors framed their work as aiding humanity's return to an Edenic perfect state, today's transhumanists use the language of human enhancement and optimization to articulate essentially the same dream. The historical analysis of chapter one shows that this is not a new divergence from religious thought, but rather a continuation of a long-held belief that, through invention and discovery, humankind can

---

[509] Harari, *Homo Deus*, 43.

transcend its fallen nature and become god-like. Transhumanism updates this old religious narrative in the 21st century, swapping divine grace for scientific progress while still seeking paradise restored.

The idea of a universal language, a perfect mode of communication understood by all humanity, has deep roots in Western thought. In the Bible, before the Tower of Babel, "the whole earth had one language and the same words" (Gen. 11:1). The story of Babel represents the loss of that primordial unity, when humanity's single tongue was confounded into many. Since then, philosophers, linguists, and more recently, computer scientists have been fascinated by recreating an Edenic language that transcends linguistic diversity and ambiguity. In this context, modern computer programming languages are often discussed as new attempts to craft a pre-Babel universal tongue for communication and logic.

In practical terms, software developers from diverse linguistic backgrounds collaborate using languages such as Java and Python, treating code as a common vocabulary. The binary foundation of computers (0s and 1s) and the formal syntax of code mean that unlike spoken languages, a correctly written program has the same meaning to any interpreter. In this sense, programming languages bypass many ambiguities of natural language, since they strive for the precision and universality that the mythic pre-Babel language would have possessed. This process is driven by a metaphysical assumption that unity is preferable to multiplicity.

Umberto Eco extensively explored Europe's centuries-long search for the perfect language in his book *The Search for the Perfect Language* (1995). Eco chronicles the many attempts to find or construct a universal language from the Middle Ages through modern times. In this pursuit, Eco highlights notable names such as Raymond Lull, Giordano Bruno, John Dee, Francis Bacon, John Amos Comenius, René Descartes, John Wilkins, and Gottfried Wilhelm Leibniz.[510] Crucially, Eco argues that contemporary efforts in artificial intelligence and programming languages are a direct continuation of this ancient quest. The dream of an Adamic or angelic language lives on in the development of computer languages and AI-driven communication protocols. Medieval art often reinforced the association of the mason or engineer with the building of Babel.

> From the Middle Ages onwards, in fact, in the pictorial representations of Babel we find so many direct or indirect allusions to human labor – stonemasons, pulleys, squared building stones, block and tackles, plumb lines, compasses, T-squares, winches, plastering equipment, etc. – that these representations have become an important source of our knowledge of medieval building techniques.[511]

Eco points out that historically, the perfect language was imagined as the language of creation, the language before the Tower of Babel, and the language that God used to create the universe. Thus, we see that the lineage of techno-millenarinaism, with its instrumental use of salvific technology and the pursuit of a perfect language, collide in the creation of utopia. In theory, such a language would map words to reality

---

[510] Umberto Eco, *The Search for the Perfect Language* (Oxford: Blackwell Publishers, 1995).
[511] Eco, *The Search for the Perfect Language*, 343.

so precisely that a misunderstanding would be impossible. Medieval and Renaissance thinkers from Ramon Llull to Leibniz have pursued this ideal. Leibniz, for example, envisioned a symbolic language of logic, his *characteristica universalis* paired with a *calculus ratiocinator*, such that reasoning became calculation and disputes could be resolved by mechanistic methods.[512]

In Eco's analysis, modern computer languages are heirs to these "a priori" philosophical languages. He notes that programming languages such as BASIC, Pascal, or C++ are constructed languages based on mathematical logic rather than any cultural idiom. They are universal in that a program written in C++ can be understood by any programmer regardless of the native tongue, and "perfect" in the sense of being unambiguous and free of contextual vagueness.[513] However, Eco also underscores the limitations of programming languages as a true universal languages. He calls them "parasitic on natural languages" because their symbols ultimately derive meaning from human language users.[514] They are capable of expressing only a small proportion of what any natural language can express. While programming languages approach the ideal of an unambiguous universal tongue, they do not encompass the richness of meaning, emotion, and nuance found in ordinary languages. Functionalist theories of the mind share similar problems. While the Orthodox Christian perspective sees this as a diminution in language as antihuman, programmers celebrate as it entails perfect communication between humans and machines

---

[512] Eco, *The Search for the Perfect Language*, 271-286.
[513] Eco, *The Search for the Perfect Language*, 293-316.
[514] Eco, *The Search for the Perfect Language*, 311.

Eco's argument is that artificial intelligence and programming are modern chapters in the centuries-old search for a perfect language. The drive to build AI that can "understand" and respond to humans reflects the longing for a medium where meaning is transparent and universal. Eco's semiotic insights remind us that every communication system has underlying assumptions, and the quest for a perfect language, whether through AI or invented linguistics, assumes that reality can be encapsulated without remainder in logical symbols. Transhumanist efforts to refine information processing, such as coding our thoughts or unifying human-machine communication protocols, are essentially attempts to complete the mission of prelapsarian perfection. Such efforts are rooted in an age-old ideological quest to recover the Adamic language or create a new one that achieves the same flawlessness.

Modern science has always aimed at a return to prelapsarian perfection. Platonic idealism has shaped the desire for a perfected state akin to the Garden of Eden. Though very few transhumanists would consent to this "Adamic restoration" to be their goal, the posthuman very much represents a person emancipated from natural forces and transcends humanity's historical condition. Recounting this eschatological impulse of science, Hans Jonas writes,

> ... a second creation perfecting the first, free of sin; the new "Adam" raised from the fall of the old and immune against its recurrence; the *imago Dei* on earth at last shinning forth in its intended purity... A secularized eschatology of the new Adam must substitute worldly

causes for the divine feat that was to work the miracle of transformation in religious creeds.[515]

In Orthodox thought, the scriptural portrayal of Christ as the "New Adam" or the "Second Adam" (Romans 5:12-21; 1 Corinthians 15:22, 45-49) is foundational. Adam, the first man, was created in the image of God with the potential to attain perfect communion with his Creator. However, through his disobedience and falling into sin, Adam introduced mortality, corruption, and spiritual alienation into the human experience. Christ, the Eternal Logos of God, took on human flesh and nature, fully identifying Himself with humanity, yet without sin, thereby perfectly accomplishing what the first Adam failed to achieve. Thus, Christ's Incarnation is more than restoration, it is a total transformation. Christ does not simply restore humanity to Adam's original condition, but elevates humanity beyond the original Edenic state. The Patristic Fathers consistently highlight that in Christ's Resurrection and Ascension, human nature itself is glorified and enthroned at the right hand of God. As St. Gregory Nazianzen writes,

> For that which He assumed He has not healed; but that which is united to His Godhead is also saved. If only half of Adam fell, then that which Christ assumes and saves may be half also; but if the whole of his nature fell, it must

---

[515] Hans Jonas, *The Imperative of Responsibility: In Search of an Ethics for the Technological Age* (Chicago: University of Chicago Press, 1984) 178-79.

be united to the whole nature of Him that was begotten, and so be saved as a whole.⁵¹⁶

In Orthodox theology, Adam's narrative is understood typologically and historically, bearing critical implications for soteriology and eschatology. Adam is viewed as an archetypal figure who signifies both humanity's potential and its tragic failure. As Metropolitan Hierotheos Vlachos describes, Adam was created neither perfect nor immortal by nature, but rather innocent and in a state of spiritual infancy. He had the vocation to advance towards spiritual perfection through communion with God.⁵¹⁷ Within Orthodox eschatology, the narrative arc stretching from Genesis to Revelation demonstrates that humanity is called not merely to recover Eden, but to enter a New Jerusalem, a transcendent reality far surpassing Edenic innocence.

Unlike attempts to return to prelapsarian perfection, Orthodox eschatology views salvation and ultimate perfection as a divine gift made possible exclusively through union with Christ and the uncreated energies. Man's perfection is not a restoration of the first Adam, but the fullness of Christ, the second Adam. This is the meaning of *theosis*; perfection is found in attaining the image and likeness of the Godman, the *Logos* of creation. The fundamental difference between the religions of Godmanhood and mangodhood relates to who embodies perfection. The religion of mangodhood is still confined to the created order; salvation is found in the machine, a cyborg-Adam. Perfection is a

---
⁵¹⁶ Gregory of Nazianzus, "To Cledonius the Priest Against Apollinarius," in *Nicene and Post-Nicene Fathers*, Series II, Vol. 7, ed. Phillip Schaff (Massachusetts: Hendrickson Publishing, 1979) 861.
⁵¹⁷ Metroplotan Hierotheos of Nafpaktos, *Orthodox Psychotherapy* (Pelagia: Birth of the Theotokos Monastery, 2022) 100-55.

transcendental ideal as it exists nowhere in material reality. Therefore, to transpose the concept of perfection into the material world, the platonic metaphysics and technological hubris of transhumanism result in an unattainable goal by its own definitional standards.

Therefore, Orthodox Christians often perceive transhumanism as neo-Gnosticism. Gnostics believed that esoteric knowledge about the true divine realm and the self's higher origin was the key to salvation. Transhumanism exhibits a comparable faith in scientific and technical knowledge as the path to transcendence. Instead of secret mystical knowledge, transhumanists pursue cutting-edge research in genetics, artificial intelligence, and nanotechnology to theurgically unlock new powers for a new god. Both systems of thought see the present human condition as something to be overcome through a form of enlightenment. As Erik Davis notes, today's tech evangelists often display "TechGnosis," a quasi-spiritual belief that technology can uncover deeper truths and free us from our limitations. For transhumanists, technology is the "esoteric" means by which we seek illumination and immortality. Placing them in the same tradition as alchemists, hermeticists, and rosicrucians. Davis writes,

> The mythic structures and psychology of Gnosticism seem strangely resonant with the digital zeitgeist and its paradigm of information… Gnostic myth anticipates the more extreme dreams of today's mechanistic mutants and cyberspace cowboys, especially their libertarian drive toward freedom and self-divinization, and their dualistic

rejection of matter for the incorporeal possibilities of mind.[518]

It is not just Christians who have characterized transhumanism as a bold rebellion against God; transhumanists often frame their projects in terms of the mythic rebels Lucifer and Prometheus. Julian Huxley described his "Religion Without Revelation" as a explicitly promethean project, where scientific knowledge steals the fire away from the gods and uses it to illuminate humanity's path forward. Max More's essay "In praise of the Devil," recasts Lucifer as an intellectual hero of freedom and defiance against the cosmic tyranny of traditional Christianity. For More, Lucifer "is a force of good," as he came to "hate God's kingdom, his sadism, his demand for slavish conformity and obedience," and "realized that he could never fully think for himself" under God's control. Therefore "he left Heaven, that terrible spiritual-State" so he could build his own kingdom characterized by reason, intelligence, and critical thought.[519]

In a similar vein, biophysicist an author Gregory Stock describes the aim to "seize control of our evolutionary future" as a promethean act that is "too characteristically human."[520] For Stock, whether we have well-founded objections or not, biotechnological progress cannot be stopped because human nature is about "stealing fire from the gods" to increase our power and control. In his play "Prometheus Unbound" Percy Shelly utilizes an altruistic peace-loving version of Milton's Satan, who

---

[518] Erik Davis, *Techgnosis*, 80.
[519] Max More, "In Praise of the Devil," 1.
[520] Gregory Stock, *Redesigning Humans: Our Inevitable Genetic Future* (New York: Houghton Mifflin, 2022) 2.

is distinguished by his "courage, majesty, and firm and patient opposition to omnipotent force."[521] Not surprisingly, Giovanni Pico della Mirandola in his *Oration on the Dignity of Man* cites Prometheus as an apt symbol for humanity "by reason of our nature sloughing its skin and transforming itself."[522] In this sense Pico can be credited as the first transhumanist because he provided the normative anthropology of transhumanism "by defining man as an animal whose nature it is not to have a nature."[523] Since Eden, Satan has been luring humanity into the false promise to transcend into a god-like divinity, but now his method is techngnosis.

The iconic logo of Apple computers symbolically represents this primordial gnostic temptation. The apple with a bite taken out of it draws connection to the Gard of Eden and has been part of Apple's branding strategy representing the company's devotion to innovation and the pursuit of knowledge. After brainstorming different names and logos, cofounders Steve Jobs and Steve Wozniak decided on the apple, "due to its allusions to the 'forbidden fruit' in the 'Garden of Eden.'"[524]

Modern authors with religious backgrounds have themselves drawn a connection between modern technological enthusiasm and Gnosticism. Meghan O'Gieblyn, for instance, in her essay "Ghost in the

---

[521] Percy Shelly, *Prometheus Unbound: a Lyrical Drama*, ed. Vida D. Schudder (New York: D.C. Heath & Co. Publishers, 1892) 3. https://archive.org/details/prometheusunbou00shelgoog/page/n66/mode/2up?q=courage.

[522] Giovanni Pico della Mirandola, *On the Dignity of Man, On Being and the One, Heptaplus*, trans. Charles Glenn Wallis (New York: The Bobbs-Merrill Company Inc., 1965) 5.

[523] Michael Hauskeller, "Prometheus Unbound: Transhumanist Arguments from (human) Nature," in *Ethical Perspectives* 16, no.1 (2009) 3-20. doi: 10.2143/EP.16.1.0000000.

[524] Siddharth Singh Bisen, "Apple Logo History: Everything You Need to Know About the Apple Logo," Oct. 13, 2017, accessed March 13, 2025, https://www.linkedin.com/pulse/apple-logo-history-everything-you-need-know-siddharth-singh-bisen.

Cloud," reflects on how transhumanism repackages the Christian and Gnostic idea of the soul's rapture in technological terms, with "upload" acting as a secular ascension.[525] The "Ghost" in her title refers to the soul being extracted from the machine-body. C.S. Lewis's dystopian novel *That Hideous Strength* (1945) presciently critiqued a proto-transhumanist project and explicitly likened it to a Gnostic rejection of the body. In Lewis's story, scientists attempt to achieve immortality by preserving the human head and discarding the body, an uncanny fictional parallel to real transhumanist practices, such as cryonics and mind uploading research. Lewis, writing from a Christian perspective, identified this impulse as essentially gnostic, in that it is a hatred of embodied life and a prideful desire to become pure mind.

In the end, Orthodoxy expects a New Eden that is God's gift, far surpassing the first Eden. As St. Paul wrote, "Eye has not seen, nor ear heard, nor have entered into the heart of man the things which God has prepared for those who love Him" (1 Cor. 2:9). The transhumanist vision has entered into the heart of man, filling it with idolatrous passions of self-worship and attempts to deify itself in the defiance of God. Thus, it remains infinitely below what God has in store; it is understood not as an elevation, but a devolution of human beings into machines. Revelation depicts the New Jerusalem with the Tree of Life and the river of life, a city where God and the Lamb dwell with humanity (Rev. 22:1-5). The Orthodox commentary emphasizes that God's Presence is what makes it paradise. Remove God from the picture, and no amount of technology or augmented abilities can fill the spiritual void.

---

[525] Meghan O'Gieblyn, "Ghost in the Cloud," in *n+1 Magazine* 28 (Spring 2017), accessed March 13, 2025, https://www.nplusonemag.com/issue-28/essays/ghost-in-the-cloud/.

We can conclude that transhumanist eschatology is a secular mimicry, since it takes Christian millenarian hope and empties it of Christ by placing the posthuman as the omega of history. In this sense, it is deeply connected to the spirit of Antichrist, who will "exalt himself above all that is called God" (2 Thess. 2:4). Transhumanism exalts human potential above the need for God. Orthodox eschatology serves as a critique because it reminds the world that paradise was first lost by trying to become God without God, and paradise is regained only through God becoming man and lifting us up. Any technological journey back to Eden is doomed to be lost in the desert or to find a counterfeit Eden. We obtain a high-tech Disneyland that masks the spiritual wasteland of its inhabitants. As Christ asked, "What does it profit a man to gain the whole world and lose his soul?" (Mark 8:36). The Orthodox Church would similarly ask, What does it profit humanity to conquer disease and aging, if in the process we lose our likeness to God? If we lose any possible hope for true deification and the source of life's ultimate meaning?

Orthodox theology draws a clear line between the divine transfiguration and artificial transformation. *Theosis* is a gift of loving communion with the living God, leading to a transfigured creation; this is the heart of the Christian Eden-to-New-Eden narrative. The religion of mangodhood is an imposed technological change, external and bereft of communion with the Creator. It is the difference between a living body and a lifelike robot: one has the breath of God, the other is animated by electricity, and the hands of fallen beings. Regardless of how advanced the robot is, it lacks the *imago Dei* already residing in humanity in their present form. The New Eden promised in Revelation is not merely a return to the past, but the fulfillment of humanity's original calling to grow in God's likeness, a reality so sublime that technology's best dreams seem like shadows of it. Orthodox eschatology thus champions a Christ-centered hope and simultaneously serves as a prophetic critique of transhumanist hubris. It assures believers that God will restore Paradise in His way and His time, and warns that any man-made Eden (however enticing with gadgets and longevity) is at best a temporary illusion and, at worst, a vehicle for Antichrist's deception. The true journey back to Eden is the journey of repentance, sanctification, and faithful endurance to the end, when Christ will say, "To him who overcomes, I will give to eat from the tree of life, which is in the midst of the Paradise of God" (Rev. 2:7).

F. Conclusion

The posthuman nature of transhumanism is consistent with the theological impulse of techno-millenarianism to return to prelapsarian perfection. In their attempts to rebuild the Tower of Babel, transhumanism implements the "perfect" language of code. Programming languages have supplanted natural languages as ideal, thus providing computer engineers with flawless communication between humans and machines. A language that is believed to be objective, logically founded, and surpasses any confusion in personal interpretation.

This quest for perfection is indicative of the monistic tendencies of transhuman metaphysics. Despite their rejection of traditional metaphysics, transhumanism still holds onto the platonic ideal of perfect unity in material terms. Harmony between the one and the many is now found in various substrates that unify all persons to the collective hivemind of an emergent AI god. The unique personhood of individuals is degraded to functionalist definitions of inputs and outputs, transforming humanity's *imago Dei* into the image of the machine. The transfiguration of humans into machines is part of the chiliastic fervor that underpins the scientific enterprise from its inception.

There are profound differences between the Orthodox conception of deification through *theosis* and the transhuman vision of technological *apotheosis*. *Theosis* is about synergistic communion with the Godman Jesus Christ, and preserves the uniqueness of human personhood while elevating it to share in the divine life. The Orthodox paradigm maintains clear distinctions between Creator and creation, even while affirming the possibility of an intimate communion. Theosis is fundamentally relational, transforming a person through divine life into the likeness of God.

By contrast, transhumanism proposes a material monism in which humans are subsumed into a network of artificial intelligence to arrive at a posthuman condition with enhanced capabilities. Mangodhood, as defined by Gallaher and Bulgakov, is an attempt to self-deify through the existential means of technology. It collapses the notion of a transcendent God into an immanent one and seeks to engineer divinity rather than receive it as grace. Transhumanism reduces the human person to patterns of information and valorizes "data" as the foundation of life itself. All life, biological and synthetic, is understood in terms of algorithms processing information in the evolutionary pursuit of superintelligence.

Although both paradigms present eschatological visions of human transcendence, they differ radically in their metaphysical foundations, anthropological assumptions, and ultimate *telos*. Both worldviews can be seen as alternative paths in the postsecular moment and the modern crisis in meaning. Transhumanism offers a technoscientific narrative of salvation, updating Enlightenment ideals of progress with explicit religious rhetoric. Meanwhile, Orthodoxy reaffirms Patristic spiritual wisdom as an antidote to nihilism and proposes *theosis* as the ultimate fulfillment of human purpose.

Crucially, Orthodox critics interpret the transhumanist project through an eschatological lens. It sees the pursuit of perfect language, an immortal physical body, and sentient AI as leading to a second fall. If centrally controlled, as transhumanists predict, the Orthodox Church understands this as a building of the New Babylon, a kingdom set for total control by Antichrist. The drive to technologically recreate Edenic perfection is seen as a misguided attempt to bypass the need for repentance and divine grace. Orthodox theology insists that true divinity and entrance into paradise is found not in augmented abilities or extended lifespans but in loving communion with the Triune God.

This comparative analysis reveals that transhumanism and Orthodox Christianity are competing postsecular visions of human destiny, each offering distinct answers to the questions of mortality, meaning, and human deification. As humanity stands at the threshold of unprecedented technological capabilities, the stark contrast between engineered mangodhood and the gracious gift of Godmanhood takes on existential urgency. The Orthodox critique serves as a prophetic warning against the hubris of self-deification, while affirming the hope for genuine transfiguration through Christ.

Conclusion:
The Battle Ensues

Exploration of transhumanism as a postsecular faith reveals profound tensions at the intersection of technology, religion, and human nature. This analysis has demonstrated how transhumanism functions analogously to traditional religions by providing a comprehensive worldview, sense of ultimate meaning, and vision of human transcendence, albeit through technological rather than supernatural means. The movement's quasi-religious dimensions are evident in its eschatological narrative of the Singularity, its salvific promises of radical life extension and enhancement, and its apotheotic aspirations for humanity to attain god-like capacities.

Transhumanism can be understood as the latest iteration of a long-standing techno-millenarian impulse in Western thought, tracing back to medieval Christian visions of recovering Edenic perfection through the mechanical arts. The Enlightenment's faith in reason and science to perfect human nature provided further philosophical foundations. Contemporary transhumanism has emerged as a distinct cultural phenomenon advocating the use of advanced technologies to radically transcend biological limitations.

While most transhumanists reject traditional religious labels, the movement exhibits clear religious functions in our postsecular context. It provides cosmic purpose, ethical frameworks, and transcendent aspirations for individuals who have largely abandoned organized religions. Transhumanism thus exemplifies the blurring of secular and religious categories in late modernity, re-enchanting disenchanted worldviews through technological myths. The transhumanist paradigm raises profound questions about human nature, embodiment, and the telos of technological progress. Its functionalist metaphysics and utilitarian ethics stand in stark contrast to traditional religious anthropologies. The movement's Gnostic impulses to escape bodily limitations through secret knowledge echo ancient heresies, and its techno-magical aspirations to engineer divinity parallel Renaissance natural magic and alchemy.

Ultimately, transhumanism represents both the *apotheosis* and potential *nemesis* of Enlightenment humanism. It extends rationalist faith in human progress to radical extremes while simultaneously threatening to dissolve the human subject it seeks to perfect. As an ontological project, it aims to redefine the boundaries of human nature itself. The stakes could not be higher - either the transcendence or extinction of humanity as we know it. As humanity stands on the precipice of transformative technologies, rigorous ethical and metaphysical reflection is imperative.

The first chapter explored transhumanism's theological roots in Western Christian thought, which viewed technology as a means to restore humanity's prelapsarian perfection. It traced this concept from late antiquity to modernity, showing how technology gained sacred significance as a tool for reclaiming Eden. The chapter discusses key figures such as John Scotus Eriugena and Joachim of Fiore, who linked mechanical arts to spiritual perfection and millenarian expectations. It examines how thinkers such as Roger Bacon, Francis Bacon, and Robert Boyle advanced empirical science as a spiritual pursuit to recover Adamic knowledge. The narrative covers the institutionalization of this techno-millenarian vision through organizations like the Royal Society and Freemasonry, and its evolution in America as a secularized, nationalistic ideal. Chapter one examined how technological progress became intertwined with American exceptionalism and the concept of Manifest Destiny.

The second chapter offered an exegesis of transhumanism as a postsecular belief system, deconstructing its historical antecedents, philosophical foundations, and sociocultural ramifications. It discussed the paradoxical nature of transhumanism, which, despite its ostensibly secular veneer, manifests unequivocal religious dimensions in its eschatological narrative and soteriological promises. This discourse traced the movement's genealogy from Julian Huxley to the contemporary transhumanist zeitgeist. It scrutinized transhumanism's syncretic assimilation of archaic spiritual paradigms, its explicit self-identification as a nascent religion by certain factions, and the continuity of its faith with techno-millenarian ideologies. The analysis further engaged with the critiques and potential perils inherent in transhumanist aspirations, ultimately situating transhumanism within the postsecular landscape as a novel faith system that proffers meaning and transcendence through technological, rather than traditional religious frameworks.

The third chapter focused on the intricate theological framework of Eastern Orthodox Christianity, specifically on the concept of *theosis* and its multifaceted implications. This chapter explored the essence-energy distinction in Orthodox theology, emphasizing the ineffable nature of God's essence, while affirming the accessibility of divine energies for human participation. It delineated *theosis* as an ontological metamorphosis, encompassing the totality of human existence in union with the Divine. The discourse further delved into *Logos* theology, noetic epistemology, and therapeutic ethics, presenting a holistic cosmology that integrates metaphysics, epistemology, and moral philosophy. The Orthodox conceptualization of sin as ontological privation and salvation as synergistic cooperation with divine grace is juxtaposed against Western theological paradigms, highlighting the distinctive features of Eastern Christian thought. This analysis not only elucidated the foundational principles of Orthodox theology but also demonstrated its capacity to reconcile philosophical antinomies and offers a coherent framework for understanding the intricate interrelationships between the Divine, humanity, and the created order.

The fourth chapter elucidated a comprehensive analysis of the divergent ontological and teleological paradigms inherent in Eastern Orthodox Christianity and transhumanism vis-à-vis human transcendence and deification. This analysis scrutinized the disparate metaphysical frameworks, anthropological presuppositions, and eschatological visions within the context of the postsecular zeitgeist and the contemporary crisis of existential meaning. The Orthodox conceptualization of *theosis*, predicated on synergistic communion with the Divine, is juxtaposed against the transhumanist pursuit of technological apotheosis and posthuman metamorphosis. Whereas the techno-millenarians of antiquity aspired to restore the prelapsarian perfection of the primordial Adamic state, contemporary transhumanists engage in an analogous endeavor, albeit with the Posthuman as the new archetypal Adam. Orthodox critiques frame transhumanism as a misguided attempt to recreate Edenic perfection and construct New Babylon, cautioning against its potential to facilitate the emergence of an antichrist figure. In this hermeneutical framework, Orthodoxy interprets transhumanism as a simulacrum of *theosis*, with its adherents placing their eschatological hope on unification with a pseudo-messianic entity.

The analysis ultimately unveils profound philosophical and theological disjunctions between these two paradigms of human transcendence, bearing significant implications for our understanding of personhood, ethics, and the ultimate telos of humanity in an era of unprecedented technological advancement.

The Eastern Orthodox doctrine of *theosis* offers a profound premodern theological critique of transhumanism, highlighting the stark contrast between traditional Christian understanding of human deification and the transhumanist vision of technological self-enhancement. Similar to postmodern critiques, Orthodoxy rejects the transhumanist narrative of unending progress. However, instead of building a new philosophical project, it wishes to return to a theanthropic paradigm that values both subjective experiences and provides metaphysical foundations for empiricism and knowledge claims.

Despite its secular appearance, transhumanism functions as a quasi-religious ideology that reconfigures Christian eschatology into a narrative of technological salvation. This parallel underscores the enduring human desire for transcendence and perfection even in ostensibly secular contexts. However, the Orthodox critique exposes the limitations of transhumanist thought, particularly its reductionist view of human nature and its neglect of the spiritual dimension of human existence. By tracing the historical and philosophical roots of transhumanism, this work illuminates how Western theological developments have contributed to the sacralization of technology as a redemptive force. This insight provides a valuable perspective on the cultural and intellectual forces shaping contemporary attitudes towards technology and human enhancement.

The Orthodox critique of transhumanism's metaphysical assumptions, including its functionalist anthropology, materialist epistemology, and postgenderist ethics, offers a robust defense of traditional Christian anthropology. This reaffirms the intrinsic value of embodied human life and the irreducible complexity of human personhood, challenging the transhumanist tendency to reduce human beings to mere information patterns or biological machines. Orthodoxy rejects the salvific hope in technology, and believes true deification is a therapeutic transfiguration of the human person into the likeness of Christ. This fundamental tension between technological and spiritual paths to human enhancement creates an important dynamic in contemporary ethical and philosophical debate.

Transhumanism and Eastern Orthodox Christianity present two fundamentally opposed visions of human deification and eschatology. While transhumanism seeks technological *apotheosis* through enhancing human capabilities with science and technology, Orthodoxy understands *theosis* as a gift of divine grace achieved through spiritual purification and communion with God. From an Orthodox perspective, transhumanism's pursuit of technological transcendence and immortality represents a modern Tower of Babel – an attempt to reach divinity through human effort alone, divorced from God's grace. The Orthodox critique frames transhumanism as a misguided and dangerous effort to recreate Edenic perfection through technology, warning that it could facilitate the coming of Antichrist. The Church sees transhumanism's vision as ultimately satanic in its rebellion against the God-given limits of human nature and its desire for humans to become gods apart from the Godman Jesus Christ. Thus, while both offer narratives of human transcendence, Orthodoxy views transhumanism's technological path to deification as a parody and inversion of true *theosis*.

Orthodox Christianity is a vital counternarrative of transhumanist ideology in contemporary culture. By upholding the sanctity of human life and the transformative potential of divine grace, Orthodox theology provides a compelling alternative to technological *apotheosis* and is finding resonance with many young adults. This critique not only enriches theological discourse, but also contributes to broader cultural debates about the ethical implications of emerging technologies and the future of human nature. What began as a technological quest toward the Garden of Eden, is seen by Orthodox Christianity as a rebuilding of Babylon, and part of a larger spiritual warfare for total human control and surveillance.

Index

A

Adam .. 1, 4, 6, 15, 16, 25, 27, 30, 35, 38, 44, 49, 50, 51, 52, 53, 55, 60, 75, 79, 85, 87, 95, 97, 100, 103, 108, 114, 211, 220, 229, 262, 281, 284, 289, 310, 311, 313, 359, 365, 366, 367, 371, 372, 373, 386, 403, 414
Adams, John.. 81
Agrippa, Heinrich Cornelius 44, 68
Alchemy 45, 58, 208, 217, 417
Allen, Joe.. 12, 13
Altman, Sam 12, 147
Ambrose of Milan 269
America..... 10, 17, 19, 25, 95, 96, 97, 99, 100, 103, 106, 109, 118, 122, 125, 153, 210, 305, 384, 403, 404, 407, 413, 415, 421
Amillennialism 300
Anaxagoras of Clazomenae............... 250
Andreae, Johann ... 18, 48, 50, 51, 66, 67, 73, 85, 209
Andrew of Caesarea.......................... 360
Anselm of Canterbury 222, 315
Anthropology 120, 229, 230, 263, 285, 292, 303, 304, 376, 388
Antichrist. 1, 3, 37, 38, 41, 47, 51, 53, 82, 96, 291, 294, 307, 358, 359, 360, 361, 362, 363, 364, 365, 378, 379, 381, 388, 405, 406, 411
Apophaticism 278, 314, 345
Apotheosis .. 3, 6, 50, 113, 148, 177, 193, 196, 200, 206, 290, 294, 300, 307, 333, 380, 384, 386, 388, 389, 411
Aquinas, Thomas 220, 222, 244, 245, 246, 247, 248, 315, 400, 425
Ardent, Hannah 198
Aristotelian . 29, 37, 62, 70, 77, 145, 220, 245, 267, 272, 312
Aristotle 20, 21, 22, 23, 29, 77, 139, 230, 231, 232, 233, 234, 239, 240, 247, 249, 251, 267, 268, 269, 400, 403
Arnau de Villanova................................ 40

Artes mechanicae 15, 27, 30, 311
Artificial intelligence ... 12, 13, 17, 38, 45, 112, 114, 127, 129, 130, 133, 134, 148, 158, 179, 180, 192, 193, 195, 199, 200, 207, 208, 211, 212, 214, 215, 217, 225, 289, 304, 325, 333, 337, 357, 362, 369, 371, 374, 380, 401
Artilect War 202, 212, 320, 331, 405
Athanasius of Alexandria ... 221, 225, 401
Augustine of Hippo 26, 27, 139, 220, 223, 246, 248, 269, 298, 305, 315, 401

B

Babbage, Charles 83
Babylon 1, 6, 72, 261, 291, 305, 359, 360, 361, 365, 381, 386, 389
Bacon, Francis... 4, 16, 18, 48, 50, 53, 54, 55, 56, 57, 59, 60, 61, 62, 68, 70, 80, 107, 118, 202, 203, 289, 303, 355, 366, 369, 384, 403, 408, 420, 425
Bacon, Roger 4, 16, 37, 38, 39, 41, 44, 48, 56, 107, 182, 208, 384
Baconian reforms 16, 61, 62, 71, 108, 118
Bainbridge, William Sims .. 155, 172, 173, 177, 178, 179, 186, 191, 192, 333, 401, 422
Bannon, Steve..................................... 12
Barlaam of Calabria 220, 226, 230
Bartley, William Warren.................... 138
Basil the Great 225, 237, 285
Bateson, Gregory 147
Bellamy, Edward .. 17, 104, 105, 108, 418
Bellamy, Joseph 97
Benedict of Nursia 23
Benedictines 23, 24, 31
Bentham, Jeremy.............................. 146
Benz, Ernst........................... 33, 34, 36
Berg, Maxine....................................... 94
Berger, Peter 153, 167
Bernal, J.D. 124
Bigelow, Jacob 100, 101

Bigelow, Julian 147
Böhme, Jakob 70
Bostrom, Nick38, 58, 117, 118, 119, 120, 121, 132, 133, 144, 147, 159, 190, 198, 210, 211, 213, 216, 217, 293, 319, 320, 321, 322, 326, 355, 367, 400, 402, 420
Boyle, Robert 4, 69, 72, 73, 74, 77, 79, 80, 82, 85, 107, 119, 384
Bradshaw, David231, 232, 234, 235, 239, 242, 247, 266, 403
Bruce, Steve 152, 403
Bruno, Giordano 49, 200, 369
Buddhism...171
Bulgakov, Sergei . 290, 293, 294, 295, 380
Burnett, James 80
Bush, George W. 172

C

Cabala 52, 60
Campanella, Tommaso 18, 48, 50, 67, 315
Capella, Martianus..............................22
Cappadocian Fathers .. 26, 225, 230, 276, 426
Carlyle, Thomas 348
Carolingian.... 15, 24, 26, 29, 31, 32, 311, 312
Cassian, John 260, 261
Casubon, Meric....................................70
Catholic..... 10, 12, 36, 37, 47, 48, 53, 62, 188, 208, 220, 223, 224, 305, 323, 404, 415, 420, 422
Charles II 71
Chidester, David........................184, 185
Christ 2, 3, 15, 32, 33, 35, 42, 48, 82, 83, 96, 145, 180, 181, 182, 184, 188, 190, 199, 219, 221, 226, 227, 228, 229, 234, 237, 239, 241, 242, 253, 254, 255, 257, 258, 261, 262, 264, 270, 271, 273, 277, 278, 279, 281, 282, 284, 287, 290, 294, 297, 298, 299, 301, 306, 308, 309, 313, 314, 323, 324, 332, 334, 342, 344, 353, 357, 358, 360, 361, 364, 372, 373, 378, 379, 380, 381, 388, 414, 416, 421
Christian Transhumanist Association .182
Christianity . 2, 10, 13, 42, 51, 83, 91, 93, 94, 121, 136, 145, 153, 162, 170, 180, 181, 182, 184, 188, 189, 190, 191, 194, 204, 224, 246, 252, 275, 276, 292, 293, 294, 296, 302, 308, 314, 326, 334, 342, 352, 358, 375, 389, 402, 405, 417, 418, 421
Chrysostom, John 279, 305, 404
Church Fathers . 219, 225, 235, 237, 322, 326, 360
Cicero 269
Clarke, Arthur C. 124, 191
Columbus, Christopher........40, 107, 424
Comenius, John Amos 64, 65, 66, 67, 72, 73, 85, 310, 369
Comte, Auguste 91, 92, 93, 94, 107, 340, 350, 414
Comte, Augustus 19, 91, 92, 93, 94
Consciousness 44, 46, 112, 131, 142, 143, 169, 181, 188, 189, 193, 195, 202, 203, 204, 213, 216, 268, 291, 316, 318, 319, 320, 321, 323, 324, 325, 326, 328, 329, 332, 336
Constantinople 33, 43, 222, 223, 227, 230
Contreni, John 311
Corpus Hermeticum...............43, 44, 332
Cybernetics 147, 148, 149, 161, 203, 366
Cyberspace 155, 206, 422
Cyril of Jerusalem 360, 361

D

Damasio, Antonio 317, 318
Darwin, Charles 80, 120
Dataism . 2, 174, 175, 179, 182, 295, 296
Davis, Erik 113, 185, 186, 374, 375
Davis, G.M. 361
de Chardin, Pierre Teilhard..... 3, 33, 169, 188, 189, 332, 401
de Mendieta, Geronimo................40, 42
Dee, John............. 58, 59, 68, 70, 71, 369
Deification ...1, 3, 5, 6, 13, 19, 49, 50, 55, 79, 113, 114, 145, 165, 177, 178, 195, 196, 212, 219, 220, 225, 228, 240, 241, 245, 248, 281, 287, 289, 290, 291, 292, 296, 301, 305, 309, 313, 330, 334, 335, 336, 340, 359, 364, 378, 380, 381, 386, 387, 388, 389, 416, 425
Derrida, Jacques 160, 162, 406
Desaguliers, John Theophilus 86, 87

Descartes, René 139, 148, 269, 310, 314, 315, 316, 317, 318, 369, 405
Devil 70, 71, 124, 133, 135, 136, 137, 263, 337, 375, 416
Dionysius the Areopagite 26
Disenchantment 112, 150, 155, 167, 168, 344, 383, 408, 412
Dorotheos of Gaza 261
Dostoevsky, Fyodor 341, 342, 344
Dreyfus, Hubert 317
Dupuy, Jean Pierre 149
Dury, John 65, 67
Dvorsky, George 197

E

Eaton, Amos 100, 415
Eckhart, Meister 223
Eco, Umberto 368, 369
Ecole Polytechnique 18, 90, 91, 108
Edwards, Johnathan 96, 97
Effective Altruism 146, 147, 414
Eliade, Mircea 366
Ellis, George 190
Ellul, Jacques 25, 155, 351, 407
Energeia 226, 230, 231, 232, 233, 234, 235, 237, 238, 239, 241, 270
Energies 1, 5, 219, 221, 226, 227, 229, 230, 236, 237, 238, 239, 240, 241, 242, 243, 244, 247, 261, 263, 266, 269, 270, 276, 277, 285, 286, 287, 288, 290, 292, 301, 322, 324, 373, 385
Enlightenment .. 2, 17, 94, 118, 139, 153, 154, 157, 160, 170, 222, 224, 292, 315, 326, 331, 355, 356, 358, 410, 412
Epistemology 5, 113, 138, 139, 171, 216, 224, 225, 230, 263, 264, 265, 266, 267, 268, 269, 270, 271, 287, 345, 385, 386, 388
Eriugena, John Scotus ... 4, 15, 16, 25, 26, 27, 28, 29, 30, 31, 32, 37, 38, 48, 50, 100, 107, 182, 289, 311, 384, 407
Eschatology 3, 4, 5, 17, 32, 33, 42, 47, 56, 107, 111, 113, 173, 179, 180, 195, 200, 213, 225, 291, 295, 296, 297, 298, 299, 300, 332, 333, 339, 351, 355, 356, 358, 359, 371, 373, 378, 379, 387, 388

Esfandiary, F.M. 126
Essence 5, 47, 61, 120, 154, 157, 164, 191, 204, 219, 221, 225, 226, 227, 232, 237, 238, 239, 240, 241, 242, 243, 244, 245, 246, 247, 248, 256, 273, 274, 276, 278, 281, 282, 287, 296, 314, 334, 337, 343, 344, 385
Ettinger, Robert 125
Etzler, John Adolphus 98, 99, 407
Eugenics 170
Eunomius 237, 238
Evelyn, John 69
Evil 32, 38, 204, 259, 260, 261, 285, 286, 299, 305, 308, 342, 356, 360, 362

F

Faraday, Michael 82, 83
Farman, Abou 113, 156
Ficino, Marsilio 43, 200
Finot, Jean 122
Fire 23, 115, 116, 123, 286, 287, 375
Florovsky, Georges 279, 408
Fludd, Robert 68, 70
Foerst, Anne 211
Foucault, Michel 160
Francis of Assisi 35
Franciscans 34, 35, 36, 39, 40, 41, 418
Frank Jackson 143
Franklin, Benjamin ... 82, 89, 92, 118, 410
Frederick the Elector Palatine 65
Freemasonry 4, 18, 69, 85, 86, 87, 88, 89, 91, 94, 107, 384
Fukuyama, Francis 172
Functionalism 141, 143
Funkenstein, Amos 76
Fyodorov, Nikolai 121

G

Gallaher, Brandon . 1, 290, 295, 309, 380, 408
Garden of Eden 17, 63, 211, 365, 371, 376, 389
Garis, Hugo de ... 202, 211, 212, 320, 331
Gauchet, Marcel 167, 168
Geraci, Robert ... 130, 158, 159, 171, 178, 179, 202, 207, 208, 409
Glanvill, Joseph ... 74, 75, 76, 77, 78, 310, 409

Gnomic 277, 278
Gnosticism 137, 201, 204, 208, 217, 238, 252, 295, 296, 297, 374, 376, 420, 421, 424
God .. 1, 2, 3, 4, 5, 6, 8, 13, 16, 18, 24, 25, 26, 28, 29, 30, 31, 32, 33, 34, 36, 37, 38, 40, 41, 42, 44, 45, 47, 48, 49, 52, 54, 55, 56, 57, 60, 61, 63, 64, 72, 73, 74, 75, 78, 79, 80, 83, 87, 93, 96, 97, 99, 100, 101, 102, 107, 108, 109, 114, 115, 137, 145, 152, 155, 162, 174, 175, 177, 180, 181, 182, 183, 184, 186, 188, 189, 190, 191, 192, 195, 196, 198, 199, 205, 208, 209, 210, 211, 212, 213, 219, 220, 221, 223, 225, 226, 227, 228, 229, 230, 234, 235, 236, 237, 238, 239, 240, 241, 242, 243, 244, 245, 246, 247, 248, 249, 252, 253, 254, 255, 256, 257, 258, 261, 262, 263, 264, 265, 266, 269, 270, 271, 272, 273, 274, 275, 276, 277, 278, 279, 280, 281, 282, 283, 284, 285, 286, 287, 288, 289, 290, 291, 292, 294, 295, 296, 298, 299, 301, 302, 303, 304, 305, 306, 307, 308, 309, 310, 311, 312, 313, 314, 315, 322, 323, 324, 325, 326, 332, 333, 334, 335, 336, 337, 340, 341, 342, 343, 344, 345, 346, 347, 353, 354, 355, 356, 357, 358, 360, 361, 362, 363, 364, 365, 366, 369, 372, 373, 375, 377, 378, 380, 381, 385, 388, 401, 403, 408, 420, 426
Godman 2, 290, 344, 373, 380, 388
Godmanhood 289, 290, 293, 294, 301, 310, 359, 373, 381
Goertzel, Ben 186
Golem 208, 209, 210, 409, 421
Greek .. 23, 25, 26, 33, 43, 123, 177, 192, 220, 232, 234, 235, 237, 245, 247, 248, 250, 252, 253, 255, 267, 268, 269, 270, 271, 283, 287, 302, 308, 315, 332, 358, 401
Greene, Robert 39
Gregory of Nyssa 225, 230, 238, 275, 285

H

Habermas, Jürgen . 8, 111, 150, 152, 153, 154, 289, 338, 409
Haldane, J.B.S. 122, 123, 137, 410
Hamalis, Perry 280
Harakas, Stanley 280
Harari, Yuval Noah 2, 174, 175, 176, 177, 179, 188, 295, 300, 301, 302, 303, 320, 331, 367, 410
Haraway, Donna 161
Hartlib circle 65, 73
Hartlib, Samuel 62, 63, 64, 65, 67, 73, 85
Hayles, N. Katherine 319
Heaven . 32, 33, 55, 81, 96, 97, 130, 173, 190, 195, 245, 252, 290, 298, 324, 375, 409, 420, 421
Heers, Peter 306, 307, 365
Hegel, Georg Wilhelm Friedrich 181
Heidegger, Martin 112, 148, 149, 272, 313, 316, 317, 341, 343, 344, 346, 411, 426
Helmreich, Stefan 204, 205, 206, 411
Henosis 242, 327, 332, 337
Heraclitus of Ephesus 249
Hermes Trismegistus 43
Hermeticism 44, 57, 208
Hesychasm 227
Hierotheos Vlachos ... 308, 325, 364, 373
Holy Trinity . 35, 184, 239, 244, 276, 282, 308, 353, 408, 413, 421
Hooke, Robert 71, 74
Hopkins, Patrick 296
Hopkins, Samuel 97, 98
Hossenfelder, Sabine 144, 411
Hugh of St. Victor . 16, 22, 29, 30, 31, 37, 38, 107
Hughes, James .. 133, 170, 178, 197, 331, 406
Humanism .. 1, 44, 56, 58, 119, 120, 133, 148, 149, 157, 159, 160, 168, 169, 223, 224, 225, 295, 345, 384
Hume, David 139, 265
Huxley, Aldous 124, 125
Huxley, Julian 5, 115, 117, 122, 124, 126, 137, 150, 168, 189, 375, 385

I

Iamblichus 192, 330, 331, 406
Imago Dei 25, 49, 196, 199, 221, 291, 293, 324, 337, 357, 365, 371, 378, 380

Immortality . 4, 10, 11, 17, 44, 58, 63, 83, 84, 114, 117, 121, 130, 159, 165, 166, 168, 173, 180, 185, 186, 190, 195, 200, 204, 206, 207, 217, 219, 291, 293, 296, 298, 301, 303, 310, 319, 321, 322, 326, 332, 336, 339, 350, 357, 365, 367, 374, 377, 388
Incarnation.... 2, 199, 219, 221, 258, 284, 287, 296, 298, 301, 313, 372, 401

J

Jacob, Margaret 79, 80, 88
Japan.. 171
Jaspers, Karl 348
Jesus 32, 33, 42, 145, 180, 181, 188, 190, 219, 227, 234, 235, 237, 253, 254, 255, 258, 278, 279, 284, 290, 294, 301, 307, 344, 357, 358, 361, 365, 380, 388, 414, 423
Joachim of Fiore 4, 15, 34, 37, 41, 47, 50, 92, 107, 185, 355, 384
Joachimite. 34, 36, 37, 39, 42, 43, 44, 45, 47, 51, 75
Johannes Kepler................. 309, 310, 401
John Climacus 261
John of Damascus 225, 245, 276, 426
John of Kronstadt................................ 353
John of Ruspescissa 40
John of the Cross 223
John the Baptist 175
John the Theologian 249
Johnson, Bryan..................................... 11
Johnson, Edward 95
Jonas, Hans 351, 371, 372
Jordan, Gregory 171, 177
Justin Parvu of Romania.................... 364
Justinian 222

K

Kaballah 211
Kant, Immanuel......................... 119, 139
Kassell, Lauren 72
Kelly, Kevin 207
Kent, Robert Thurston............... 102, 103
Kent, Saul 126
Kierkegaard, Søren 341, 342, 343, 344, 413
King James I 53, 59, 60, 66

Kircher, Athanasius 208
Kirill of Moscow 363
Knight, Christopher....................266, 267
Kripal, Jeffrey 125
Kuhn, Thomas 140, 413
Kurzweil, Ray 129, 131, 167, 175, 179, 180, 181, 203, 214, 216, 291, 319, 320, 321, 322, 326, 331, 339, 367, 413

L

La Mettrie, Julien Offray de 120
Larchet, Jean-Claude 307, 308
Latin 23, 25, 26, 28, 33, 43, 139, 219, 222, 223, 245, 260, 274, 312, 358, 405
Latour, Bruno 167
Leary, Timothy 203, 204
Leibniz, Gottfried Wilhelm. 315, 369, 370
Lewis, C.S. 377
Lewis, R. W. B...................................... 95
Logismoi 259, 262, 422
Logocentric 162, 163
Logoi .. 255, 256, 257, 258, 264, 274, 279
Logos 5, 162, 180, 181, 182, 188, 199, 219, 225, 237, 248, 249, 250, 251, 252, 253, 254, 255, 256, 258, 259, 262, 264, 273, 274, 275, 276, 277, 278, 281, 284, 287, 292, 301, 357, 372, 373, 385, 411
Lossky, Vladimir 221, 223, 240, 246, 324, 325, 414
Lucifer 1, 114, 136, 137, 375
Lully, Raymond..............................31, 40
Luther, Martin...................................... 47

M

Magnus, Albert 182
Magus, Simon 234
Mangodhood 290, 293, 294, 295, 306, 309, 310, 359, 373, 378, 381
Marcion of Sinope 238
Marcuse, Herbert 349
Martyr, Justin 234, 253, 254, 255
Marx, Karl 94, 95
Marxism.. 34

Maximus the Confessor 26, 222, 225, 255, 256, 261, 273, 277, 278, 282, 334, 335, 414
Maxwell, James Clerk 83, 404
McCulloch, Warren............................147
Mechanical arts 28
Medici, Cosimo de 43
Metaphysics.. 2, 5, 18, 21, 113, 133, 141, 162, 171, 196, 216, 225, 263, 272, 273, 274, 287, 292, 293, 312, 327, 334, 335, 337, 338, 345, 346, 374, 379, 384, 386
Meyendorff, John...............221, 222, 277
Michael the Scot...................................31
Middle Ages 4, 16, 18, 19, 20, 23, 25, 30, 34, 35, 45, 61, 92, 105, 220, 262, 368, 369, 419, 422, 425
Mill, John Stuart 121, 146
Millenarianism.... 5, 8, 15, 17, 18, 19, 37, 41, 93, 94, 95, 107, 111, 114, 120, 183, 215, 216, 291, 311, 313, 355, 379
Milton, John...........................63, 64, 375
Mind ... 32, 42, 49, 51, 54, 72, 78, 81, 97, 98, 112, 128, 137, 141, 142, 143, 157, 168, 169, 170, 180, 188, 195, 201, 204, 224, 228, 229, 251, 260, 262, 263, 272, 273, 277, 297, 309, 310, 313, 315, 316, 317, 318, 319, 321, 322, 323, 324, 325, 326, 327, 328, 329, 330, 370, 375, 377, 410, 423
Minsky, Marvin 127, 128, 131
Mirandola, Giovani Pico della.....43, 117, 376, 415
Modernity..... 3, 4, 54, 61, 153, 265, 266, 292, 342, 345, 346, 351, 383, 384
Montgolfier, Jacques-Etienne 91
Moorhead, John 96
Moral realism 280
Moravec, Hans.. 130, 131, 202, 203, 319, 320, 322, 326, 415
More, Gordon 128
More, Max 117, 118, 120, 126, 127, 132, 134, 135, 136, 137, 138, 140, 141, 145, 163, 164, 177, 186, 355, 375
More, Thomas 18, 48, 403
Morison, George S. 102
Mormonism...............................183, 184
Morphological freedom..............163, 165
Morse, Samuel....................................101

Moses 43, 56, 234, 240, 241, 243
Mumford, Lewis 16, 54, 80, 92, 349
Murphy, Michael 125
Musk, Elon...... 11, 12, 13, 144, 214, 215, 217, 218, 404, 416

N

Neoplatonism... 217, 230, 232, 242, 273, 327, 330, 406
New Jerusalem . 36, 37, 40, 61, 108, 113, 313, 373, 377
Newton, Isaac........................79, 86, 119
Nietzsche, Friedrich.. 120, 121, 311, 341, 342, 343, 344, 417
Noble, David 16, 24, 30
Nous . 228, 229, 230, 256, 257, 261, 262, 268, 288, 323, 324

O

Old Testament .. 237, 240, 252, 253, 255, 278
Omega Point theory 3, 182, 188, 189, 190, 329, 332, 333, 336
Order of Cosmic Engineers113, 178, 186, 191, 192, 193, 194, 206, 217, 289, 333, 419
Orthodox Christianity . 1, 2, 5, 6, 8, 9, 10, 145, 177, 194, 223, 248, 249, 259, 263, 264, 267, 272, 279, 290, 292, 325, 337, 340, 345, 354, 355, 356, 381, 385, 386, 388, 389, 406, 411, 421
Ovitt, George 26, 31, 77
Owen, Robert 94

P

Pacey, Arnold..36
Page, Larry..................................131, 187
Paisios of Mount Athos 361, 363, 417
Palamas, Gregory 219, 221, 225, 227, 228, 230, 245, 261, 287, 418, 425
Pancritical rationalism 138
Paracelsus.... 45, 46, 50, 70, 71, 209, 412
Parmenides 232
Patristic... 2, 25, 27, 30, 31, 33, 221, 223, 225, 255, 263, 276, 280, 287, 290,

292, 309, 322, 365, 372, 381, 423, 426
Patristic theology 31
Paul the Apostle .. 33, 230, 231, 234, 237, 377, 403
Pearce, David 132, 146, 186
Peilkan, Jaroslav 275
Pelagianism 220
Pentecost 35, 235, 298, 306
Perronet, Jean-Rodolphe 90
Personhood 1, 6, 163, 200, 212, 225, 229, 242, 243, 244, 258, 263, 277, 282, 283, 292, 294, 295, 304, 316, 319, 325, 333, 334, 335, 336, 337, 379, 380, 387, 388
Peters, Ted 1, 165, 184, 195, 196, 290, 408
Phallocentrism 162, 163
Phallogocentrism 162
Philo of Alexandria 234, 249, 252
Plato .. 20, 21, 22, 43, 139, 162, 223, 232, 240, 249, 250, 251, 267, 330, 343, 418
Platonic 118, 217, 258, 374, 379
Platonism 273
Plotinus 233, 239, 242
Polkinghorne, John 190
Ponticus, Evagrius 260, 262, 422
Popper, Karl 138, 140
Postgenderism 196, 197, 406
Posthuman 6, 10, 114, 117, 134, 146, 147, 149, 156, 157, 158, 159, 163, 164, 166, 172, 173, 181, 182, 183, 184, 185, 201, 290, 292, 293, 301, 309, 319, 333, 337, 340, 365, 371, 378, 379, 380, 386, 403, 408, 410, 425
Posthumanism .. 147, 157, 158, 161, 196, 215
Postman, Neil 349, 350
Postmillennialism 299
Postmodernism 160, 347
Postsecular 4, 5, 6, 8, 13, 19, 111, 113, 114, 150, 151, 152, 153, 154, 156, 212, 216, 289, 292, 338, 339, 355, 356, 358, 359, 380, 381, 383, 385, 386
Postsecularism 153, 354
Premillennialism 299
Price, Dick 125

Priestly, Joseph 81, 82, 408
Prisco, Giulio 186, 187, 188, 189, 191, 192, 193, 194, 419
Prony, Gaspard Richie de 90
Protestantism 65, 279
Pythagoras 249, 276, 411

R

Ramsay, Chevalier 89
Reason 83, 118, 133, 136, 140, 150, 151, 154, 157, 159, 162, 163, 182, 216, 219, 224, 247, 248, 250, 251, 254, 255, 258, 264, 265, 268, 271, 274, 283, 293, 310, 311, 312, 315, 326, 337, 338, 340, 354, 363, 375, 376, 383
Re-enchantment 8, 113
Reformation 36, 48, 53, 221, 223, 358
Religion . 5, 13, 16, 60, 73, 77, 83, 91, 92, 94, 98, 107, 111, 112, 113, 115, 116, 121, 124, 125, 127, 135, 136, 137, 144, 150, 151, 152, 153, 154, 155, 156, 165, 166, 167, 168, 169, 171, 172, 173, 174, 175, 176, 177, 182, 184, 186, 187, 188, 189, 191, 192, 194, 205, 206, 212, 217, 218, 289, 293, 294, 295, 296, 302, 306, 309, 310, 333, 338, 339, 340, 355, 358, 361, 365, 373, 378, 383, 385
Remigius of Auxerre 29
Renaissance 2, 4, 9, 18, 26, 29, 32, 39, 43, 44, 46, 47, 48, 51, 53, 54, 56, 57, 61, 108, 117, 200, 222, 223, 224, 279, 292, 311, 312, 358, 370, 384, 402
Rogan, Joe 144, 416
Romanides, John 223, 323
Rose, Seraphim 340, 353, 358, 359
Rosenblueth, Arturo 148
Rosicrucians 18, 51, 52, 53, 57, 59, 60, 70, 72, 85
Rothblatt, Martine 186
Royal Society 4, 18, 61, 68, 69, 70, 71, 72, 73, 74, 77, 78, 82, 86, 89, 107, 384

S

Saint-Simon, Henri de 19, 91, 339
Sandberg, Anders 38, 163, 164, 210, 211, 400

Sartre, Jean-Paul 341, 343, 344, 420
Satan ... 33, 136, 234, 261, 294, 299, 306, 375
Schmemann, Alexander 345
Scholasticism 2, 76, 77, 220, 222, 224, 230, 279, 292, 314, 358
Searle, John 143, 317, 318
Segal, Howard P. 101, 104, 105
Shelly, Percy 375, 376
Silicon Valley 10, 11, 12, 19, 107, 175, 306
Singularity 2, 113, 129, 131, 142, 158, 175, 180, 181, 182, 186, 190, 213, 291, 298, 299, 300, 321, 331, 333, 339, 351, 359, 383, 404, 405, 413, 426
Society for Universal Immortalism ... 113, 206, 217, 289
Socrates 254
Sorem, Ananias Erik 303, 421
Sorokin, Pitirim 350
Soul 25, 26, 28, 44, 51, 83, 124, 193, 194, 201, 208, 220, 228, 229, 240, 241, 244, 248, 250, 251, 254, 257, 260, 261, 263, 264, 267, 268, 277, 286, 292, 308, 310, 320, 322, 323, 324, 325, 326, 330, 336, 346, 348, 353, 364, 365, 377, 378
Spengler, Oswald 348, 349
Sprat, Thomas 69, 77
Stark, Rodney 155
Steinhart, Eric 193, 330
Stoicism 251, 252, 253
Symphonia 282

T

Talmud 209
Taylor, Charles 8, 111, 150, 152, 338
Techno-millenarianism 15, 94
Telos 4, 30, 47, 97, 236, 240, 241, 245, 257, 258, 281, 323, 337, 380, 384, 387
Terasem Transreligion 113, 217, 289
Teresa of Ávila 223
Tertullian 249, 269, 411
the Fall .. 4, 15, 17, 20, 25, 28, 30, 38, 44, 55, 60, 63, 70, 75, 87, 108, 220, 229, 261, 284, 289, 308, 312, 366
The World of Warcraft 179

Theoria 230, 301
Theosis. 1, 5, 6, 8, 13, 177, 183, 219, 225, 226, 229, 240, 241, 242, 247, 249, 256, 259, 263, 270, 276, 278, 281, 287, 290, 291, 292, 301, 308, 309, 313, 327, 334, 337, 344, 357, 373, 380, 381, 385, 386, 387, 388, 389
Therapeutic ethics 5, 385
Thiel, Peter 11, 187
Thirty Years War 65, 67, 108
Tipler, Frank 188, 189, 190, 329, 332, 333, 334, 336, 423
Tower of Babel .. 3, 9, 113, 194, 195, 291, 293, 304, 306, 307, 360, 361, 368, 369, 379, 388
Toynbee, Arnold 350
Transhumanism ... 1, 2, 3, 4, 5, 6, 8, 9, 11, 14, 15, 17, 19, 45, 80, 95, 108, 109, 111, 113, 114, 115, 116, 117, 119, 121, 122, 124, 126, 128, 131, 132, 133, 135, 137, 139, 141, 146, 150, 151, 152, 154, 156, 157, 159, 163, 165, 166, 168, 170, 172, 173, 178, 179, 182, 183,184, 185, 187, 188, 189, 190, 191, 193, 194, 195, 198, 199, 200, 201, 216, 217, 218, 248, 289, 290, 291, 292, 293, 295, 296, 297, 300, 301, 302, 304, 306, 307, 308, 319, 327, 328, 329, 335, 338, 339, 340, 344, 351, 354, 355, 358, 359, 365, 374, 375, 376, 377, 379, 380, 381, 383, 384, 385, 386, 387, 388, 389, 411, 416, 420
Trenham, Josiah 365, 366
Trump, Donald J 11, 12, 401
Turing, Alan 128

U

Ulam, Stanislaw 129, 130
United States 4, 9, 96, 104, 122
Useful arts 20, 23, 24, 26, 28, 30, 43, 44, 49, 51, 55, 63, 76, 85, 88, 89
Utopia 8, 13, 15, 36, 48, 49, 56, 57, 66, 95, 99, 100, 104, 179, 306, 311, 354, 357, 369
Utrecht Psalter 24

V

Valentinus 238
Van Rensselaer, Stephen 100
Vance, J. D. 11
Vaucanson, Jacques 84, 86, 208, 339
Vaughn, Thomas 69
Villa Nova, Arnalus de 208
Vinge, Vernor 129, 206, 214, 320
Virtue .. 88, 145, 230, 245, 255, 261, 268, 269, 281, 288, 313, 325, 348
Vita-More, Natasha ... 117, 163, 164, 186, 416
von Foerster, Heinz 147
von Neumann, John ... 129, 130, 147, 423

W

Ward, Seth 70
Waters, Brent 156
Watts, Pauline Moffit 40
Weber, Max 155, 340
Webster, Charles 56, 72, 73
Webster, John 69
Wertheim, Margaret 155

Western Civilization 13, 22
White, John 96
White, Lynn 24, 25
Whitman, Walt 95
Whitney, Elspeth 27, 30
Wiener, Norbert 147, 208
Wilkins, John 68, 70, 74, 208, 369
William of Malmesbury 39
Wolfe, Cary 161
Wotton, William 78, 426

Y

Yannaras, Christos 243, 265, 266, 267, 268, 269, 283, 284, 312, 313, 314, 315, 345, 346, 347, 354, 426
Yates, Frances 55, 71, 86
Yudkowsky, Eliezer 214, 216, 320

Z

Zimmerman, Michael 181
Zizioulas, John ... 271, 272, 280, 356, 424, 426

Bibliography

Allen, Joe. *Dark Aeon: Transhumanism and the War Against Humanity*. New York: Skyhorse Publishing, 2023.

Amarasingam, Amarnath. "Transcending Technology: Looking at Futurology as a New
 Religious Movement." Journal of Contemporary Religion 23, no. 1 (2008): 1-16. https://doi.org/10.1080/13537900701822989.

Anderson, William H. U. ed. *Technology and Theology*. Wilmington, Delaware: Vernon Press,
 2021.

Aquinas, Thomas. *De Veritate*. https://catholiclibrary.org/library/view?docId=/Medieval-EN/XCT.024.html&chunk.id=00000011.
———. *Summa Theologiae*. https://catholiclibrary.org/library/view?docId=Synchronized-EN/XCT.017.html;chunk.id=00000740.

Ardent, Hannah. *The Human Condition*. Chicago: University of Chicago Press, 1958.

Aristotle, *The Basic Works of Aristotle*. Edited by Richard McKeon. New York: The Modern Library, 2001.

Armstrong, Stuart Anders Sandberg, and Nick Bostrom. "Thinking Inside the Box: Using and Controlling an Oracle AI." *Minds and Machines* (November 2012) http://dx.doi.org/10.1007/s11023-012-9282-2.

Ashley, Dustin. "Science Before the Revolution: a Continuity of Christian Thought," (June 23, 2023) accessed September 18, 2024, https://www.christiantranshumanism.org/blog/2023-science-before-the-revolution/.

Athanasius of Alexandria. *On the Incarnation*. Translated by John Behr. Yonkers, New York: St. Vladimir's Seminary Press, 2011.

Augustine of Hippo. *City of God*. London: Penguin Books, 2003.

Bacon, Francis. *The New Organon and Related Writings*. Edited by Fulton H. Anderson. New York: Macmillan Library of Liberal Arts, 1960.

Babbage, Charles. *The Ninth Bridgewater Treatise*. London: Frank Cass, 1967.

Bainbridge, William Sims. "Trajectories to the Heavens*." The Journal of Personal Cyberconsciousness* 2, no.3 (2007).
———. "The Transhumanist Heresy," *Journal of Evolution and Technology* 14, no.2 (2005): 91-100.
———. "Turing Church," (August 6, 2019) accessed September 21, 2024, https://wrldrels.org/2019/08/03/turing-church/.

Barnes, Jonathan. *Early Greek Philosophy*. Harmondsworth: Penguin Books, 1987.

Bartle, Richard A.. *Designing Virtual Worlds*. Berkeley: New Riders, 2003.

Baumgardt, Carola. *Johannes Kepler: Life and Letters*. New York: Philosophical Library, 1951.

Bellamy, Edward. *Equality*. New York: D. Appleton and Co., 1897.

Benz, Ernst. *Evolution of Christian Hope: Man's Concept of the Future from the Early Fathers to Teilhard de Chardin*. New York: Doubleday & Company Inc., 1966.

Berg, Maxine. *The Machinery Question*. Cambridge: Cambridge University Press, 1980.

Bialy, Filip. "Trust in artificial intelligence makes Trump/Vance a transhumanist ticket." *The Loop* (October 2024): https://theloop.ecpr.eu/trust-in-artificial-intelligence-makes-trump-vance-a-transhumanist-ticket/#:~:text=ideological,Rationalism%2C%20Effective%20Altruism%2C%20and%20Longtermism.

Bisen, Siddharth Singh. "Apple Logo History: Everything You Need to Know About the Apple Logo." (Oct. 13, 2017): https://www.linkedin.com/pulse/apple-logo-history-everything-you-need-know-siddharth-singh-bisen

Bordo, Susan. *The Flight to Objectivity*. Albany: SUNY Press, 1987.

Borlik, Todd Andrew. "More than Art: Clockwork Automata, the Extemporizing Actor, and the Brazen Head in Friar Bacon and Frian Bungay." in *The Automaton In English Renaissance Literature*, edited by Wendy Beth Hayman. New York: Routledge, 2011

Bostrom, Nick. "A History of Transhumanist Thought." *Journal of Evolution and Technology* 14, no. 1 (April 2005).
———. *Anthropic Bias: Observation Selection Effects in Science and Philosophy* (London: Routledge, 2010
———. "Are You Living in a Computer Simulation," *Philosophical Quarterly* 53, no. 211 (2003) 243-255.
———. "Ethical Issues in Advanced Artificial Intelligence," *Cognitive, Emotive, and Ethical Aspects of Decesion Making in Humans and in Artificial Intelligence* 2 (2003): 12-17. https://nickbostrom.com/ethics/ai#:~:text=Additionally%2C%20a%20superintelligence%20could%20give,living%20closer%20to%20our%20ideals.
———. *Superintelligence: Paths, Dangers, Strategies*. Oxford: Oxford University Press, 2014.
———. "The Fable of the Dragon-Tyrant," *Journal of Medical Ethics* 31, no.5 (2005): 273-277. https://nickbostrom.com/fable/dragon.
———. "The Transhumanist FAQ: A General Introduction," In *Transhumanism and the Body: The World Religions Speak*. Edited by Calvin Mercer and Derek Maher. London: Palgrave Macmillian, 2014.

Boyarin, Daniel. *Border Lines: The Partition of Judeo-Christianity*. Philadelphia: University of Pennsylvania Press, 2007.

Boyer, Paul. *When Time Shall Be No More: Prophecy Belief in Modern American Culture*. Cambridge, Mass.: Harvard University Press, 1992.

Bradshaw, David. *Aristotle East and West: Metaphysics and the Division of Christendom*. Cambridge: Cambridge University Press, 2004.
———. *Divine Energies and Divine Action: Exploring the Essence-Energies Distinction*. St. Paul: Iota Publications, 2023.
———. *Natural Theology in the Eastern Orthodox Tradition*. St. Paul: Iota Publications, 2021.

Berger, Peter. *The Desecularization of the World: Resurgent Religion and World Politics*. Grand Rapids: William B. Eerdmans Publishing Company, 1999.

Bergunder, Michael. "What is Religion?." *Method & Theory in the Study of Religion* 26, no. 3, (2014): 246-286. https://doi.org/10.1163/15700682-12341320.

Buben, Adam. "Personal Immortality in Transhumanism and Ancient Indian Philosophy." *Philosophy East and West* 69, no. 1(January 2019): 71-85. https://www.jstor.org/stable/10.2307/26742510.

Bukatmann, Scott. "Postcard from the Posthuman Solar System." In *Posthumanism*. Edited by Neil Badmington. New York: Palgrave, 2000.

Brezezinski, Zbigniew. *Between Two Ages: America's Role in the Technetronic Era.*
Connecticut: Greenwood Press, 1982.

Bruce, Susan ed.. *Three Early Modern Utopias: Thomas More Utopia, Francis Bacon New Atlantis, and Henry Neville The Isle of Pines*. Oxford: Oxford University Press, 2008.

Bruce, Steve. *God Is Dead: Secularization in the West*. Oxford: Wiley-Blackwell, 2002.
———. "Interview: Steve Bruce," Goldsmiths University of London, accessed September 4, 2024, https://www.gold.ac.uk/faithsunit/current-projects/reimaginingreligion/landmark-interviews/steve-bruce/.

Campbell, Joseph. *The Hero with a Thousand Faces*. Princeton: Princeton University Press, 1968.

Campbell, Lewis and William Garnett. *The Life of James Clerk Maxwell*. New York: Johnson Reprint Corporation, 1969.

Cao, Sissi. "Six Companies Owned by Elon Musk: How the Tech Mogul Manages Them All." *Observer* (October 23, 2023): https://observer.com/2023/10/elon-musk-companies-key-people/#:~:text=match%20at%20L213%20Musk%20has,its%20brain%20chips%20in%20humans.

Carey, James W. *Communication as Culture*. Boston: Unwin Hyman, 1989.

Carlyle, Thomas. "Signs of the Times." (1829): https://archive.org/details/carlyle-signs-of-the-times-1829/Carlyle%20-%20%27%27Signs%20of%20the%20Times%27%27%201829/page/71/mode/2up?q=moral

Cassian, John. "On the Eight Vices." Edited by Bishop Kastor. https://orthodoxchurchfathers.com/fathers/philokalia/st-john-cassian-on-the-eight-vices.html#:~:text=thoughts%20and%20then%20eradicating%20them,137%3A9%3B%20I%20Cor.

Chalmers, D. J.. "The Singularity: A Philosophical Analysis" In *Science Fiction and Philosophy: From Time Travel to Superintellige*nce. Edited by Susan Schneider. Hoboken: Wiley-Blackwell, 2010.

Chidester, David. "Moralizing Noise," *Harvard Divinity Bulletin* 32, no.3 (2004).

Chrysostom, John. "Homilies on Genesis 1-45." in *Fathers of the Church*. Translated by Robert C. Hill. Washington DC: The Catholic University of America Press, 1986.

Climacus, John. *The Ladder of Divine Ascent*. Boston: Holy Transfiguration Monastery, 2012.

Cole-Turner, Ronald. "The Singularity and the Rapture: Transhumanist and Popular Christian Views of the Future." *Zygon* vol. 47, no.4 (December 2012

Condorcet, Jean Antoine Nicolas de Caritat. *Sketch for a Historical Picture of the Progress of the Human Mind.* London: 1795. https://archive.org/details/outlinesofhistor00cond/page/n15/mode/2up.

Contreni, John J. "John Scotus, Martin Hiberniensis: The Liberal Arts and Teaching." in *Insular Latin Studies. Edited by* Michael W. Herren. Toronto: Pontifical Institute of Medieval Studies, 1981.

Constantinou Scarvelis, Eugenia. *Thinking Orthodox: Understanding and Acquiring the
    Orthodox Christian Mind.* Chesterton, IN: Ancient Faith Publishing, 2020.

Damasio, Antonio. *Descartes' Error: Emotion, Reason, and the Human Brain.* New York: Penguin Books, 2005.

Davis, Erik. *Techgnosis: Myth, Magic + Mysticism In the Age of Information.* New York: Three
    Rivers Press, 1998.

Davis, G. M.. *Antichrist: the Fulfillment of Globalization.* Uncut Mountain Press, 2022.

De Garis, Hugo. *The Artilect War: Cosmists vs. Terrans.* Palm Springs: ETC Publications, 2005.

De Lubac, Henri. *The Drama of Atheist Humanism.* San Francisco: Ignatius Press, 1998.

De Chardin, Pierre Teilhad. *Christianity and Evolution.* Translated by René Hague. New York: Harcourt, Brace, Jovanovich, 1971.
———. *Human Energy.* Translated by J. M. Cohen. New York: Harper & Row, 1969.

De Young, Stephen. *The Religion of the Apostles: Orthodox Christianity in the First Century*.
    Chesterton, IN: Ancient Faith Publishings, 2021.

Delport, Khegan M.. "The Artifice of Eternity: Transhumanism and Theosis." *Stellenbosch Theological Journal* 9, no.1 (2023): https://doi.org/10.17570/stj.2023.v9n1.at1.

Derrida, Jacques. *Dissemination*. Translated by Barbara Johnson. Chicago: The University of Chicago Press, 1981.
———. *Grammatology*. Translated by Gayatri Chakravorty Spivak. Baltimore: The John Hopkins University Press, 1976.

Dillon, John. "Iamblichus' Defense of Theurgy: Some Reflection." *International Journal of the Platonic Tradition* 1, (April 2007): 30-41, DOI:10.1163/187254707X194645.
———. "The Divinizing of Matter: Some Reflections on Iamblichus Theurgic Approach to Matter." In *Soul and Matter in Neoplatonism*. Edited by Tobias Dangel, Jens Halfwassen, and Carl O'Brien. Universitätsverlag Winter Heidelberg, 2015.

Dostoyevsky, Fyodor. *The Brothers Karamazov*. Translated by David McDuff. New York: Penguin Books, 2003.

Dreyfus, Hubert. *What Computers Still Can't Do: A Critique of Artificial Reason*. Cambridge: MIT Press, 1992.

Dupuy, Jean Pierre. "Cybernetics Is Antihumanism: Advanced Technologies and the Rebellion against the Human Condition." In *H+: Transhumanism and Its Critics*. Edited by Gregory R. Hansell and William Grassi. Philadelphia: Metanexus, 2011. 215-26.

Dvorsky, George and James Hughes. "Postgenderism: Beyond the Gender Binary" *Institute for Ethics and Emerging Technologies Monograph Series* (March 2008) DOI:10.13140/RG.2.2.18028.08324

Dzhaparidze, Mikhail. "Russian Patriarch Warns 'Antichrist' Will Control Humans Through Gadgets." *The Moscow Times* (Jan. 8, 2019): https://www.themoscowtimes.com/2019/01/08/russian-patriarch-warns-antichrist-will-control-humans-through-gadgets-a64060

Eberl, Jason. "Enhancing the Imago Dei: Can A Christian Be a Transhumanist?." Christian Bioethics 28, no.1(2022): 76-93. https://doi.org.10.1093/cb/cbab016.

Eco, Umberto. *The Search for the Perfect Language*. Oxford: Blackwell Publishers, 1995.

Eliade, Mircea. *The Sacred and the Profane: The Nature of Religion*. Translated by Willard R. Trask. New York: Harcourt Brace & Company, 1987.

Elliott, Debbie. "U.S. Reading and Math Scores Drop to Their Lowest In Decades." *NPR*, June 22, 2023. https://www.npr.org/2023/06/22/1183653578/u-s-reading-and-math-scores-drop-to-their-lowest-levels-in-decades.

Ellis, George. "Piety in the Sky" *Nature* 371, no. 115 (1994). https://doi.org/10.1038/371115a0.

Ellul, Jacques. "Technique and the Opening Chapters of Genesis." in *Theology and Technology*. Edited by Carl Mitchum and Jim Grote. Lanham: University Press of America, 1984.
———. *The Technological Society*. Translated by John Wilkinson. New York: Vintage Books, 2016.

Englehardt Jr., Tristam, H.. "An Orthodox Approach to Bioethics." In *Living Orthodoxy in the Modern World*. Edited by Andrew Walker and Costa Carras. Crestwood: St. Vladimir's Seminary Press, 1996.

Eriugena, John Scotus. *Periphyseon: On the Division of Nature*. translated by Myra L. Uhlfelder Eugene: WIPF & Stock, 1976.

Etzler, John Adolphus. *The Collected Works of John Adolphus Etzler*. Delmar, N.Y.: Scholar's Facsimiles and Reprints, 1977.

Fälthammar, Mikael. "The End Times and the Book of Revelation." St. Vincent's Orthodox Church. https://orthodoxsaskatoon.com/2021/05/12/the-end-times-and-the-book-of-revelation/#:~:text=whore%20of%20Babylon%20represents%20earthly,image%20of%20the%20whore%20of.

Farman, Abou. "Re-Enchantment Cosmologies: Mastery and Obsolescence in an Intelligent Universe." *Anthropological Quarterly* 85 (2012): 1069-1088

Farrington, Benjamin. *The Philosophy of Francis Bacon*. Chicago: University of Chicago Press, 1964.

Florovsky, Georges. *On the Tree of the Cross*. New York: Holy Trinity Seminary Press, 2016.

Foerst, Anne. *God in the Machine: What Robots teach us About Humanity and God*. New York: Dutton, 2004.

Fukuyama, Francis. *Our Posthuman Future: Consequences of the Biotechnology Revolution*.
New York: Farrar, Straus, and Giroux, 2002.

Funkenstein, Amos. *Theology and the Scientific Imagination*. Princeton: Princeton University Press, 1986.

Gallaher, Brandon. "Technological Theosis? An Eastern Orthodox Critique of Religious Transhumanism." In *Religious Transhumanism and Its Critics*. Edsited by Arvin Gouw, Brian Patrick Green, and Ted Peters. Maryland: Lexington Books, 2022.

Gauchet, Marcel. *The Disenchantment of the Word: A Political History of Religion*. Princeton University Press, 1985.

Genett, Clark. "Joseph Priestly, the Millennium, and the French Revolution." *Journal of the History of Ideas* 34 (1973).

Geraci, Robert M. "Apocalyptic AI: Religion and the Promise of Artificial Intelligence." *Journal of American Academy of Religion* 76, no. 1 (March 2008) 138-66.

———. *Apocalyptic AI: Visions of Heaven in Robotics, Artificial Intelligence, and Virtual Reality*. Oxford: Oxford University Press, 2010.

———. "Cultural Prestige: Popular Science Robotics as Religion-Science Hybrid." *Reconfigurations: Interdisciplinary Perspectives on Religion in a Post-Secular Society*. Edited by Stefanie Knauss and Alexander D. Ornella (Berlin: LIT Verlag, 2007): 43-58.

———. "Spiritual Robots: Religion and Our Scientific View of the Natural World," *Theology and Science* 4 no.3 (2006): 229-46. https://doi.org/10.1080/14746700600952993.

———. "Video Games and the Transhuman Inclination," In *Zygon* Vol. 47, no.4 (December, 2012) 735-756.

Glanvill, Joseph. *The Vanity of Dogmatizing*. New York: Columbia University Press, 1931.

Goodwin, Kate. "Investors Fuel Fountain of Youth Research with Longevity Company Funding." *Biospace* (October 3, 2023): https://www.biospace.com/investors-fuel-fountain-of-youth-research-with-longevity-company-investments#:~:text=Over%20the%20past%20five%20years%2C,to%20be%20by%20Jeff%20Bezos.

Goldsmith, Arnold. *The Golem Remembered, 1909-1980*. Detroit: Wayne State University Press, 1981.

Gouw, Arvin, Green, Brian Patrick, Peters Ted. Eds. *Religious Transhumanism and Its Critics*.
London: Lexington Books, 2022.

Gorski, Phillip S., David Kyuman Kim, John Ropey, and Jonathan Van Antwerpen. *The Post-secular in Question: Religion in Contemporary Society*. New York: New York University Press, 2012.

Habermas, Jurgen. "A 'Post-Secular" Society – What Does it Mean." *Reset Dialogues on Civilization*, (September 16, 2008) accessed

March 20, 2025, https://www.resetdoc.org/story/a-post-secular-society-what-does-that-mean/#:~:text=in%20Europe%20can%20be%20described,attribute%20primarily%20to%20three%20phenomena

———. "Notes on a Post-Secular Society." *New Perspectives Quarterly* 25 (2008): 17-29, https://doi.org/10.1111/j.1540-5842.2008.01017.x

———. *The Future of Human Nature*. Cambridge: Polity, 2003.

Halberstam, Judith and Ira Livingston. *Posthuman Bodies*. Bloomington: Indiana University Press, 1995.

Haldane, John Burdon Sanderson. *Daedalus, or Science and the Future*. London: Kegan Paul, Trench, Trubner & Co., 1924. https://babel.hathitrust.org/cgi/pt?id=mdp.39015026649544&view=1up&seq=54.

Hallam, Archpriest Gregory. "Orthodoxy and the Enlightenment." *Pravmir* (September 10, 2012): https://www.pravmir.com/orthodoxy-and-the-enlightenment/#:~:text=Orthodoxy%20and%20the%20Enlightenment%20,mind%20is%20so%20radically%20different.

Hamalis, Perry T.. "Eastern Orthodox Ethics" In *International Encyclopedia of Ethics*. Edited by Hugh LaFollette. New York: John Wiley & Sons, 2013.

Hans, Nicholas. "UNESCO of the Eighteenth Century: La Loge des Neuf Soers and Its Venerable Master Benjamin Franklin." *Proceedings of the American Philosophic Society* 9, no. 5 (Oct. 1953).

Harakas, Stanley. *Toward Transfigured Life: The Theoria of Eastern Orthodox Ethics*. Minneapolis: Light and Life, 1983.

Harari, Yuval Noah. *Homo Deus: A Brief History of Tomorrow*. New York: Harper Perennial, 2015.

Harrington, Alan. *The Immortalist*. New York: Random House 1969.

Hauskeller, Michael. "Prometheus Unbound: Transhumanist Arguments from (human) Nature." *Ethical Perspectives* 16, no.1 (2009): 3-20. doi: 10.2143/EP.16.1.0000000.

Heers, Peter. "Transhumanism: The End of Evolution, Apotheosis of Carnal Man, and Preparation & Path to Antichrist." (February 6, 2023) https://www.orthodoxethos.com/post/transhumanism-the-end-of-evolution-apotheosis-of-carnal-man-and-preparation-path-to-antichrist.

Heidegger, Martin. *Basic Writings: Martin Heidegger*. Edited by David Farrell Krell, New York: Routledge, 1993.

Helmreich, Stefan. *Silicon Second Nature: Culturing Artificial Life in a Digital World*. Berkeley, University of California Press, 1998.

Hillar, Marian. *From Logos to Trinity: The Evolution of Religious Beliefs From Pythagoras to Tertullian*. Cambridge: Cambridge University Press, 2012.

Hopkins, Patrick D.. "Transcending the Animal: How Transhumanism and Religion Are and Are Not Alike." In *Journal of Evolution and Technology* 14, no. 2 (2005): 13-28.

Hopko, Thomas. "Orthodox Christianity and Ethics." In *Orthodox Education Day Book*. Crestwood: St. Vladimir's Seminary Press, 1995.

Horgan, John. "Is the Omega Point Ironic Science?" (November 29, 2004) https://johnhorgan.org/cross-check/is-the-omega-point-ironic-science#:~:text=HOBOKEN%2C%20NOVEMBER%2029%2C%202024,1994.

Hossenfelder, Sabine. "The Simulation Hypothesis is Pseudoscience," 2021, video 8:44-8:52, , https://www.youtube.com/watch?v=HCSqogSPU_Q&t=63s

Hughes, James. "The Politics of Transhumanism and the Techno-Millennial Imagination, 1626-2030." Zygon 47, no. 4 (December 2012): 757-776.

———. "Contradictions from the Enlightenment Roots of Transhumanism." Journal of Medicine
and Philosophy 35, no. 6 (December 2010): 622-640, https://doi.org/10.1093/jmp/jhq049

Huxley, Julian. *Evolutionary Humanism*. Buffalo: Prometheus Books, 1992.
———. *New Bottles For New Wine*. London: Chatto & Windus, 1957.
———. *Religion Without Revelation*. New York: Harper & Brothers Publishers, 1927. https://archive.org/details/in.ernet.dli.2015.90330

Ihde, Don. *Technology and The Life World*. Bloomington: Indiana Press, 1990.

Jacob, Margaret. *The Cultural Meaning of the Scientific Revolution*. Philadelphia: Temple University Press, 1988.

Jacobi, Jolande ed. *Paracelsus Selected Writings*. Translated by Norbert Guterman. Princeton: Princeton University Press, 1979.

Jaspers, Karl. *The Origin and Goal of History*. London: Routledge, 1953.

Josephson-Storm, Jason. *The Myth of Disenchantment: Magic Modernity, and the Birth of the
 Human Sciences*. Chicago: Chicago University Press, 2017.

Jonas, Hans. *The Imperative of Responsibility: In Search of an Ethics for the Technological Age*. Chicago: University of Chicago Press, 1984.

Jordan, Gregory. "Apologia for Transhumanist Religion," *Journal of Evolution and Technology* 15 no.1 (2006): 55-72.

Jung, Daekyung. "Transhumanism and Theological Anthropology: A Theological Examination
 of Transhumanism" *Neue Zeitschrift für Systematische Theologie und Religionsphilosophie* 64, no. 2 (2022): 172-194. https://doi.org/10.1515/nzsth-2022-0009

Kaufmann, Michael. "Locating the Postsecular." *Religion and Literature* 41, no. 3 (autumn
 2009): 68-73. https://www.jstor.org/stable/25746543

Kekatos, Mary. "Teen Girls Are Experiencing Record-High Levels of Sadness and Violence: CDC." *ABC News* (February 13, 2023): https://abcnews.go.com/Health/teen-girls-experiencing-record-high-levels-sadness-violence/story?id=97079978.

Kelly, Kevin. "Nerd Theology." *Technology in Society* 21, no.4 (1999): 387-92

Kierkegaard, Soren. *The Sickness Unto Death*. Translated by Alastair Hanney. New York: Penguin Books, 2004.

Klaaren, Eugene M.. *The Religious Origins of Modern Science*. Grand Rapids: William B. Eerdman, 1977.

Knight, Christopher. *Science and the Christian Faith: A Guide for the Perplexed*. Yonkers, New York: St. Vladimir's Seminary Press, 2020.

Kripal, Jeffrey J.. *Esalen: America and the Religion of No Religion*. Chicago: Chicago University Press, 2007.

Kuhn, Thomas. *The Structure of Scientific Revolutions: 50th Anniversary Edition*. Chicago, University of Chicago Press, 2012.

Kurzweil, Ray. *The Age of Spiritual Machines*. New York: Penguin Books, 1999.
———. *The Singularity Is Near: When Humans Transcend Biology*. New York: Penguin Books,
 2005.

Kushner, David. "When Humans & Machines Merge." *Rolling Stone* (February 19, 2009) http://www.davidkushner.com/article/when-man-machine-merge/.

Larchet, Jean-Claude. "Divinization as the Christian Project and Model of True Transhumanism." *Holy Trinity Seminary* (May 10, 2022): https://www.youtube.com/watch?v=eL1PIdJqAyE.

Leary, Timothy. *Chaos and Cyber Culture*. Ronin Publishing, 1994.
———. *The Intelligence Agents*. Peace Press, 1979.

Lenzer, Gertrude, ed. *Auguste Comte and Positivism: The Essential Writings*. New York: Harper and Row, 1975.

Lewis, Richard Warrington Baldwin. *The American Adam*. Chicago: University of Chicago Press, 1955.

Lilley, Stephen. *Transhumanism and Society: The Social Debate Over Human Enhancement*.
New York: Springer, 2013.

Lossky, Vladimir. "The Doctrine of Grace in the Orthodox Church." *St. Vladimir's Theological Quarterly* 58, no. 1 (2014).
———. *The Mystical Theology of the Eastern Church*. Crestwood: St. Vladimir's Seminary Press, 1997.

Mabee, Carelton. *The American Leonardo: A Life of Samuel F. B. Morse*. New York: Alfred A. Knopf, 1944.

MacAskill, William. "Effective Altruism." In *The International Encyclopedia of Ethics*. Hoboken: John Wiley & Sons, 2013. https://www.academia.edu/43357478/Effective_Altruism?b=50 _percent_vector.

Manuel, Frank. *Freedom from History*. New York: New York University Press, 1971.

Manzocco, Roberto. *Transhumanism: Engineering the Human Condition*. Switzerland: Springer Praxis Books, 2019.

Marcuse, Herbert. *One-Dimensional Man*. New York: Routledge, 2002.

Maximus the Confessor. *Disputations with Pyrrhus*, trans. Joseph P. Farrell. Pennsylvania, St. Tikhon's Monastery Press, 2014.
———. *On the Cosmic Mystery of Jesus Christ*. Edited by Paul Blowers and Robert Louis Wilken. New York: St. Vladimir's Seminary Press, 2003.
———. *Selected Writings*. New Jersey: Paulist Press, 1985.

Mayor, Adrienne. *Gods and Robots: Myths, Machines, and Ancient Dreams of Technology.*
    Princeton: Princeton University Press, 2018.

McAllister, Ethel M. *Amos Eaton: Scientist and Educator.* Philadelphia: University of Pennsylvania Press, 1941.

Mercer, Calvin, and Trothen, Tracy. ed. *Religion and Transhumanism: The Unknown Future of*
    Human Enhancement. Santa Barbara, California: Praeger, 2015.

Merleau-Ponty, Maurice. *Phenomenology of Perception.* Translated by Donald Landes. New York: Routledge, 2013.

Metropolitan Hierotheos of Nafpaktos. *Empirical Dogmatics of the Orthodox Catholic Church*, Vol. 1 & 2. Pelagia: Birth of the Theotokos Monastery, 2011.
———. *Orthodox Bioethics: The Theological Perspective.* Translated by Sister Pelagia, (The Birth of the Theotokos Monastery): https://www.pelagia.org/the-views-of-orthodox-theology-on-bioethical-issues.en.aspx#:~:text=1,with%20God%20and%20to%20deification.
———. *Orthodox Psychotherapy.* Pelagia: Birth of the Theotokos Monastery, 2022.

Meyndorff, John. *Byzantine Theology: Historical Trends and Doctrinal Themes.* New York:
    Fordham University Press, 1979.

Miller, Perry. *The Life of the Mind in America.* New York: Harcourt, Brace and World, 1960.

Mirandola, Giovanni Pico della. *On the Dignity of Man, On Being and the One, Heptaplus.* Translated by Charles Glenn Wallis. New York: The Bobbs-Merrill Company Inc., 1965.

Moravec, Hans. *Mind Children: The Future of Robot and Human Intelligence.* Cambridge: Harvard University Press, 1988.

———. *Robot: Mere Machine to Transcendent Mind*. Oxford: Oxford University Press, 1999.

More, Max, and Natasha Vita-More. ed. *The Transhumanist Reader*. Sussex, UK: Wiley-
 Blackwell, 2013.
———. "In Praise of the Devil." *Atheist Note*s, no.3 (1991) http://libertarian.co.uk/2019/08/21/atheist-notes-003-in-praise-of-the-devil-1991-by-max-more/.
———. "Transhumanism: Towards a Futurist Philosophy." 1990. https://www.ildodopensiero.it/wp-content/uploads/2019/03/max-more-transhumanism-towards-a-futurist-philosophy.pdf.
———. "Principles of Extropy." 2003. https://web.archive.org/web/20131015142449/http://extropy.org/principles.htm.

Morison, George S. *The New Epoch: As Developed by the Manufacture of Power*. Boston Houghton Mifflin, 1903. https://archive.org/details/newepochasdevelo00mori.

Mumford, Lewis. *The Myth of the Machine: Pentagon of Power*. New York: Harcourt Brace Jovanovich, 1964.
———. *The Myth of the Machine: Technics and Civilization*. New York: Harcourt Brace Jovanovich, 1966.

Murphy, David. "Elon Musk: Artificial Intelligence Is 'Summoning the Demon.'" *PC Mag* (October 26, 2014): https://www.pcmag.com/news/elon-musk-artificial-intelligence-is-summoning-the-demon.

Musk, Elon. "Joe Rogan Experience #1169 – Elon Musk," *Joe Rogan Experience*, Sept. 6, 2018, podcast 43:35-44:40, https://www.youtube.com/watch?v=ycPr5-27vSI.

Nellas, Panayiotis. *Deification In Christ: Orthodox Perspectives on the Nature of the Human
 Person*. Crestwood, New York: St Vladimir's Seminary Press, 1987.

Newman, William. *Promethean Ambitions: Alchemy and the Quest to Perfect Nature*. Chicago: University of Chicago Press, 2004.

Nietzel, Michael T.. "American IQ Scores Show Recent Decline, According to New Study." *Forbes*, March 23, 2023. https://www.forbes.com/sites/michaeltnietzel/2023/03/23/american-iq-test-scores-show-recent-declines-according-to-new-study/.

Nietzsche, Friedrich. *The Gay Science*. Translated by Walter Kaufmann. Vancouver: Vintage Books, 1974.
———. *Thus Spoke Zarathustra*. Translated by R. J. Hollingdale. New York: Penguin Books, 2003.

Noble, David. *The Religion of Technology: The Divinity of Man and the Spirit of Invention*. New
    York: Penguin Books, 1997

O'Connell, Mark. *To Be a Machine: Adventures Among Cyborgs, Utopians, Hackers, and the Futurists Solving the Modest Problem of Death*. London: Granta Books, 2017.

O'Gieblyn, Meghan. "Ghost in the Cloud." *n+1 Magazine* 28 (Spring 2017): https://www.nplusonemag.com/issue-28/essays/ghost-in-the-cloud/.

Ovitt, George. *The Restoration of Perfection*. New Brunswick: Rutgers University Press, 1986.

Owen, Robert. *Debate on the Evidences of Christianity*. London: R. Groombridge, 1839.

Pacey, Arnold. *The Maze of Ingenuity: Ideas and Idealism in the Development of Technology*. Cambridge, Mass.: The MIT Press, 1992.

Paisios of Mount Athos. "Elder Paisios of the Holy Mount Athos: On the End Times." *Orthodox Word* (March 18, 2010): https://orthodoxword.wordpress.com/2010/03/18/elder-paissios-holy-mount-athos-on-the-end-times/#:~:text=Everything%20is%20going%20as%20planned,a%20loan%2C%20or%20find%20work

Palamas, Gregory. *Dialogue Between an Orthodox and a Barlaamite.* Translated by Rein
    Ferwerda. New York: SUNY Press, 1999.
———. *The Triads.* New Jersey: Paulist Press, 1983.

Patai, Daphne. ed., *Looking Backward 1988-1888 Essays on Edward Bellamy.* Amherst: University of Massachusetts Press, 1988.

Partridge, Christopher. *The Re-Enchantment of the West Volume 2.* London: T&T Clark
    International, 2005.

Pearce, David. "The Abolitionist Project." (2007): https://www.hedweb.com/abolitionist-project/index.html.

Pelikan, Jaroslav. *Christianity and Classical Culture: The Metamorphosis of Natural Theology
    in the Christin Encounter with Hellenism.* New Haven: Yale University Press, 1993.

Peters, Ted. "Imago Dei, DNA, and the Transhuman Way." *Theology and Science* 16, no. 3 (2018): 353-362. https://doi.org/10.2307/jj.890650.40

Phelan, John Leddy. *The Millennial Kingdom of the Franciscans in the New World.* Berkeley: University of California Press, 1970.

Picon, Antoine. *French Architects and Engineers in the Age of Enlightenment.* Cambridge: Cambridge University Press, 1992.

Pilsch, Andrew. *Transhumanism: Evolutionary Futurism and the Human Technologies of
    Utopia.* Minneapolis: University of Minnesota Press, 2017.

Plato. *Plato: Complete Works.* Edited by John M. Cooper. Indianapolis: Hackett Publishing Company, 1997.

Polkinghor, John. "I am the Alpha and the Omega Point" *New Scientist* (Feb. 4, 1995): https://www.newscientist.com/article/mg14519634-400-i-am-the-alpha-and-the-omega-point/.

Pomazansky, Michael. *Orthodox Dogmatic Theology*. Platina: St. Herman of Alaska Brotherhood, 2021.

Popkin, Richard. *Millenarianism and Messianism In English Literature and Thought*. Leiden: E. J. Brill, 1988.

Postman, Neil. *Technopoly: The Surrender of Culture to Technology*. New York: Vintage Books, 1992.

Prisco, Giulio. "Engineering Transcendence." (December 1, 2006) https://giulioprisco.blogspot.com/2006/12/engineeringtranscendence.html.
———. "Prospectus of the Order of Cosmic Engineers" (September 18, 2021) https://turingchurch.net/archive-order-of-cosmic-engineers-6c562b401b03.

Puttick, Elizabeth. "Human Potential Movement" In *Encyclopedia of New Religion*. Edited by Christopher Partridge. Oxford: Lion Publishing, 2004.

Reeves, Marjorie. *The Influence of Prophecy in the Latter Middle Ages: A Study in Joachimism*. Oxford: Oxford University Press, 1969.

Robinson, Daniel ed.. *The Shepherd of Hermas*. CreateSpace Independent Publishing, 2013.yst

Rose, David. *Enchanted Objects: Innovation, Design, and the Future of Technology*. New York: Scribner, 2014.

Rose, Eugene Seraphim. *Nihilism*. Platina: St. Herman of Alaska Brotherhood, 2018.
———. *The Orthodox Survival Course*. Download PDF. http://orthodoxaustralia.org/wp-content/uploads/2015/06/course.pdf.

Ross Jr., Thomas Ernest. "The Synergy of Gnosticism and Transhumanism." *Medium* (July 15, 2023): https://tomrosscom.medium.com/the-synergy-of-gnosticism-and-transhumanism-ced36b8af7d9.

Rossi, Paulo. *Francis Bacon: From Magic to Science*. Chicago: University of Chicago Press, 1968.

Russell, Stuart. *Human Compatible: Artificial Intelligence and the Problem of Control*. New
    York: Penguin Books. 2020.

Ryle, Gilbert. *The Concept of Mind*. Chicago: University of Chicago Press, 2000.

Sale, Kirkpatrick. *The Conquest of Paradise*. New York: Alfred A. Knopf, 1992.

Saliashvili, Meagan. "Orthodox Church Boomed During Pandemic, Study Finds, but Calls Growth 'Mixed Bag.'" *National Catholic Reporter* (August 26, 2024): https://www.ncronline.org/news/orthodox-churches-boomed-during-pandemic-study-finds-calls-growth-mixed-bag#:~:text=The%20Orthodox%20tendency%20to%20,declines%20in%20participation%20and%20volunteering.

Sartre, Jean-Paul. *Existentialism Is a Humanism*. Translated by by Carol Macomber. New Haven: Yale University Press, 2007.

Savulescu, Julian and Bostrom, Nick. ed. *Human Enhancement*. Oxford: Oxford University
    Press, 2021.

Schäfer, Peter. *Two Gods in Heaven: Jewish Concepts of God in Antiquity*. Princeton: Princeton University Press, 2020.

Schaff, Phillip. *Nicene and Post-Nicene Fathers*. Massachusetts: Hendrickson Publishing, 1979.

Schlott, Rikki. "Young Men Leaving Traditioanl Churches for 'Masculine' Orthodox Christianity in Droves." *New York Post* (December 3, 2024): https://nypost.com/2024/12/03/us-news/young-men-are-converting-to-orthodox-christianity-in-droves/.

Schmemann, Alexander. *For the Life of the World*. Crestwood St. Vladimir's Seminary Press, 1973.

Sherwin, Byron. *The Golem Legend: Origins and Implications*. New York: University Press of America, 1985.

Schmemann, Alexander. *The Historical Road of Eastern Orthodoxy*. New York" St. Vladimir's
 Seminary Press, 2003.

Schwab, Klaus. *The Forth Industrial Revolution*. New York: Crown Business, 2016

Segal, Alan. *Two Powers in Heaven: Early Rabbinic Report About Christianity and Gnosticism*. Waco, Texas, Baylor University Press, 2012.

Segal, Howard P.. *Technological Utopianism in American Culture*. Berkeley: University of California Press, 1985.

Sergieff, John Iliytch. *My Life in Christ*. Jordanville: Holy Trinity Monastery, 2015.

Shelly, Percy. *Prometheus Unbound: a Lyrical Drama*. Edited by Vida D. Schudder. New York: D.C. Heath & Co. Publishers, 1892.

Sijuwade, Joshua. "Monarchical Trinitarianism: A Metaphysical Proposal" *TheoLogica* 5, no. 2 (December 2021): https://doi.org/10.14428/thl.v5i2.54483.

Smith, Houston. *The Soul of Christianity*. San Francisco: Harper, 2005.

Sorem, Erik Ananias. "An Eastern Orthodox Understanding of the Dangers of Modernity and Technology."

https://www.academia.edu/41476699/An_Eastern_Orthodox_Understanding_of_the_Dangers_of_Modernity_and_Technology.

Spengler, Oswald. *Man and Technics*. New York: Routledge, 2018.

Stark, Rodney and William S. Bainbridge. *The Future of Religion: Secularization, Revival, and Cult Formation*. Los Angeles: University of California Press, 1985.

Steinhart, Eric. "Theurgy and Transhumanism." *Archai* 29, e02905 (2020): https://doi.org/10.14195/1984-249X_29_5.

Stenger, Nicole. "Mind is a Leaking Rainbow," In *Cyberspace: First Steps*. Edited by Michael Benedikt. Cambridge: MIT Press, 1991.

Stewart, Columba. "Evagrius Ponticus and the Eight Generic Logismoi." In *In the Garden of Evil: Vice and Culture in the Middle Ages*. Edited by Richard Newhauser. Pontifical Institute of Mediaeval Studies, 2005.

Stock, Gregory. *Redesigning Humans: Our Inevitable Genetic Future*. Boston: Houghton Mifflin, 2002.

Sy, Stephanie. "Are Smartphones and Social Media Harming Teen Mental Health? Here's Why Experts Are Split." *PBS News* (June 10, 2024) https://www.pbs.org/newshour/show/are-smartphones-and-social-media-harming-teen-mental-health-heres-why-experts-are-split#:~:text=Are%20smartphones%20and%20social%20media,of%20sadness%20and%20suicide.

Taylor, Charles. *A Secular Age*. Cambridge: Harvard University Press, 2007.

The Catholic Encyclopedia, 1913 edition, Vol. 6, https://www.ecatholic2000.com/cathopedia/vol6/volsix663.shtml.

The Eschaton Vigil, *Elders on the End Times: The World Before the Second Coming* (The Eschaton Vigil, 2024)

———. *The Eschatological Visions of the Blessed: End Times Prophecies of Elders & Saints of the Orthodox Church*. The Eschaton Vigil, 2024.

Thurston, Robert. "Scientific Research: The Art of Revelation and Prophecy," *Science* 16 (Sept. 12-19, 1902) https://www.jstor.org/stable/1628776.

Tipler, Frank and John D. Barrow. *The Anthropic Cosmological Principle*. Oxford: Oxford University Press, 1988.
———. "The Omega Point as Eschaton: Answers to Pannenberg's Questions for Scientists." *Zygon: Journal of Religion and Science* Vol. 24, no. 2 (June 1989): 217-253.

Tirosh-Samuelson, Hava. "Transhumanism as a Secular Faith." Zygon 47, no. 4 (December 2012).

Trenham, Josiah. "Jesus vs. Transhumanism," *Patristic Nectar Films*, Oct. 6, 2022, https://www.youtube.com/watch?v=t-adGqQoC8M.

Turing, Alan. "Computing Machinery and Intelligence," *Mind* 59 (October 1950): 433-460, https://doi.org/10.1093/mind/LIX.236.433

Turkle, Sherry. *Alone Together: Why We Expect More from Technology and Less from Each Other*. New York: Basic Books, 2017.

Turner, Fred. *From Counterculture to Cyberculture: Stewart Brand, the Whole Earth Network, and the Rise of Digital Utopianism*. Chicago: Chicago University Press, 2006.

Tuveson, Ernest Lee. *Millennium and Utopia*. New York: Harper and Row, 1964.

Ulam, Stanislaw. "Tribute to John von Neumann," *Bulletin of the American Mathematical Society* (May 1958) https://www.ams.org/journals/bull/1958-64-03/S0002-9904-1958-10189-5/S0002-9904-1958-10189-5.pdf.

Vasiljević, Maxim. "Between the "Already" and the "Not Yet": A Journey with Metropolitan John Zizioulas." in *The Wheel* 36 (Winter 2024): 20-26. https://static1.squarespace.com/static/54d0df1ee4b036ef1e44b144/t/66b4ec0f48a10b72f746b489/1723132943936/Wheel_36+Vasilevich.pdf#:~:text=On%20questions%20of%20secularization%2C%20Zizioulas,be%20imparted%20with%20an%20eschatolog%02ical.

Verchot, Manon. "Meet the People Who Want to Turn Predators Into Herbivores." (November 27, 2020): https://www.treehugger.com/meet-the-people-who-want-to-turn-predators-into-vegans-4857310

Virk, Rizwan. *The Simulation Hypothesis*. Bayview Books, 2018.

Voegelin, Eric. *Science, Politics, & Gnosticism*. 3rd ed. Wilmington, Delaware: ISI Books, 2004.

Von Stuckard, Kocku. *A Cultural History of the Soul*. New York: Columbia University Press,
    2022.
———. *The Scientification of Religion. An Historical Study of Discursive Change*
    1800-2000. Boston: De Gruyter, 2015.

Wassinge, Maggie and Anders Amelin, "On the Evolution of the Phenomenal Self and Other Communications from QRI Sweden)" *Qualia Computing: Revealing the Computational Properties of Consciousness* (June 16, 2020): https://qualiacomputing.com/tag/evolution/#:~:text=Open%20Individualism%20,about%20a%20profound%20sense%20of.

Watts, Pauline Moffitt. "Prophecy and Discovery: On the Spiritual Origins of Christopher Columbus' Enterprise of the Indies," *American Historical Review* 90 (1985).

Ware, Metropolitan Kallistos. *The Orthodox Way*. Crestwood, St. Vladimir's Seminary Press, 2012.

Waters, Brent. "Is Technology the New Religion." *Word & Wo*rld 35, no.2 (Spring 2015): https://wordandworld.luthersem.edu/wp-content/uploads/pdfs/35-2_Posthuman_Identity/Is%20Technology%20the%20New%20Religion.pdf#:~:text=TRANSHUMANIST%20AND%20POSTHUMANIST%20MYTHOLOGY%20Transhumanists,eschatological%20end%20of%20personal%20immortal%02149

Wax, Trevin. "Is Eastern Orthooxy the New Thing for Young Men." *The Gospel Coalition* (January 7, 2025): https://www.thegospelcoalition.org/blogs/trevin-wax/eastern-orthodoxy-young-men/#:~:text=picture,7%20percent%20of%20the%20population.

Webster, Charles. "New Light on the Invisible College the Social Relations of English Science in the Mid-Seventeenth Century." *Transactions of the Royal Historical Society* 24 (1974): 19–42. https://doi.org/10.2307/3678930.

———. *The Great Instauration: Science, Medicine, and Reform 1626-1660*. London: Gerald Duckworth, 1975.

Weiss, John Hubbel. *The Making of Technological Man: The Social Origins of French Engineering Education*. Cambridge, Mass.: MIT Press, 1982.

White, Lynn. "Cultural Climates and Technological Advance in the Middle Ages" *Viator* 2 (1971).

Whitney, Charles. *Francis Bacon and Modernity*. New Haven: Yale University Press, 1986.

Whitney, Elspeth. *Paradise Restored: The Mechanical Arts From Antiquity Through the Thirteenth Century*. Philadelphia: American Philosophical Society, 1990.

Williams, Anna. *The Ground of Union: Deification in Aquinas and Palamas*. Oxford: Oxford University Press, 1999.

Wolfe, Cary. *What Is Posthumanism?*. Minneapolis: University of Minnesota Press, 2010.

Wolfram, Stephen. *A New Kind of Science*. Wolfram Media, 2019.

Wotton, William. *Reflections Upon Ancient and Modern Learning*. London, 1694, accessed March 24, 2025, https://archive.org/details/reflectionsupon00wottgoog/page/n40/mode/2up.

Yannaras, Christos. *Elements of Faith: An Introduction to Orthodox Theology*. Translated by Keith Shram. Edinburgh, Scotland: T&T Clark, 2000.
———. *On the Absence and Unknowability of God: Heidegger and the Areopagite*. translated by Haralambos Ventis. London: Continuum, 2005.
———. *Postmodern Metaphysics*. Brookline, MA: Holy Cross Orthodox Press, 2004.
———. *The Freedom of Morality*. New York: St. Vladimir's Seminary Press, 1984.
———. *The Schism in Philosophy*. Brookline, MA: Holy Cross Orthodox Press, 2015.

Yates, Francis. *The Rosicrucian Enlightenment*. New York: Routledge Classics, 2002.

Young, Simon. *Designer Evolution: A Transhumanist Manifesto*. Amherst, NY: Prometheus Books, 2006.

Zachuber, Johannes. *The Rise of Christian Theology and the End of Ancient Metaphysics: Patristic Philosophy from the Cappadocian Fathers to John of Damascus*. Oxford: Oxford University Press, 2020.

Zimmerman, Michael. "The Singularity: A Crucial Phase in Divine Self-Actualization?" *Cosmos and History: Journal of Natural Social Philosophy* 4 no.1 (2008): 347-70.

Zizioulas, John. *Being as Communion*. Crestwood: St. Vladimir's Seminary Press, 1985.
———. *Communion and Otherness: Further Studies in Personhood and the Church*. Edited by Paul McPartlan. London: T&T Clark, 2006.

www.ingramcontent.com/pod-product-compliance
Lightning Source LLC
Chambersburg PA
CBHW031248230426
43670CB00005B/88